GOING BONKERS:

THE WACKY WORLD OF CULTURAL MADNESS

I0118872

Also by Charles W. Sasser

Nonfiction

The Walking Dead (with Craig Roberts)
Homicide!
Shoot to Kill
One Shot-One Kill (with Craig Roberts)
Always A Warrior
Last American Heroes (with Michael Sasser)
In Cold Blood: Oklahoma's Most Notorious Murders
Smoke Jumpers
First SEAL (with Roy Boehm)
Doc: Platoon Medic (with Daniel E. Evans)
Fire Cops (with Michael Sasser)
At Large
Arctic Homestead (with Norma Cobb)
Taking Fire (with Ron Alexander)
Raider
Encyclopedia Of Navy SEALs
Hill 488 (with Ray Hildreth)
Pathways: Magic Steps To Writing Success
Patton's Panthers
Crosshairs on the Kill Zone (with Craig Roberts)
Going Bonkers: The Wacky World of Cultural Madness

Novels

No Gentle Streets
The 100th Kill
Operation No Man's Land (writing as Mike Martell)
Liberty City
The Return
Detachment Delta: Operation Punitive Strike
Detachment Delta: Operation Iron Weed
Detachment Delta: Operation Deep Steel
Detachment Delta: Operation Aces Wild
Detachment Delta: Cold Dawn
Dark Planet

GOING BONKERS:

THE WACKY WORLD OF CULTURAL MADNESS

Charles W. Sasser

AWOC.COM Publishing
Denton, Texas

Published by AWOC.COM Publishing, P.O. Box 2819, Denton, TX 76202, USA. No part of this publication may be reproduced, stored in a retrieval system, or transmitted in any form or by any means, electronic, mechanical, recording or otherwise, without the prior written permission of the author.

Manufactured in the United States of America

ISBN: 0-9707507-6-5

Visit the author's web site: http://www.CharlesSasser.com

Dedication

To all who remain sane in the midst of lunacy

ACKNOWLEDGMENTS

Over the decade during the research for and writing of this book, I have been encouraged, influenced and supported by a great number of people, either person-to-person in discussions and interviews or through many books and publications. Quite obviously, not all the ideas, anecdotes and thought for or in this book are original with me. A considerable number of people are beginning to recognize the cultural insanity that has infected our society and, breaking with it, to raise their voices. I should like to acknowledge the following people and publications, in no particular order of importance, who and which have greatly influenced the writing of this book. I realize this is only a partial list, so please forgive me if I have overlooked or neglected anyone.

William Pollack; Ann Davis; The Miami *Herald; The Limbaugh Letter;* Jeff Jacoby; Rush Limbaugh; T. Kelly Rossiter; George Will; Kenneth Smith; Richard and Karla Hauk; *Reader's Digest; Human Events;* Michael Fumento; *The American Spectator;* Mark Steyn; *Insight;* Robert Stacy McCain; Bruce R. Hare; Benjamin J. Stein; John J. Miller; Paul Greenberg; Ann Coulter; Michael Savage; *Heterodoxy; Orthodoxy; U.S. News & World Report; National Review; Time; Harvard Law Review;* Thomas Sowell; The Seattle *Times*; John Leo; William Raspberry; Cal Thomas; The Washington *Post; Associated Press;* Gayle M.B. Hanson; Fred Reed; San Francisco *Chronicle;* The Detroit *News;* Minneapolis *Star Tribune; Ms. Magazine;* Mike Royko; Carol Iannone; Randall Robinson; John Stossel; Walter E. Williams; F. Carolyn Graglia; *Accuracy In Academia...*

The Chicago *Tribune;* Woody West; David Broder; Paul Craig Roberts; P.J. O'Rourke; Candace de Russy; Kenneth Lee; Jon Reisman; Georgie Ann Geyer; Richard A. Zeller; Ralph R. Reiland; Dinesh D'Souza; Craig Roberts; Benjamin Kepple; Leon Janoff; James C. Rees; Sandra Stotsky; Emily Sarchar; Alan Charles Kors; Harvey A. Silverglate; David Horowitz; Sylvia Ann Hewlett; Cornell West; Philip Rieff; Jane Robelot; Keith Laub; Darrell and Ann Turner; Ellen Goodman; Stephen Keene; L. Brent Bozell III; Dan Case; Stephen Goode; Mel Gibson; Charlton Heston; Bill O'Reilly; Jay Nordlinger; Stephen Goode; Suzanne Fields; Julia Duin...

William Powers; Larry Elder; Carl S. Ely; *The Weekly Standard;* Don Feder; The Boston *Globe;* Stephanie Gutmann; Kelly Patricia O'Meara; Oliver North; *Military* Magazine; Walter A. McDougall; *Commentary* Magazine; The Washington *Times;* David Hackworth; John Corry; Colin Powell; Atlanta *Journal & Constitution;* Jim Minter; Terence Hunt; C.R. "Corky" Johnson; Tom Bethell; *New Oxford Re-*

view; James J. Kilpatrick; Los Angeles *Times;* Ernest W. Lefever; Peter Hitchins; Joe Sobran; Julia Gorin; *New Times;* Maureen Dowd... Mark Stuart; Michael A. Wilson; St. Paul *Pioneer Press;* Charles Socarides; *Web Today;* Don Feder; Mona Charen; Paul M. Weyrich; Jim Myers; *World Washington Bureau;* Rod Dreher; Deborah Mathis; *Reuters News Service;* New York *Post;* Randy Fitzgerald; Robert Whelan; *National Directory of Environmental & Regulatory Victims; Farm Bureau Journal;* Muskogee *Phoenix;* Tony Snow; Al Gore; *Heritage Foundation;* Edwin Feulner; Dr. Laura Schlessinger; Aimee Welch; Balint Vazsonyi; James Bovard; Linda Chavez; David Weaver; *America's 1ˢᵗ Freedom; Wall Street Journal; American Guardian;* H. Brand Ayers; Pat Buchanan; *Esquire;* Trent Lott...

The *Advocate;* Morton Kondracke; Joseph Farah; Al Hunt; Gary Aldrich; James B. Stewart; Joe Eszterhas; Henry Ruth; David Limbaugh; Thomas Disch; Tim Russert; James Q. Wilson; *The Nation;* William Tucker; Jim Olsztynski; *Imprimis;* Bob Barr; *Reason* Magazine; W.A. Borst; Bruce Tinsley; Ted Nugent; George Koether; R.J. Rummel; Sean Hannity; Matt Drudge; Kenneth Starr; Joanna Jacobs; David Bauder; Paul Johnson; Andrew Delbanco; Heather MacDonald; Daniel Patrick Moynihan; Alan Bodine; Roy Boehm; Galen Kittleson; Ron Alexander...

Finally, I should like to thank my wife, Donna Sue, for her patience and forbearance during the writing of this book; my mother and father, Mary and George Wells; my brother Joe Sasser, and my children whose bright minds and strong opinions greatly contributed to this work—David Sasser, Michael Sasser, Joshua Sasser, Darren Cagle, Mike Haworth and Dee Ann Schisler.

If, however, as must be occasionally true in a work of this scope, I have made minor errors of interpretation or fact, I must bear the full responsibility...

Charles W. Sasser

Table Of Contents

"I have been drinking the middle third of my early morning urine for almost twenty years and feel that it has enhanced my well-being. Along with a regular hatha yoga practice and a healthy vegetarian diet, drinking one's urine can truly improve your health. It is an easy, cost-effective adjunct to a healthy regimen. Once you overcome the cultural bias against "pee," you will find that it is not at all unpleasurable to the taste—in fact, it's quite palatable. It becomes another morning bathroom habit, like washing and brushing your teeth."

David Ackerman

Yoga Journal, May/June 1996

INTRODUCTION

There was a time not so long ago when people chuckled to themselves, clucked their tongues and wagged their heads over the bizarre antics of eccentrics, peculiars and funny Uncle Freds on the fringes. No one ever took their ravings and capers *seriously*; the more disconnected were even locked in padded rooms to prevent harm to themselves and others.

Today, however, via some remarkable combination of hypersensitivity, tolerance, concern for self-esteem, "inclusiveness," and biases against being "judgmental," the nation has thrown itself on the mercy of these seriously disturbed people. Rantings of hard metal rock stars and rappers chanting about "ho's" and "bitches" carry equal weight with the treatises of Nobel prize winners. The feel-good notion that all opinion, regardless of how outlandish, is equally valid has led to its all being taken seriously. The more outrageous the message, the more attention it commands. Better to be a fool and attract other fools than to point out the folly of such drivel and be considered insensitive and judgmental.

"(T)hose whom the gods wish to destroy," observed Britain's Lord Tibbet, "they first make mad, and these ideas have been fermented in minds which are gravely imbalanced."

If individuals can go wacky, eating bugs off the sidewalk, talking to sofas and sipping urine, is it not possible for an entire culture to go mad in the same way?

When I first proposed writing this book, an editor of the major publishing house with whom I had published a dozen previous books immediately took umbrage. I was "reactionary." What may seem wacky to some, she said, is perfectly reasonable to others.

Is it wacky or reasonable, I submit, for a professor of drama to be sacked for teaching the classic theater of Shakespeare, Aeschylus and Ibsen because "feminists are offended by the selection of works from a sexist European canon?" That instead of *Othello* or *The Cherry Orchard,* the theater department should approve the production of *Betty The Yeti,* about a logger who becomes an environmentalist after having sex with a lady Sasquatch in the Pacific Northwest?

Is it wacky or is it reasonable that children should be denied the opportunity to see the ballet *Romeo & Juliet* because their school felt it to be a "blatantly heterosexual love story?"

Is it wacky or is it reasonable for feminists to insist that men should sit or squat to urinate because for them to stand at the function, which women cannot, is "overtly macho" and therefore offensive?

3

I have no difficulty discerning the difference between wacky and reasonable.

Cultural madness becomes cultural norm. America, and indeed much of Western society, has been conditioned to accept, endorse and promote virtually *anything.* That which is tolerated by one generation is accepted by the next and embraced by a third. Go along with the tenets of the "tolerant" society and you join the gelded herd to be praised, rewarded and celebrated. Sound off like you got a pair and you find yourself accused of hating and intolerance, branded as homophobic, sexist, racist, specie-ist, able-ist, or any of a dozen other similar labels through which saner and more judicious voices are drowned out.

In 1943, the Moscow Central Committee devised a plan for its communist followers to use in dealing with critics. "Members and front organizations must continually embarrass, discredit, and degrade our critics," the committee decreed. "When obstructionists become too irritating, label them as fascist, or Nazi, or anti-Semitic... The association will, after enough repetition, become 'fact' in the public mind."

The same script on how to deal with "obstructionists" could have been written by modern Lefties who continue to push for collectivism. Senator Ted Kennedy gloated over what he perceived to be America's post 9-11 goal of "facing down individualism." Senator Chuckie Schumer cried in glee that "the era of shrinking federal government is over."

The Left Coast and the Liberal Northeast cannot bear knowing that people in between prefer to live life their own way outside the progressive agenda. That they eat beef, stop for fast foods, go hunting and fishing, smoke tobacco, have rodeos, say prayers at football games, drive SUVs and keep guns. Ironically enough, folks in flyover country are perfectly willing to tolerate the "progressive" coasts while the "progressives" are willing to tolerate virtually anything except "obstructionists." These "right wingers"—a handy term which always means "bad guys"—must be dealt with. So call them names. Name calling, as the Moscow Central Committee understood, works. It's almost impossible to express conservative ideas today without sounding apologetic.

For a while after 9-11 we toyed with the false assumption that sanity might return to the American culture. Pundits declared that a new era of understanding and tolerance was descending upon the country, that political, philosophical and cultural differences would be shoved back to make room for America to "come together." It was even suggested that America would return to its former morality and values, that the terrorists had knocked us back to our senses.

Don't believe it.

There was a lull, a very short lull, and then the wackiness resumed madder than ever. In Pennsylvania, a city councilwoman accused a police dog of being "racist." An eight-year-old was suspended from school for pointing his finger like a gun and playing "cops and robbers." Protestors marched against "racial profiling" Islamic terrorists.

Unabomber Ted Kacysinski was a dangerous nut who went around blowing up people to demonstrate his opposition to industrial society. Although he is somewhat of an icon among Leftists, even his twisted mind was astute enough to recognize modern Leftism for what it really is. In his Unabomber Manifesto he wrote, "...(Y)ou asked leftists to make a list of all the things that was wrong with society, and then suppose you instituted every social change that they demanded. It is safe to say that within a couple of years the majority of leftists would find something new to complain about, some new social 'evil' to correct because, once again, the leftist is motivated less by distress at society's ills than by the need to satisfy his drive for power by imposing his solutions on society."

Don't suppose for a second that the attacks on traditional morals, standards and common sense will let up. Not everyone who wants to harm the country is a radical Islamic armed with a box cutter. The Cultural Wars threaten the future of the nation more than terrorist attacks. In a very significant way, Cultural Madness is terrorism. We are in effect succumbing to terrorism whenever we censor ourselves and constantly make concessions to maintain peace and get along, when fewer and fewer people are willing to confront public ridicule and speak out, when we remain silent and concede away our core beliefs and values. The outcome for society underneath all the wackiness is as serious as a dead baby.

In writing *Going Bonkers*, I am quite aware that I will offend and that, in offending, I will be branded as reactionary or worse. I wrote it and, out of dread, had second thoughts about sending it out to a publisher. Frankly, it takes guts to write or to publish against the "progressive" takeover of our institutions.

Yet, far too many conservatives have been intimidated and gone AWOL in what may be the last great fight of our society. If we remain silent out of intimidation and stoically accept the madness of our Brave New World, we will eventually concede away the final remnants of liberty. It isn't civility to remain silent; it's cowardice. The disintegration of culture begins with conditioning people to accept everything in silence. If I go down, I prefer to go down firing from the bulwarks rather than with a whimper in the shadows of madness and tyranny.

SECTION I
VICTIMS

CHAPTER ONE

We don't live in America anymore, at least not in the America I know. Envy used to be a human failing; today it is a major industry. Politicians, journalists, and academics are all part of the "victim industry," which the more Enlightened call "social justice." Since virtually everybody is worse off than someone else, in at least some aspect, there are nearly unlimited opportunities to pander to people's sense of victimhood and entitlement. Hey, if you ain't a victim, you ain't cool.

We have created a culture that worships helplessness, impotence, weakness and frailty, whether it be physical, mental or moral. Pity and the courting of pity have become a national obsession. You simply aren't playing fair unless you're poor, ignorant, crippled, fat, gendered, or a minority. It seems nobody can cope with even life's minor uncertainties without unending whimpering, a dozen self-help books and a support group.

Mack, whose letter appeared in the Syracuse *Herald American,* claimed victimhood by virtue of *loneliness.* You can almost hear the violins playing.

"As Father's Day approaches," he laments, "I am disappointed to say I cannot receive any honor or respect on this day... You see, I am a single bachelor without a soul mate and without a child of my own... I would like to establish a day for all singles. Single people deserve a day of honor too. It is a tough life as a single. It's tough not finding the right one and being lonely..."

Maybe his congressman could pass a law to issue this poor fellow a soul mate.

Victimhood is a growth industry that makes Microsoft and Chrysler seem virtually sluggish by comparison. You're healthy only if you're *not* healthy. Everyone is afflicted with *something*, whether it be real, perceived, contrived or imagined—race, gender, alcoholism, obesity, flat feet, poor upbringing or halitosis. Ingenious new ways are invented to create fresh categories of suffering martyrs seeking their rightful share of victimhood spoils.

A Florida woman, she a left-hander, became the first "sex worker" to win a worker's compensation settlement after she sued on the grounds that she developed carpel tunnel syndrome while regularly masturbating at her post in providing "phone sex."

Support groups exist for virtually every affliction. The Tulsa *World* and other newspapers regularly publish a full page of them, in small print: Alcoholics Anonymous; Youth Emotions Anonymous; Workaholics Anonymous; National Association to Advance Fat Acceptance; Dieters Anonymous; Families of Sex Offenders Anonymous...

Addicted shoppers and debtors have formed support networks. One

group shores up those who "drink a little too much but not too much
Coca Cola." Still another bunch formed the Support Group for People
Civically Abused.

Civically Abused? That's right. According to the Monterrey
County *Herald,* "They're trying to fight city hall, and when city hall
fights back, they seek a few kind words, support and advice from each
other... There is a place to turn to when the bureaucrats don't seem to
be listening..."

If you have more than one malady, you can always join Dual Disorders Anonymous. One guy I knew belonged to five different support
groups. They were his social life. A woman named Nadean Cool required so much support that a psychiatrist convinced her she had 120
distinct and separate personalities, each of which required sustenance.
Parts of her were devils, angels and ducks. She sued—and as Dave
Berry says, I'm not making this up—her shrink for malpractice after he
charged her insurance company for *group therapy.*

Hello. My name is America, and I'm dysfunctional...

My sister-in-law belonged to a support group called Adult Children of Dysfunctional Families. My brother, who makes Paw Kettle
seem urbane by comparison, refused to accompany her to meetings. So
I went.

After the usual hugging and weeping, we sat in a circle around the
room while everyone got up in sequence to relate dramas of alcoholism, abuse, desertion and wreckage. It was a lot like the *Sally Jessy
Raphael Show.*

I sat back for a moment when it came my turn. What I wanted to
do was get up and say, *Get over it, for God's sake. So life ain't fair.
Move on and stop wallowing in self-pity.* Instead...

Well, I'm a writer. I scribble stories for fun and profit. I know how
to do a story. There wasn't a dry eye in the house by the time I finished.
Two women were openly sobbing. My sister-in-law descended on me
with both feet when she got me out of there.

"Wasn't that what they came for?" I defended myself. "They all
had a good time."

Call me insensitive, but can only insensitive people tell the difference between a simple nuisance and a raging catastrophe? It seems
everything is a disaster for America's hordes of emotional cripples. It is
calculated that the number of victims in America reaches 374 percent
of the population. Statistically, that means each of us belongs to 3.74
different victim categories. This is the way it works:

I'm an American Indian, therefore a victim of racism. I was born
out of wedlock; that accumulates victim points for a "dysfunctional
family." I can claim poverty and geographic points for having been
reared in shacks, chicken houses and barns in the Ozark Mountains.
Call me a "senior citizen" and I'll shout "age-ism." I'm fairly short

(size-ism) and not particularly handsome (look-ism). I'll soon fall under the Americans With Disabilities Act if my eyesight continues to fail...
I'll stop here. I've exceeded my 3.74. Next thing you know, I'll begin feeling sorry for myself, whimpering, seeking a support group and demanding preference and deference.

I was raised with the idea that common sense was a better thing to have than a fancy education. Today, simple common sense has become an endangered species, replaced by excessive emotionalism and groupthink. I'm going to throw up out the window of my pickup truck if one more goofy Hollywood celebrity presumes to raise my awareness, admonishes me about some group's precious self-esteem, or reproves me for lack of tolerance of drunken bums and lazy welfare cheats.

In a society gone bonkers, there will come a day, mark my word, when *all* God's children will be aggrieved and *everyone* will be a victim.

CHAPTER TWO

The question asked on Census Form 2000 about the respondent's race provided 126--Dave Berry again, I'm not making this up—possible choices: Spanish-Hispanic-Latin ethnicity; black, African-American or Negro; American Indian or Alaskan Native; Asian Indian; Korean, Filipino; Guamanian or Chamorro... If *none* of these 126 matched you, you had a final option of "Some other race."

Human race was not included among the choices.

Were we a nation of canines, few of us would be eligible for registration as pure breeds in the American Kennel Club. Most of us are a "Heinz 57" blend of different herbs and spices. No "multiracial" box, however, was included in the Census Form. The "race industry" lobbied against it out of concern that it would dilute minority political influence and cut the amount of public guilt cash pouring into race coffers. Jesse Jackson, the Reverend Al Sharpton and Louis Farrakhan might actually have to go out and find *real* jobs.

We have turned into a nation neurotically obsessed with *diversity*, be it of race, gender, or some other favored minority status. Diversity is based upon a person's identity and status as a member of a group, not upon his individual character or abilities. We distinguish, celebrate, apologize for, and martyr every single drop of blood that does not come from Western Europe and the white male. Once you have accepted victim status, you are open to recognize affront, insult and disrespect in every shadow of daily life. From here to eternity, amen.

The assistant dean at the Howard School of Public Health, Deborah Prothrow, charged that the movie *Jurassic Park* was an "outrageous insult" because finicky dinosaurs knocked off people of color while light-skinned blond people—heroes of the film—escaped death or maiming. Nothing was said about the fat white thief who ran off the road and was presumably devoured. The ancient denizens were probably prejudiced against people of heft as well as being racists.

To escape charges of racism and simultaneously promote diversity, a directive from the Department of Defense directed officials to obtain special permission to promote any white male to a senior management position—unless the white male was disabled in some way that would allow him to fall under a victim category.

The New Jersey school board, faced with having to lay someone off, fired a white teacher based solely on her race. They argued that her absence from the faculty would improve diversity numbers in the school.

And poor, poor Barbie Doll. Don't let her inoffensive appearance fool you. Even before charges of racism hit her—Yep, Barbie is a racist—she had already had face lifts, tummy tucks, boob and butt jobs in order to appease various victim groups. Her breasts were too big, so they were reduced to mollify the smaller boobs lobby. Plumpies thought her slim, shapely figure damaged little girls' self-esteem, so they corn-fed her on gravy and potatoes. The physically challenged wanted to cripple her and put her in a wheelchair. Her boyfriend Ken turned up gay in a purple outfit. Boys and girls in switched bodies demanded a transgender Barbie. It's hard to imagine Barbie with a... Well, you know. An extra appendage. Probably removed from Ken.

That wasn't enough. Barbie was still, God forbid, *white.*

Her debut as a Puerto Rican created what was referred to as "a heated debate among Puerto Ricans on the United States mainland." That you or I might not have heard of this imbroglio attests perhaps to our lack of diversity sensitivity. Critics carped that her skin was still too light and that, in wearing a cotton dress with ruffles, she dissed the entire Puerto Rican community. She should have worn *what*—skintight slacks and spiked heels?

"Barbie looks very, very Anglo," pundits accused.

Besides that, Barbie was *still* too damned skinny for the fatties.

"It's a start that they have a person-of-color Barbie," conceded a University of California-Berkeley professor, "but they should make it look like the person's eaten in the last millennium."

Go figure. Try to please everybody and this is what you get. It's a doll, folks. A *doll.* Why not a short, fat, dark-skinned, lesbian Barbie with thick thighs, pimples and a gimpy leg. She'll walk on crutches while living on a street grate and suffering from drug addiction and AIDS. She has two fathers who are priests accused of molesting alter boys and a mother madly in love physical-wise with her Doberman.

Sound far out? The sensitive, the compassionate, the guilt-ridden will go to ridiculous lengths to have their "concerns" satisfied. All you have to do is breath the word "racism" to start such folks hopping around like toads on a hot plate. Take, for example, the case where the Western Mohegan Indian tribe filed a legal motion in New York laying claim to Ellis Island.

"Ellis Island is ours and so is the Statue of Liberty," insisted Sachem Ron Roberts, who also calls himself Chief Golden Eagle. Why does it always have to be an *eagle?* Why not Chief Golden Chicken or Chief Golden Lizard? "We may consider giving the island to New Jersey and give the statue back to France."

Thirty years ago, Chief Golden Eagle would have been re-dubbed Chief Squatting Dog and told to find a fireplug. But in today's wacky cultural climate, lawyers actually argued the merits of the case. "What *will* we do with the Statue of Liberty?"

Under the Native American Graves and Repatriation Act, *all* cultural materials dating before 1492 (Columbus came that year, for the information of you public school graduates) are deemed to be "Native

American," therefore to belong to "Native Americans." Indians living near an archaeological site are "culturally affiliated" and therefore may claim any discoveries as their rightful and legal property. A Viking boat uncovered on the coast of Maine would be "Native American."

In 1996, two college students digging in the banks of Washington State's Columbia River found a 10,000-year-old skeleton known archaeologically as "Kennewick Man." A problem arose because of the remain's Caucasoid features, suggesting "Native American" may *not* have been the *first* American. Such an outrageous supposition threatened politically-correct doctrines of "white oppression" and "original ownership" of the continent, never mind the logical conclusion that *anything* 10,000 years old couldn't possibly belong or be traced to anyone particular living today. Who could care anyhow about great-great-great (two more pages of great-greats) Uncle Running Mastodon who wasn't fast enough to escape a saber-toothed cat?

Never mind. The Colville Indian Confederation (no full-bloods left?) demanded possession of the bones so they could be properly reburied; they also demanded that the site and all records pertaining to it be destroyed. *We don't want to know what's there or what it means— and we don't want anyone else to know either. That's* an enlightened, scholarly point of view.

Over the objections of scientists, anthropologists and Congress itself, the Clinton administration ordered the Army Corps of Engineers to bury the Kennewick site under 500 tons of rock to prevent further study. Nothing, including the truth, must be allowed to contradict established tenets of race and multiculturalism.

Talk about the sins of our fathers. If you are white in our society, there can never be redemption for what your ancestors did. Prejudice in the victim culture is virtually always ascribed to Caucasians. From the Enlightened viewpoint, *all* whites are bigoted merely by privilege of birth.

"All white individuals in our society are racists," asserts a training manual for the New York State Insurance Fund. "Even if a white is totally free of all conscious racial prejudice, he remains a racist, for he received benefits distributed by a white racist society through its institutions."

Beat me, kick me, call me a bitch and make me like it. I deserve it every day and twice on Sunday for the white blood in my veins and for what my great-great-great-great grandfather *might* have done to my other great-great-great grandfather. Can you Harvard and Yale grads figure that one out on your own?

America has fielded an army of diversity managers, affirmative action officers, EEOC (Equal Employment Opportunity Commission) bureaucrats and consulting companies to root out hidden racism. There seems to be no conceivable limits to how far multiculturalism and political correctness will go in seeking out, accommodating and paying tribute to perceived victims of race.

When John Dalton was Secretary of Navy, he devised what was called a "Diversity 12-12-5" Plan to recruit Navy and Marine Corps officers. All future volunteers, he said, must meet a formula of diversity which he described as 12 percent black, 12 percent Hispanic, and 4.25 percent Asian-American and Pacific Islanders.

To which I indignantly reply: Wait just a cotton-picking minute there, Kemo Sabe. That is blatant discrimination against the Indians, Irish-Americans, Jewish intellectuals and assorted Heinz 57 hillbillies. Where's *our* quotas? After all, Census Form 2000 listed 126 possible combinations of race. What's wrong with a 12-12-5-5-5-4-4-4-3-3-3-2-2-2-2-1-1-1... Plan?

It seems you can even be a victim of racial discrimination by being *too successful.* When Yvonne Lee was commissioner of the Federal Civil Rights Commission, she declared (not tongue-in-cheek either) that being "stuck in the upper rank is a civil rights problem" for Asian-Americans. Folks, I'm not making this up.

"Asian-Americans are over represented in middle management, technical and professional ranks," asserted Ms. Lee, who obviously didn't have sufficient other matters to keep her busy. "They've been shifted toward that area because they were thought to be smart in math and all technical areas... (which has) shielded them from other social studies (and denied them) the opportunity to be exposed to other aspects of education."

Did she ever think that maybe Asian-Americans *are* smart in math and technical areas? Perhaps the Chinese should go back to building railroads and working in laundries where they wouldn't be so disadvantaged.

Mr. Randall Robinson, who "teaches" at Dutton, argues that American society is "stubbornly, poisonously racist...a still unfolding massive crime... Many blacks—most, perhaps, though I can't be sure—don't like America."

Perhaps I'm being indelicate in pointing out that I don't see lines of black folk at the airports happily brandishing one-way tickets to Kenya or the Sudan. I've been to Africa and seen the ignorance, squalor and disease, and, yes, the blatant racism that compels groups of *black people* to attempt to wipe out other groups of black people. Were I a black man, I'd get down on my knees and thank God (or Allah or whoever is in charge in the spirit world, in order that I be politically correct) that somebody's great-great-great grandfather *brought* my great-great-grand grandfather's black ass across the Atlantic.

Wait a minute. I'm supposed to keep my mouth shut, aren't I, when it comes to matters of race, unless of course I obediently toe the "oppressed victims" line? Only the "Enlightened point of view counts. The rest of us don't really matter. After all, we're undoubtedly racist, insensitive, narrow-minded and wear sheets and hoods and burn crosses on dark nights. But more on religion later.

In 1997, President Bill Clinton decided to solve the "race problem" once and for all, as he had similarly solved other problems—by convening a "National Dialogue on Race." Wise and notable participants would study and make recommendations for attaining racial harmony and equality in American society. However, it became immediately apparent that anyone who opposed group preferences and affirmative action or who questioned standard race orthodoxy would not be permitted dialogue in the Dialogue.

A white man who somehow made it as far as the audience had the temerity to point out that the commission was a farce because no white people were included. He was ordered expelled from the room. What else did you expect? It seemed black people were dialoguing with other black people of matching sentiments and persuasions. John Hope Franklin, the black historian who headed the "National Dialogue," was asked if Ward Connerly might join the discussion. Connerly is the black man who led the fight for California's Proposition 209 opposing affirmative action.

Franklin's response was predictably unequivocal: "No. Mr. Connerly would have nothing to contribute."

You couldn't have taken a jackhammer and a pry bar and stuffed an opposing point of view through a crack in that "Dialogue's" collective mind.

Out of such "dialogue" emerged the insane conviction that individuals, families and businesses who profited from slave labor or discrimination (painting with a broad brush) should be identified and coerced into making "reparations." Dutton University's Mr. Randall Robinson, among a growing group of fellow travelers, apparently believes that scoundrels who possess the bad manners to have chosen the wrong ancestors should be charged a special tax over and above regular taxes the rest of the country is paying. A powerful group of civil rights and class-action lawyers, taking time off from suing "Big Tobacco," "Big Fat Foods," "Big SUVs," "Big Guns," and "Big Religion," formed the Reparations Assessment Group to file lawsuits to solicit reparations for American blacks descended from slaves.

Few in the public arena have had the gonads so far to say what a lunatic and destructive idea this is. They've all been gelded out of fear of being branded racists. Instead, they mealy-mouth around the point. Congressman Ton Hall (D-Ohio) introduced legislation calling on Congress to formally apologize to black Americans whose ancestors were slaves. President Bill Clinton floated the idea of a national executive apology for slavery. Apologizing, as it were, for the unalterable facts of history in which none of us presently living had a role. I can apologize, even pay reparations, for something *I* might have done. But for what my great-great-great Uncle Toby or great-great-great Uncle Sitting Chipmunk might have done—that's a different story.

"An apology is in order," agreed the Right Reverend Jesse Jackson, "but you must not only apologize with your lips. Repent, repair, and remedy go together."

In other words, bring money. Jesse is a preacher who, for more than thirty years, has preached only once in any church. He has been too busy leading protests and raising money. Mostly raising money.

If reparations are finally deemed, how would the payments be made? Who will pay them? A little scenario might explain the process. These days, everything has to have a *process*. Peace Process, Education Process, Civil Rights Process... Why not a Reparations Process?

Let us begin by determining *who* will pay.

First of all, it appears to me that Africans, Arabs and Europeans *all* bear an equal percentage of guilt for the slave trade. Black people didn't simply walk down to the beach and shout, "Massah, take me!" Slavery was aided and abetted by Africans selling other Africans to Arab traders who sold them to European shippers. Of course, Africans and Arabs aren't about to pay any slavery reparations; some of them still engage in the slave trade.

Who pays then? Americans. But not black Americans.

Wait a cotton picking minute!

What about Indians? Shouldn't we be exempt from the tax? I think White America should also apologize to the Noble Red Man and offer reparations for The Trail of Tears, the Battle of The Little Big Horn, firewater, and other instances of oppression against Native Americans, who had it good before that idiot Columbus blundered across the Atlantic.

While we're on the subject of exemptions, what about the Irish, the Italians and the Jews? Shouldn't their descendants be offered "repent, repair and remedy" for the discrimination they confronted in the New World? As a matter of fact, most such immigrants came to America *after* the slavery era. Why should we tax their innocent progeny at all?

Come to think of it, most southern whites never owned slaves. That's right, *most*. The white side of my ancestry could hardly afford a mule, much less a slave. On top of that, many whites died in the Civil War fighting against slavery. Have they not redeemed themselves? Cannot redemption be passed along through the gene pool in perpetuity the same as guilt?

Then *who* finally pays? But first, *who* do they pay?

Not all African-Americans are of pure African descent. The "Heinz 57" formula again. In fact, a majority of black people may also have

European, Asian or Indian blood. Golfer Tiger Woods is a perfect example. A modern black American may be descended from *both* slaves
and slave owners. Is it not only fair that the parts of him descended
from slave owners pay at least a portion of the reparation tax?

We're down now to the part of the actual tax. This is the process: I
go in to the tax man to make my annual apology and pay my reparations tax.

"That'll be three hundred dollars." Or whatever some government
bureaucrat determines the price of our individual guilt to be.

"I'm a quarter-breed Creek Indian."

"That'll be seventy five dollars."

"My great-great-great grandfather on my father's side was shanty-
town Irish. He didn't come here until 1874."

"So how much Irish are you?"

"He also married a Jewish lady. Aren't Jewish a protected class?"

"Let me deduct the points. So you're Native American—"

"Yes. I'm Native American, I was born here. I'm also Indian."

"—and you're Jewish. Any African-American?"

"I have curly hair. Will that lower my tax?"

"Hold it up. Here's a list of races and other exemptions. You figure
out exactly which proportion of each race you are—and then we'll
compute your tax based on that."

Don't we see how preposterous the whole thing is? Whatever happened to Martin Luther King's wanting his children to be judged "not
by the color of their skin, but by the content of their character?"

CHAPTER THREE

Sylvia Quarles got married on a lovely Sunday at the Ramada Hotel in Southfield, Michigan. What made this story unusual enough to hit the news was not that she got married but, instead, *who* she married. No, not a lesbian. That doesn't make news anymore, unless thousands line up hand in hand with gays in Boston to be proclaimed "bride and bride" and "groom and groom." You see, Sylvia married *herself.* That's right. It was a *solo* wedding. Sylvia exchanged vows with herself, promising mutual "positive self-love, tranquility and peace."

It says a bunch about the mental stability of a society when a woman having a wedding without a groom no longer seems all that weird. Nonetheless, even weirder and more schizophrenic things are happening in the perplexing world of feminism. Feminists may be even more paranoid over their perceived victim status than race minorities. The fairer half (half plus another one or two percentage points, which makes it odd in looking at females as a *minority)* is simply not going to accept its traditional role anymore. Radical women, as Sylvia demonstrated, don't even *need* men—even though you just can't go out and shoot them. Again like Sylvia, they are learning to celebrate themselves.

Take, for example, sex and private parts, a subject weighted heavily in favor of men. No pun intended. An essay in *Rites,* a monthly publication by the Women's Center of Chico State University, complained that "many women do not even know what to call their genitals."

What about Patsy or Joanie?

"...And many," the article went on, "had never been taught by their mothers, fathers or schools what the clitoris was... It took all my power to keep from screaming, 'Why not?' Men look at their penises every day! They touch them, play with them, look at them, name them, inspect them, take pride in them, and are encouraged to do so their whole lives."

Oh, come on now. You mean women completely ignore *their* parts?

"I believe strongly," the article concluded, "that we, as women, need to cherish our vulva, ovaries, uterus, cervix and, of course, my favorite, our clitoris."

A lot of women apparently agree with her. In a ludicrous movement to replace Valentine's Day with *Vagina* Day, more than 150 colleges and universities celebrated female private parts by staging productions of *The Vagina Monologues,* a play in which women actors portray talking vaginas. The image of vaginas sitting around having polite intercourse, as it were, was enough to inspire sarcastic criticism

from a Georgetown University columnist—who was promptly fired for
his audacity.

How dare he speak out against something as sacrosanct as a gaggle
of vaginas bent on being taken seriously. In the victim game, victims
set the rules. You can be kicked out of the game if you object to the
way it is played.

Feminists have become so adept at spotting an insult and playing
the "sex card" that they detect offense in everything from museum
presentations and street signs—*Curves Ahead, Soft Shoulders*—to cartoons and the Constitution of the United States.

Feminists threw a tantrum and came down on the Smithsonian Museum of Natural History with both little slippered feet for "reinforcing
sex-role stereotypes" in a display of a male lion standing while the female reclined. They wouldn't have uttered a peep, of course, were the
male lying as he rightfully should at the feet of the female while she
kept watch and protected him. Being a sensitive, modern entity, the
Museum responded by posting an apology alerting visitors that *Female
animals are being portrayed in ways that make them appear deviant or
substandard to male animals.*

How utterly precious.

That loveable cartoon character Bugs Bunny drew the ire of more
than Elmer Fudd in an episode entitled "Bewitched Bugs." In it, wily
Bugs escaped the clutches of a witch by blowing her up with magic
powder, transforming her into a gorgeous girl bunny. As Bugs and she
strolled off arm in arm, Bugs quipped, "Ah, sure, I know. But aren't
they all witches inside?"

Duck! The cartoon was "anti-woman." Canadian biddies charged it
violated the nation's Sex-Role Portrayal Code. Yep, Canada has a Sex-
Role Portrayal Code. Look for it to come to your neighborhood soon.

It seems the first thing victims lose is their sense of humor. Other
victim groups joined in the clamor for poor Bugs' head to be delivered
to them on a platter, the macho, sexist slob. Witches rejected the stereotype of witches having warts and riding brooms. Gun control people
protested the "violence" of the witch's being blown up, disregarding
the improvement in her appearance. The race cartel claimed the cartoon
depicted latent bigotry. Gays thought Bugs should have turned the
witch into Stevie or Ken, with whom he then strolled off into the sunset.

Cartoons are one thing, the Declaration of Independence quite another. Nonetheless, any public reading of the Constitution or of the
Declaration of Independence may soon be deemed *unconstitutional*
because of offense to women in particular and other victims in general.
Feminists, for example, went sonic when the New Jersey State Assembly voted to require public schools to daily recite the famous lines from
the Declaration of Independence—"We hold these truths to be self-

evident, that all men are created equal..."

Men? *Men?*

Elizabeth Volz, president of the New Jersey chapter of NOW, declared the idea "dangerous." A dissenting member of the New Jersey
house objected that "at the time those words were written, only white
men, and only white men with property were perceived to be the bene-
ficiaries of these words. To have it repeated every day that all *men* are
created equal...does not meet the present-day expectations of these
young women in these schools."

It's mankind, idiot. *Mankind.* Sorry. *Person*kind. Oh oh. There's
the male word *son* in that word. Change it to *personhood?* Humankind?
Nope. There's that *man.* Oh, Lord, protect me from the wrath of the
Enlightened as I struggle to dehumanize language and reduce it to
complete inoffensiveness.

* * *

In the same way that all whites are guilty of racism, especially
white *males*, so it is that *all* males are guilty of sexism. Radical feminist theologian Mary Daly characterized men as "lethal organs of a
rapist society" who feed upon "benign female energy" to keep women
subservient. Because we men are dangerous to females, therefore, we
must be controlled and "properly" socialized for the overall good and
ultimate survival of society. While we are being conditioned to conform to feminist standards and to swallow all the goofy assertions
about the sameness of the sexes, we are admonished to keep our
mouths shut and do nothing except feel guilty and inadequate.

Young women in Europe and Australian have gone so far as to insist men should *sit* while urinating. I'm really not making this up. If a
woman can't stand and do it, then neither should a man. Feminist
groups at Stockholm University are campaigning to ban all urinals from
campus. A Swedish elementary school has already removed them. Can
the University of California-Berkeley be far behind?

"(A) man standing up to urinate is deemed to be triumphing in his
masculinity and, by extension, degrading women," explained *The Spectator*, an English magazine, adding that it was a "nasty macho gesture"
suggesting male violence.

Imagine *John Wayne* sitting down to pee! In such sensitive times,
you don't swagger in and order your steak raw out of fear of engendering the wrath of ladies and embarrassing all the gelded males who
possess less and less brawn and confidence and more and more empathy and tears. Swag a brewski, cast an admiring glance at a pretty girl's
behind, laugh at an off-color joke...

Huh uh. *Huh uh!* That kind of behavior has to be nipped in the bud.
And it all starts from standing up to... Real men *piss*, damnit. Standing
up.

"The distinctions between the sexes seem to be narrowing," declared Chuck Edgley, professor of sociology at Oklahoma State University.

Soon, we *will* all be sitting down to pee, comfortable with our new status.

Writer Mark Simpson coined the word "metrosexuality" to explain how the idea of manhood is changing in the West and how trends are moving culture in an androgynous direction. The term refers to heterosexual men, usually urban, who have common habits similar to gay men. It's fashionable, for example, to enjoy pedicure and have one's hair *styled* at a salon rather than cut at a neighborhood barber shop.

"The typical metrosexual is a young man with money to spend, living in or within easy reach of a metropolis—because that's where all the best shops, clubs, gyms and hairdressers are," Simpson explained.

So-called "gender experts" — What the hell is a *gender expert?* — believe boys who are being wrongly "masculinized" must be rendered less competitive, more emotionally expressive and sensitive. Early traits of masculinity must be swiftly eradicated. To such "experts," gender inequity is a "health problem," like cigarettes, guns, Twinkies and driving SUVs.

"The cult of masculinity is the basis of every violent, fascist regime," declared feminist Gloria Steinem. "We need to raise our sons more like our daughters, with empathy, flexibility, patience and compassion."

In other words, sissy boys who will be *delighted* to sit down to pee after visiting their favorite hairdresser and buying a new pair of earrings.

You can go to any gay parade, said author Tammy Bruce, and see a fair share of men dressed up like their favorite female movie stars. "But I don't think I want some guy dressed as Dolly Parton running the Department of Defense," she added.

Are we totally bonkers yet or what?

A mother came to fetch her son from day care and was told that he was sent to the "time out" chair. His offense? "He's a hugger," Mommy was told. "We are not going to put up with it."

The little boy was three years and he was already harassing women.

Twelve-year-old Sal Santana asked a classmate at Magoffin Middle School in El Paso to be his girlfriend. When she declined, Sal stuck his tongue out at her. School administrators suspended him for three days while they considered placing him in an alternate school. The charge? Sexual harassment.

Senator Ted Kennedy (D-Massachusetts) co-sponsored a "gender equity" education bill which attacked the "crisis" of "sexual harassment among the young." This is the same guy who drove a young woman off a bridge and left her to drown. Talk about sexual harassment. "You have first, second and third-grade harassers," Kennedy rationalized. "You have kindergarten harassers. We're reaching out and identifying them at the earliest grades, disciplining these individuals. As with every aspect of health care, early intervention can have a big impact."

All I have to say is keep your grubby mitts off my five-year-old.

One of the ironies and unforeseen consequences of feminism as victimhood is that greater and greater numbers of men, since they are no longer responsible for leading, protecting and providing for families, are stepping back and letting women take over. Many military recruiting posters, for example, show women in alert, heroic poses prepared to defend the motherland against all enemies, foreign and domestic, while young men in uniform fade into the background. As F. Carolyn Graglia put it, the more bureaucratic, layered, protected and controlled a society is, the more hospitable it is to women and to the "effete, attenuate, androgynous male who fits within the feminist mold of manhood... Being willing and often very competent to institute and enforce a minute regulation of other people's lives, women thrive in the security of bureaucracy, the bastion of females and feminized males."

Decades ago, D.H. Lawrence forecast that the "vast human farmyard" was starting to fall out of scheme.

"All the cocks are cackling and pretending to lay eggs," he wrote, "and all the hens are crowing and pretending to call the sun out of bed. If women today are cocksure, men are hen sure. Men are timid, tremulous, rather soft and submissive, easy in their very hen like tremulousness. They only want to be spoken to gently. So the women step forward with a good loud cock-a-doodle-doo!"

CHAPTER FOUR

Woe, woe, woe is me;
I'm downtrodden and it ain't fair.
It ain't my fault.

These may well become the first lines of the new national anthem whining from sea to shining sea. These strange days Americans identify with so many different victim groups that we almost need federal ID cards in order to establish our protected statuses. This neurotic society is obsessed with ensuring *fairness* for everyone—the short, the fat, the ugly, the lonely, the dateless, the criminal, the gendered, the engendered... No matter what our perceived affliction, no matter what threatens our health, safety and, above all else, our fragile self-esteem, we all know one thing: *It ain't my fault. And it ain't fair.*

Instead of accepting responsibility for his crimes after President Bill Clinton pardoned him out of prison for his role in a series of bombings, Puerto Rican terrorist Ricardo Jimenez blamed—who else but the proprietors of the restaurants and taverns he blew up.

"I think all precautions were taken, you know, (by us terrorists) to make sure all human life was preserved," he declared in presenting himself as a sensitive, compassionate terrorist who really cared, "and in the end the measures were not taken that were necessary by the people who owned those establishments."

He was a victim of *their* oversight and carelessness in their not protecting their customers against him.

The concept that a person is in command of his own behavior and therefore responsible for it has all but vanished from modern American life.

"That bum sitting on a heating grate, smelling like a wharf rat?" radio talk show host Neal Boortz pointed out. "He's there by choice. He is there because of the sum total of the choices he has made in life. This truism is absolutely the hardest thing for some people to accept, especially those who consider themselves to be victims of something or other—victims of discrimination, bad luck, the system, capitalism, whatever. After all, nobody really wants to accept the blame for his or her position in life. Not when it is so much easier to point and say, 'Look! He did this to me!' than it is to look into a mirror and say, 'You SOB. You did this to me!'"

Twin sisters Karen Sutton and Kimberly Hinton desperately wanted to be commercial pilots, but American Airlines turned them down because both were badly nearsighted. That's tough, but, hey, I wanted to be heavyweight boxing champ of the world. Except I was five-nine and weighed one sixty. I suppose I could have followed Karen and Kimberly's example. They sued under the Americans With

Disabilities Act, claiming they were being discriminated against because they were disabled. I know I would have felt very secure flying to fight Big George Foreman or Lenox Lewis in a plane flown by a pilot who may not have been able to tell the airport from U.S. 40.

Definitions of "discrimination" and "rights" expand to cover greater and greater numbers of people in the lunacy of pursuing and wiping out all signs of victimization and insensitivity. Feelings of "doing something" and "making a difference" count more than any reality of near-sighted pilots and midget heavyweights for "victims" and their supporters. It's an easy thing to rectify discrimination and feel good about it.

First, you discover a certain category of people in need of special protection. Say, for example, shorties who want to play with the National Basketball Association. You raise everyone's awareness about the new victim group—"Shorties need love and appreciation of NBA fans too"—and brand anything negative about it as "discrimination" or "hate." You pass a law or regulation restricting behavior toward that group and providing it privilege. Don't you absolutely feel great about yourself for having "made a difference?"

Under guidelines issued by the Federal Equal Opportunity Commission (EEOC) covering "myths, fears and stereotypes" about mental conditions, an employer is prohibited from asking a job applicant if he has ever been hospitalized for a mental illness. Don't we think it's important for an employer to know that the guy he's about to hire to teach sixth graders once went to the loony bin for molesting children? Or that the new mall security guard, armed, was once committed for shooting up a post office?

Employers are further informed that "problem workers" are protected under the Americans With Disabilities Act if their problems "may be linked to mental impairment." Chronic tardiness, absenteeism, poor judgment, screaming at supervisors, picking boogers while serving a Big Mac or scratching your crotch behind the counter at Wal-Mart may all have to be tolerated unless you want to be dragged into one sweet federal lawsuit for failure to "make reasonable accommodation to disability."

If someone enters your personnel office picking flies out of the air, passing gas in public and chattering about a "vast right wing conspiracy," maybe you had better do the safe thing and hire him. He's probably protected, and may even be a liberal Enlightened presidential candidate. You can always adjust *your* schedule and *your* requirements in order to accommodate him—build him a visual barrier if he's schizophrenic; install a plant-wide filtering system to accommodate his allergies; put up a sign saying picking your nose and scratching your crotch is actually very healthy and multicultural.

Adam Cohen of the American Civil Liberties Union (ACLU)

chose ugly people as needing special protection against "look-ism."

"People don't realize how pervasive the preference for the beautiful is in our society," he explained. "There is nothing wrong with giving these (homely) people who have a hard life a legal remedy. We can always set enforcement priorities later."

Now *that's* chilling. First set the offense, then provide the punishment. It's *my* fault for noticing if you walk in with tentacles and scabs and one eye in the center of your head, an offense of observation which, if I'm not careful, can get me tossed into jail or into Sensitivity Training. Given the choice, I'll take jail.

By the time of Super Bowl a decade or less from now, I predict the Dallas cheerleaders will "look like America," with a full quota of fatties, one-legged streetwalkers, plug uglies and transgendered former truck drivers. We mustn't "discriminate" or "hate."

I call it insanity. The insanity of good intentions, perhaps, but still totally bonkers.

Another prime example of cultural madness is Section 504 of the Rehabilitation Act which intends to blend "disabled students" into regular public schools. It expanded the category of "disabled" to also protect "behavior difficulties." Protected behaviorally-challenged students are those with "an inability to learn which cannot be explained by intellectual, sensory or health factors...(of) inappropriate types of behavior or feelings under normal circumstances..."

What this psychobabble really means is that teachers cannot punish bad boys, kick them out of school, or even complain about them. They are behaviorally disabled. They are therefore a protected class. Again, I'm not making this up.

"I've walked miles shadowing my charges while they destroy school property, bang on classroom windows, and scream obscenities to both students and staff," said junior high teacher T. Kelly Rossiter. "These students are not mobility-limited, blind or mute. They're what Section 504 terms 'behaviorally disabled,' a loose category of students who receive the educational equivalent of diplomatic immunity.

"I've seen teenagers who failed all their classes because they refused to open a book, who smashed a picture frame because they were 'pissed off,' who told the school principal to 'go fuck your slutty mother.' Recently, while trying to talk one of my students down from his desktop perch, where he stood simulating masturbation in front of the class, I heard this explanation, 'Don't lecture me, Mr. Rossiter. I'm behaviorally disabled. I can't listen to lectures, they make me angry. And I can't control my anger.'"

At the risk of sounding impolitic, I think this kid's crude, bad-tempered, insulting butt should have been dragged down from that desk top and thrown out the door on said butt. When did we reach the point of accommodating all behavior at the expense of everyone else?

Yet another example of victim bloat, if you'll pardon the pun, is *size-ism.* That's right. Lard butts. The EEOC now considers fat, "under appropriate circumstances," to be a disability. "It is not necessary," said the EEOC in a statement, "that a condition be involuntary or immutable to be covered." Fatties as victims now outnumber transgendered witches, left-handed sex workers and all other victim groups combined. Society offends and transgresses against them at every turn—and they ain't gonna take it no more.

"At last, fat people are on the march!" roared an activist for NAAFA, the National Association to Advance Fat Acceptance. But only after a couple of Twinkies for the road and a pair of Whoppers and a Diet Coke from the drive-thru.

NAAFA targeted Eddie Murphy's movie *The Nutty Professor*, claiming it sorely offended them by its treatment of the weight-challenged. That, even though the Association's founder, Sally Smith, admitted, "We haven't seen the movie. The theaters have no seats big enough."

NAAFA was quite reasonable even though their members were weightily insulted. Representatives offered to work with Paramount on future projects to replace "nutty professor" fat jokes with ones more "affirming of fat people's self-esteem." Paramount rejected the offer in an act of rare common sense—perhaps because they already had a full stock of sensitivity representatives to protect every other victim group in America.

You can literally take your life in your hands these days by dissing someone's priceless self-esteem.

In Texas, a suspicious husband shadowed his wife to her weekly Weight Watchers meeting because she seemed to be making no progress. He discovered that she was pigging out at a local steakhouse instead of attending meetings. He confronted her that night in bed. Perhaps foolish men should also be a victim class. She grabbed a pistol from the nightstand and shot him.

Foolish woman. She couldn't go on the lam because she was too fat to get out of bed without his help. All she could do was lie there with her poor dead husband and her damaged self-esteem and wait for the cops to come.

Naturally, it wasn't *her* fault. It wasn't *his* either. Then whose fault was it, you might ask? Foolish reader. It was *food's* fault. Food and those who sell food.

First there was tobacco, then guns, then SUVs, then... It ain't gonna stop, folks. The victim industry is growing, pun intended. In 2000, a New York lawyer sued *McDonald's, Wendy's, Kentucky Fried Chicken* and *Burger King* on behalf of his 272-pound client, Caesar Barber, charging that the fast food industry was responsible for Barber's weight gain and extensive health problems. Apparently, about a dozen or so servers and quick cooks tossed the struggling customer to the floor and stuffed barbecue chicken thighs, whoppers, and McNuggets down his gullet. That was just the beginning. The next year, San Francisco lawyer and publicity hound Stephen Joseph sued Oreo cookies, demanding that Kraft cease selling the cookies in California because they contain "dangerous" amounts of partially hydrogenated vegetable oil. Lawyer John F. Banzhaf II, who led America's anti-tobacco litigation, wrote to six of the world's largest fast food companies warning them that they were "deeply vulnerable" to litigation. Other lawyers and legal health advocates likewise warned major ice cream chains of lawsuits if they ignored the dangers of ice cream-induced obesity. New Zealand's health minister is considering a bill to make it a crime to sell junk food like soft drinks, pies, sweets, and chocolates to children.

It's not difficult to imagine your local drug pusher now dealing in contraband Hershey bars and Bama pies. Psst! Psst! Hey, kid. Interested in either a Milky Way or a bag of Mexican grass? Condoms? Nah. You can get your condoms from your teacher.

Look for something like *The Extremely Pure Food & Drug Act* to come to Congress soon. All products containing "unhealthy" ingredients will be illegal. Food Police will clamp down on our borders and declare a War on Fast Foods. Fast food restaurants will close, replaced by Twinkie smugglers. Ain't life fun in a world gone bonkers?

America's "Victim List" was relatively short in the early 1980s compared to today's "inclusive" tally. So far, even a partial list of current victim classes—and therefore, as such, legally protected—includes such groups as: cross-dressers; people with AIDS; dope sufferers; alkies; the homeless; ex-convicts; people of accent; people of color; women; transsexuals or otherwise "gendered;" left-handers; schizos; fatties; skinnies; the lazy; the poor; shorties; uglies; mentals...

Lawyer greed fed by government greed encourages the search for further victims, the most cutting edge now being victims of "health issues." Shakespeare might have been right in suggesting we kill all the lawyers in order to preserve civilization.

For the past forty years cigarettes have borne dire warnings on every pack: *The Surgeon General has determined that cigarette smoking causes cancer.* What part of that don't we understand? What else do we need? Skulls and crossbones? So we suck smoke into our lungs for most of our lives and, sure enough, we catch cancer. Rather, it catches us; that's why we're victims. What do we do? What else? Sue the bastards! It's the American way.

Woe, woe is me;
It ain't my fault...

West Virginia is even considering whether the tobacco industry should be forced to spend $500 million on doctors' examinations for healthy people who, despite the warnings, keep smoking.

Tobacco, Big Macs and SUVs are not the only suspects by far in the frenetic search for "health issue" victims. Underarm deodorants, perfumes, after shave lotions are all potential offenders of human health and dignity. That's right. Watch out Ban, Jergens and Old Spice. Lawyers and their client sufferers of MCS (Multiple Chemical Sensitivity) are on your scent—and on the scent of your money.

"While the dangers of second-hand smoke have been widely studied and publicized," charged a spokesperson of the Fragranced Products Information Network, "both the scientific community and the press have largely ignored the dangers of exposure to fragrances... Fragrance products worn by people a block away adversely affect the chemically sensitive..."

A *block* away? You're kidding me, right?

San Francisco's Ecology House produced a list of fragrance items that might adversely affect MCS sufferers-victims. The list included the following products: perfumes; cologne or after shave; hair spray; mousse; scented shampoo; hair conditioners; scented deodorants; lotions; lipsticks; recently dry-cleaned clothing; scented laundry detergents; fabric softeners; shoe polish; chewing gum...

Naturally, those sensitive to the sensitivities of the sensitive jumped on the wagon like ducks on June bugs. Two professors at Western Connecticut State University in Danbury distributed a list of what their students could not wear or bring to class, such list including many of the items categorized by the Ecology House. How would you like to be in either one of these classes on a warm July afternoon? Talk about *fragrance sensitive!*

Citizens attending town meetings in Shutesbury, Massachusetts, are now sorted out according to how they smell. The old whiff test. One section of the meeting hall is set aside for those Enlightened who *never* use perfume, scented deodorants or other fragrances—and who, incidentally, probably never shave their legs and underarms. Another section is devoted to those people who admit shame-facedly to *occasionally* using fragrances. The third section, of course, is cordoned off exclusively for the perfumed and beetle-browed savages.

Guess where I'd rather be seated? They must be very short town meetings. Some inspired wag suggested a new bumper sticker: *If Giorgio is outlawed, only outlaws will wear Giorgio.*

"Basically, we want to destroy the fragrance industry," declared the late activist Jackie Kendall. "Why should we have brain damage because people are wearing toxic chemicals?"

I think it's too late. Brain damage may already have occurred.

It almost seems as though thin-skinned Americans go around *seek-*

ing ways to be offended. It may actually increase their self-esteem. *We're picked on more than you are.* They clamor to be accommodated to by the rest of us. Society has become a crazy quilt pattern of demand, accommodation and counter-demand. Consider:

Former National Energy Secretary Hazel O'Leary did away with different levels of security badges at nuclear plants because they discriminated against those with lower classifications, "made them uneasy," and damaged their self-esteem;

The National Federation of The Blind jumped on Disney for producing the movie *Magoo*, deemed offensive to the visually impaired;

The Alliance for The Mentally Ill denounced presidential candidate Ross Perot for using the Patsy Cline tape *Crazy* as his theme song;

Disney pulled ads for a children's bath soap featuring the stuttering Piglet from *Winnie The Pooh* and apologized to the National Stuttering Project for "any unintended offensive use of stuttering;"

The Iowa City Community School District sent letters to parents cautioning against children wearing offensive and politically-incorrect Halloween costumes such as gypsy, witch, slave, hobo, devil or American Indian princess;

And in Britain some teachers avoid using the word "brainstorming" since it might offend students with epilepsy. They advise to use "word storm" or "thought showers."

It has become modern fashion plate for celebrities and social activists of various stripes of immaturity to showcase how deeply they feel about society's victims. One victim group this month, another next. Actor Martin Sheen, for example, slept on a street grate for a night to accentuate the plight of the homeless and "raise awareness." He shed a couple of tears for the camera, then went home to Hollywood secure in the realization that everyone knew how much he *cared*. I suspect stars and starlets hire publicity agents to select for them causes that will most likely appeal to their fans.

"How about pro-choice?"

"No, no. I had that one last month. Maybe we could do... Uh... How about racial profiling?"

"That may be too controversial since 9-11. Let's do something tried and true—pro-choice or women's rights."

Some of the solutions for social problems proposed by these ribbon wearers are so wacky you have to think they've fallen off their rockers and can't get up.

San Francisco, that bastion of conspicuous compassion, wanted to alleviate the suffering of street bums by giving them free shopping carts so they could push around their recyclable Coke cans, half-empty wine bottles, free hypodermic syringes and other personal treasurers. Amos Brown, supervisor of the city's Coalition On Homelessness, went absolutely goo-goo over how this remedy would "give them a sense of ownership... We could have designated areas for people to park their carts and have them locked."

Talk about fostering human dignity and self-esteem. My very own Albertson's shopping cart—and I didn't even have to steal it. Every "homeless" person in San Francisco receives a monthly check from the city merely because he's a bum. It's good work if you can get it. A subsidized panhandler can do all right for himself without having to work like other poor stiffs. Recently, the city offered one further innovative idea on how to help the homeless—credit cards.

I swear I'm not making this up. Bums and panhandlers would be "empowered" by presenting them with credit card machines with which, for your ease and convenience, they could more easily process your handouts. Mayor Willie Brown enthused that the scheme "empowers homeless persons to take responsible actions for their lives." Is this guy smoking something or what?

Do you take MasterCard or Visa?

Sorry. I only accept American Express.

After an initiative was placed on the ballot to curb panhandling in San Francisco, Democratic Senator John Burton threatened to file a lawsuit to prevent it, even if voters passed it into law. Hey, the City on The Bay is proud of its deadbeats; it keeps electing them.

I must admit I'm old-fashioned in that I look at a panhandler as a panhandler whether he's thrusting a grimy hand at me for my change or demanding credit card charity. I fail to see "empowerment" here. No wonder citizens can't walk the street downtown without being button-holed or threatened.

This is liberal fundamentalism at its purest: Protect parasites and law breakers at the expense of everyone else. The old admonition to "grab ahold of your boot straps and pull yourself up" does not apply in the victim culture. You aren't "playing fair" if you're industrious, ambitious, productive and contribute to society instead of sucking from it. "Equality" means leveling society to the lowest common denominator. Lower the standards if the standards can't be met by *everyone*. We are expected to cater to the lesser among us, no matter what it is.

"Peoples Park" in Berkeley was overrun with dopers, panhandlers and a wild assortment of other deadbeats who made the intergalactic bar scene in *Star Wars* appear tame by comparison. Berkeley shelled out more than a million dollars in taxpayer funds to build volleyball courts in an attempt to make Peoples Park "less scary."

The volleyball courts were then torn down in a couple of years because, to quote activist Eric Robinson, "volleyball is kind of an upper-class game and that's why it offended."

That's right. People, he said, were *offended* by volleyball.

Basketball courts remained, however, because basketball "is an inner-city game." The park, Robinson said, should be primarily enjoyed by the "downtrodden." Removing elitist volleyball would "make the park a place for everybody."

Are these people *serious?* They are. Do they see the irony? They do not.

The victim game has now reached the point where white heterosexual Anglo-Saxon males, traditionally excluded from victim lists since everyone knows they are universal oppressors, may themselves join the protected ranks. A federal judge ruled that *white men* are socially disadvantaged and thus eligible for affirmative action if—yep, you guessed it—*they* have been victims of affirmative action.

Who else does that leave to claim victim status? My God, we're *all* victims!

SECTION II
POLITICAL CORRECTNESS

"When co-workers discuss their spouses, the use of terms such as 'husband' and 'wife' may be too exclusive. If co-workers use the more inclusive terms such as partner, domestic partner, or significant other, more people will feel part of the conversation."

Chairman, Gay and Lesbian Employees Forum

CHAPTER FIVE

In George Orwell's futuristic social novel *1984*, unorthodox (read *politically incorrect)* opinions were to be rendered obsolete in two ways. First, undesirable words were either diminished or stripped of their original meanings. Second, new words were constructed in order to impose a desirable political attitude upon the people. Reality and truth were whatever the Party held to be real and true. There would come a time when people would believe whatever they were told to believe because words would not exist to believe anything else.

George was an insightful man; he didn't even miss the date, 1984, by much, if any. All you have to do to confirm his novel is look at our sensitive and politically correct times when it is a trauma for some to drink from a *Dixie* cup or turn on the radio and hear a song by the *Dixie Chicks*. When some nations now make it a hate crime to refer to someone as "obese" or to mutter such felonious words as "elderly," "married," "disabled," or "aged." These are now four-letter words akin to slapping someone in the face but with harsher penalties.

We are rapidly losing words from our language while the meanings of other words are being obfuscated or transformed into witless psychobabble. *Differently abled, significant other, undocumented alien...* The old words are much clearer. *Crippled, husband, wetback...* Language and the facts language symbolize are being refashioned to conform socially and politically to a fashionable but wacky ideology. Orwell called it *Groupthink*. We are being conditioned to suppress individual thought in exchange for correct *approved* opinion, to guard our tongues out of fear of uttering something that might offend someone else and thus get our thoughtless and insensitive butts fined, tossed into the hoosegow or dispatched to be reeducated in Sensitivity Training.

Honest thinking men are unable to disagree without one being branded with an "ism" label to shut him up—*racism, sexism, able-ism, look-ism...* There are dozens of them. Many topics have thus been rendered taboo to discussion. You simply mustn't talk or write about these "sensitive" issues, unless, of course, you follow the correct party-approved line.

"A man who deliberately inflicts violence on the language will almost certainly inflict violence on human beings if he acquires the power," wrote philosopher Paul Johnson. "Those who treasure the meaning of words will treasure truth, and those who bend words to their purposes are very likely in pursuit of antisocial ones. The correct and honorable use of words is the first and natural credential of civilized states."

Who can forget the Bill Clinton quote on the meaning of "is?"

After I wrote my novel *Liberty City* satirizing political correctness

(AmErica House, 2000), I re-read it and suffered an overwhelming compulsion to apologize for it. It was like I had been caught having sex with a farm animal, only incomparably worse. In our tolerant social climate, sodomy with a cow or a sheep could be understood and forgiven provided I apologized to the animal, sought counseling, and joined a support group. What would be less readily understood and forgiven in an age of acute sensitivity was my daring to venture into unpopular thought. I would be accused of every modern "ism" imaginable. I would be charged with *hating*. I felt I should run through the streets begging forgiveness from every stranger I met: *Look at me! I don't hate anybody!*

I grew up in the Ozark Mountains of a hillbilly clan of Indians and farm workers. Admittedly, we were a ragged, ignorant, backward bunch. My dad could neither read nor write; the only books in our tin-roofed shack were *Sears & Roebuck* catalogues, and only those because of their utilitarian value in the outhouse. But what we hillbillies possessed instead of sophistication was a fiercely independent nature and a rough-spoken language that expressed our worldviews directly, clearly, and left no doubt as to meaning. If a man thought you an idiot, he called you an idiot and to hell with your self-esteem.

Contrast that to today's Groupthink that seeks to limit and make subject to poll approval not only words but also thought and behavior. Social idealists who believe they and only they possess the enlightened keys to remaking society and building a "New Person" have found in language and the use of language the means to control thought, expression and behavior.

"Don't you see that the whole aim of Newspeak is to narrow the range of thought?" Orwell wrote. "In the end we shall make thought crime literally impossible, because there will be no words in which to express it."

CHAPTER SIX

If you look at the growing numbers of "victim" groups in our society, the act of being offended has become a full-time political vocation for many. While they talk in the rhetoric of concern about "hate" and "violence," what they are really up to is social control. It's about power. It always is when some people want to bridle others.

Free speech, argues Professor Catherine MacKinnon of the University of Michigan Law School, is "a chimera in sexist, racist America where most people are members of subordinate groups." Government, she insists, has a Constitutional *duty* to suppress all expression that exacerbates any "historically oppressed" group's subordinate status. In other words, keep your mouth shut. Do not offend anyone. If Professor MacKinnon and her cohorts have their way, a virtuous government would adopt the goal of establishing equality by imposing upon society a "progressive consciousness."

You have to translate such terms. "Progressive consciousness" means keep your mouth shut and go along.

Naturally, it's up to the Enlightened and the Progressive to lead us common yeomen out here in the hinterlands to social awareness, to destroy old speech and the old thought that goes with it and replace both with a contemporary construction. The movement to make language totally inoffensive and therefore as incapable of holding thought as a sieve is of holding water continues to flood the country. One notes remarkably little resistance. The whole thing would be absolutely hilarious but for its unfunny consequences.

For example, Washington D.C.'s black mayor Anthony Williams forced his white aide David Howard to resign because of a statement Howard made in speaking of a funding program.

"I will have to be niggardly with this fund because it's not going to be a lot of money," he said.

Whoa there, Nellie! Sound the offense alarms. Word spread throughout this sensitive city on the Potomac that Howard had used a racial slur. Never mind that in my Funk & Wagnall's "niggardly" is defined as miserly or stingy. What a word *means* doesn't really matter if someone is sorely and irreparably offended by it.

"I don't agree with him saying that kind of word," went one enlightened comment. "He should be punished because it's so close to a degrading word."

The mayor agreed. Howard had to go.

"He didn't say anything that was in itself racist," the mayor admitted. *However,* "we're trying to bring our city together" and officials must "exercise utmost judgment, discretion and caution" in their choice of words. Decent people, he went on self-righteously, must avoid words that could *sound* offensive to someone who didn't know better.

Sounds reasonable to me. I think we *should* pander to the hypersensitive and the ignorant. You can encounter any number of words that *sound* offensive if your total workaday vocabulary consists of 400 words.

The New York University at Albany was going to sponsor a student/faculty picnic. They distributed flyers promoting the picnic. All plans went in reverse, however, when students—the more enlightened, sensitive ones naturally—began protesting the word *picnic*. They insisted the word had been used at one point in American history as a synonym for racist lynching. It wasn't true of course, but who gives a damn about truth? *Don't confuse me with the facts, my mind's made up.*

New flyers were distributed with the word *picnic* deleted. You expected something else? It took some real creativity to come up with a substitute word. *Outing*, for example, was rejected by gay leaders who warned its use would open different sensitivity issues. No one objected to *event*, although a few tried, so the university finally had an *event* in the park in which lunches were brought and eaten picnic-style. I mean, *event*-style.

Naturally, we are reassured that in weeding out words that make offensiveness and thought crime possible, in reducing vocabularies to no more than 400 words, each of which must be vetted and approved, we are promoting *inclusion* by a process of *exclusion*.

"... In the course of daily interaction, inclusive language allows everyone to be a part of the workplace," wrote National Institute of Health employee Nick D'Ascoli in *Diversity Digest*. "When co-workers discuss their spouses, the use of terms such as 'husband' or 'wife' may be too exclusive. If co-workers use the more inclusive terms such as partner, domestic partner or significant other, more people will feel part of the conversation..."

Over 300 students protested the use of the word "marriage" in a publication at Barnard College, New York. They accused, tried and found the word guilty of being "heterosexist."

There was a time not that long ago when parents wanted their children to read in order to expand both their vocabularies and their understanding of the world. Today's politically-correct pedagogics want to control and limit children's range of thought, and therefore their vocabulary. Even very young children are targeted by thought police. Get them early enough and they'll grow up hugging trees, nibbling carrots and wearing little colored *I Care* ribbons to demonstrate their sensitivity.

"I'm on a mission to create a new body of children's literature that is both entertaining and positive..." declared Bruce Lansky of his children's book, *The New Adventures of Mother Goose*. "We need to replace traditional children's literature that is archaic, scary, violent,

intolerant, and sexist with literature that reflects contemporary values."
Contemporary values! Now, that is scary.

So, Mr. Lansky in his superior contemporary wisdom rewrote *Mother Goose* in today's politically correct vernacular. Remember *Georgie Porgie?*

> *Georgie Porgie, puddin and pie,*
> *Kissed the girls and made they cry.*
> *And when the boys came out to play,*
> *Georgie Porgie ran away.*

That's *sexual harassment.* Three-year-old boys get kicked out of day care for kissing little girls. Mr. Lansky's version is so much more sensitive and correct.

> *Georgie Porgie, what a shame.*
> *Kids call you such a silly name.*
> *Now I think you know it's true,*
> *That teasing isn't nice to do.*

Isn't that just absolutely so precious, so...so *today?*

Language usage and the possibility of its being viewed as offensive has reached the point where the University of Missouri School of Journalism, one of the nation's most "prestigious," found it necessary to create something called a "Multicultural Management Program" and to publish a *Dictionary Of Forbidden English.* The dictionary, a sizeable tome, listed words that no self-respecting culturally-aware wordsmith must ever use in his copy. Forbidden or objectionable words included:

Dutch treat. Why? It implied Dutch people were cheap.

Fried chicken. "A loaded phrase when used carelessly and stereotypically referring to black cuisine."

Gorgeous. "Must be used carefully" in describing female physical attributes. Seeing a woman as *gorgeous* is an insult?

The Los Angeles *Times* was one of the first newspapers to catch on to the trend. Its writers and editors were issued "Guidelines to Ethnic, Racial, Sexist or Other Identification," which, among other things, banned certain common words and phrases. *Mailman, mankind* and *man-made* got the ax because they "appeared to exclude women." *Co-ed* was out because, for some reason I'm not enlightened enough to understand, it "appears derogatory to female students." God forbid *normal* be used because it implies activities such as having sex with your dog or murdering your neighbor is "not normal."

Niggardly was not included in the "Guidelines," possibly because the *Times* leadership felt its staff was already too "decent" to contemplate its usage.

A "Diverse Quotes" policy accompanied the "Guidelines." In imposing a "quote quota" on reporters, it required them to include quotes from women and minorities, no matter what the story was about. Can't you just see the copy? *Two women, an African-American, a Chinese and a lesbian had these comments about the ten-car pileup on the LA Freeway this morning...*

It's a holocaust! Words and phrases are being slaughtered all over the nation. Ink is running knee deep in the glory of inoffensiveness and sensitivity. Casualties are piling up.

Pregnant is now "parasitically engaged." *Fat* is "horizontally challenged." *Lying* is "spin control." *Hobo* is "homeless." *Body odor* is "non-discretionary fragrance." The Clinton State Department declared that "rogue states" would heretofore be known as "states of concern" out of concern for these states' self-esteem.

Politically correct wordsmiths are striving to eliminate all negative and casual references to the color black in popular speech. *Black magic, blacklist* and *blackboard* should, they say, be liquidated. One school official complained of a report that said a student suffered a "black eye." Children now sing "Baa, Baa, Green Sheep." An editorial designer for a New York publisher censored the phrase "colored markers" from a children's book.

Mad, crazy, and *manic* are "offensive to some with mental health problems." *Cripple* and *queer* should only be used when "reclaimed" by the differently abled and differently oriented. Animal rights groups insist the village of *Fishkill,* New York, be changed to something more compassionate, like *Fishsave.* Legislatures are eradicating *squaw* from state maps and signs. "Blatantly sexist" street signs like *Yield, Soft Shoulders* and *Curves Ahead* are disappearing. Longmont, Colorado, eliminated *Dead End* signs because they reminded some residents of death. Massachusetts wanted to change its *Slow Children* signs because they were insensitive to retarded kids.

Make the mistake of using "niggardly" or some other word that even *sounds* offensive, as David Howard learned to his dismay, and the enlightened community will jump on your incorrect ass faster than flies can swarm a pile of slaughter house guts. Of course, *who* you are makes as much difference in the use of language as *what* you say. Ugly name calling is perfectly acceptable when you're mocking the "right wing rabble," but heaven help you if you so much as let out a peep to criticize the Enlightened.

No objections were voiced, for example, when George Stephanopoulos called Senator Jesse Helms a "terrorist" or when CNN pundit William Schneider compared him to "Old South slave owners." On the other hand, when Reverend Jerry Falwell referred to gay activist actress Ellen DeGeneres as "Ellen Degenerate," he was verbally beheaded.

"We have ways of making sure you keep your mouth shut."

CHAPTER SEVEN

In the Brave New Sensitive Society it is not enough for me to be merely tolerant, to live and let live, to say that I really don't give a damn what people do in the privacy of their own homes as long as they aren't tossing their garbage on my front porch. Huh uh. What is required, *demanded,* is that I enthusiastically embrace and celebrate the New Culture of Madness. I must either come to *believe*—or face the wrath of the Enlightened.

"American society is racist and sexist," declared Donna Shalala, former Secretary of Health and Human Services. "In the 1960s, we were frustrated about all this. But now, we are in a position to do something about it."

And "do something about it" the Enlightened are—by creating a totalitarian atmosphere in which you guard your tongue at all times for fear of being ostracized and punished for inadvertently saying something in which some sensitive other soul might take umbrage. It is so *easy* to offend the oh-so-sensitive in our society.

When Shalala was chancellor at the University of Wisconsin, she imposed a broad speech code on her faculty to protect against an "intimidating or demeaning environment." It covered "all expression, teaching materials, student assignments, lectures or instructional techniques (which) gender, race, cultural background, ethnicity, sexual orientation or handicap...might find objectionable."

Might, mind you. Talk about having to walk around on intellectual tiptoes and doublethink every single word.

The Enlightened are big on reeducation. Not so much *education*, which has been taken over by self-esteem and feel-good courses, but rather by *reeducation* that smacks of political reeducation camps. Sensitivity and diversity training by universities, state and federal agencies, and even private employers are the big guns of the new consciousness and awareness police.

Anyone who has ever ridden a New York subway cannot totally disagree with observations made by Atlanta Braves pitcher John Rocker. "Imagine having to take the Seven train to the ballpark," he said in an interview, "looking like you're riding through Beirut, next to some kid with purple hair, next to some queer with AIDS, right next to some dude who just got out of jail for the fourth time, right next to some twenty-year-old mom with four kids. It's depressing."

It *is* a bit depressing, and scary, for some guy off a farm or from a small town down South or out west (But not as far West and left as San Francisco). I'm a former Green Beret soldier and I feel a bit queasy on the subway, watching some bum take a leak against the wall while everyone walks on by, stepping over dopers and panhandlers, crowding into a train with some guy with spiked blue hair and his tongue split and pierced, next to a six-foot-tall dude dressed up like Whitney Houston. Hey, if you don't take a second look at *this*, you aren't human, you are blind, or you have rings through your own pierced nipples and scrotum.

On top of all this, California's then-Governor Gray Davis signed a bill imposing heavy fines on employers who refused to hire such people. Under the bill, a former wrestler named Bubba has the *right* to dress up like Dolly Parton and work at your Christian bookstore. Either you hire him or you pay a fine of $150,000.

Rocker's troubles began because he actually voiced his observations. From the public reaction, you might have thought he had nuked Manhattan. Rocker "brought dishonor" to himself and major league baseball. He was fined $20,000, suspended from playing baseball, ordered to a psychiatric screening, made to apologize to everybody in the world and their pets, and *then* shipped off to "sensitivity training" in order for the diversity folks to rearrange his brain.

Wonder if all that made a *believer* out of him? From now on, ole John won't notice such stuff and if he's ever mugged he will *understand* how tormented his mugger must have been to knock him over the head and take his money. The lesson we are all supposed to learn, with Rocker as the example, is that if you are foolish enough to sing anything other than the approved melody you are going to be rightly subjected to reeducation, social pressure, civil or criminal action, and legislation.

Lenin and Stalin established political camps in which dissidents were "rehabilitated" through thought control and brainwashing. After all, you had to be "insane" if you opposed the regime's socialist ideals of "equality and fairness." It must have seemed to poor Solzenitsyn writing from the gulags that the asylum inmates were in charge and locking up everyone else.

Just before his recall election, Governor Gray Davis of California announced that he would sign legislation providing for "intolerance and hatred control training" for all teachers—whatever the hell that means other than political reeducation. Sometimes it's good to be *intolerant* and to notice the insanity around you lest you become part of it.

As it stands, however, the only time intolerance can be practiced is when it's directed toward someone who disagrees outside the Enlightened realm. Take radio "family and marriage" talk show host Dr. Laura Schlessinger. Dr. Schlessinger believes gay people are "entitled to respect and kindness as fellow human beings" but that homosexual behavior is unnatural and that marriage is a sacred contract between a man and a woman, not between Jack and Bob or Sue and Joanne. Children, she thinks, are entitled to one mother and one father, not two mothers or two fathers.

Instead of merely voicing their opposition to her viewpoints, the Enlightened in a supreme example of their self-touted tolerance set out to destroy her, to *silence* her. All across the nation, it seemed, people were outraged at the audacity of her rejecting the orthodoxy of conventional wisdom. A gay website called her "Queen of Hate Radio." The San Francisco Board of Supervisors warned her against "making inaccurate statements about gays and lesbians that incite violence and hate." A number of her sponsors crumpled like the no-balls cowards they are and withdrew advertising from her show.

All that chatter, naturally, came from the Enlightened. Everyone else cowered in corners for fear of being branded along with her. Hardly anyone dared to publicly stand up and defend *her* First Amendment rights. Not so much as a peep came from that bastion of righteousness, that defender of civil and constitutional rights, the American Civil Liberties Union. I suppose the ACLU was too busy defending a "free speech issue" of the North American Man-Boy Love Association (NAMBLA), whose motto is "Sex by Eight—Or It's Too Late."

Hurt feelings trump any residual freedom of speech. Those very institutions of a society that should oppose censorship and thought repression, such as education and the press, are the very ones manning the bulwarks in defense of it. In academia especially, that bastion of the world's remaining true believers of socialism, you are expected to toe the line of political correctness and trumpet its glory.

Nearly every college and university has initiated "verbal behavior" codes to limit speech. Brown University prohibits "verbal behavior" that produces "feelings of impotence, anger or disenfranchisement, whether intentional or *unintentional.*" (emphasis added) In other words, a mere slip of the tongue, a careless phrase, an unguarded moment, can get you *reeducated.* Which is most difficult considering you probably haven't been *educated* to begin with.

The University of Connecticut goes further than that. "Inappropriately-directed laughter, inconsiderate jokes, conspicuous exclusion from conversation, stereotyping..." can get you sentenced to a term of "sensitivity training." Watch your words; also watch your laughter. Watch your *thoughts.*

Or, how about the University of Vermont, which demands that its students not only not offend but that they all "appreciate each other?"

A kind of "consciousness-raising" D-Day has struck a beachhead against "inappropriate" or "insensitive" school symbols. As with speech codes and other politically-correct aspects of education in the Age of Cultural Madness, even symbols must be restructured to conform to the enlightened melody.

Thus, the University of Massachusetts' "Minuteman" was "too macho, white and violent." Also, there was concern "with the single-gender ethnicity of the Minuteman, and the fact he's carrying a firearm." Perhaps he should have been a transvestite of mixed heritage tiptoeing through daisies. I'm really not making this up.

The University of Wisconsin at Madison wanted to reject all symbols and nicknames that derived from anything *alive.* It also refused to play ball against any other college team whose mascot was derived from Indian culture. *Braves, Redskins, Seminoles* and the like were somehow considered insensitive and racist.

Even the traditionally-conservative Deep South is not immune against the PC virus. Objections were raised against the distinctly comic "Norseman" at the University of Alabama, who appeared "too masculine to represent female students." He is probably too masculine to represent many of the male students.

"It was—I hate to use the word—too *Aryan...*" delicately explained the sports information director. "Some people objected because (the Norseman) was too white, too male, or too violent, or scared little children..."

Heaven—and the Enlightened, of course—forbid anything being too white, too male, too macho, too competitive, too... God, if I may be so presumptuous, please protect me from the do-gooders.

Students at the University of California, Riverside, got together to discuss plans for erecting a new mural on the commons. It must have been the Mother of all meetings, if Saddam Hussein will forgive me for copping his phrase.

First of all, reported the student newspaper *Highlander*, "There was some concern voiced by the senate about the contents of the mural."

One student objected that he saw "pilgrim invaders," which "reminds me of my colonization and I don't like that."

No, no, no cried another student. Those weren't *pilgrims.* Heavens, no. They were *Shakespearean* actors.

Some other student wanted to know if white cranes depicted in the mural were appropriate. They weren't. They were changed to birds of color.

There was still a problem. Where, oh, where, was the same-sex couple? What an unforgivable oversight. The same-sex couple was added, after which the amended mural was dutifully approved.

Officials at the Massachusetts College of Liberal Arts refused to grant student groups permission to hold a pig roast on campus because it might offend vegetarians. A carrot roast, now, that would be permissible, providing the carrots consented.

Indiana University's Commission on Multicultural Understanding (Does that title provide insight into its makeup or what?) presented graduate student B. Afena Cobham an award for insisting the student newspaper fire its editor for publishing an editorial cartoon critical of affirmative action.

"His action," claimed the honored student in testimony against the editor, "is not protected free speech and has no place on a college campus."

No free speech, it seems, is free speech unless the Enlightened approve of it.

"The heresy of heresies," George Orwell explained in his novel *1984*, "was common sense." Common sense is no longer, well, *common*.

Should social pressures, accusations, and reeducation fail to advance the worthy cause of inoffensiveness, the law can always step in to ensure "fairness." And to hell with the Constitution if it stands in the way of social progress and social justice.

In one of the broadest restrictions of speech in American legal history, the California supreme court issued a list of words that cannot be used in any workplace in the state, on penalty of going to the slammer or attending diversity training. I think the slammer might be preferable over diversity training.

Again in California, the most "progressive" state in the union, West Hollywood police file reports on racist remarks. Should you tell an ethnic joke that is overheard and reported, your name goes into a police file as a potential "hate crime" perpetrator. New York does the same thing with a "Bias Crime Investigations Unit" to investigate racist actions and "hateful remarks."

Europe takes hate crimes speech even more seriously. In Gloucester, England, undercover police hang around local restaurants listening for offensive language that can land the detestable miscreant in the slammer. The European Union recently decided to outlaw "racism and xenophobia" by enacting draconian laws to throw violators in jail for such things as calling someone a "dirty little geek" or " a lazy wop." Insulting Christians or white males is probably not offensive.

For example, Abdullah el-Faisal, a Jamaican living in London, gave lectures calling for Muslims to kill "filthy Jews." His passport was seized, but he remains in Britain with his wife and four children, drawing welfare from the European Development Fund, while he applies for permission to remain in England.

On the other hand, senior barrister Gordon Pringle, a white man, called a clerk lawyer a "black moor," for which offense he was found guilty by a disciplinary tribunal and sentenced to a heavy fine and a one-year suspension of his right to practice law.

Don't say it can't happen here. It will. Look for your own city to start cracking down on "hate speech," as New York and California already are. That sexist remark, that racist joke, that comment against affirmative action, that slip of the tongue about the stevedore in high-heeled pumps and a blond wig...can get you slapped into the hoosegow doing hard time with *other* dangerous criminals.

Personally, I believe it boorish and bullying to insult or diminish another human being without cause. But that isn't the point. Government has no business keeping track of speech if it really is protected under the Constitution. Sensitivity training and reeducation are merely steps down a one-way road. Offensive speech cannot be suppressed today without tomorrow bringing the burning of books, the trashing of newspapers, and the jailing of those who would speak out against the madness.

SECTION III
EDUCATION

"They have filled their campuses with intellectually lazy people who are bored by books and always ready for some soul-searching debate or gaudy march. They would all be better off guzzling beer or cheering the local mud wrestlers."

Editorial, The American Spectator

CHAPTER EIGHT

I attended a one-room schoolhouse on the edge of the Ozarks where classes First through Eighth were taught by a man and his wife, the Lowrimores. Each class had its own row of desks. You started out over by the windows and moved up a row year by year until you reached Grade Eight's row next to the door. Your next move was out the door.

Understand that my dad was an itinerant sharecropper and harvest worker who could not even read his own name. But—and this is a big *but*—Dad understood to some degree that the only way for us kids to get out of the cotton fields was through education. Mr. Lowrimore and his wife understood the same thing—and they taught the way they believed. I daresay that by the time I left that one room in the hills I knew much more about history, English, math and government than today's average high school grad. These two dedicated teachers taught the basics upon which all subsequent knowledge and learning could build upon.

My, how the field of education has changed. The governing idea behind modern public education seems to be the *Wizard Of Oz* philosophy. The scarecrow went to see the Wizard because he didn't have a brain. The Wizard issued him one, no effort required on the scarecrow's part, and just like that he was doing calculus and geometry. Why should a student have to put out effort to actually *learn* anything when he can simply be issued a diploma—and *viola!*--he's now "making a difference" and working for "social justice," even though he probably can't even spell *justice.*

American kids are not scarecrows; they have brains, although perhaps the same can't be said for many of those who purport to teach them. I knew a teacher, a *teacher*, mind you, who said she had not read a book in ten years. Americans are being dumbed down because they have traded the three R's taught by the Lowrimores for the governing idea that no student be offended or challenged by any idea to which he might be exposed in the classroom. The three R's have been converted to "equity," "fairness," "multiculturalism," and "self-esteem." Teaching has verged from its traditional role of conveying the nation's intellectual heritage to creating "agents of change."

There was a recent photo in the newspapers of a seven-year-old boy protesting budget constraints by holding up a sign demanding more money for his school while he thrust his fist in the air. He hadn't the slightest idea what he was doing, other than what his teacher told him to do for a photo-op. He didn't need to know. What mattered was that he was learning to vent his feelings by becoming an activist for "social change." He was learning how to protest when the poor little kid would have been better served in the classroom learning that two and two *do* make four.

No wonder that almost forty percent of the units taken by first year students at many of the schools in the California State University system are remedial courses designed to teach reading, writing and arithmetic, subjects that should have been learned at least by high school.

So *what* are our public schools teaching? Schools which once extolled the classical literature of Plato and Shakespeare have replaced the masters with more challenging and *relevant* works such as *Heather Has Two Mommies* or *Earth In The Balance*. A Massachusetts educator warned teachers against using *The Story of Babar* because it "extols the virtues of a European, middle-class lifestyle and disparages the animals and people who have remained in the jungle." Another educator of "radical math literacy" warned against bombarding students with "oppressive pro-capitalist ideology." Practical math applications such as totaling a grocery bill, he said, should be avoided because such an exercise carried a message "that paying for food is natural."

Horrors! No student must be taught to pay his own way, not when the government will seize from someone else to pay it for him. What kind of idiocy is this?

A teacher in New Jersey proudly described how she taught her fourth graders that Columbus was a greedy man and a murderer who did not "discover" America. He stole it. Equally proud teachers of elementary-grade students chronicled their part in building a new non-competitive citizen by banning "aggressive" children's games such as Musical Chairs which "promote aggression and allows the biggest and strongest children to win." Musical Statues was better because "everybody wins."

Average students in other industrialized countries are more proficient in math than America's *best* students. The *highest*-scoring American school falls below the *lowest*-scoring Asian school. A Roper Poll of top seniors in 55 leading *colleges* and *universities* discovered that while nearly 100 percent of them knew cartoon characters Beavis and Butthead and rapper Snoop Doggy Dogg, only 34 percent knew that George Washington was the American general at Yorktown.

Such general knowledge was even more deplorable among public grade and high schoolers. Seven out of ten thought Illinois, California and Texas were part of the original thirteen colonies. Only seven out of 100 knew what occurred on July 4, 1776.

Take a look at recent adult products of American education. A study of 1,882 young adults revealed that less than half knew it takes a year for the earth to orbit the sun or that early humans did not coexist with dinosaurs. Sixty percent could not name the president who ordered the dropping of the atomic bomb on Japan. Most of them couldn't find the Persian Gulf on a map, only half knew the location of Central America, and 43 percent couldn't find England. A full fourteen percent couldn't even find the United States.

Folks, these are not illiterates like my dad who grew up during the Great Depression. These are high school *graduates.*

Can't we see what's wrong when, in the average U.S. school, a student can get an A simply for answering a question, not on whether his answer is right or wrong? So what if two plus two comes out five? Tell him he's getting *close.* Merely *trying* is sufficient. Accuracy is optional if there's a chance that correcting him will damage his precious self-esteem.

Seeing all this, need we wonder why so many people fall for every goofy politically correct trend that comes along? Perhaps more of us should go looking for the Wizard of Oz.

In spite of all evidence to the contrary, however, it can't be the fault of the school curriculum if Little Johnny can't read and write and subtract two from four. We are repeatedly assured that the *real problem* is social and economic. Asking victims of economic circumstances, ethnic identity, biological sex or some other "root social stigma" to spell, speak properly, or read "Run, Jane, run" is applying inappropriate or excessive standards. So what do we do? We lower our expectations and reduce standards even further. It's much easier to teach "social justice" and "self-esteem."

Who cares if I can't find Texas on a map? I still feel good about myself. Besides, government will take care of me. All I have to do is vote for candidates who promise to take from the smart and the rich and distribute it among my home boys and me.

America's education continues to provide further evidence that the nation is rapidly on its way to going bonkers. In fact, Bonkers 101 appears to be the major of choice at many schools and universities.

CHAPTER NINE

Like Thomas Sowell, one of my intellectual heroes, I grew up so poor that even poverty was a step up. And, like Tom, I *ached* to go to college. But how could a ragged kid from the Ozark Mountains ever go to college?

I was 28-years-old, married, with two kids by the time I made it to Florida State University on scholarships. Disillusionment set in immediately. I was an outsider with thought patterns formed by the real world. I was a military veteran, had been to Vietnam, and, on top of all that, I was an ex-cop. Cops were known in academia as "pigs." I arrived with a cast on my leg from injuries suffered during the racial rioting in Miami that accompanied the 1968 Republican National Convention.

Education, I was repeatedly informed, was the long-term solution to bringing about change. I could live with that. Change is the nature of our world and the human condition. However, it became immediately clear that any change in either academia or society had to be along socially engineered lines. For example, one of my first professors "proved" on the blackboard that political and social liberals were more intelligent than and therefore superior to conservatives. Another prof offered to give Vietnam veterans an automatic gentlemen's "C" if they *didn't* attend classes.

It was abundantly clear that academia did not want the intrusion of outside thought as it went about "making a difference" and "bringing about change." Hells bells, Adolf Hitler brought *change.* So did Josef Stalin. Adolf Eichman and Pol Pot *made a difference.*

I have since taught high school, at junior colleges and at a four-year college where I was director of the Criminal Justice program. What I have discovered, and what the evidence clearly supports, is that the radical young associate professors, graduate assistants and students of the 1960s and 1970s have assumed control of education from kindergarten through PhD programs and have turned campuses into reeducation camps where armies of "diversity teachers," "multicultural educators" and "sensitivity trainers" mold young skulls full of mush into their own "progressive" image. Education's goal of preparing students to live as independent, responsible, *thinking* citizens of a free society has been subverted by all the goofy trash intellectuals like to call "liberating forces." As with poor Winston Smith in Orwell's *1984,* students must have their "false consciousnesses" purged in order for them to fit in with Utopian images of a "New World Order."

It doesn't really matter if Johnny and Joanie can read or find Texas on a map as long as they feel *good* about themselves, as long as they remain dumbed-down receptacles to receive and accept the wacky spew of our "enlightened" betters. Education's role has been watered down to make it "relevant" and accessible to the lazy, the slothful and the uninspired. My old granddad, admittedly an uneducated man who could barely sign his own name and only then by first touching the lead of the pencil to his tongue, had a marked talent for putting things in perspective. "If you step in bullshit," he said, "and you can see it and smell it and there's a bull in the pasture, you can call it whatever you like, but it's still bullshit."

There is definitely a bull in education's pasture. If you doubt that the inmates have taken over the education of our kids, take a look at the modern approach to education in America.

First of all, where are the adults who might put a damper on things?

"Every semester when I would ask my students what they believed the role of a teacher should be," wrote Maureen Stout, a professor of education who teaches future teachers, "the replies would be the same: To be a student's friend. To get the students to feel good about themselves. To get them to see me as one of their peers."

Is *that* really the role of a teacher? Whatever happened to teaching the three R's so the little darlings can at least read their unemployment applications? Oh, yes, I forgot. Here's what has taken the place of Readin', 'Ritin', and 'Rithmetic...

Respected universities offer any number of challenging courses and programs designed to stimulate the intellect, perpetuate the best of our culture, and mold youth into strong and principled citizens. One-third of all U.S. colleges are obligated to enroll students in at least one course on cultural pluralism, while virtually all other courses of "higher education" have been changed to meet ideas of political correctness. Two areas come particularly to mind—sex studies; black studies.

More and more campuses offer "academic" courses in pornography—as in Larry Flynt and *Hustler*, as in XXX-rated porn movies, as in sadomasochism, bondage and homosexuality. Kinky sex has become a liberal arts academic discipline like Women's Studies or Black History. Can anyone recognize parody when it kicks you in the butt?

"Several students have complained of pressure so intense to engage in lesbian sex," reflected Candace de Russy, a trustee of State University of New York (SUNY), "that, in the words of one of them, 'I hardly know any longer if I have the right to be heterosexual.'"

SUNY features tutorials on sadomasochistic lesbian sex, workshops on anal intercourse, and courses in bisexuality and female masturbation. At Wesleyan University, Professor Hope Weissman requires her students to make a sex film, to stage a pornographic performance, or to write a porn story. The hotter it is, I suppose, the nearer the students gets to earning an A.

Pornographers recently shot part of an X-rated movie on the campus of Indiana University, featuring twenty to thirty male and female students who signed up to "act" in the film. At San Diego State University, prospective teachers were required to take "Education 451," a course which included segments on homosexuality where straight students stood up in class and proclaimed themselves gay, discussed their feelings about it, and took "cultural plunges" in gay bars so they could "better understand what it feels like to be different."

How about schools *really* being different and offering a true education?

Responsible intelligentsia came crawling out of the baseboards when the University of California sponsored "Gender and Sexuality Week." Out, first of all, crawled English Professor James Kinkaid, whose book *Erotic Innocence: The Culture of Child Molesting and Child Loving* redefines sex between adults and children as loving play instead of a crime. Celina the "Condom Queen" appeared for a "love fest" while her learned colleague, the owner of a sex shop, demonstrated the use of dildos, vibrators and bondage gear. Female-to-male transsexual Loren Cameron extolled the bliss and self-fulfillment of either having everything whacked off or added. Former Episcopalian chaplain Elizabeth Davenport promoted her "creative workshop" with a flyer saying, "If you've ever suffered from the sex/guilt/shame/aaargh syndrome—whether because of your minister, or God, or anyone else for that matter—this creative workshop is for you."

Let it all hang out. Do what feels good. Never feel guilty—even if you *should.*

As for "Black Studies," racism is not only accepted, it's encouraged. Black people who claim genetic superiority of race are offered tenure at respected universities. Any white foolish enough to assert the same about whites would be issued a hood and a robe and hounded out of Dodge as a member of a "hate group."

The core of the so-called "Afrocentric Movement," now taught in universities and high schools and designed to acquaint U.S. blacks with "their long-ignored African heritage and raise pride and self-esteem," is a tall tale based on the assumption that ancient Egyptians were blacks who mastered flight with gliders, invented electricity, discovered quantum mechanics, anticipated Darwin's theory of evolution, plotted the solar system, smelt steel, founded irrigation and, in their spare time, discovered America first. In short, African people of color founded, invented, learned or at least anticipated about everything worth anything to modern people.

Such advancements, according to the theory, were possible because of a magical substance called neuromelanin, which is present to a greater degree in the brains of darker-skinned people than in those of people with lighter skins. Black people were therefore the *real* creators of civilization. The nasty white heterosexual male *stole* everything from them and appropriated it as his own, thereby leaving, I suppose, much of Africa still living in grass huts, drinking cow's blood and practicing clitorectomy.

"Give a professor a false thesis in early life," wrote critic John Jay Chapman a century ago, "and he will teach it till he dies. He has no way of correcting it."

Academia is full of false thesis, none of which was more absurd, more insane, than that "progressive" schools attempted to hustle in under the guise of "Ebonics." According to the rationale of the Oakland Unified School District, black people have a genetic predisposition toward "black English," more appropriately known as ghetto slang dressed up as "Ebonics." It's easy to see how Ebonics almost entered the curriculum to be taught as a second language, like Spanish or French. After all, it's far easier on the teacher and on the self-esteem of the pupil if students are accepted as they are rather than have them face the rigors of actually learning anything.

"'I ain't got none' means the same thing as 'I haven't got any' ('I haven't any')," explained Kirk Hazen, Linguistics professor at West Virginia University when he argues that teachers should let students speak the way they want, mispronunciations, bad grammar and all. "Teachers shouldn't tell their students how they're saying something is wrong. What teachers should tell them is that there are different varieties of the English language. I don't think it's the job of the schools to correct dialect features..."

Ain't nobody got no beef with that, right? Pardon me while I go outside and scrape the bull off my boots. I ask you, can you think of a more condescending and destructive means to make sure kids, especially poor black kids, remain stuck in poverty and ignorance?

The pathetically undereducated people who staff public schools, along with the pathetically undereducated ones who man the politically correct bulwarks of colleges and universities, have taken upon themselves the task of reshaping society by "dumbing down" Americans. We're in trouble if ole' Abe Lincoln was right in asserting that Democracy could only survive on the shoulders of an enlightened electorate. All you have to do to understand how wacky education has become is look at what is now taught and not taught.

For example, school bosses in Farmington, Michigan, dropped "American Government" for seniors, replacing it with a "current events" program centered on "Peace Studies." As far as I can tell, Peace Studies programs now thriving on over 250 colleges and universities across America and gradually sifting down into public schools are actually little more than breeding grounds for the next generation of anarchists, socialists and anti-American subversives. In such studies, every example of conflict and social injustice is America's fault. Cynthia Keppley Mahmood, Peace Studies professor at Notre Dame, declared that the goals of terrorist suicide bombers are no different than those of soldiers in the U.S. military. She wrote that the U.S. would be much better off if we established a "dialogue" with Osama bin Laden rather than responding with violence and "patriotic machismo."

Give peace a chance. I feel your pain. Never think critically. Turn the other cheek, but never mention Jesus. Better yet, don't even think about any of it. The Enlightened will take care of the thinking part, God help us all, while students go out and take courses which preclude that nasty business of thought.

At the University of Virginia, you can take "Dracula" as a required humanities course. The University of Alabama trumps it with "History of College Football." Georgetown comes up with "Prison Literature," while Duke challenges its students with "Soap Operas." Boudoin College touts "Music and Gender," Cornell teaches "Queer Theory and Literature of The Body," whatever the hell that is, and Harvard challenges with its "Feminist Biblical Interpretations." The University of Michigan dropped its Religion major, citing lack of staff and resources, but conveniently recovered both staff and resources in time to offer "How To Be Gay: Male Homosexuality and Initiation." You need someone to teach you how to be gay, that being such a desired quality?

The University of California, Santa Barbara, listed 62 different courses on "Chicano Studies." In contrast, there were only a few courses on either the Revolutionary War or World War II, and only a few classes on the Civil War. And in New York City, Harvey Milk High School opened the first public high school segregated for gay, lesbians, bisexual and transgender students. What on earth can come next?

It almost seems as though ignorance is cultivated; the ignorant are, after all, more tractable and therefore easier led across the bridge into a Brave New Century where there will be a carrot in every pot. In Education, facts and truth no longer matter, since both are situational. If historical facts don't agree with you, why, hell, there's an easy solution: *Change* the facts so they do.

Professors at the University of California at Los Angeles endeavored to rewrite a history textbook to make it more "relevant" to today's restless and increasingly-illiterate or semi-illiterate youth. Naturally, *In The Course of Human Events* was oh so sensitive and politically correct. What else did you expect?

In the "relevant" history, George Washington became a cold man of "ordinary talents...not completely successful as a military man nor as a president." That was about the extent of his accomplishments. Susan B. Anthony, Harriet Tubman, "Mother Jones," and Caesar Chavez received more ink than he did. Quick, without looking it up, tell me what each of these "historical figures" accomplished.

The chapter on World War II focused on labor and ethnic strife in the home workforce rather than on military operations in which millions of young Americans risked their lives to rid the world of Fascism. American Japanese *Nisei* placed in interment camps used up as much space as D-Day and all the Pacific Campaigns up through 1944. Women were depicted as a beleaguered minority like slaves and Indians. The Internet—which Al Gore invented? — received more print than America's entire religious and intellectual heritage.

Ronald Reagan came along. You could almost read the cursing and blackguarding between the lines. He won the presidency only because he was in league with "Big Business" and "the New Right." "Slashing" cuts in welfare had "profound negative effects on the economy and government services." Military buildups and covert operations under his administration were dangerous and illegal and led to "worsened relations" with the Soviet Union. The book failed to even *mention* that Reagan policies spearheaded the end of the Cold War or that economic inflation was completely out of control when he assumed office. *Don't confuse me with the facts, my mind's made up.*

The text ended on a scary note: "The application of the ideas of liberty, equality and justice on which this democracy is founded are constantly evolving in response to changing times."

Perhaps *devolving* might be a more appropriate word. California textbooks are leading the way toward an ultimate stated goal of "advancing multiculturalism" by changing, eliminating or destroying any thought, idea, or concept that conflicts with political correctness. The Thought Police are alive, well, and working hard.

In all new California textbooks, facts and reality must be altered to correspond with pre-conceived ideas of correctness. For example, women must not be depicted as caregivers or shown doing household chores. Men cannot be lawyers, doctors or plumbers; they are nurturing, sensitive helpmates in support of women. Old people are never feeble or dependent, they are out jogging and repairing the roof, reveling in having shed the "senior citizen" tag in favor of the new PC term "older person."

Anything that might remotely be construed as racist, sexist or any other "ist" is purged. "Founding Fathers" has been replaced by "The Framers" to avoid, I suppose, offending "Founding Mothers." Mount Rushmore can't be mentioned because "it appears to offend" some American Indians. American Indians can't be depicted with long braids, in rural settings, or on reservations—even though many American Indians wear long braids and live in rural areas or on reservations. *Snowmen* aren't allowed; *snowpersons* are. "Rain forest" is the PC term, not the negatively connotative of "jungle." Yachts mustn't be mentioned at all, since they are elitist and the "common people" don't own them. SUVs, of course, are banned. California educational authorities warned publishers not to picture or even mention "unhealthy" and "naughty" foods such as French fries, coffee, bacon, butter, ketchup, hot dogs, and even birthday cakes. You will never see McDonald's golden arches in a California classroom, unless, of course, the fast food chain finds itself becoming the subject of a lawsuit for making kids fat by holding their mouths open and stuffing them with Big Macs.

Is it any wonder that an entire generation is turning into an army of ignorant, self-righteous, self-absorbed underachievers?

A few years ago, the National Endowment for The Humanities (NEH) gave professors at the University of California at Los Angeles money to research and produce a book prescribing what U.S. public schools ought to be taught about their country. When *National Standards For United States History* was finally released, it was so full of multiculturalism, anti-Western bias, and politically correct bull that the U.S. Senate denounced it by a vote of 99 to one. Even Ted Kennedy voted against it. *Standards* said not a word about Paul Revere, Thomas Edison, the Wright Brothers, Albert Einstein, General Douglas MacArthur... It was the first time, said American Federation of Teachers CEO Al Shanker, that government had ever attempted to teach children to "feel negative about their country."

"They have filled their campuses with intellectually lazy people," went an editorial in *The American Spectator*, "who are bored with books and always ready for some soul-searching debate or gaudy march. They would all be better off guzzling beer and cheering the local mud wrestlers."

Maybe we would all be better off.

CHAPTER TEN

Ever wonder why the average eighth grader is on a level with the average fifth grader of forty years ago? Why today's college degree is roughly equivalent to yesterday's high school diploma? Wonder no more. There's an easy but bizarre answer: The world of education has gone completely bonkers. Yep. Nutso. It's like the formula has been laid out to produce graduates steeped in political correctness but void of intellectual curiosity and capacity. The formula goes like this: dumb down the teachers; dumb down the students by indoctrinating them properly; and, above all else, keep those little darlings' minds clear of any thoughts or influence that might corrupt and lead them away from Enlightenment—as defined, naturally, by the Enlightened, our betters.

Albert Einstein would likely never have received tenure anywhere in today's academic world. He was too intelligent. You don't need *intelligence* to be a modern teacher. In fact, intelligence might be a handicap, because it means you have the capacity to question rather than simply mimic all the clap trap produced by modern education's curriculum. Rather than individual ability and knowledge, today's "educators" are selected and retained primarily on the basis of gender, race, sexual preference, and the politics of class—and to hell with other qualifications.

It doesn't *really* matter if I can teach or not. I can indoctrinate the little tykes. *Anybody* can do that.

Let me add here that there *are* good and dedicated teachers, thank God. But they are good teachers in spite of the system, not because of it. I don't intend to indict all of them, merely the system.

One third of all active teachers in New York City flunked the state certification exam *three or more times*. More than 50,000 applicants for minority teaching positions failed the California Basic Education Skills Test. In a sane world, they would have had their butts kicked out of the system and reached their appropriate level flipping hamburgers with Elvis in Memphis. But not in sensitive, caring America. Teachers in both New York and California screamed "*Racism!,*" even though not all were minorities. New York immediately backed down and sent its teacher failures, its "best and brightest," back out to teach. In California, flunkees who failed the test demanded back pay and damages for psychological trauma.

How clear the message: If I can't cut it, hire me anyhow so you don't bruise my oh-so-precious self-esteem. Don't discriminate against me because I'm unable to compete against a two-by-four. I can teach multiculturalism with the best, even if I can't spell it.

Purveyors of modern "education" are going to make sure that when you graduate from institutions of learning you're not too smart and your head is filled with the nonsense of political correctness. Who needs to find Texas on a map anyhow? You can always find a home-schooled grad to do it for you.

Indoctrination starts early. A state law in Minnesota requires "cultural dynamics" training for all licensed child Day Care workers so they can begin cultural indoctrination of their tiny charges. A group called Cultural Dynamics Education Project spent seven years blowing public money before it came up with a proper curriculum. Do you dare speculate on some of the highlights?

To begin with, the program portrayed America as a horrible place dominated by a corrupt "non-disabled European-American culture." *Non-disabled!* White people, those damned white people again, led lives of privilege, "an unearned entitlement to and attitude of superiority and advantage (which) perpetuates their cultural heritage and imposes it upon others... (White people) got the power first and they made sure they didn't give it up..."

This in *Day Care.* How *dare* any of those little tykes to be born white! How unfair! How insensitive! Poor Martin Luther King. He must be restless in his grave, moaning aloud on the night wind at how education has institutionalized the destructive division of race and class.

And that's how it goes all through public school and then college. Education on the easy plan, designed without expectations. After years of this kind of bull, many high school grads are so ill-equipped to handle college entrance exams that most universities are—naturally—lowering requirements for admission. In the Newspeak of today, traditional tests like SAT and ACT aren't "sophisticated" enough to reveal important talents like "initiative, teamwork and leadership." Therefore, some universities are admitting students based on their ability to *play with Legos.* Had I written this thirty years ago, you would have laughed and accused me of making it up. I'm not. You read it correctly. *Legos, plastic blocks* "aimed at recruiting diverse students who otherwise might not win admission."

Do they really mean that it doesn't matter if I can read or not, that I will be admitted to the brotherhood of scholars if I'm an Indian kid and can play with Legos? President George W. Bush called it "the soft bigotry of lowered expectations."

"Diversity" and "multiculturalism" are the twin icons at whose alter "progressive" educators pay homage, to the dominance of which everything else, such as real learning, is irrelevant.

Harvard law school students filed a lawsuit alleging they were receiving an inferior education because the law school faculty did not have enough diversity—too few women, minorities, and homosexuals. Forgive my confusion, but what difference does it make to my learning of torts and corporate law by knowing what my instructor does to another man in his bed?

It is no longer the quality of the material. Its ethnicity is what counts.

"We are now the first district in the nation to *require* the reading of nonwhite authors," chortled a proud member of San Francisco's school board. "We also voted for a requirement that writers who also are lesbian, gay, bisexual or transgender be identified."

How wonderful. Maybe we should go further and identify pedophiles, sadomasochists, and beastie lovers and likewise *require* reading them in the name of diversity and fairness.

The climate in American education has reached the point that it is difficult to distinguish parody and satire from normal school days. Conservative students at Dartmouth lampooned the system by having the student government approve a club dedicated to bestiality. Lampooners at the University of Miami at Ohio formed the Miami Masturbation Society. No one, *no one*, publicly questioned the authenticity of either club. That says a lot for what academia considers normal on campus.

In the 1960s, I joined the NAACP as an auxiliary member (being white and Indian) because I opposed segregation and thought it wrong to discriminate against individuals based on the color of their skins. I still think it's wrong. However, ironically enough, segregation has returned as politically correct on modern American campuses. In the name of diversity (don't ask me to explain it), it is now possible for students to live in virtually segregated housing, attend ethnic courses taught by teachers of color waving texts written by authors of color, and graduate without having to associate at all with the dreadful whites.

For example, new students arriving at Tufts attend separate orientations according to race. Dartmouth and Cornell permit "residential program houses" for minorities but not for whites. Stanford allows blacks, Asians, Hispanics and Indians to request roommates of the same ethnic background. It's considered "bigotry" for a white kid to make the same request.

The University of California, Berkeley, sponsors segregated graduation ceremonies for blacks, Hispanics, Asians and Indians. Brown University's Third World Center holds a yearly invitation-only champagne reception for graduating minorities. The University of Michigan and UCLA both take it a step farther and offer separate ceremonies for graduating homosexuals.

And we call the proponents of this crap "progressive."

Students are supposedly getting only what they demand. And exactly what is it they are demanding? Speech codes, mandated sensitivity seminars, affirmative action programs, feel-good courses catering to race and gender, the abolishment of a "core curriculum" of Eurocentric white male accomplishments which was no doubt stolen

from Black Africa in the first place. If you look closely enough, I daresay you'll find the hand of the "Enlightened Elite" stuffed up the
darling little puppets' behinds to manipulate their mouths as they go
about refashioning society.

The question remains: Refashioning it into *what?* It's a scary
thought to contemplate.

Stalin and Lenin discovered in the Soviet Union that propaganda
and curriculum did not go far enough to ensure compliance to the
Party's dictates. Much of the unenlightened rabble simply ignored it,
making it necessary to form secret police, gulags and leagues of true
believers with the passion to keep an eye out for incorrectness. Pardon
me if I see a great deal of correlation in Stalin's Soviet Union and
American college campuses, much of the difference being merely a
matter of degree. In the early days of communism, believers behaved
very much like today's believers burrowed into American academia.

There is a great deal of blather within the hallowed ivy walls about
"communities of scholars committed to free and open discussion and to
tolerance of differing views." Oh, really? Behavior directly contradicts
freedom of speech and all that claptrap about open discourse. You can
say anything you want, true, but only as long as it follows the party
line. Step over that line and there's hell to pay.

A residential director at the University of Central Arkansas disagreed with a column published in *Echo*, the university newspaper. He
went around campus collecting all the newspapers he could find, while
flyers distributed by his cohorts invited students to attend a bonfire to
"watch the *Echo* burn."

Sounds like free and open discourse to me.

Meanwhile, at the University of Pennsylvania, activist students
protesting a conservative campus columnist seized 14,000 copies of
The Daily Pennsylvanian and dumped them in trash bins. Listen to the
softshoe offered by University President Sheldon Hackney. "Two important values—" he said, "diversity and open expression—seem to be
in conflict."

Any guess as to which value trumped the other?

"Not only are the papers free," Hackney hedged, "but there exists
no explicit restrictions on the number of papers that any given student
may remove."

And we were appalled at Nazi book burnings. By the way, Hackney was later President Bill Clinton's nominee for the National
Endowment for The Humanities. These people have absolutely no
sense of irony.

When a column in Yale student magazine *Light & Truth* poked fun
at a "condom race" in which new students raced to sheath a wooden
phallus, counselors themselves confiscated and trashed 700 copies of
the publication because it was an "offensive issue."

Outraged counselor Tom Cantey was "incensed" by the publication because, he said, it criticized "programs important to campus safety." Seems reasonable. No dangerous wooden phalluses must remain un-condomed.

In addition to "book burning," American schools are employing the tools of reeducation camps, brainwashing and other means of coercion in order to stifle opposition to a "correct" agenda meant, in the words of the Enlightened, to promote an "un-hostile atmosphere" and ensure "common decency." It is not *we* who are mad, they seem to say, it is *you*—and you must submit to "sensitivity training" and multiculturalism indoctrination until you agree with us that we are right.

In a prime example of open-mindedness and tolerance, Vice Provost Mary Ellen Ashley of the University of Cincinnati snapped that anyone who disagreed with the university's policy on diversity should find work elsewhere.

Bowling Green school administrators deemed "illegitimate" a course Professor Richard A. Zeller proposed to teach on "political correctness." These same administrators had previously sanctioned a credit course on the roller coaster, which included field trips.

The director of the Office of Equal Opportunity and Affirmative Action offered to send a "Classroom Climate Advisor" to the University of Minnesota to monitor classes and "help" students whenever they found "a classroom discussion about race or gender disrespectful or insulting." In other words, Nurse Ratchett was going to sit in on classes and monitor them for proper political content.

Stanford PhD candidate Steven Mosher visited China as part of his doctoral program and wrote a best-selling book exposing forced abortion in that country. That's a big no-no to America's Enlightened, first of all because abortion is a "woman's right of choice," apparently whether coerced or not, and China is a brave republic on its way to socialist Utopia. The Chinese government protested—and Stanford President Donald Kennedy suddenly discovered all sorts of principles of conduct Mosher had violated. Mosher was kicked out of the PhD program. How dare the little upstart criticize that great example of human rights and human equality!

Liberal activists, media personalities and government officials of the right bend—which means bent sharply to the left—dominate academia's pulpits. As such, they determine who is and is not allowed to voice an opinion in the hallowed ivy halls, resulting in blatant and outrageous examples of mind, thought and speech control. Rarely is any conservative personality allowed to open his mouth on campus. Leftists, old pony-tailed radicals, and leftover Fellow Travelers from the Cold War are eagerly received and embraced. If Stalin and Lenin were still alive, they would be swamped with invitations to speak.

Avowed communist and former Black Panther Angela Davis is

welcome almost anywhere there's ivy. So is convicted cop killer Mumia Abu-Jamal, providing he can get out of slam long enough to do a speaking tour. Made an "honorary citizen" of Paris, which tells a lot about the French, this serial criminal and brutal cop killer actually delivered the commencement address by telephone at Antioch College in Ohio in 2000. "Think of the lives of those people you admire," he admonished the grads. "Show your admiration for them by becoming them."

I'm not making this up—a cop killer standing bald-faced and requesting to be admired and emulated. Has American truly gone bonkers? Have we run out of real heroes?

Remember actress Jane Fonda, ex-wife of communications mogul Ted Turner, who had her picture taken with communist North Vietnamese during the Vietnam War, proprietress of the observation, "I would think that, if you understood what communism was, you would hope, you would pray on your knees that we would become communists?" *She* is a very popular speaker on campus

So is former President Bill Clinton, who added new words—"Get a Lewinsky"—to the American lexicon, who introduced young Americans to the idea that a blowjob is not really sex, and who was proclaimed an "extraordinary good liar." He is, after all, a liberal, a "progressive." In contrast, former President Richard Nixon after Watergate—*before* Watergate, for that matter—was about as welcome in the beatified halls of learning as a good stiff dose of common sense.

Even on those rare occasions when speakers with whom the Enlightened disagree *are* permitted on campus, school administrators and activist students attempt to make it as difficult for them as possible.

Former Secretary of State Henry Kissinger's speech at the University of Texas was canceled at the last moment out of fear of violent protests by campus Lefties who claimed he was "nothing more than a war criminal."

Immigrant Dinesh D'Souza, author of *Illiberal Education*, which criticizes political correctness in American colleges and universities and illuminates the "dumbing down" of students to conform to a "progressive" mindset, is clearly a minority member but without the minority mindset. A "sensitivity coalition" of students wearing rattling chains intended to represent slavery greeted him when he arrived to speak at Tufts University. Student activists had to be repeatedly warned during his appearance against throwing things at him and shouting him down. An outraged African-American professor accused him of having "the white man's obsession with big words," of possessing "a white perspective" and a preference for "rationality... and sexual restraint."

I suppose this meant D'Souza didn't rant and rave on the podium using easily understood platitudes of the Left, and that his argument zipped right over the esteemed professor's indignity.

Leave it to Brandeis University and Columbia to really make a speaker feel welcome. Campus hosts at Brandeis invited Charlton Heston to speak when he was President of the National Rifle Association. They must have been out of their minds to beard the liberals like that in their own den. Instead of outright refusing him, the university used a back door approach in efforts to discourage Hollywood's most famous and, some say, *only* conservative. It imposed the extra expense of requiring bomb-sniffing dogs, airport-style metal detectors, scores of extra guards, and four units of Heston's blood type. All of which says a lot about how far the Left might be willing to go to deny a podium to anyone with whom it disagrees.

Censorship went even more blatant at Columbia University when Accuracy in Academia attempted to stage "Conservative Ideas in Higher Education," almost an oxymoron in itself. Protestors magically appeared hissing and stomping and booing, mouths open and minds closed as always, while they waved placards reading *Racists Not Allowed at Columbia* and *There's No Place At The Table For Hate.* Citing a security risk, administrators sent guards to block all entrances to the conference site.

"We're not censoring your event," proclaimed Faculty House Director John Hogan.

Speakers, he said, would not be denied entrance to the conference. There simply would not be an *audience.* Speakers could talk to empty seats all they wanted, on any topic they chose. How utterly *liberal,* how *tolerant,* how completely *typical.*

The conference adjourned to nearby city-owned Morningside Park. Jubilant protestors chanted, "Ha, ha, you're outside. We don't want your racist lies."

The follow-up column in *The Columbia Spectator* denied that driving the conservatives off-campus violated their freedom of speech. After all, the conservatives possessed a "dark, dangerous point of view..."

The message here and from nearly every corner of academia can't be clearer: Ideas are dangerous things which must be contained or eradicated if they contravene the accepted orthodoxy. Tyranny has always been, *always*, the result of ignorance imposed ideologically and often with good intentions. If a hostile power wanted to destroy America, it could hardly do a better job than American education is doing. From Day Care to graduate school, students are being systematically indoctrinated in political correctness while robbed of their true intellectual and cultural inheritance. After all, bright individuals who think for themselves are not required in the Enlightened World. Thinkers are dangerous upstarts who refuse to be folded, spindled and mutilated.

If there is any doubt of that, look at the new school chartered in 1999 in San Juan Capistrano, California. It is a school for the academically so-so, the C-average student who aspires to go no further. Students there are ideal for Enlightened manipulation. They are neither more gifted nor less than the average man. Upon graduation, they are, well, expected to come out *average*. I'd like to hear a commencement address delivered to that bunch.

Score another one for collectivism. No one is different than anyone else, not better nor worse, and they *don't care* if they can't find Texas on a map. What these average students *can* do, however, is cite rote all the requirements of feminism and gay rights and racial rights and...

Citizens educated for the Brave New World. Are we really going bonkers or what?

SECTION IV
FAMILY

"I think we can...take some bolder steps, especially where children need to be protected... I think we need some more guidance counselors, some more mental health care options..."
Al Gore, Vice President

CHAPTER ELEVEN

Keep track of this. I'm not making it up. In a Boston court in August in the year of our Lord 2000, while we are all being led enlightened across the Bridge into a Brave New World, a judge ruled that a child born to one lesbian woman from an egg donated by her girlfriend and fertilized by an unidentified sperm donor had *two* mothers and *no* father. "Father" on the baby's birth certificate was crossed out and replaced by a second "mother."

It seems that men can finally be consigned to the periphery of the American family. We aren't really needed, are we? In its new Statement of Purpose, the National Organization of Women (NOW) eliminated all positive references to men. "We envision a world," the Statement proclaimed, "where patriarchal culture and male dominance no longer oppress the earth."

A little point of fact: Seventy two percent of all teenage murderers grow up in homes without a father.

In retaliation, I suppose, comes the announcement that science is about to make it possible for a *male* to give birth, thereby consigning *women* to the periphery of the American family. That's right. It's almost possible to surgically implant a womb in a man. It's a simple procedure after that. Medically insert a fertilized egg in the guy's womb and, *Presto!,* he's complaining of morning sickness and swelling feet for the next nine months.

Couple such stunning developments with the movement to legally recognize "gay marriage" and we are well on our way to redefining marriage and family to mean two lesbians, three Rottweilers, a gerbil and a gay man in a "loving relationship." Sound wacky? It is, but it wasn't that long ago that people with common sense (now *that's* an oppressed minority) called wacky the idea of Stevie and Bob standing before a clergyman and vowing to "love and honor till death do us part."

An issue of *Bride's* Magazine ran a full-page article on same-sex weddings. "We looked at what was happening in the wedding industry," said Millie Martini Bratten, the magazine's editor-in-chief. "We were hearing from various retailers that same-sex couples had become an important part of their gift registries. And we were answering more readers' questions: 'If two women were getting married (to each other), what was the appropriate attire?'"

And as for that clergyman before whom they stand to take their vows? He may well be the Right Reverend V. Gene Robinson, the Episcopalian Church's Bishop of New Hampshire, who divorced his wife and abandoned his two daughters to establish a "relationship...sacramental for me" with his best buddy.

The family throughout time has been the basic building block of a society, the collapse of which invariably leads to the collapse of the society. Look what happened to the Soviet Union where family ties were broken in an attempt to tie people to the state. Immediately after the Bolshevik Revolution, laws against divorce were loosened, promiscuity was encouraged, and marriage was redefined as a "bourgeois institution." Vladimir Lenin said the act of sex should "be as simple and unimportant as drinking a glass of water."

Sound familiar?

"Sex is not harmful," wrote Judith Levine. "It is a vehicle to self-knowledge, love, healing, creativity, adventure, and intense feelings of aliveness. There are many ways even the smallest children can partake of it."

The American family is on the skids when it reaches the point that we can no longer define what *marriage* and *family* mean. While a principle aim of American government should be to reinforce the family, we find government aiding and abetting policies that promote just the opposite while media outlets drumbeat for lesbianism, abortion on demand, child sex and pornography. It's become a crazy world created by Jerry Springers.

Social engineers look upon the traditional family as a roadblock to perfecting human nature. In order to change the structure of society, they must first destroy old virtues and replace them with new. In June 2000, a block of developing nations introduced to the UN Special Session for Human Rights a statement saying, "The family is the basic unit of society and is a strong force in social cohesion and integration and its stability should be strengthened."

The United States opposed the statement. *Opposed* it.

"We increasingly have volumes of social science data to show the redefinition of the family and tinkering with the traditions developed over the millennia undermines the family and the society," said Austin Ruse, a leader against antifamily practices. "Families are dropping like flies because they are under assault. Societies fall when their keystones are destroyed. Look at the divorce rate and the number of single mothers with kids. All these are attributable directly to the destruction of the family. Both a father and a mother under the same roof are necessary to raise their kids—and, if both are not there, hell can follow."

Hell *will* follow.

CHAPTER TWELVE

I was in a Taco Mayo one afternoon munching a couple of tacos when a little boy of about ten or so approached. He wasn't shy. "Do you have any money?" he asked.

"Why?"

He wanted to buy a particular toy.

He received from me instead a gentle lecture against an able-bodied young man going around begging, as though assuming strangers ought to give him whatever he wanted. I offered him a small job so he could earn money for his toy. *Work?* He went to another man who, apparently filled with compassion and sensitivity, dumped a load of change on him while shooting me a look that asked, "What kind of hard-hearted SOB are you?"

This guy had done the kid no favor. He merely reinforced a growing sentiment in this country that the world owes him a living. The kid probably went home and told mom and pop what he had done and received praise for getting something for nothing. After all, this is the era in which welfare recipients march in protest over not receiving enough handouts, rephrased now as "entitlements." Some states have gone so far as to redistribute the wealth by taxing the more wealthy to give to the less wealthy. This kid probably felt similarly entitled.

Thirty or forty years ago, parents generally counted on the culture to reward and reinforce values they wanted to instill in children: truthfulness, honesty, respect for faith, independence, hard work... These days it's just the opposite. Society seems to reward those who lie and cheat; who become dependent on government and others for their livelihood; who wheedle and cajole their way through life, giving the least while demanding the most.

An Associated Press news release announced this wonderful news: *Woody Harrelson's latest role—husband. The 'Natural Born Killers' star married his former assistant, Laura Louie, in a private ceremony in Costa Rica...*

In an afterthought, the article added: *It was the first marriage for both. The couple has two daughters...*

We've turned everything upside down. Other than the fact that glamorous Hollywood is The Land of Musical Beds and an inspiration for every little oversexed munchkin in the universe, aren't we supposed to get married first, *then* have children? I know that's an old-fashioned and outdated concept, but no wonder children practice slipping condoms on carrots in school and are eager to play rabbit and try out their machinery as quickly and as often as possible. They only practice what they see in the adult world.

It's getting harder and harder, it seems, to even *find* a real adult.

Back during the 1960s when much of today's wackiness started, parents began cowering before their own children, warned by Dr. Spock and other "experts" that imposed discipline might stunt the little darlings' emotional growth. A single catch-phrase trumpeted from the tops of the nation's lungs: "Our children are trying to tell us something." It was as though children somehow embodied the voice of reason, that *they* were the wise ones who knew what was best for society. *They* were going to teach the adult world, these callow, pimply-faced youth throwing a national tantrum. Unbelievably, adults wilted and abdicated their time-honored role of passing along the culture from one generation to the next.

The notion rose that children could raise themselves, create a new culture and a new moral universe virtually overnight, and bring peace, love and flower power to the world. "I can give them my opinion, tell them how I feel," said a modern mother, "but they have to decide for themselves."

Please! Isn't that just too precious? George Orwell remarked that some ideas are so stupid that only an intellectual could believe them. "No ordinary man would be such a fool."

Two fourteen-year-olds, opposite sexes if that makes a difference in this crazy world, were getting it on in the boy's bedroom when his mother surprised them in the act. She ordered them to cease and desist. He told her in no uncertain terms to take her outdated sense of morality and shove it. She called the cops. Now, the little twerp is suing his mother for violating his "right of privacy."

"Many parents wonder why they lose their children to a whole new value system," wailed a parent.

It is no accident. Nationwide efforts in every aspect of education and the culture work to detach children from their parents as a way of promoting "social change." The entire moral structure of society, starting with the family, is systematically being undermined through such misnamed programs as "values clarification." Authority once lost, as parents are finding out, is difficult to regain as we relinquish much of our parental authority to government and myriads of social workers who warn us *never* to do anything that may harm the little darlings' highly inflated self-esteem.

Spank a child? That's violence; the United Nations issued a resolution demanding that Britain repeal a law that allows parents to spank their children. Scold little Jimmy? Oh, no. You'll *alienate* him In fact, don't discipline the little reprobates at all. They shouldn't have to do *anything* they don't want to do—and you, the parents, have no right to complain of messy behavior, nose piercing, foul language, sloth, disrespect... Children are being taught early to reject authority and to expect little from adults except praise and indecision and "understanding." My dad would have *understood* me all right had I stood up in his face and told him to go intercourse himself; I wouldn't have been able to sit down for a month, and deservedly so.

Who would have dreamed even thirty years ago that an entire ideology would rise favoring government and "expert" takeover of parental roles? Who would have dreamed that our children would become the tool by which the institution of family is destroyed?

Hillary Clinton decided that "we," meaning government, must do something to fix the way people are raising their kids. Parents are not doing the job properly. Therefore, she said in her book of the same title, it takes a village.

"As we stand here at the end of the century," she lectured, "I don't think we have done as much as we could... We do not do enough to help families do a better job of caring for their children... We are going to have to do some serious thinking in this country about how we can take more control over what our children see and experience."

Take *more control?* By that, she naturally means government will take more control, the Enlightened will take more control to make sure our kiddies grow up to be good little *progressives* in support of wacky causes, without minds of their own.

"I think we can...take some bolder steps, especially when children need to be protected," asserted Algore, then-vice president. "I think we need more guidance counselors, some more mental health options..."

More *experts* are exactly what we need.

At the present rate of growth, counselors in schools will soon outnumber teachers. Ever notice how anytime anything happens in the world, no matter how remote or trivial, flocks of do-gooder counselors with their shorts in a bind descend upon their bemused charges to help them through the "healing process?" At one school, counselors evoked the "healing process" over global warming. At another, students were perceived to have been so traumatized by a video camera planted inside a girls' locker room that it took a week's counseling to work them through it.

Kids must come to understand early that they simply cannot function without the help of a compassionate and caring government. "Experts" take over in Day Care and public schools while mommy seeks her "full potential" and daddy runs from child support payments. After all, as Hillary implied in *It Takes A Village,* it is society's responsibility to rear children, not the parents'.

A cartoon in *Human Events* depicted how liberal "experts" protect and rear our children. The cartoon was in six frames, each of which showed protestors reacting to an event. The first frame dealt with cigarette smoking. *Eeek!* went the horrified reactors. *Eeek!* they went in response to frames of not wearing seat belts, eating fatty foods, corporal punishment, and compelling students to pledge allegiance to the flag. The last frame showed two men, arms around one another, with two little children standing looking up at them. "Bobby, Alice...meet your new mom." Was there an *Eeek?* Not on your life. The reaction was a yawn and the protestors turning and nonchalantly walking away. After all, to the delight of the elite, Massachusetts legislators had just vowed to make laws allowing a man to take another man as his wife; and our own Supreme Court found a Constitutional right to homosexual sodomy.

Children's Defense Fund, Planned Parenthood, National Organization of Women, Human Rights Campaign, Gay and Lesbian Task Force... Teachers, shrinks, armies of social workers, the "professionals..." They're all hammering out their agendas, assaulting the traditional family, and exhorting over a new era of tolerance. The family can only take so much "tolerance" before it disintegrates. The family has become a major battleground in the Cultural Wars.

Public schools force upon teens and young children graphic and offensive sex education. The "moral uprightness" of being gay is preached to Christian families by government institutions, classrooms, the media, the workplace and even some churches. Our taxes pay for Internet porn sites in public libraries while at the same time all public religious expression is silenced. Gay extremists visit schools and pass out cards advertising local gay hangouts while Christians handing out Bibles are kicked off campus. "Multiculturalism" is pushed, along with the values of being "nonjudgmental." Everything is relative in the New Village, including right and wrong, moral and immoral, good and bad.

"The women's movement brought changes and power to millions of American females," declared Jane Robelot, co-host of CBS' *This Morning.* "Virginal brides surrendered to the sexual revolution. Modern fashions exposed body parts previously reserved for the bedroom... The search for pleasure leads some women to shop (for videos and sex tapes) and some to stray... And experts say many husbands and wives can become stronger individuals, and on rare occasions, might even find that cheating recharges their marriages."

Hasn't this woman looked at the divorce and birth-out-of-wedlock rates in this country? Mothers are taking off. Fathers have less and less incentive to stick around. There are so many unwed births that states' Vital Records Divisions all over the nation are removing the last-name section in the birth-certificate process. This means that if your name is Rogers and the daddy's name is Callahan, junior or miss doesn't have to be named either. He can be named Gable, Hepburn or Clinton. Any last name you want.

"I think society has changed," said John Burks, the Oklahoma registrar for vital records. "We're just conforming."

Aren't we ever?

Contrary to popular opinion, it is not the damned male macho pig who breaks up most marriages either. Two-thirds of all divorces involving children are now initiated by mothers. Usually the break ups aren't over male adultery or wife abuse either. They are over the graver concerns of *Oprah* and other similar cultural icons who preach about "losing a sense of closeness," "not feeling loved and appreciated," or "failing to meet my full potential as a woman." Over and over you hear of the modern woman who breaks up a home in order to go out and "find herself."

You don't even have to keep your kid if you don't want it. Professor Peter Singer at Princeton advocates that parents should be able to kill their baby up to the first thirty days of its life if it does not contribute to the "happiness" of the parents or family. Sort of like taking unwanted newborn kittens out and drowning them in a sack. Except, you could go to jail for drowning the kittens.

A number of states have passed laws providing legal immunity to parents who abandon unwanted newborn infants. Say you have the kid and decide you don't want it. You merely carry it out like a bag of trash to the nearest hospital waiting room and dump it. Transfer the responsibility of caring for it to someone else while you go out and pierce your tongue, get a tattoo on your butt, look around for a new stud and seek your "full potential."

What a wonderful country!

And we wonder why fourteen-year-old kids go to school and shoot up the place; why you see gangs of eleven- and twelve-year-olds hanging around with purple spiked hair, nose rings and baggy trousers, smoking cigarettes and saying "Fuck!" to each other; why teachers both male and female are having sex with their students; why movies for prepubescents get raunchier and more violent; why government scolds parents not to correct little Johnny—self-esteem, you understand—and schools teach him he has "rights" in government that supercede those invested in parents...

With all respect due, if any, to Hillary Clinton, a village cannot raise a child. Especially not when the village is run by the village idiot. Especially not when that village is promoting a family composed of two transgenders and a gerbil; when Johnny and Judy make up their own rules while mom and dad go out and play golf or join a swingers group; when family decision-making is based on the consensus of counselors, support groups, child welfare reps and any other politician or child rights "expert" who forces his way into the family circle; when child-rearing practices focus on emotional temperature-taking and "self-esteem" rather than on the conscience and the intellect; when a "don't bug me" attitude prevails when it comes to manners, tact, orderliness and plain simple good behavior; when there is a fixation on the gruesome, ugly and prurient in movies and music and, for those who can still read, print; and, finally, when there is tolerance for all behavior, no matter how outlandish or destructive, while vestiges of self-

discipline, personal responsibility and standards of behavior once nour-
ished within families are condemned.

The village certainly cannot raise a child when it is riding hell-for-
leather to destroy the family that should be rearing the child.

SECTION V
ARTS & CULTURE

"The contents of this exhibition may cause shock, vomiting, confusion, panic, euphoria and anxiety."
Warning at the Brooklyn Museum of Art

CHAPTER THIRTEEN

Were Edgar Allen Poe alive today, he who wrote of insanity in the darkest depths of man's soul and psyche, he might have been nominated head of the National Endowment of the Arts. The NEA was established during President Lyndon Johnson's era of The Great Society to bring "art" and "culture" to the backwoods. At taxpayer expense, of course. It created a State Art approved and funded by government. If art in its various forms-canvas, print, film and performing—reflects a society's values and represents how society sees and understands itself, then perhaps it's time for our culture to sit down with a shrink in a padded room and start interpreting Rorsarch ink blots.

Perhaps intentionally, but more likely unintentionally, the NEA is helping to provide the mirror into which America can look at its own madness. We have built a society that has gone so backward, especially when it comes to "arts," that we now glorify the sick and denigrate the normal and healthy. Poe indeed would have loved it.

Shirley Finkleheimer of Dallas, Texas, received a $20,000 NEA grant for an oil painting of the wart on the end of her nose. It was reported that the Clinton White House was so impressed she was commissioned to paint Hillary Clinton wearing a pair of the President's boxer shorts.

Norbert Gooch of Brooklyn, New York, received $27,500 to doodle on the back of a box of Argo starch while having phone sex with a talking chicken.

Grover Turnipseed of Boaz, Alabama, was awarded $10,000 to snap a photo display of tobacco spit from the parking lots of various truck stops.

Loody Hogarth of Columbia, South Carolina, copped $61,000 to exhibit some of the really cute sugar-sprinkle designs she and her nine-year-old daughter put on some donuts.

This is only the surface. Remember Andres Serrano's *Piss Christ*, the crucifix in a jar of urine? Or Robert Mapplethorpe's exhibit that featured one photo of an unzipped man in a polyester suit letting it all hang out and another with a bullwhip handle rammed up a man's rectum?

Compliments of the NEA and our government in action.

How about a display featuring a mound of synthetic excrement in the background of which a film shows a man stuffing his head up another's rectum; a "performance artist" who smears herself with chocolate to dramatize how the United States treats its women as "nothing but shit;" a papier-mâché sculpture of naked women on all fours, buttocks smeared with feces and excrement hanging down; a display of dead flies and maggots lying alongside the head of a dead cow; a bucket of water containing two dead flies; a Times Square exhibit featuring bright yellow mannequins clad in clothing made of condoms...?

Need we wonder why the Brooklyn Museum of Art banned children under sixteen years old from one of its exhibits and posted a "health warning" caution: *The contents of this exhibit may cause shock, vomiting, confusion, panic, euphoria and anxiety?*

Art is art if you *say* it's art. You're an artist if you *say* you're an artist. It's all part of the New Age of "inclusiveness." Talent? Who needs *talent?* Nothing must be excluded from being art if all people are equal. The grosser you are, the more *common*, the greater your artistic esteem. We no longer elevate great men to where they should be; instead, we take the lowly and elevate them to where they shouldn't be.

Naked Carolee Schneemann received an NEA grant to pull a rolled scroll from her vagina for her audiences to read, assuming that most of them *could* read. Others who received your tax money include: a lesbian Elvis Presley impersonator performing as "Elvis Herselvis;" Vito Acconi performing "Seedbed" in New York's Sonnabend Gallery by masturbating while visitors passed by and watched...

Thank you, Uncle Sam, for bringing us these wonders to uplift, inspire and encourage. And thank you, taxpayers, even though many of you are too stupid or unenlightened to appreciate "true art."

John Baldessori admitted in a statement about one of his canvasses that, "Everything is purged from this painting but art. No ideas have entered this work."

That was obvious.

I have been a professional freelance writer for twenty six years. I went through lean years working on developing my talents and honing my skills. I competed in the open market and have published, so far, over forty books and novels and a couple of thousand or so magazine articles and short stories.

I know a college professor who also wants to be a writer but is unwilling to make the requisite sacrifices and effort. Instead, he applied to the NEA and received a $30,000 grant to write a *literary* novel. It was never published, but the money was his to keep.

Does that make any sense? While I was writing and paying taxes from it, he was writing and leeching off those taxes. Why can't he compete on the open market if anyone actually wants to read his scribbles? Why should society continue to pay for the mediocre and the crude?

What we must understand is that in art the politics of rebuilding society takes precedence, as it does in every other area of modern culture. Art has turned into a medium by which to push through an agenda. The NEA itself declared in its annual report that art should be useful in serving today's themes of multiculturalism, "pulling us as diverse groups and cultures together...shred(ding) the veil of academic elitism."

In other words, it should celebrate the mundane and the coarse—and in the process destroy even the definition of art.

We are lectured on how contemporary art is "liberating" us from age-old norms and habits, making artists more creative because they are no longer "party to biases of race, gender and class that have so marred previous art."

I certainly feel "liberated" when I see a bullwhip stuck up a man's butt... Masturbating in public...A woman pulling a scroll from her vagina... I certainly see how previous art must have been marred before it was liberated.

So help me here. I'm just a little Indian hillbilly, uncultured and all, and I'm having a tough time understanding "creative" and "liberating."

Maybe artist/writer Lisa Phillips can help: "(A) vast underground that included radical political organizations, gay-rights activists and feminists helped fuel a transformation in American life by demanding status for special interest groups," whose *progressive* visions contributed to the development of art.

Now I understand.

"It reminds me of the Cultural Revolution," commented Chen Shi-Zheng, a naturalized U.S. citizen from China, "when things that have no relevance to artistic debate take over, like ideology and politics."

CHAPTER FOURTEEN

Virtually the *only* rule of our insane art culture is that it may be as obscene and offensive as it chooses on the single condition that it not insult any of the various victim groups or violate any politically correct dogma. It's all right, however, to stomp on the sensitivities of trailer trash girls, rednecks, right-wingers, Dr. Laura Schlessinger, Christians, Republicans, white males as long as they're heterosexual and not crippled, stay-at-home moms, Rush Limbaugh, successful people, gun owners and black conservatives. That celebrated progressive tolerance for which the Enlightened remains so smugly self-congratulatory need not extend toward us unenlightened slobs.

Visitors to the Biennial Exhibition at New York's Whitney Museum shelled out six bucks apiece and were awarded a little pin that proclaimed *I Can't Ever Imagine Wanting To Be White.* Monitors explained that "whiteness is a signifier of power" and wearing the button permitted whites to "absolve themselves of some of the privileges of cultural imperialism."

Beat me, kick me, call me a bitch and make me like it. I am so sorry—can't you see I'm down on my knees?--that I was born with the blood of white oppressors in my veins.

Naturally, much of the Whitney exhibit was "victim art." Plastic vomit on the floor introduced one large section devoted to "women's rage." Included were huge grotesque casts of women's larynxes and tongues made out of lipstick. They allegedly represented the "silencing of women through the use of specifically-gendered material."

American art in the new century is indeed a savage place full of ridiculous situations and idiotic people. A good starting point in the disintegration of culture and the social conditioning of people to accept "change" in silence is to legitimize the depraved and convince people that the vulgar is "beautiful." The objective of so-called *avante garde* art appears to be to destroy all common social standards and norms through assaults on propriety, common sense and common decency.

Oleg "Mad Dog" Kulik stripped himself naked, put a dog collar around his neck, and moved into a bare exhibit room at the Deitch Art Gallery in New York. Art aficionados could watch through barred windows as this talented genius barked savagely, munched Purina Dog Chow, and paced around on all fours with his bony, naked butt stuck in the air. I'm not making this up. Go figure what the object of the exhibit was.

At the San Francisco Art Institute, Jonathan Yagge received the permission of his instructor to create a masterpiece he called "Art Piece #1...to explore Hegel's master-slave dialectic and Kant's theories on freedom of thought and action." See if you can find any of *that* high-minded Barbra Streisand (BS) in *this*.

He bound and suspended a naked male outdoors in the middle of the campus, then stripped himself. "I engaged in oral sex with him and he engaged in oral sex with me... I had given him an enema, and I had taken shit and stuffed it in his ass. That goes on, he shits all over me. I shit on him. There was a security guard present. There was an instructor from the school present. It was videoed, and the piece was over."

Surely you are astute enough, sensitive enough, stupid enough to recognize this as *art*.

The NEA granted the Manhattan Theatre Club $31,000 to fund the production of *Corpus Christi,* in which Christ is crucified as "King of The Queers." First of all, that's tax money. That's public money. That's *our* money.

The script was filled with stereotypical gay sexual comments and behavior such as obsession with the penis and lots of crotch grabbing. Joshua (the Christ figure) presided over a "wedding" between James and Bartholomew. He had sex, mostly offstage, with Judas and Philip. "I hope you have rubbers," Philip cautioned. "HIV, you know." The Apostles pretended to urinate on stage, with appropriate sound effects, after which Joshua proclaimed then all divine, saying, "Fuck your mother, fuck your father, fuck God."

The play ended with an actor saying, "If we have offended you, so be it."

The New York *Times*, naturally, raved over it, adding a small apology that "only one sexual encounter, a non-explicit one with an HIV-positive street hustler, takes place in any form on stage."

Only *one?* Well, then, give this play a PG rating.

In 2003, London's Tate Gallery awarded its annual Turner Prize for the year's most outstanding and important artwork to Grayson Claire Perry, a transvestite potter in pornographic and pedophile imagery. Mister or Miss, as the case may be, produces decorative motifs of child abuse, erotica and "angry social comment."

How about the runner-up? It was a tableau of two inflatable dolls going at it, mutilated corpses being consumed by maggots and a bronze tree festooned with rotting apples.

Sounds like prize-winning artwork to me.

The brigands on the Far Left continue to discover ways to destroy vestiges of what it nauseatingly refers to as *ad infinitum* as an "oppressive and repressive American society." Performance "artist" Stelare, whose website describes his work as "exploring and extending the concept of the body and its relationship with technology," announced plans to have a human ear grown in a biotech laboratory and permanently grafted onto his arm. How about an anus attached to his forehead?

The Quentin Tarantino movie *Wild Bill*, a "reflection about our culture and about ourselves," is a study in gratuitous violence—

shootings, stabbings, slashings, disemboweling, decapitations, plucking
out of eyeballs, severing of limbs, biting off of tongues... At the same
time, England's Channel 4, which airs reality programs, broadcast a
documentary called *Beijing Swings* that featured "performance artist"
Zhu Yu eating the corpse of a dead baby.

Nihilism is a philosophy of life that takes the point of view that
traditional values and beliefs are unfounded and that existence itself is
senseless. It denies any objective ground for truth, especially for moral
truth. Concepts of right and wrong, moral and immoral, good or bad
simply do not exist. Ultimately in a world where nothing matters, evil
will win the day by filling the moral vacuum left behind.

After Rigoberta Menchu won the Nobel Peace Prize for her dia-
tribe in favor of revolutionary violence, of the left wing variety
naturally, it was discovered that most of her "autobiographical" book
may have been made up of exaggerations, half-truths and outright lies.

"Whether her book is true or not, I don't care," harped a Wellesley
professor. "We should teach our students about the brutality of the
Guatemalan military and the U.S. financing of it."

See what I mean? He *doesn't care*. Ideology and agenda are more
important than any truth. Truth can go to hell in the proverbial hand
basket. It is considered righteous to censure, censor or condemn anything that fails to support the liberal tenets of the Brave New World. It
makes no difference whether those tenets are based on falsehoods or
straight lies.

As long as you are an artist with the "correct" mindset, you may be
lauded, praised and rewarded. Cross the line, however, and offend the
wrong persons and you become toast in the world of the Enlightened,
who are all oh-so-sensitive and cultural.

Catholics and Christians complained of being offended by the
Brooklyn Museum of Art's display of Chris Ofili's *Holy Virgin Mary,* a
"painting" composed of scrap porn magazine photos and elephant
dung. That's *shit* for those of you in Palm Beach County, Florida. All
the usual suspects jumped up to defend it and to attack those with the
temerity to question the judgment and tastes of their intellectual betters.
Steve Martin, Norman Mailer, Arthur Miller and Kurt Vonnegut were
some of the more than one hundred luminaries who ran a full-page
"pro-dung" ad in the New York *Times.* The *Times* art critic gushed over
how the painting "does what all good art should do: it makes you
think."

Well, okay. Suppose I go along with that? How then do you explain the arrest of art dealer Mary Boone at her Manhattan gallery?
Mary had the audacity to permit exhibitor Tom Sachs to show a display
of homemade guns (now, *that's* obscene) while inviting visitors to take
home a 9mm bullet as a souvenir. Police seized the exhibit and charged
Mary with illegal distribution of ammunition and resisting arrest. Her

real crime was that she crossed the artistic line to offend sensitive, caring, progressive people who are, naturally, all anti-gun.

Everything in art has protection under the First Amendment. However, on one side of the line symphony orchestras may be too elite, distant, exclusive, arrogant and "possibly racist." Get rid of them. They serve as poor role models for our youth.

On the other side of the line, the NAACP nominated rapper Tupac Shakur for an NAACP Image Award, never mind that he had been charged with sodomy and sexual abuse while out on bail accused of shooting two off-duty police officers. Now, *he's* a suitable role model for our sensitive youth.

The contempt these *artistes manques* (that's French for those who know more than the rest of us) display toward us mortals is personified in arts & design student Jubal Brown. Jubal contends that Rembrandts and all the world's other masterpieces are oppressive. He has therefore set out on a mission to "liberate individuals and living creatures" from them—by going around to museums and vomiting on the paintings. Puking on them, he says, is itself an art. Looks like art to me. It wouldn't surprise me if he received an NEA grant.

Maybe one day you can go to a museum and view a Brown (a Gauguin smeared in puke) on display next to an award-winning abstract created by a talented chimp.

CHAPTER FIFTEEN

Art is no longer allowed to be a matter of taste; it must be a matter of politics. In his heyday, Stalin threatened punishment to any artist who did not support his socialist goal of propagating and enforcing his version of political correctness. It was surprising and a bit daunting to realize the number of good little socialists, true believers they, who would turn in an unreformed artist in order to have him sent to the gulags and thus silence him. It is just as daunting today to realize the number of good little socialists out there willing to silence *you* to enforce the American version of political correctness. You're sadly mistaken if you think they won't send you to the gulags once they have the power. If you don't go along with the roadmap of the Enlightened... Well, put the cat out, as this letter to the editor of the Vermont *Valley News* suggested.

"The comic strip *Garfield* is neither humorous nor insightful..." it began. "The cat is blended from all the Biblical faults—sloth, greed, envy and meanness... The violence is assumed to be natural and justified because the victims...are a special class because they look different... Garfield celebrates the killing of spiders for no reason other than they are spiders... We hold that it's not all right to kill, curse or deny an education or a job because of differences of appearances. That's prejudice. I resent being exposed to an unregenerate proponent of prejudice in my daily paper... Please put the cat out, for good..."

Puh-*leese!* You really have to stretch to see prejudice in a comic strip cat swatting a spider. But it only serves to illustrate how dead set these people are on destroying anything—and I mean *anything*—that fails to toe the line of the Enlightened, however ephemeral, transit and constantly moving that line might be. Even the funny papers cannot escape their pursed-mouth scrutiny. But isn't it odd how indignant they can become over a comic cat while hardly twitching a sphincter over a steady TV fare about necrophilia, abortion, incest, masturbation, homosexuality, pedophilia, doctors sodomizing anesthetized patients, and passing gas?

Fox TV's "Family Guy" threw in every conceivable obscenity along with a steady diet of references to pornography, masturbation and necrophilia. The characters were never so crass, however, as to swat a spider and therefore risk accusations of prejudice. "Will & Grace" was rife with homosexual humor, always, naturally, in a positive non-spider-swatting way. In one episode, gay Jack was alarmed at being aroused by a female stripper—until he learned the stripper was really a transsexual-in-the-making who still possessed proper male plumbing.

"Thank God," he exclaimed. "I'm still gayer than Christmas."

Shock and offend however you want, as long as you shock and offend us low-browed Garfield types, and you can be declared creative and *avante garde* and a celebrated leader of the New Generations. Question—and it's out with the cat. Plenty of folks out there are most willing to toss out the cat to make sure political correctness in the "arts" is adhered to. You have to understand that art is only art if it's the *proper* art.

NAACP's Kweisi Mfume, whose real name was originally Harold Brown or Otis Smith or something, opened up a Pandora's box when he made a deal with NBC-TV that the networks had to hire at least one black writer for any second-season TV series. That was to make sure blacks were *always* shown in a positive light.

He hadn't even stepped out of the way before a pack of Hispanics, Asian-Americans, Indians, gays, women, and Lord only knows who else descended upon the network executive braying for the same privilege of censorship and control of content. Dare you contemplate how long it will be before law mandates that every TV program, movie, magazine, and book publisher, etc., include representatives from all groups—a lesbian, a one-legged dwarf, a Puerto Rican, two transsexuals, and a poofter from San Francisco...

Hey, I can still say what I want, politically correct or not. Whether it will be published in this climate, however, is entirely another matter. Maybe I ought to have one of each of the above sitting here with me to vet my material—and undoubtedly cut it down to about two pages maximum.

But, hey, TV producer Ed Weinberger was so impressed with the gay dentist from New Jersey that NBC hired to vet all homosexual jokes to make sure they depicted gays in a positive light that he chortled, "There really is a tooth fairy!"

Most of the Enlightened don't have that kind of humor. This business of transforming art to transform the multitudes is serious stuff. What's important in art is not truth but instead what the truth by right *ought* to be. Reality re-created.

Artist Mike Alewitz designed a mural for the downtown office building of the Associated Black Charities of Baltimore to celebrate the heroic saga of Harriet Tubman, the woman who led slaves to freedom along the Underground Railroad prior to the Civil War. Everything came to a halt when Alewitz revealed sketches of his work-in-progress. Heavens! Tubman was being shown with a rifle in one hand and a lantern in the other as she led frightened slaves to freedom. The gun had to go.

"As much as we want her on our building, we have to look at how people will interpret it," said Barbara Blount Armstrong, director of community services and grants for the Charities. "(The gun's) something I probably was aware of, but *it's not how I thought of her.*" (Emphasis added)

See what I mean? The mural must be politically correct. And since political correctness is anti-gun, historical accuracy be damned.

You should have heard the clamor when Washington's Fine Arts and Memorial Commission designed a Franklin Delano Roosevelt memorial. As you probably know, every disparate and itinerate Leftwing group from Gay Jaywalkers to Single Mothers For Little Green Men claim FDR as one of their own sent to them from... Well, not from God since God is dead, but from...somewhere. Anyhow, they all wanted to make sure ole Franklin and First Lady Eleanor were depicted in a proper progressive light.

Therefore, the animal rights bunch protested Eleanor wearing her trademark fur piece. So that was discarded. Anti-tobacco is fashionable, so FDR's ever-present cigarette and holder vanished. Although of the more than 35,000 photos taken of Franklin, only two ever showed him in a wheelchair, the Americans With Disabilities bunch insisted he ride a wheelchair into bronze-and-stone immortality. Go figure. Most of us probably won't even recognize him.

It's like that everywhere. Realities of an unsuitable past erased and replaced by a more acceptable present vision. A courthouse in New England removed a Civil War cannon from its lawn because it was, *Shriek!*, a *gun*. Bronze generals all over the South are being toppled from their horses; they were racists, you know. Sculptures of poor Chris Columbus have been shattered into door stops, good enough for him considering he was a bigoted imperialist. Fly a Confederate flag at your own peril. In another decade or so, the Stars and Bars will not only not exist, it will never have existed in the first place. That was the way the PC folks of George Orwell's *1984* handled things; they simply erased what was offensive and, lo, it never existed to begin with.

There is no room for compromise with the Enlightened. There is no middle ground. The cultural elite know what is good and true for us schmucks out here. Everything must either support the True Belief—or be silenced or altered to reflect the proper faith.

West Side Story, the musical, was banned as racist by the Amhurst-Pilham Regional High School in Massachusetts. I'm not even going to try to understand *why*. My mind doesn't work that way in seeing offense in every nuance and vowel.

The same school decided the way Indians were portrayed in *Peter Pan* was somehow offensive, so its students turned Indians into woodland sprites when it performed the play.

Pennsylvania's branch of the NAACP declared Mark Twain's *Huckleberry Finn* "racist" and demanded the book be removed from library shelves. It was.

Protests by black employees at the Library of Congress led to the dismantling of an exhibit about slavery. Controversy prompted the Smithsonian Institute to cancel an exhibit on the Vietnam War and replace it with an elaborate *safe* exhibit of Hollywood's fictional *Star Wars*...

And, so, thus it goes, on and on, re-creating a sterile environment safe from all tainting of the past. In the process, we can almost be afraid heaven will fall on our heads if we do a painting, write a book, stage a play or make a film that is recognizable, uplifting, requires talent, and is not obscene in some manner. And, oh, yes, is not free of all bugaboos that might be considered offensive by the one hundred and one different groups out there who wait like vultures to comb through anything looking for the slightest suggestion of offense, whether intentional or unintentional. If we commoners enjoy and appreciate something, you can be certain the ribbon-wearing, pony-tailed herd that kicks out Huck Finn, Peter Pan and Garfield will want to kick us out as well.

For example, look at the accolades critics heaped upon *Party*, a play appealing to the modern hipster, as compared to the lack of same awarded to Mel Gibson's *The Passion Of The Christ* or *The Patriot*, considered movies for the Nascar crowd.

Kara Swisher, the Washington *Post's* drama critic, described *Party* as "sexually-oriented party games, a lot of liquor and seven naked gay guys...perhaps one of the sweeter and more innocent plays now on Washington stages... The play's appeal is certainly due in part to the complete nudity of all the characters by play's end, but also its frothy, shamelessly entertaining nature."

What are those people in D.C. watching, and smoking, if they consider this one of the "sweeter and more innocent" plays?

In contrast, critic Arion Burger of the *Washington City Paper* lit into *The Patriot* with all claws. The movie, he snipped, "is right-wing hogwash. Now the disgruntled, home-schooling, SUV-buying, pro-militia-but-cautious-suburban-family-values man has a movie to call his own..."

Whoa! Say all that in one breath, making sure you get in everything you despise about the ordinary American. Well, throw me out of the trailer park and send my red Indian ass to sensitivity training. It must be I'm simply not cool, not with it, which undoubtedly also means I'm a bigot, a homophobe, a sexist, a... Fill in the blanks. Does it make me all those things, and a prude to boot, to expect some level of morality and decency in one's life?

For a six-week period, artist Stephen Keene painted original landscapes and sold over 17,000 of them quite inexpensively in a window of Goldie Paley Gallery at the Moore College of Arts and Designs in Philadelphia—and is not devastated that not one of them hangs in the New York Museum of Modern Art. To listen to how the elitists in the art world blistered, denigrated, and condemned him, however, you might have thought he set back art two centuries and insulted everyone from Mad Dog Kralik to Chris Ofili.

"It's schlock," whined Academic Dean Wayne Morris. "It's also mean-spirited and cynical."

Let me make sure I get this straight: This is a guy who paints landscapes for ordinary people and *that's* mean-spirited and cynical!

Ex-*cuse* me! I think I'll take Stephen Keene any day over Lucy Lippard's *Eccentric Abstraction* of soft furniture liberally studded with phallic imagery; over Robert Morris' clumping a pile of rock on the gallery floor to make an artistic statement (the janitor didn't know it was art and cleared it out); over Tracey Emin's *My Bed* which critics adored and described as "her own unmade bed, complete with torn pillows and wine-stained sheets, surrounded by ashtrays full of smoked fags, a box of sanitary towels, medicine, nylons, soiled underpants, a candle, a pregnancy test..."

"Art attempts to address the human condition," carped Moore College faculty member Moe Brooker, "and you don't trivialize the human spirit."

Somehow I don't feel nearly as trivialized by looking at a pleasing oil of a sunrise over Mount Rainier as I do by a "conceptualist" who rides the Trans-Siberian Railway for sixteen days, burns his notes, smears the ashes on a slate, and exhibit's the slate as "art."

I swear I'm not making this up.

"People are being told they bought a piece of art (from Keene)," added Dean Wayne Morris, "and they haven't, which is condescending... It's a bad joke."

And a photo of a guy with a bullwhip handle stuck up his anus *is* art, *not* condescending, and *not* a joke? I told you these people have no sense of humor or of parody.

Permitting Keene's work to show at the Paley, Morris went on, legitimized something that "has no merit" while "serious artists" receive no such stage.

I see. *Serious artists?* Like those who create *Piss Christ* and sprinkles on donuts and a repetitive five-minute audio of a person's breathing superimposed upon short blasts from aerosol spray cans?

If you look for something truly creative and immortal in your art, for something to revere, something heroic and self-sacrificial... Well, forget it. Jubal Brown will probably make "real art" out of it by coming around and vomiting on it. What art in the Brave New World offers instead is deviancy defined down to the lowest common denominator, a leveling of both the human spirit and the human condition, bodily functions on display.

"It's not possible," wrote Alexandra Jacobs in the New York *Observer,* "to have a society where people give the finger to everything."

Not for long it isn't.

SECTION VI
THE MEDIA

"There are many kinds of eyes, and consequently there are many kinds of 'truths,' and consequently there is no truth."
Nietzsche

CHAPTER SIXTEEN

"There are many kinds of eyes," said Nietzsche, "and consequently there are many kinds of 'truths' and consequently there is no truth." Apparently, judging from events at the New York *Times* and elsewhere, the mainstream media agrees with Nietzsche. Movie-making mogul Oliver Stone, producer of distorted epics like *JFK*, argues that truth twisting is justified as long as it makes the point you want to make. There you have it, folks, straight from the horse's mouth. Truth is no longer objective, not even an attempt at truth. It is relative and ambiguous. You use it to make whatever point you choose.

Most Americans form our opinions and develop a world outlook through the media—newspapers, magazines, radio, and particularly TV. While no one who thinks beyond slogans and platitudes believes there is a conspiracy as such among the media to "silence the opponents," the media is nonetheless largely biased toward the Left and dedicated to pushing a "progressive" agenda. Even seventy percent of honest self-described liberals think the press is biased in their favor.

What we common folk are expected to do is sit on our fat behinds, watch TV, swill another drink and let the media tell us what to think and believe. Here's an example of how it works:

Bryant Gumbel began his CBS-TV prime-time special "Racial Attitudes and Consciousness Exam" by assuring viewers that "this test is not going to tell you whether you're a *racist or a liberal*." (My emphasis) Did you get that? If you're not a *liberal,* you fall into the broad category of *racist.* There is no other choice.

Look at how columnist Ellen Goodman, while lamenting the lack of liberal talk show hosts to rival Rush Limbaugh, described two fellow media personalities, one liberal and therefore agreeable, the other conservative and therefore despicable.

"The belovedly bellicose James Carville," she wrote, "once said, 'If your opponent is drowning, throw the son of a bitch an anvil.'"

"The most recent person to mourn the lack of civilized political debate was Ann Coulter," Goodman wrote, "who said, 'The country is trapped in a political discourse that resembled professional wrestling.'" Ellen then snidely added, "That's like Arnold Schwarzenegger complaining that voters pay too much attention to body image."

Carville is *belovedly bellicose;* Coulter may as well be a lady mud wrestler.

Let's go back to Bryant Gumbel one more time. The man is about as subtle as hitting an infant with a sledge hammer.

During an interview with Bob Knight of the Family Research Council on *The Early Show*, Gumbel scowled, then laughed in Knight's face after the guest said he supported the Boy Scout policy of excluding homosexuals as scout leaders because they might steer boys in a dangerous direction.

"I got to let that stop there," Gumbel snapped.

After Knight left the studio, Gumbel turned to another guest and, apparently thinking himself off-camera, contemptuously referred to Knight as a "fucking idiot."

A CBS spokesman later apologized for the remark: "All our anchors are unbiased." He said it with a straight face too.

"I'd settle for being civil," Knight responded.

Shortly thereafter, Knight was scheduled to appear on Peter Jennings' *ABC News* to balance Evan Wolfson, attorney for homosexual James Dale who had been denied leadership in the Boy Scouts. Wolfson, however, flatly refused to appear with Knight. Care to make a wager on which of the two got scrubbed? You are correct! ABC booted Knight and interviewed Wolfson exclusively. After all, Wolfson's vision of "truth" was the one that really counted.

Liberals never seem to get it though. They have myopic vision, seeing only what they want to see, and what they do see is severely tilted off-center. Irving Kristol described a liberal as "a person who sees a fourteen-year-old girl performing live sex acts on stage and wonders if she's being paid the minimum wage."

The New York *Times* (among others) hasn't changed its viewpoint since at least the 1930s when the Enlightened first looked upon communism as mankind's salvation. Back then, *Times* correspondent Walter Duranty swore there was no government-induced famine in the Soviet Union when in fact he knew Moscow was deliberately starving peasants, even allowing children to die after their parents were hauled off to gulags for the hideous and unforgivable crime of attempting to own private property. He even won a Pulitzer for his reporting—awarded him, naturally, by like-thinking fellow travelers.

The media, sympathetic toward the goals of the Brave New World and hostile toward those who question them, have replaced "truth" with "fairness." Their deepest loyalties extend to special causes such as ultra feminism, gay marriages, environmentalism, wealth redistribution, gun control... Right and wrong, *truth,* have taken such a beating that we are no longer sure what they are. Selfish agendas pushed by those who *know* what is best for us, moral relativism, have eaten into society like a cancer.

Media figures used to have roots within the common people. I was a newspaper reporter for a while; I came from a shack in the Ozarks. Today, most journalists, especially those in the upper echelon, have fallen out of touch with the Great Unwashed and aligned themselves with the country's special elites, people who wear fashionable factory-faded jeans, ponytails and "I Care" ribbons.

A New York *Times* poll confessed that 82 percent of people in the media favor abortion on demand; 89 percent support gay rights. Journalists disapprove of prayer in school by a margin of three to one while the general nincompoop public approves of it by a margin of four to one. Journalists voted overwhelmingly for Democrat Bill Clinton during the 1992 elections--89 percent. *Ninety* percent voted for him again in 1996 after all the scandals and evidence of corruption.

You would have to be as wacky as the rest of the world to believe this does not affect the way journalists select subject matter and approach it, the tone of their reporting, and even the way journalists are selected and hired. Journalists, film producers, TV personalities and others of the "media" are constantly praised for contributions in which even hard-core pornography is viewed as valuable "free speech."

When she was president of the ACLU, Nadine Strassen attended the World Pornography Conference to praise porn stars and adult-film makers for their "vital work" in protecting "freedom of sexual expression." Freedom of sexual expression in this instance being to get it on in as many different combinations as possible, including with Rover, Spot and Tabby, and in a variety of ways to include bondage, S&M, and pissing in each other's faces, all for the viewing pleasure of other sickos in darkened rooms.

"I want to thank and applaud you for your fight and contribution for First Amendment freedom," she exhorted, "and to galvanize you to 'keep it up,' so to speak."

And *keep it up* is exactly what the media is doing, cajoling and coaxing the public in the proper direction of a Utopia where anything and everything goes. What I find most disturbing, excluding the insanity of all this, is why we go along with it with rarely a pathetic bleat of protest. Maybe it's because we are so dumbed down and conditioned by the daily onslaught of wackiness that we no longer think about it in terms other than those defined for us by the media and the Enlightened Elites. What's really scary is how much of our standards, principles, morality and freedom we seem eager to concede to those inmates who have taken over the asylum.

The New York-based First Amendment Center published a study on how Americans view such constitutional rights as freedom of speech, press, assembly and religion. Now, are you ready for this? Thirty-seven percent, over a third of the United States, could not name even one of the five freedoms guaranteed by the First Amendment—freedom of religion, speech, press, assembly, and the right to petition government for redress of grievance. No wonder we're willing to give them up, or have them redefined for us, when so many of us don't even know what they are.

That may explain why a "significant number" in the study were "willing to allow government to control, restrict, or ban material that *some* find offensive" Of course, you understand that "offensive" means such as "hate speech" and not a film of a woman getting it on with Rover.

For example, thirty six percent said they approved of laws banning public remarks offensive to racist and minority groups. Like, perhaps, commenting unfavorably on homosexuality? Twenty percent said freedom of religion "was never meant to apply to religious groups that the majority considers extreme or fringe." Like, perhaps, Jerry Falwell? Thirty one percent said a group should not be allowed to hold a rally if its cause is "offensive" to some in the community. Like, perhaps, a Christian revival?

Thomas Jefferson said a democracy cannot survive without an *enlightened* electorate. It's disturbing to think that it's left up to the media to keep the American people *enlightened.*

CHAPTER SEVENTEEN

Very few controversial subjects in the mainstream press receive fair and impartial coverage. You can always predict what the press will say if it's a matter of consciousnesses "being raised." Journalists view counter viewpoints as impediments to advancing social agendas of political correctness.

Take two reports published in *Archives of Pediatrics and Adolescent Medicine.* One supported the "progressive" theory that spanking children encourages aggression and violence. The other upheld that spanking, done judiciously, does not increase aggression and violence. All the major networks—CBS, NBC, ABC—and more than one hundred newspapers went with the anti-spanking story. Even though the second report was more conclusive and better researched, not one network and only fifteen of the same newspapers even mentioned it.

The same kind of twisted reporting was directed at radio talk show host Dr. Laura Schlessinger and at George W. Bush during his 2000 presidential election campaign.

Dr. Schlessinger's views on homosexuality, marriage and family offended the gay movement and earned her the title "Queen of Hate Radio." If you've noticed, TV, newspapers and magazines are chock full of touching stories about faithful, monogamous gay couples caring for each other for a lifetime while struggling to maintain dignity in an unjust and ignorant world. Any mention of gays must make them appear more "normal" than normal and show them in a positive light. Seldom is there a dissenting or discouraging word. They simply mustn't be criticized in a sensitive society. To do so is to bring down the ire of the Enlightened.

Gays launched a campaign to prevent Dr. Schlessinger's show from airing on TV. They warned the media that dissenters should never be heard in stories about gays. To give the opposite viewpoint on homosexuality, said one gay activist, is the same thing as asking a Nazi to provide an opposing view in a news report about Hanukkah.

Naturally, the media acquiesced to gay clamor. Stories about Dr. Schlessinger's row with the gay activists overwhelmingly depicted a very kind and loving woman as a hater and gay basher.

Now to George W. Bush. During his election campaign he took a great deal of heat when confessed rapist and convicted murderer Gary Graham faced execution in Texas, where Bush was governor. Major news stories ran more than thirty stories suggesting Bush was killing an innocent man. Cable channels held death row vigils. Jesse Jackson ran frantically all over the countryside spouting his tasteless rhyme comparing Bush to Pontius Pilate.

Bill Clinton had confronted a nearly-identical situation when he ran for president in 1992 and was governor of Arkansas. He dropped his campaign long enough to fly home to personally authorize the execution of convicted murderer Ricky Ray Rector, a man so mentally disturbed he asked guards to save his pecan pie for when he returned from the electric chair. How was Clinton viewed by mainstream media? Were there candle light vigils, Jesse Jackson spoutings, anguished cries from the press?

Hardly. Get this. He was lovingly called "a different kind of democrat" who would be tough on crime. There were a total of *two* mainstream news stories about the case, one before and one after the execution, both brief and favorable to the candidate. Jesse stayed home and campaigned for Bill.

What was the difference between George and Bill, you might ask? That's an easy one. George was a conservative, Bill a liberal. Bill was the man of the party of the Enlightened. That was what counted, that was the *only* thing that counted. We Injuns saw forked tongues.

During California's governor recall elections in 2003, the Los Angeles *Times* and other papers, the same ones who defended Bill Clinton's peccadilloes with Monica, lambasted candidate Arnold Schwarzenegger over allegations that he had groped women. Feminists, also the same ones who defended Clinton's Lewinsky, or remained conspicuously silent, were outraged. The difference?

"The difference," said Patricia Foulkrod, an activist at an anti-Schwarzenegger rally, "is that Clinton was so brilliant."

There you have it, folks. Nothing counts against you if you're a member of the Enlightened Elite. You're too smart, too sensitive, too compassionate, too *everything* to be held to the same standards as the dastardly villains who burn black churches, send people to gas chambers, make war on misunderstood minorities, and think there are such things in the world as evil, sin and immorality. Common sense goes once liberalism takes over.

How the press selects stories and the slant it puts on them reflects the way a liberal, politically correct press wants us peasants out here to see the world; we are deemed too stupid to look at both sides and make up our own minds. Besides, that's too dangerous; we might choose the "wrong" side.

We are expected to agree that spanking a child is wrong, that Dr. Schlessinger hates gays, that George W. Bush is a monster for supporting the death penalty...

A few years back, a black teen named Tawana Brawley accused a group of prominent white men of gang raping her. An incensed press rocketed Reverend Al Sharpton, who championed her, into the national political limelight while it railed against racism and discrimination. Sharpton rode the press coverage to become a prominent "black leader" and a candidate for president. Politicians like Al Gore and Hillary Clinton made pilgrimages to his doorstep to kiss his... Well, to kiss his ring.

It turned out that, to coin a Mary McCarthy quip, every word the young woman spoke, including *and* and *the*, was a bald-faced lie. Sharpton himself may even have known she was a liar. But so what if it didn't *really* happen? It *could* have happened because of all the racism in the country.

Not once did the media apologize to Brawley's falsely accused assailants for besmirching and scandalizing their names. Months passed before most of the press even owned up to having been taken in by Brawley and Sharpton.

Ask yourself this: What would have been the reaction if Louisiana's white extremist David Duke had championed a white girl who falsely accused prominent black men of rape? See what I mean? Do you think he would ever have been swept into the presidential race and had pols lining up at *his* doorstep to kiss his...ring?

The use—and misuse—of language and words is a powerful and important weapon used by the media. The term "illegal immigrant," for example, is now taboo when speaking of wetbacks. They are now, and I'm not making this up, "undocumented *citizens.*" No matter how violent they are, rioters are always referred to as "demonstrators," unless they're marching for pro-life or in favor of the death penalty, at which point they become a "mob." The New York *Times* still refers to Osama bin Laden as an "*alleged* terrorist." The Boston *Globe* won't use the word "terrorist," not even when referring to those who crashed air carriers into the World Trade Center because it "condemns rather than describes." Huh? Certainly it isn't for us to *condemn* these murderers.

Media propaganda can and certainly does win, convert, and direct a culture. Politically correct language helped advance the gay movement's meteoric rise into the mainstream to the point that Johnny and Stevie are gonna get married and everything. First, there was sodomy, an act. Sodomy became homosexuality, a condition. Homosexuality evolved into gay, an identity. Once homosexuality turned from a criminalized act to an identity, like being Hispanic or black, you are forced to accept it wholeheartedly as perfectly normal or risk being called a bigot.

Coverage of religion—not religion per se, *Christianity*—is where all stops come out and neon signs start flashing to tell you *This is the right way to believe! This is the wrong way!* That's because your chances of bumping into an Orthodox Jew, a traditional Catholic, a Mormon, or a born-again Christian in the mainstream media is, as the Center for Media and Public Affairs put it, about like "encountering a rapper at a chamber music recital." Believers are commonly portrayed as provincial, fanatical and violence prone, a bunch of poor, uneducated redneck crackers led into denying everyone else his right to fornicate in public, enjoy kiddie porn, and marry his boyfriend or her pet poodle.

In the press, Evangelical Protestants are always "fundamentalists" or "the Christian Far Right." Torah-based Judaism is "ultra-orthodox." You may be "enlightened and compassionate" if the press agrees with you, such as when the National Conference of Catholic Bishops spoke out against capital punishment and welfare cuts. On the other hand, you may be "mean-spirited and anti-First Amendment," such as when the National Conference of Catholic Bishops disapproved of same-sex marriage.

"Divisiveness" in the media means that the opinions of most people, the rabble and the unenlightened, differ from those of the media and the Enlightened.

An article about the Supreme Court and school prayer began with "Prayer in public schools, for forty years a divisive and politically-charged issue..." Seventy five percent of Americans support school prayer, but it is still "divisive."

Abortion and gay marriage, however, are rarely characterized as either "divisive" or "politically-charged."

Where liberalism takes over the minds of a nation, common sense soon goes. Liberalism is a dangerous mental disorder, as Michael Savage put it, that attacks the way we live, how we conduct our business, the way we worship, the choice of the car we drive and the place we live, the food we eat, our very freedom. Social insanity and the death of culture, Savage goes on, are where the liberal mind ultimately takes a nation that fails to resist. If we continue to follow where the media leads, we're all bound to wake up bonkers in the middle of a nightmare.

CHAPTER EIGHTEEN

What you can't see in the media these days isn't worth mentioning. The general attitude is "anything goes and I'm all right with it." The media triumphantly leads the way into the lowest possible reaches of popular culture. But just when you think it can't get any lower, it does.

If everything keeps sliding deeper into the chaos of insanity, *The Jerry Springer Show* (Springer, incidentally, is a delegate to the 2004 Democratic Convention) might well be looked upon in a few years as tame, even a standard bearer of a higher culture. After all, it presents sights for your entertainment, amusement and edification that merely reflect America, right? Like an extremely-pregnant stripper who takes it all off for the camera and then, near naked, proceeds to lecture the rest of us on our lack of sensitivity and compassion for not insisting the federal government grant *paid* maternity leave for exotic dangers and other seedy sorts. In case you're from Palm Beach County, Florida, and don't understand a dangling chad from a dollar, that means we should be ashamed of ourselves for not ponying up more of our hard-earned money through taxes for the less-privileged. Spell it more socialism.

Howard Stern always tops Jerry Springer for sheer depravity—like, for example, a female guest who blows out a candle and tosses a ping pong ball with a part of the anatomy once considered unmentionable but which is highly mentionable and showable these days. Don't ask me how she does it. Talent finds many roots.

In today's media you can find these and many other instances of everything you don't want to know about penis envy, pedophilia, bestiality, adultery, oral or anal sex, or anything else focusing on mankind's baser nature. And bad taste, lots of bad taste. Two women strippers frolicking in slime with a bunch of toads, as in amphibians, not lounge lizards. Two men munching maggots while a young lady licks the armpits of a sweaty weightlifter. Cartoons about third-graders encountering Satan and Saddam Hussein as a passionate gay couple.

This used to be considered madness. Now it's *art.*

CBS aired an assisted suicide, *live,* so to speak. *Action TV* offered a woman who urinated in her boss's salad, with no follow up of whether he liked it or not. Rufus Griscom, editor of *Nerve* Magazine, described how he relished sex with girls while they were having bowel movements. The Reform Party—*Reform* Party, mind you—launched Donald Trump's presidential campaign in 2000 by Trump's boasting that he and his girlfriend sometimes had sex more than once a night.

Bravo cable network has gone gay with *Queer Eye For The Straight Guy* and *Boy Meets Boy*, suggesting that homosexuality is somehow superior and naturally more sensitive than being straight.

Tony Snesko, founder of Protect Our Children, complained that "at

103

ten o'clock at night (a Seattle TV station) had these three homosexuals, not scrambled at all, sodomizing each other...right there on public access television."

Did anyone listen to his complaint? Hardly. After all, the station was upholding free speech and human rights and "freedom of sexual expression" under the First Amendment.

Little Johnny and Jamie, latchkey kids, got one hell of a sex education with all the juicy, lip-smacking details televised about the Lewinsky President Bill Clinton received from Monica in the Oval Office. It tells a bunch about the level of sanity of our society that neither Clinton nor Monica had the good grace or shame to appear embarrassed—and that many of us were not even embarrassed for them.

In fact, Monica is getting rich off the scandal with "tell it all" books and TV appearances. Telling what? How she manipulated the President's...? Well, you know. Clinton as ex-President receives $100,000 a pop to speak, demurely grinning whenever Monica's name is brought up. His wife Hillary won a Senate seat on the "I'm a victim, you're a victim, and I'm all right with it" ticket. And hospitals report that the name "Monica" has reached a new popularity as a moniker for newborn girls. I suppose modern thinking goes something like this: *I want my baby girl to grow up to be just like Monica and go to the White House and...*

I don't know about you, but I'm just an Indian kid from the hills who finds all this more than a bit sick.

Roman emperors encouraged orgies and offered the coliseum's blood games to divert the masses from real issues when Rome was going down the tubes. You don't need to think about old-fogy concepts like freedom, morality and principle when you can frolic with four naked women, a bisexual and two sheep dogs. Give the ignorant *hoi polloi* an orgy and why should they care if the Enlightened, insane or not, takes control of their lives?

By and large, the media supports a liberal agenda that denigrates, ridicules and diminishes any point of view contrary to that held by Elites. Certain topics are considered taboo unless they are approached the "correct way" with "sensitivity," "compassion" and care to avoid being seen as, heaven forbid, "judgmental." Rarely will the popular press assume any view that goes counter to the Enlightened landscape. They have prescribed ways of dealing with these "divisive" issues. For example:

Black people must always be seen as underdogs battling for liberation from racism. Unless, of course, they are either successful or conservative, at which point they are considered to have had unfair advantage not available to others of their race;

Women are portrayed as underpaid, trapped by the "glass ceiling," victimized, little more than slaves. Or, they are superhuman, superior to men in every way—plus, as one-hundred pound heroines in arms, they kick the butts of brutish, overweight men;

You'll rarely see a homosexual in the media who isn't a creative, sensitive, superior human being discriminated against even though he's probably more "normal" than heterosexuals;

AIDS is a disease contracted like a flu virus and not through the victim's own behavior with contaminated needles and blood in fecal matter. We are *all* "at risk;"

Homelessness remains a paycheck away for each of us. There beneath the bridges and on the grates go we all but for luck and the grace of God. It has nothing to do with alcoholism, drug addiction and poor choices;

The First Amendment covers free expression like burning the American flag and protecting the North American Man-Boy Love Association's advocacy of child seduction. It does not cover "hate speech" such as baseball player John Rocker's utterances about the New York subway crowd or Dr. Laura's voicing her opinions on homosexuality.

Americans are thus constantly told what is correct and what is not, what is acceptable in a PC world and what is taboo. If we simply go along and keep our mouths shut, we can be left alone and even rewarded in subtle ways. *Not* being called a racist or a sexist is a reward in this society. Heaven help you, your ancestors and all your progeny, however, if you dare take an opposing stand.

During the 2000 presidential campaign, the Republican Ideas Political Committee ran a TV ad in favor of school choice. The narrator in the ad, a white woman, lamented the condition of many public schools in the country by explaining how her public schooled son "started hanging with the wrong crowd... We didn't want him where drugs and violence were fashionable. That was a bit more diversity than we could handle. So we sent him to a private school run by our church. There, he gets more attention, and the moral expectations are higher."

You can't ridicule "diversity" when it has been expanded to cover behavior as well as physical traits. That's *blasphemy.* The national media attacked the commercial as "race baiting," "wrong-headed," "racist." The Washington *Post* called it "repugnant to all Americans." It was accused of containing sentiments similar to those that led to the Holocaust.

The ad wasn't repugnant to me. It made common sense, a rare thing nowadays. Incidentally, the piece was immediately pulled because of the onslaught. It seems no one has the guts to stand up to all this insanity.

It goes on and on. The "correct" side gets heard, the "incorrect" side is suppressed, ignored or ridiculed.

The New York subway system accepted billboard ads for pro-abortion but rejected anti-abortion ads. The manager of the Toledo Public Library in Ohio refused to allow George Grant's *Killer Angel* on its shelves because the book criticized Planned Parenthood founder Margaret Sanger's views on race and her association with Nazi eugenics officials. Explained the library's history section manager: "(T)he author's political and social agenda, which is strongly espoused throughout the book, is not appropriate."

What he didn't mention were the two dozen other books the library displayed on Sanger. These, of course, *were* appropriate since they lauded Sanger's politically-correct agenda of pro-abortion and did not mention her politically-incorrect association with Nazis.

Author George Grant explains the library's position better than I can, calling it "simply Orwellian. In the name of intellectual freedom, they man the barricades anytime anyone suggests the removal of child pornography from a library. But if anything conflicts with their political agendas, then censorship imposed by the library hierarchy is completely acceptable. They're encouraging libraries to set up their own Politburos to test books for political correctness."

The attitude by the media that *We're right, you're wrong* and *We need to be heard but you don't* bleeds over into all areas of public communication. The media panders to political correctness, to its vast insanity, because when it comes to the Left ideology trumps truth and substance every time. The Left wants to "remake the world." In its own image, naturally. Therefore, it will support Satan himself if it thinks Satan will further socialist goals. Nothing better illustrates this tendency than the New York *Times'* odd endorsement of Hillary Clinton for the U.S. Senate.

"The investigative literature of Whitewater and related scandals is replete with evidence that Mrs. Clinton has a lamentable tendency to treat political opponents as enemies," the *Times* admitted. "She has clearly been less truthful of her comments to investigators and too eager to follow President Clinton's method of peddling access for campaign donations. Her fondness for stonewalling in response to legitimate questions about financial legislative matters contributed to the bad ethical reputation of the Clinton administration."

Having said all this, the *Times* still endorsed her. So what if she's dishonest and a scoundrel? She's a *liberal.* She's one of *us.* That's what counts with the media. She's *our* scoundrel. Besides, concluded the *Times,* "Mrs. Clinton is capable of growing beyond the ethical legacies of her Arkansas and White House years."

Even if she doesn't, what difference does it make? Haven't you heard? Ethics are situational. They only apply if you're an enemy of the Enlightened, at which time you'd better be as clean as the driven snow all the way back to the womb or face being mercilessly trashed. Arnold Schwarzenegger found that out.

With rare exception, only white heterosexual conservative males sound of mind and body are free game when it comes to press coverage and media depiction. Unlike we Noble Red Men or Fine African-Americans, it's okay to show them white guys as coarse, crude, un-couth, dull-witted, beer-guzzling, pot-bellied, loud-belching, farting, insensitive, uncompassionate louts. To avoid the Homer Simpson stereotype, the modern white male must be a metrosexual like Hugh Grant or Leonardo DiCaprio. Sensitive, open, liberal, politically correct, and more than a little effeminate. The sissier the better.

The characters on the sitcom *Ally McBeal* all share a unisex bathroom at the law firm. Ain't that just so precious, so...so *politically correct?* Should the mean, nasty, unapologetic male troglodytes of a macho era walk in—like John Wayne, Clint Eastwood or Charlton Heston—the entire cast, male and female, would all run and hide in the unisex john.

Try showing a black guy driving up in a pickup truck with a rifle rack and a bumper sticker, getting out with a bottle of *Night Train Express* wine and a *Camel* cigarette burning, scratching his crotch and talking "hate speech." Jesse Jackson would be all over the networks and calling the Rainbow Coalition to arms.

"All that stored-up tension from being careful not to offend women, black people, gay people, animals rights activists, or any nationality on earth comes out in the creation of grotesque male characters in popular culture," journalist Anita Gates observes.

Modern liberalism in the media is heavily emotional while portraying conservatives as rich white males who go out and run down old ladies in wheelchairs, starve orphans, and deprive the homeless of free chow. Although the media is quick to howl that it is objective, how objective can Ted Turner's CNN be, for example, when the Turner Foundation awards annual multimillion dollar grants to Planned Parenthood and the National Abortion and Reproductive Rights League to help identify pro-choice voters and train activists in key states where Democrats run tight election races against anti-abortion Republicans? How objective when the Turner Foundation awards grants to radical environmental groups like Greenpeace that, while rioting at the World Trade Organization in Seattle, distributed free vivid green condoms bearing slogans condemning the WTO? *Green condoms!* Is that where great minds focus?

In order to avoid the "objective" controversy, Rosie O'Donnell thought to hide her liberal Democrat label when her TV show started in 1996. Then, she said, "I realized: what Republicans are watching daytime television? They're too busy trying to make more money than anybody else."

It's called *having a job,* Rosie. So, I suppose, we can support through our taxes all those who *do* watch daytime television while it depicts conservatives as... Well, you know...

SECTION VII
MILITARY

"Private needs to come in from the field. Her husband is complaining that the child is crying and will not go to sleep. Request her presence immediately to breast-feed the child."
Message sent to an Army field training exercise

CHAPTER NINETEEN

Even the U.S. military cannot escape a society going bonkers. I enlisted in the navy for four years and then joined the army to complete a total of 29 years in the military, active and reserve. I retired shortly after returning from *Desert Storm*, the War in The Gulf. (The first war). I was in a man's army for most of my career—paratroops, scouts, Special Forces. I remember the disgust I felt the first time I saw a female at Fort Bragg wearing a green beret, the sacred symbol of the elite Special Forces.

Green Beret soldiers were *men*, snake eaters, the subject of ballads and legends. We jumped out of perfectly good airplanes and chewed up commies for lunch. Now here came this slip of a girl strutting across the grinder wearing a green beret. There had been a lawsuit or something to allow women to wear it if they were clerk typists or in some kind of support position. It wouldn't be many more years before the Secretary of Army issued an order authorizing *everybody* in the army to wear a beret. You wouldn't have to earn it, just wear it and your self-esteem was automatically elevated.

"Next thing you know," I muttered, "women will be wanting the army to issue them balls."

I was wrong. What they *would* be wanting was to take away what balls the military had.

"We are in the process of weeding out the white male as a norm," declared Barbara Pope, Assistant Secretary of Navy for Manpower and Reserve Affairs.

Duke University law professor Madeleine Morris, a paid consultant to President Clinton's Secretary of Army in 1997, wanted to change the "military culture from a masculine vision of unalloyed aggressivity to an engendered vision."

Engendered? I am not making this up. You know, gays, transvestites, transgenders, men who love their poodles, the pink beret bunch. Earth to Madeleine: In case you haven't heard, the military exists to kill people and break things when the nation is threatened. That *requires* masculinity, aggressiveness, men with balls.

The USS *San Antonio*, an ultramodern troop carrier, is being designed to accommodate 700 Marines plus a *female* cadre of 250. The ship, according to news releases, is being built with "women in mind, from the keel up...the heads won't have urinals." The "bathrooms" will be "ladylike" with increased ventilation "due to hair spray" and will have extra electrical outlets and mirrors for hair and makeup. The navy is also concerned about the "delicate nature of women's undergarments in today's industrial-strength shipboard laundry facilities," about chemicals that hurt fetuses, and about "reducing heat and noise and improving the health of the entire crew while supporting standards developed to protect pregnant sailors."

Now look at this a second time. Folks, this is supposed to be a *warship*.

When I was activated to duty from the Army Reserves to serve in *Desert Storm*, I was assigned as First Sergeant to ramrod a military police company of 120 soldiers, 21 of whom were females. Until then, I had seldom worked with females in the military other than with nurses and support personnel. Hey, I'm just as sensitive as the next crusty old sergeant who has been to six wars and been shot once, knifed once and led men in combat. But war, I was to discover, was nothing compared to what I was about to face in the new, sensitive coed army.

The official word from throughout the defense and political establishment is that women are proving themselves to be more than equal to male soldiers in every respect. Military spokesmen go to great lengths to cover up statistics or information that might indicate otherwise. The "warrior culture" is out, they say, replaced by the "gender-neutral New Age army."

I like women; I *love* them. I didn't want to be branded a chauvinist pig by rejecting female soldiers outright. Still, I had my reservations when it came to women actually serving in my combat army with me. I had learned a few things over the years about men and women together. If it turned out I was wrong, then I'd hush up and choke on it. But if it turned out I was right and a man's army should still be a man's army, then I'd talk about that too. Loudly. And to hell with political correctness. Truth is truth and it's seldom pleasant. There seems to be precious little of it around anymore.

As the *Desert Storm* call-up began, newspapers and magazines filled with stories and photos of cute rifle-toting blonds from Texas and buxom warrior brunettes from California. You would have thought women were going to fight the whole war themselves as the media fell into politically correct mode. Cutesy stories such as *Nanny Wears Combat Boots* and *Papa Stays Home With Junior While Mommy Defends The Nation* made me acutely nauseous. *Life's* cover story asking if women were ready for full combat equality alongside men had the answer already built in. Of course they were.

In spite of "smart bombs" and high-tech equipment, war is still no push button affair. The grunt is called a grunt because battle requires strength to hump heavy loads, endurance to stay in the fight while running, jumping and lifting, and a certain male aggressiveness to win that the average female simply does not possess. No amount of legislation, lobbying or bullshit to satisfy feminism and all the other liberal elements is going to make a 110-pound female do anything but sit on a 100-pound combat rucksack.

The weaker sex in uniform is routinely protected and catered to while maintaining a pretense that women can handle anything as well as men. When I needed an advance party whose tasks required a certain amount of labor, my NCO-in-charge begged, "Top, please don't send any of the females. We're talking about lifting and carrying 100-pound duffel bags."

I sent him ten men. I needed a job done. I didn't need five men working while five women struggled and finally stood aside to watch.

"We don't have camp followers anymore," a platoon sergeant commented. "We don't need 'em. We recruit 'em and bring 'em with us."

My supply sergeant lugged in three hefty bags full of *condoms. Army-issued* condoms. He dumped them on the orderly room floor. We had stretched rubbers over the muzzles of M16 rifles on jungle patrol to keep out rain, mud and dust. But even if my company were going to be patrolling, we wouldn't be doing *that* much patrolling.

"The company that screws together stays together, First Sergeant," the supply sergeant quipped. "Make sure to tell the soldiers when we pass out the rubbers to keep the screwing within the company. No use raising the morale of some other outfit."

It quickly became apparent that my company would be burning far more rubber than gunpowder. Even though we issued condoms, ten of my 21 women turned up pregnant within six months. The same thing has happened every time since. In the initial steps of the Bosnia mission, for example, servicewomen had to be evacuated for pregnancy on the average of every three days. The same thing is happening in the current Iraqi War (2004).

Rumors about who was sleeping with whom, where and how many times reminded me of a bizarre juxtaposition of M*A*S*H with *Love Boat* and *Dallas*. The commander and I stopped reporting pregnancies to division headquarters. Division raised hell about it. What were we supposed to do? Issue corks?

"We could use a cork," admitted one of my platoon sergeants. "Specialist C...has gone through every swinging jock in the platoon and is starting all over again. I don't have soldiers. I have a pack of dogs in heat, and they're starting to fight each other over the bitch."

Every time a female killed the rabbit, I had to replace her with a male, even if that meant he did double duty. How could you run an army when your soldiers kept turning up pregnant and couldn't work or fight? Ten percent of my company, the female percentage, took up ninety percent of my problem-solving time. Every time someone burst in breathlessly with "Top! Top!" my first reaction was "Calm down. Which one of my females is pregnant now? Or which one has killed the other?"

One afternoon I found myself bunkside waiting for an ambulance while one of my female specialists suffered a miscarriage. She wept uncontrollably, while I awkwardly held her hand and stroked her cheek. I stared at the wall, a little confused by it all.

I had been to war, spent much of my life as a tough sergeant in combat outfits. I had shot it out with Central American guerrillas and parachuted onto the Korean DMZ. I had been wounded in battle. Had it all come down to this—refereeing a bunch of women in uniform, half of whom were pregnant?

What had the U.S. Army become when unwed women waddled about in maternity *combat* uniforms? When morale and fighting effectiveness were being leeched away? When tough sergeants found themselves handling miscarriages and settling female spats? The feminization of the American military is destroying its ability to wage war.

It used to be that tough old sergeants like myself stood ramrod straight in front of an equally-tough outfit and shouted, "All right, men! Sound off like you got a pair!"

Not anymore. That's sex and gender discrimination. Besides, I'm beginning to doubt there's anyone left in the military with a working pair left. It takes more balls these days to face the strong political lobby that keeps pushing to put women in fox holes than it does to stand up before an enemy.

"Everybody knows it's a system built on a thousand little lies," said ex-army officer John Hilten, "but everybody's waiting for someone that's high-ranking who's not a complete moral coward to come out and say so."

CHAPTER TWENTY

The United States is today the only serious military power in history to contemplate the thorough sexual integration, or "engendering," of its armed forces. The biggest lie ever told about the New Age Military is that "inclusiveness," which means an infusion of women and gays, actually makes the armed services *better*. Such goofy social experimenting will inevitably destroy the military—which, I suppose, many liberals consider a good side effect. After all, one year after Osama bin Laden staged his massive assault against America, a Democratic senator praised him for his good work in building day care centers. Other liberal politicians, including ex-presidents, are always popping up in places like Cuba, North Korea and Iran, which hate America and would like to see us bombed back to our stone age ancestors. In 1984, the Democratic leadership of the House of Representatives sent Comrade Danny Ortega, the Soviet-backed Marxist despot in Nicaragua, a "Dear Commandante" letter commending him for his efforts to bring democracy to his country. One of the letter's backers was Senator John Kerry, later a Presidential candidate for the Democratic Party.

Israel experimented with using women as combatants in its 1948 War of Independence. Quite predictably, discipline fell apart. Male soldiers lost control when they saw women blown apart and sexually brutalized. Not much different than what happened when American women were on the front lines in both Iraqi wars. General Moshe Dayan said women greatly reduced Israel's combat effectiveness and would never again be placed in direct combat.

Don't we learn *anything* by such examples? It's like with socialism. It has failed dismally wherever it has been attempted, claiming literally millions of lives, and yet our good little socialists in America claim it was because it hasn't been tried the "right way." God protect us from the good the do-gooders do.

War is inherently masculine. How much common sense does it take to understand and accept it? Apparently, more than most of the Enlightened possess. They have proved themselves notoriously short of it again and again.

There was a time when young men were encouraged to go out, seek adventure, and work out male aggressiveness without a woman's soft hand holding down their rowdy heads. A man could escape and *feel* like a man, build his reputation as a man among men. The rise of diversity and all the other dogma of political correctness changed that. Feminization of everything, a "softer, gentler" touch, is considered a desirable thing, even in the military.

When the evening news ran a highly critical segment on "blood

115

pinning" by the army Green Berets, the sensitive public was aghast at sight of all those big tough men "hoo-yaaaing!" *Oh, my God! What have we created! Is it society's fault? Is it the fault of violence-filled military training?*

Blood pinning is an old custom by which new paratroopers have the pins of their "blood wings" pounded into their chests as a form of initiation and bonding. It's not as though they are maimed or anything. The pins are only about a quarter-inch long. I was a Green Beret; I'm proud of my tiny, almost invisible scars.

Still, such *violence* shouldn't be allowed in a brave and sensitive New World. Earth to you people: War *is* violence. I suppose new paratroopers now bond with a cup of tea in the shade with the ladies.

Much of the public and even the upper ranks of the military—Ever notice how many military women there are these days in high leadership positions?--are embarrassed and uncomfortable with the warrior culture. It must therefore be changed to get rid of overt macho behavior and make it tolerable for females and gender-questionables, therefore melding it into a mirror image of the wackier side of mainstream culture.

There have always been idealists and kooks on the fringes demanding to implement their particular visions of Utopia. In the past, however, they were consigned to the freak sideshows where they could amuse without causing too much harm. Not anymore. Banshees are attacking the military in blood-sucking hordes all across the fruited plains, intent on destroying it in order to let the new Phoenix rise from the ashes.

"(T)he nineties were a decade in which the brass handed over their soldiers to social planners in love with unworkable (and in many cases undesirable) visions of a politically-correct Utopia," Stephanie Guttman wrote in *The Kinder, Gentler Military.*

"We're about changing the culture," crowed Barbara Pope, then-Secretary of the Navy for Manpower.

Into *what?* One big, happy, diverse family where there is no such thing as war, where everyone has "equal opportunity," even if it means "disabled" parking spaces in front of Airborne headquarters and toilets for at least three different genders, and where there is so much niceness and sensitivity that guns have corks in the barrels? I could almost throw up in my corn flakes.

Cora Weiss of the Peace and Security Funders Group, one of those wacky sects with influence in feminizing the military, said she absolutely detested "men in uniform with guns." What was needed, she said, and I'm not making this up, is a more "sensitive" armed force in which every UN peace-loving soldier was compelled to attend gender and cultural sensitivity training.

"This is not your father's army anymore!" approved General Claudia Kennedy, Army Deputy Chief of Staff for Intelligence.

She was speaking at the annual Meeting of Sergeants Major at Fort Huachuca, Arizona, this to introduce her new politeness program which she called COO—"Consideration of Others." In a background note, Claudia was the officer who accused a colonel of sexual harassment when he attempted to kiss her, forcing him to give up his career and resign while she received another star. Getting rid of the colonel was probably a good move, since any man who attempted to kiss *this* female obviously displayed poor judgment.

Anyhow, after the kissing incident, Claudia drafted a new army policy statement redefining sexual harassment as when "his hand lingers on your back. He touches you on your upper arm, and you can't tell if he's a touchy-feely type person. All you know is that he gives you the creeps."

This stalwart female warrior, a leader of men, women, lesbians, and gays—and a touch on the arm gives her the creeps! How about the touch of an enemy soldier up her--?

To further emphasize her point that male savages need to be further tamed, she introduced COOing. She had the crusty old Sergeants Major squirming in their seats. As one sergeant major described it: "She informed us old timers how we should conduct our COO sensing sessions back at our home stations. She also made it clear to the sergeants that those who did not participate in COO sessions are 'resistant and insensitive to others.' Such behavior will not be tolerated, she said. She giggled, much like a little girl, as she inferred we had not been COOing at those bases."

"Anybody who thinks a three-star general COOing a room full of professional NCOs is not attacking the institutional war-fighting ethos is somebody who is ready for a lobotomy," declared a U.S. Marine general.

Thank God for the Marines.

Quite predictably, the New Age military cowered and capitulated in response to feminist demands and the insane transfer of society to political correctness. No longer are men men, women women, and everyone in between a hair dresser.

The U.S. Navy went down first. It began assigning females to non-combat ships in the early 1980s. In 1993, women won the right to serve on combat ships. Politically incorrect male sailors sarcastically refer to the USS *Eisenhower* as "The Dyke" instead of "The Ike" and to the USS *Abraham Lincoln* as "The Babe" instead of "The Abe." The navy now takes for granted the statistic that at least ten percent of its sailors will return pregnant from long cruises. Do the calculations yourself. Hundreds having morning sickness and swollen feet.

Then-Secretary of Navy John Dalton saw nothing wrong with this. "Pregnancy and parenthood are compatible with a naval career," he insisted. The challenge, he said, was "to ensure equality of opportunity... An expectant mother can remain on sea duty until her sixth month and no harm done to operational readiness."

What is this guy smoking? The challenge is to ensure the security and survival of the nation, *not* equality of opportunity. Have we reached such a ridiculous point that we entrust national defense to girls and pregnant women while men are feminized and taught to COO?

When the going gets tough, the tough get pregnant.

Crewmembers aboard one gender-neutral warship paired off for sex when it went to sea. With one little unforeseen problem. There weren't enough females to go around.

"The inescapable feeling of resentment, competition and anger...created a powder keg of emotions that cannot help but affect morale, discipline and attention to duty," observed former Secretary of Navy James Webb.

Surprise! Surprise! I propose the only logical solution: issue every male serviceman one each standard female. On second thought, you can't win this kind of game either. Officers and senior enlisted who get first pick are likely to be resented by the lower ranks. You might end up with one like...

"The purple fingernail polish and the dreadlocks covering her face and the hole in the side of her nose where she wears a diamond stud on weekends were bad enough," groaned an army command sergeant major. "But then Specialist Flake asked me if she had to take that 'pointy sticky thing that goes on my gun' when she went to the rifle range."

Hoo-ya! COO that girl.

The wacky jargon of feel good therapy—*I'm okay, you're okay, we're okay*—has invaded the military. While the military *says* it does not lower standards to *engender* the armed forces, that's another of the thousand and one lies that make up a society gone neurotic about its very existence. For those of you who haven't noticed, or who are afraid to notice because you might offend, women *are* different. To start with, they're physically different than men. The average woman is five inches shorter with lighter bones, more fat tissue and less muscle. She possesses at least fifty percent less upper body strength and a heart that is only eighty percent as efficient. Add to that lighter, weaker frame all that complicated reproductive equipment, and then get her pregnant on top of everything else... Have we all gone nuts!

The standard PC rationalization is: *Well, we really don't need all that brawn on the battlefield anyhow.* So, what we need is a kinder, gentle, weaker, *pregnant* soldier?

Everything in the military has been gender-normed *down*. Overall standards keep getting lower to accommodate a coed military more intent on COOing than in fighting and winning a war. It starts in basic training where it's almost impossible for a recruit to flunk out.

Take, for example, the gender-normed grenade throw. The main objective has become merely to get the damned thing out of the foxhole. There are also gender-normed pushups, runs, marches, all performed at half-speed and half-distance. Running with heavy weapons is a no-no, since it's too hard on the ladies. Obstacle course events requiring upper body strength have been eliminated to also mollify the ladies. All I can hope for is that, at the present rate of deterioration, opposing forces send in their ladies to take on our ladies. Otherwise, it will not be a pretty sight to see.

As in education and in other of our institutions gone PC, actual achievement is out of fashion in the military. What counts is mere effort.

"I don't care how fast you go or how slow," warmly lectured a drill instructor before beginning a coed physical training session. "This is just to have a good time. Go at your own pace. At least give it a try. This is mostly an exercise in teamwork. That playground area there is a stress reliever."

The poor guy was actually begging those greenhorn boot maggots to get with the program. *Please? Please?* It would be *his* fault for not properly developing the little darlings' self-esteem if the spoiled brats washed out or quit.

Oh, yes, you can now *quit* if the going gets too tough.

"It is essential that the (training) cadre develop the soldiers self-esteem, self-confidence and positive attitude..." states an army training manual. Training must not be "intimidating, hostile or offensive."

Whatever happened to: All right, you lazy puke maggots! Get off your fat butts. You're slow, you're sloppy, your breath stinks and you don't love Jesus! COOing General Claudia is right: this ain't your daddy's army anymore.

"The pull-up is an exercise where some of your teammates are gonna need some help," a DI wooed his sniggering sorry excuse for a training platoon. "If you see them hanging there and they can't pull themselves up, don't just walk by. Grab 'em by the legs and push 'em up. But I don't wanna see any hands on butts, or thighs. You can grab the calves, the knees..."

Does no one but us old vets see the absurdity in all this? The total insanity?

"It's strenuous and it can get hard, but it's okay to cry," counseled a recent grad of the Great Lakes Naval Training Base when she was invited to inspire a new class of boots.

It's okay to cry!

If you believe mixing the sexes has no effect on order, morale and discipline, let me sell you some seaside property in Oklahoma. It's nothing less than grotesque hypocrisy to believe otherwise. Modern drill instructors spend more time keeping the sexes apart than they do building soldiers. Look, for example, at the reason why these boot camp trainees had to be disciplined:

Wrongfully allowing a soldier of the opposite sex to massage your feet...

Wrongfully sharing your care package with two females and smiling at them instead of sharing your package with your battle buddy...

Wrongfully passing love notes in class...

Holding hands...

Kissing...

Smiling suggestively and uttering sexually-tinged language...

Engaging in public sex in a coed barracks in Mississippi...

Wrongfully sitting between the feet of a female recruit...

One post installed alarm systems and surveillance cameras in an attempt to keep men and women apart in a same-floor male and female quarters. Other posts have simply given up and started issuing free condoms. The military now manufactures *combat* maternity uniforms, holds special exercise classes for pregnant and postpartum soldiers, tacitly encourages abortion and allows mommies in the ranks to take "bonding breaks" with their children.

"Private needs to come in from the field," went a message sent to a female soldier's commander during a field training exercise. "Her husband is complaining that the child is crying and will not go to sleep. Request her presence immediately to breast-feed the child."

Stop the war! Stop the war!

Even military language has been altered, censored and censured to accommodate and sooth new combat sensitivities. Time-honored Jodie marching calls have been outlawed...

Two old women lying in bed...
One looks over to the other and said,
'I wanna be an Airborne Ranger...'

Watch it! Watch it! There are women and gays in the ranks. Don't offend 'em.

Call a trainee *wus, maggot* or *flabby civilian puke* and it is definitely trainee abuse and could even be *assault.* All military jargon is carefully scrutinized for "sexist" or "homophobic" content. Don't dare utter *cockpit, leg* (non-airborne personnel) or *box.* Can't you see how sexist they are? An airplane *cockpit* is now referred to as a "flight station." Ask for a pair of *dykes,* a common name for pliers or wire cutters, and you can almost count the minutes before you have Equal Opportunity officers swarming all over you.

Since Vietnam, *cherry* has been a common term for a new soldier. Not anymore. "Any other fruit would be fine," stated a memo from the brass—and then the memo's author was chastised for using the word *fruit.*

Gash, a mark for waving off carrier planes, was abolished because it had connotations of a part of the female anatomy.

Throughout the services, the image has become that of a smothering mommy who, as Stephanie Guttman puts it, "corrects your language...takes away your booze, who slaps you if you gawk at a woman or tell a dirty joke, who worries overbearingly about danger and prescribes tomes of tiresome safety procedures..."

On and on it goes...

"If the navy had its way," lamented one male chauvinist sailor, "it would neuter everybody."

On each officer's or NCO's fitness report or evaluation report is a blank to be checked indicating whether or not he "supports equal opportunity." It's the kiss of death for the career of any soldier who fails to at least pay lip service to women's rights and gay rights. This report is so important that careerists routinely lie about the activities of women—and now gays—or they exaggerate these minorities' feats because they fear their own careers might otherwise suffer.

Military spokesmen were eager to demonstrate their compliance to the party line during Operation *Just Cause*, the 1989 U.S. invasion of General Manuel Noriega's Panama. They played it up in the media over the role a female military police lieutenant supposedly played in routing a heavily-armed Panamanian force. She supposedly was at the head of her platoon, leading it against heavy resistance. That was what the news stories said.

The reality was quite different. Turned out she barely got within sight of the objective—a dog kennel. Enemy defenders resisted only half-heartedly. The most she could have suffered under the circumstances was a hangnail, for which I'm certain she would have received a Purple Heart and quite possibly a Bronze Star.

Elsewhere in Panama, two female truck drivers broke into tears and refused to drive a supply truck through a minimally hostile area. Male dogfaces took over the mission. Males displaying such cowardice would have been court martialed. But the army takes care of its camp followers. Public affairs officers valiantly covered up details of the incident, even going so far as to deny it even occurred.

Similar incidents cropped up, with frequency, during the *Desert Storm* war against Iraq in 1991 and again in 2003. According to the publicity, those brave Amazons of the desert were superwomen. But what *really* happened?

One woman got lost in the desert and was captured by the enemy. She was well on her way to becoming a national celebrity and hero before someone discovered she was having a romance with a fellow soldier, who was leaving his wife and children for her. Just another one of those little things about putting men and women together.

A female soldier named Cindi was asked by network news: "And what's your job? What are you doing over here?"

"I'm the camp whore," the girl shot back with more candor than the public was deemed prepared to accept. The footage never aired.

The army also squelched a report about a woman noncom who earned $10,000 in just a few weeks by engaging in the world's oldest profession. Army investigators quietly shipped her home.

At Abu Ghraib prison in Baghdad following the 2003 Iraqi War, the prison abuse scandal revealed a female MP soldier who had sex with multiple partners in front of the prisoners. It was referred to as "torture."

I was a Military Police first sergeant during *Desert Storm* and personally witnessed much of this lunacy. Although I had retired and was too old to be activated for the 2003 Iraqi War, I *know* what goes on there. Things haven't changed. If anything, the hypocrisy has become even more institutionalized.

To begin with, there is something tragically wrong about sending mothers of small children into combat. That's beyond shameful. It's *criminal* when a mother of a four-year-old son and a two-year-old daughter can be killed on the battlefield, as PFC Lori Piestewa was on 23 March 2003. The Defense Department shows that more than half the 212,000 women in the military are mommies. Why aren't we embarrassed at seeing two-year-olds hanging onto their mothers' legs while mommies dressed in combat uniform prepare to depart for a war zone?

Why aren't we even more embarrassed at the hypocrisy? Remember the officer and the NCO fitness and evaluation reports where lies have to be spread in order to comply with the demands of women's rights? The same thing happened in 2003 Iraq that happened in Panama and in 1991 Iraq. Any woman that so much as busts a thumb nail receives at least a Purple Heart while the obliging press already steeped in PC is willing and eager to "prove" that a woman can do the same job as a man.

PFC Jessica Lynch received a Purple Heart, a POW Medal and a Bronze Star medal with a "V" for valor after her supply train got lost and ambushed. The BSM citation reads: "For exemplary courage under fire during combat operations to liberate Iraq, in support of Operation Iraqi Freedom. Private First Class Lynch's bravery and heart persevered while surviving in the ambush and captivity in An Nasiriya..."

Now, as Paul Harvey says, for the rest of the story.

"There's nothing they won't stoop to spin," said retired Marine Lt. Colonel Roger Charles. "The army needed a female hero to boost female recruiting and PR efforts, so they went and invented one."

Lynch hid in the Hummer during the ambush until, by her own admission, she jumped out on the street and started praying until she passed out. She was taken to a hospital where she "fought back" by staying comatose until Special Forces troops rescued her. She didn't fire a single shot, didn't fight back, never resisted. She didn't do anything but get carried off, for which she was dubbed a hero. The males in her unit who *did* fight back received nothing, not even an honorable mention.

Why do we do this? Smile. It's all part of the cultural madness that now grips much of America. What kind of insane society have we become if, in the name of equal opportunity, we brutalize the feminine side of our culture while feminizing the masculine side so that we are no longer capable of defense? The Israeli officer who noted that any nation which uses its women in combat is not worth defending certainly has it right.

Better men in combat units try to protect women. It's an inherent trait. Worse men try to take advantage. The solution has been to change the men to cater to the women. It makes little sense to blunt the warrior culture to accomplish and encourage such behavior.

Soldiers who are natural warriors in the modern military find it difficult to get promoted because they tend to be outspoken and make insensitive remarks. As a result, they are fleeing the military in droves, leaving behind the managers, ass kissers, COOers and others of the politically correct genre. A General George Patton or a General Douglas MacArthur would not likely make it through a first enlistment in today's politically correct army. If they didn't quit in disgust, their no-balls superiors would nail them on their fitness reports and force them out to make room for a gay dentist, some dude from LA with earrings and purple hair, and a pair of cute blonds from Des Moines.

CHAPTER TWENTY-ONE

Political correctness in the military did not start with the Clinton administration, but it certainly accelerated. During Clinton's first inauguration ceremonies, military pilots performed an impressive show of power in a fly-by. Hollywood actor Ron Silver turned to a friend and indignantly demanded to know why the "damn military" was doing this during the "Festival of Freedom." His companion soothed him with a smile, reassuring him that, with Clinton's election, "those are *our* planes now."

Clinton immediately set the tone for the military. His first policy decision was to declare the rights of gays and lesbians to serve in the armed forces. He preferred them to serve openly, but finally settled for a "Don't ask, don't tell" policy. Feminization of the military, it seemed, was not enough. Now, the formerly over-macho military had a new sex angle with which to contend. Pentagon officials began soliciting suggestions on how to solve homosexual harassment in the military, seeking ways to curb offensive speech, jokes and derogatory remarks.

One soldier at Fort Campbell, Kentucky, outlined a hypothetical situation to his "sensitivity instructor" in which he was asked out on a date by a gay soldier. Did that, he asked, constitute prohibited conduct under "Don't ask, don't tell."

"No," he was told. "It's just associational behavior. Going to a gay bar, having a gay roommate off base, marching in a gay parade—that's associational behavior. That is not against the policy."

What *was* homosexual conduct then, which the Uniform Code of Military Justice still prohibits?

Well, explained the "sensitivity instructor," if you should visit the home of a gay and his lover in off-post quarters and witness them French-kissing, groping each other's genitals and the like...

Yes? Yes?

...That *could* constitute prohibited conduct. However, it should not be reported without first talking to military lawyers.

What a wacky military it became with the world's most famous draft dodger as commander-in-chief of planes, tanks, ships and soldiers. He had spent time in Russia during the Vietnam War and actually went to foreign countries to protest the war. For a man who openly stated he abhorred the military and who wanted U.S. Marine guards at the White House to change out of their uniforms into civilian clothing, he used the military more than the three previous presidents combined. He called it "peace keeping" and "nation building."

"What's the point of having this superb military...if we can't use it?" demanded Madeleine Albright, Secretary of State during the Clinton occupation of Washington.

Naturally, the game was played politically correct, starting from when "rogue nations" were redefined as "nations of concern" in order not to offend them.

It is okay to bomb people if your *intention* is honorable. When NATO planes mistakenly bombed a refugee convoy in Kosovo, NATO spokesman Jamie Shea explained that, "He (the pilot) dropped the bomb in good faith."

You blow up my mother and my brother and leave me blind—but what the hell! You dropped it in good faith.

Clinton ordered the bombing of Iraq during the last week of December 1998, the first major strike against the recalcitrant Saddam Hussein since *Desert Storm*. But first, he postponed the attack out of concern for Ramadan, the Muslim world's most sacred religious holiday, and bombed instead during Christmas, the Christian world's most sacred religious holiday. Then, he gave advanced notice, something along the lines of "the bombing will commence at midnight against the following targets."

Sensitivity, you understand. Concern. I feel your pain.

Aboard the USS Enterprise, a sailor scrawled a message on one of the bombs: *Hey, Saddam. Here's a Ramadan present from Chad Rickenberg.*

Oh, my God! Poor Chad was disciplined for his crudeness and insensitivity. The U.S. Secretary of Defense dispatched an apology to Iraq, saying the U.S. was "distressed to learn of thoughtless graffiti mentioning the holy month of Ramadan written on a piece of ordnance..."

Meanwhile, sailors on the flight deck of the *Enterprise* were led in a caroling of *You Make Me Feel (Like A Natural Woman).*

Lead bullets, deemed harmful to the environment, were replaced with environmental-wacko tungsten-core bullets which were more expensive, less reliable and only slightly more friendly to the environment, if at all. The U.S. has no tungsten resources; the metal to make the bullets will have to come mainly from *Red China.*

"We can work with other militaries round the world to share with them our policies on environment and health safety that we have been implementing..." said Sherri Goodman, Deputy Undersecretary of Defense.

As a combat soldier, I feel so much better knowing someone is concerned about my health when he shoots me with an environmentally friendly bullet.

Even when confronted with the War On Terror and the invasion of Iraq, the environmental wackiness continues. The Endangered Species Act and other federal environmental laws and regulations often restrict the ability of American military forces to undergo realistic training.

On May 16, 2002, Paul Mayberry, deputy Under Secretary of Defense for readiness, and Raymond DuBois, Deputy Under Secretary of Defense for installations and environment, requested that military training facilities be at least partially exempt from environmental laws.

"The most fundamental military readiness principle is that we must train as we intend to fight," they testified before the House Armed Services Subcommittee on Military Readiness.

They provided examples of how training was being restricted.

"When Navy SEALs land on the beaches at Naval Base Coronado, California, during nesting season, they have to disrupt their tactical formations to move in narrow lanes, marked by green tape, to avoid disturbing potential nests of the western snowy plover and California least tern," they testified.

Camp Pendleton, California, training ground for 40,000 Marines, has been forced to restrict its off-road movement in military vehicles because of environmental concerns. "To be frank," said Colonel Thomas Waldhauser, "we are not providing our drivers, small unit leaders, and commanders with realistic training in their fundamental aspect of modern combat... Wildlife and habitat preservation regulations force amphibious planners to execute tactically unsound plans."

These now-restricted beaches are where Marines practiced for Iwo Jima during World War II. Perhaps some future tyrannical enemy will be so accommodating as to mark out lanes in green tape to protect birds, snails, and crabs on a future Iwo Jima.

Army National Guard troops are prohibited from live-fire training on the Massachusetts Military Reservation in order to protect Cape Cod's sole-source aquifer. Instead, they must travel hundreds of miles to alternate locations.

In March 2002, a federal judge ordered the navy off its bombing range in the Northern Mariana Islands because of migratory birds. In October, another federal judge ordered the navy not to use low-frequency sonar because the sonar "bothered" whales. The sonar is designed to monitor the movement of enemy submarines.

Were the training exemptions granted? You have to be kidding. Marine spokesman captain Stewart Upton predicted environmental lawsuits could shut down even more training.

Environmental policy is not the only thing the United States seems to be sharing with the rest of the world. In May 2000, President Clinton promised to share any new missile technology with U.S. allies, which presumably included Russia and China, because "it would be unethical" to keep it solely for the protection of the United States. The man had chutzpah, lecturing the world on *ethics*.

While the Chinese government actively prepares for a future war with the United States, even saying as much, the U.S. government approved trade agreements which actually *gave* China the ability to produce and deliver nuclear weapons. What China didn't receive as gifts, it blatantly stole while our government looked the other way.

"Clinton and advisors," said Colonel David Hackworth, "are so incompetent that I'm surprised they didn't threaten to carpet-bomb Nevada when weapons of mass destructions were reported there."

One morning during the Vietnam War, F-4 fighter pilot Larry Corrigan and other POWs suffering in the Hanoi Hilton prison camp were jerked from their cells and cleaned up for a "peace delegation" visit. The delegation turned out to be actress Jane Fonda.

The captives devised a plan to get out the word that they were still alive. Each man would palm Fonda a sliver of paper with a message for his family. "Hanoi Jane" accepted them without a change of expression as she walked down the line of POWs, asking, "Are you grateful for the humane treatment from your benevolent captors?"

The POWs thought this to be an act until, to their shocked disbelief, she turned to the North Vietnamese officer in charge and handed him her little collection of papers. Three Americans died from the subsequent beatings.

The celebrated draft dodger in the White House wanted to strip U.S. Marines of their uniforms while hosting Jane Fonda and others of her ilk in the Lincoln Bedroom.

Bill Clinton, wrote columnist Mona Charen, "can point with pride to a feminized, hollow, demoralized, politically-correct military."

Once implemented, political correctness is almost impossible to eradicate, as we are discovering in all aspects of our culture. It's as difficult to cure insanity in a society as it is in an individual.

A navy officer who retired in protest penned his assessment of the New Military. "There is an absolute state of terror in regards to open discussion of the women in combat issue," he wrote. "It is now clear that all dissension has been squelched... Resentment is building rapidly against the social engineering, and the longer the lid is held on, the more the pressure builds... The absolute truth of combat will probably only become apparent to a lot of career feminists when missiles start tearing gender-integrated ships in half and turning them into rapidly sinking hells. Right now, their air-conditioned interiors are deceptively protective. I hope that someone can come up with a gender-normed 190-pound bayonet-wielding enemy fairly quickly, or we are going to pay a tremendous price in human lives for our politicians' inability to lead."

SECTION VIII
RELIGION

"You have demonstrated at least in my adult lifetime a higher commitment to the kind of moral leadership that I value in public service and public policy than any person that I have ever met... Our prayer for you today and for the First Lady and for the vice president and for Tipper is that you will continue to provide the kind of moral leadership to this country that has enriched the life of virtually every citizen."
Steve Grossman, National Chairman of the Democratic Party, offering prayer for impeached President Bill Clinton

CHAPTER TWENTY-TWO

In Saratoga Springs, New York, kindergartener Kayla Broadus held hands with classmates to recite "God is great, God is good, thank you, God, for my food." An alert teacher went ballistic, reprimanding the little girl and reporting her to the school administration. The principal sternly warned Kayla's parents that she could not pray aloud in school.

At Lynn Lucas Middle School near Houston, two sisters carrying Bibles were blocked at the classroom doorway. Another alert teacher (thank God for alert teachers) marched them to the principal, who warned their mother that she would be reported to Child Protective Services for the offense of allowing her children to bring Bibles to school. The teacher threw the Bibles in the wastebasket, shouting, "This is garbage."

At the same school, school administrators told students that the Ten Commandments constituted "hate speech."

After the September 11 terrorist attacks, signs saying "God Bless America" went up all across the country. City attorney Chet Adams of Sparks, Nevada, became worried that someone would sue over the signs displayed at City Hall. He ordered the word "God" deleted, whereupon the sign then read "Bless America."

"I don't know who is blessing America," Adams waffled. "I think a court would say the word 'bless' is okay... Maybe it should just say 'America' on there."

Who could possibly make up this kind of lunacy?

Christians are increasingly viewed as impediments to a Brave New World Utopia and are therefore under bombardment all across the landscape by moral idiots. Christianity in the context of American history and society is the last bastion of morality, values and decency. It must be destroyed in the pursuit of freedom by those who first embraced license and have now thrown off all restraints and moved on to licentiousness. Nothing shames us anymore. Look at the Paris Hilton sex tapes; the girl didn't even have the self awareness to be embarrassed— and we're no more embarrassed for her than we were for Monica on her knees in the Oval Office john with the President of the United States. In modern America, anyone who claims to be moral is considered a bigot.

What we are witnessing is the death of right and wrong, the suspension of our own sense of moral judgment, and the destruction of the concepts of good and evil. Having driven the Judeo-Christian value system from the public square, the Enlightened now want all remnants of it erased.

Georgetown University taught a course labeled "The Bible and Horror" which described the Bible as "a scary book" that "often reads more like horror than religious literature." The class would examine the question of "What might religion and horror (or the monstrous) have in common."

Patriotic songs now offend people because, to quote one of the offended, "there are so many people who don't agree with the songs." For example, the deeply offended went on, *God Bless America* is "very exclusive" because it mentions God.

At the Oxnard, California, Pleasant Valley School District, directors of a school "cinematic" show changed the title of Lee Greenwood's song *God Bless The USA* to *I Love The USA* when a student wanted to sing it. The student was told that "God" might violate laws separating church and state.

It has gotten so wacky a school employee in Frederick County, Maryland, was barred from passing out Christmas cards because it "may not be a legally protected right on a public school campus."

"May God continue to bless America," a typical closure for speeches by President George W. Bush, brought a complaint from Constance Hilliard, associate professor of history at the University of North Texas. "We are, after all," she carped, "a pluralistic society." She suggested Bush might add to his closing "And Allah bless America too."

What we are witnessing is the de-Christianizing of America and the growth of the Promethean spirit, the belief that mankind can do better without God. During the summer of 2003, "The Godless March," the first of its kind, attracted 2,500 atheists to Washington D.C. Ellen Johnson, president of American Atheists, announced the formation of a new PAC—the Godless Americans' Political Action Committee—to support atheist politicians. The hero behind the Supreme Court ruling that "under God" in the pledge of allegiance is unconstitutional led the crowd in reciting the new "Godless" pledge.

While I'm not sure Americans are ready to support atheist politicians (or at least ones openly admitting it)--"Hi, I'm Senator Arnold and I'm an atheist running for president of the United States"—don't discount the movement too quickly. Who would have thought twenty years ago that two men could marry each other in a church or that it would become against the law to sing Christmas carols in school or whisper God's name in a courthouse?

What is most suspicious, however, is the selectiveness of these politically correct enlightened crusaders. You see, at the same time that "God" is being banished like a leper, Satanists, New Age gurus, atheists, nature worshippers, and assorted other star gazers and witches have all become politically correct and embraced as "inclusive." Even God can come in as long as he is referred to as Allah.

Take a look at what I mean:

Tupelo, Mississippi: School administrators purged Christmas carols of all religious content, then led children in chanting "Celebrate

Kwanzaa;"

Katy, Texas: Christmas songs are banned; students who refuse to sing songs celebrating other religious faiths are threatened with grade reduction;

New York: Nativity scenes in public schools outlawed; the Islamic star and crescent may be displayed;

California: The legislature mandated a three-week immersion course in Islam for all seventh graders in which students adopt Muslim names, plan a trip to Mecca, pray to "Allah the Compassionate" (He's probably a Democrat), and chanted "Praise to Allah, Lord of Creation!;"

Broken Arrow, Oklahoma: City bus service enacted a policy that prohibited passengers from discussing religion on a public bus;

Brooklyn: A mural on school property featuring Jesus Christ was painted over; Muslim students allowed time off to worship in school during holy month of Ramadan;

Ohio: ACLU forces four schools to take down Ten Commandments display;

Plattsmouth, Nebraska: Ten Commandments monument in a public park, there for over 40 years, ripped out because of ACLU lawsuit;

Alabama: Chief Justice Roy Moore lost his job for refusing to take down a Ten Commandments display in his courtroom...

Need I go on? All this while the craziness continues—Macy's Thanksgiving Day parade 2003 featured a gay transvestite as Mrs. Santa; Denver refused to issue a Columbus Day Parade permit unless the organizers promised there "will be no reference, depictions or acknowledgment of Christopher Columbus during the parade;" a fat teenager sued the San Francisco Ballet for not accepting her, accusing it of "weight discrimination;" and, of course, coming soon, ACLU lawsuits against "In God We Trust" on U.S. currency and swearing an oath on the Bible to tell the truth...

I heard it somewhere: If God doesn't get rid of San Francisco and New York, he owes Sodom and Gomorrah an apology. Problem is, San Francisco and New York may have already gotten rid of God, at least in public. Can the rest of the country be far behind?

God is dead, if He ever existed in the first place. He is going to be replaced. Lo, *man* is God and government his supreme source. The Enlightened can't mess with rights that come from God, but if these rights only come from government... Well, everything is up for grabs and Enlightened Personkind will fill planets and universes with Utopians where all forms of life will live in love and harmony—self-created heaven, if you will—forever and ever, amen. God did such a lousy job that we will get rid of Him and, to coin an old Frank Sinatra phrase, *do it our way*

If contemplating that outrage and considering the ends of Utopians created through communism and socialism isn't scarier than a mass murderer on Halloween, I don't know what is. You have to think things can't get any wackier.

But they can.

CHAPTER TWENTY-THREE

A Methodist minister once told me he did not believe the Bible was ever intended to be taken literally, that it was merely a guide, a "living document" that had to be changed to meet changing times. Sort of like the Constitution of the United States, I presume.

If, in these strange times that try men's souls, you don't like a particular historical document, you simply "correct" it. That means, naturally, to make it *inclusive* and *non-offensive*. The Bible as well as other history has been subjected to "corrections"

A band of American protestants rewrote *The New Testament and Psalms* and turned it into *The New Testament and Psalms: An Inclusive Version* (Oxford University Press, 1995), the objective being to eliminate or rephrase "all gender-specific language not referring to particular historical individuals and all pejorative references to race, color, religions or physical disability."

"God" in this proper revised edition becomes "our Mother-Father in Heaven;" "the Son of Man" morphed into "the human one;" all references to brother, as in "love thy brother" became "love they brother or sister."

In this goofiness, *no one* must be left out of an *Inclusive Version.* In 63 Psalms, "Thy right hand upholds me" was replaced with "They strong hand upholds me" out of deference to left-handers who might feel excluded.

I really am not making this up.

It is such a *sensitive* new work that I can barely suppress the urge to regurgitate. References to "darkness" equating with sin, evil or ignorance was eliminated to avoid offending "people of color." It was particularly sensitive to women and thereby suitably de-masculinized. "Kingdom" became "dominion" because a king is a male figure. Children, in turn, were urged merely to "heed" their parents rather than "obey" them. Heavens! We can't have children *obeying.* I'm surprised *sinner* wasn't purged, as its use must certainly damage the self-esteem of thieves, adulterers, murderers and assorted other scumbags.

Protestants aren't the only ones entering the New Age. Rabbi Rebecca Alpert of Philadelphia proposed removing all sexist and dominant references to God in Jewish prayers by making God a transsexual. How utterly appropriate in this goofy New Age. God would be called "She" and "Queen" and "Mother." Also, "She" would hereafter be referred to as "lover, friend, companion, partner" to erase "images of inequality between the exalted divine and the lowly human."

We mustn't bruise our precious self-esteem by elevating *God* above *man.* Sometimes I feel like I'm the only sane man caught in a rabbit hole nut house.

"Inclusive." "Pluralistic." These seem to be the greatest goals of the New Clergy. Everyone must be embraced, no matter his beliefs or behavior. Redemption? Huh-uh. That implies that man is flawed; everyone knows man is not flawed, and even if he is it's God's fault for making him that way. Even witchcraft and Satanism are "recognized religions" on a par with Christianity. Exorcism, I suppose, is discriminating toward the Devil and therefore a hate crime.

Mankind loses its moral compass once the Bible's moral standards are amended, cast aside, deleted or compromised to meet lowered human expectations, leading deeper into depravity. Naturally, it shouldn't be called *depravity*, since that word offends the depraved.

On August 5, 2003, the Episcopal Church approved its first openly gay bishop, V. Gene Robinson, who had left his wife and daughter to live homosexually with "partner" Mark Andrew, thereby defying Scripture and 2,000 years of church teaching. Eyes rolled and expressions went to polite exasperation when the Bible's plain teaching was referenced. We were told it was time to move on, that the Bible had not kept up with the times. After all, we reactionaries were assured, "God changes God's mind." Practitioners of a sexual style for which Sodom and Gomorrah were destroyed suddenly find themselves celebrated as respected Christian teachers.

If God doesn't take action, He indeed owes Sodom and Gomorrah an apology.

God, under these new provisions, is nonjudgmental about everything—premarital sex, abortion, homosexuality, adultery, murder, blasphemy... No need to repent or stop sampling your neighbor's wife. He's nonjudgmental about *sin*, period. No one can *possibly* go to hell. Everyone ends up *equal* in Heaven, Nirvana, Valhalla, or the Happy Hunting Grounds. I can hardly wait to see in the afterlife Hitler and Stalin and all the cold-blooded killers I arrested when I was a homicide cop.

What can be expected of the rest of us if even the clergy refuse to take a moral stand? All behavior becomes equal and therefore accepted if there is no good and evil, moral or immoral.

Steve Grossman, then-national chairman of the Democratic Party, offered a prayer to President Bill Clinton's "moral leadership." The man, believe it or not, didn't even blink when he began praying.

"You (Bill Clinton) have demonstrated at least in my adult lifetime a higher commitment to the kind of moral leadership that I value in public service and public policy than any person that I have ever met. Our prayer for you today and for the First Lady and for the Vice President and for Tipper is that you will continue to provide the kind of moral leadership to the country that has enriched the life of virtually every citizen..."

What? Was he talking about "I did not have sex with that woman"

Bill Clinton? Bill Clinton of the Blue Dress and "oral sex is not sex?" Makes you wonder what kind of people ole Steve hangs around with if Bill Clinton is his ideal of moral leadership.

Almost anything that remotely touches on the spiritual as redefined by the Enlightened can pass these days as religion. In Florida, New Agers and fantasists worshipped, a la Stonehenge, a collection of holes in the ground called the "Miami Circle." The state spent several million dollars to "save" the holy relic, no matter that local old-timers kept trying to point out that the congregation was worshipping the remnants of an old septic tank.

Witchcraft and Satanism are becoming the new affirmative action religions as practitioners demand equal consideration with Christians, Jews and Muslims. The U.S. Supreme Court even ruled that the military must consider Satanism (that's the worship of Satan for those of you in Palm Beach, Florida) on an equal basis with other religions. What the hell. Devil worshippers need love too.

"We want religious freedom for the entire United States," clamored Terry Riley, a high priest of the "Motami Coven" of witches, as he led a religious freedom march in Jonesboro, Arkansas. Represented among the various witches, pagans, and other conjurers, enchanters, necromancers and sorcerers was a cult that killed and ate dogs, two of whose members were charged with beating to death three eight-year-old boys in West Memphis.

Consider this conundrum from a letter seeking advice in a Washington *Post* column: "My fiancé and I are getting married next spring. Both sets of parents want the wedding to be if not in a church, then at least with a Christian minister performing the ceremony. However, that is not an option for us because of our beliefs (born-again Wiccans)... My parents refuse to accept my religion, and his know (he is a witch) but he doesn't care what they think... How do we tell them it's a Wiccan wedding ceremony or we elope?"

First of all, what is a *born-again* Wiccan? Second, in my opinion, the two of them can get on their brooms and fly off together into the sunset. Is that insensitive or what?

Life in an age where anything goes and there is no social foundation—or what there is of it is crumbling—can become terribly confusing and convoluted. Take fifteen-year-old fresh*person* Jamie Schoonover of Maryland, a devotee of Wicca. When she was suspended from school for allegedly casting a spell on another student, her "mother" showed up to protest. Mommy Dearest turned out to be a transsexual cross-dresser who in reality was her *father*. And we wonder why so many kids are screwed up.

The Witches Education Bureau of Salem, Massachusetts (Yes, Virginia, there really is a Witches Education Bureau) accused the low-budget movie, *The Blair Witch Project*, of casting a negative stereotype on Wicca and insisted on a disclaimer denying that the film sought "to represent witches or witchcraft as evil." Will it be long before *Broomhilda* is banned from comic strips as insensitive to Wiccans and assorted other practicing broom riders?

I'm bound to be vilified as a racist for pointing out this kernel of truth, but perhaps the biggest hoax fostered upon a naïve and gullible population is the semi-religious holiday called Kwanzaa, which has replaced Christmas among many black people. Black minister and presidential candidate Al Sharpton said it performed a valuable service by "de-whitizing" Christmas. While Kwanzaa allegedly originated among black African tribes, the ancestors of American slaves, it was actually the creation of a 1960s black militant who calls himself Malanga Ron Kerenga.

Kerenga first hit big-time fame when he led his "soldiers" in a gangland-style gun battle with another group of Black Panthers inside the school cafeteria at UCLA, during which two people were killed. Shortly thereafter, he went to prison for torturing two female followers by whipping them with electrical cords, beating them with a karate baton, sticking a hot soldering iron in their mouths, tightening vices on their toes, putting detergent and running hoses in their mouths... You get the picture.

And then, and *then*, while in prison, he invented Kwanzaa. The rest, as they say, is history. Kwanzaa, the brainstorm of a vicious criminal, is now celebrated religiously. The creative ex-convict, now *Doctor* Mulanga Ron Kerenga, resurfaced as the head of Black Studies at California State University at Long Beach. Wonder what he teaches his students.

Wackiness can be accepted, elevated, even worshipped as long as it is the politically correct variety approved of by the Enlightened. Everyone knows God is on the side of political correctness.

"God has spoken," began an editorial letter in the San Francisco *Chronicle.* "He sent a message via His press secretary, Mother Nature. Texas and Oklahoma baked all July long, the sun so hot it warped railroad tracks and dried up every drop of water... Clearly, God is punishing Texas, Oklahoma and the whole general region for its ongoing attacks on gays..."

Tolerance extends to those who worship trees, rocks, ferrets or old septic tanks. You're branded immediately as intolerant, narrowminded, and even bigoted if you dare criticize witchcraft, devil worshippers, Kwanzaa or dog eating. I wouldn't be surprised were San Francisco to erect a huge phallus surrounded by prayer benches. At taxpayer expense, naturally.

What cannot be accepted is mainstream Christianity with its message of morality and sin, redemption and hell. Christianity is often equated with the "Far right...the Religious Right," paired with Hitler and attacked as "cultic, detestable...criminal...a worse threat than communism." Though Lord knows the Enlightened have seldom viewed communism as a threat. Too often men who support the teachings of the Church and the Bible, especially on matters of sexual morality, are condemned as "rigid and uncharitable homophobes" while those who reject such teachings and "come out of the closet" become bishops. Is that turning everything upside down or what?

Christianity's influence on traditional American society must be diminished and ultimately destroyed if the Enlightened ever hope to implement the New Age and the New Man. Stalin and Lenin thought so too when they were creating a new society in the old Soviet Union.

CHAPTER TWENTY-FOUR

In the 1970s and 1980s, some friends of mine used cars with hidden compartments to smuggle Bibles to clandestine churches behind the Iron Curtain. Bringing a Bible into Czechoslovakia or Hungary or any number of Soviet-dominated nations was a crime for which you could serve a long prison term. We were appalled at the Godless nature of a society that actually banned the Bible. However, I predict that it won't be many more years before the possession of a Bible on public or government property in the United States will likewise be a jailable offense. You can clearly see the trend as our loving and benevolent government strives to save us from at-risk situations in which men and women with Bibles run about attempting to corrupt the society.

Through a bizarre twist of logic, Americans are being incrementally conditioned to see God and religion, especially Christianity, as against the tenets of a free and "fair" society. The courts have taken a constitutional prohibition on the establishment of a national church and transformed it into a ban against any connection between government and religion. Sometimes it requires the skills of a contortionist to see the connection in order to outlaw the undesirable behavior.

Take, for example, how it is considered religious discrimination, and therefore *illegal*, for California real estators to advertise a house as being near a church or synagogue. Or how the Federal Communications Commission attempted to restrict religious broadcasting on *religious radio stations* by issuing an edict that would have required the stations to reserve at least fifty percent of their programming for "educational, instructional, or cultural" purposes. No "religious exhortations, proselytizing, or statements of personally held religious beliefs," no hymns, no sermons, church services, or prayer would be allowed during the faith-free zone. It was Big Nanny's way of saying she disapproved of religious broadcasters getting *too* religious.

In Memphis, Tennessee, the government cancelled federal funding for a large homeless shelter because it required the homeless to attend religious services before they received a free meal and a place to flop. Presumably, prayer would contaminate these wandering bums, bruise their precious self-esteem, and violate their inalienable right to be taken care of by the rest of us.

A first grade teacher in Medford, New Jersey, rewarded her best reading students by allowing them to read their favorite stories before the class. Everything went okay until Zachary Hood chose to read *The Beginner's Bible: Timeless Children's Stories.* The teacher and the school principal informed Zachary's mother that the story was "inappropriate" since it was the equivalent of praying and might offend Muslim, Hindu and Jewish students. "There is no place in a public

140

school for reading the Bible," the mother was told.

But there seems to always be a place in public school for reading *Heather Has Two Mommies.*

Is it just me, or is it really a scary turn of events when reading a Bible is offensive to the American public but saying the "F" word on family hour TV isn't; when consensual sodomy is a sacred right while consensual public prayer is embarrassing and unlawful; when we tolerate corrupt and immoral politicians yet ridicule a president who admits he prays to God; when New York Judge Elliott Wilk can proudly display a portrait of communist revolutionary Che Guevara while Alabama Justice Roy Moore loses his job by refusing to remove a plaque of the Ten Commandments; when it's laudable for participants in Gay Day parades to dress up in whips and chains and beat each other while simulating homosexual sex but scandalous for the deputy undersecretary of defense to admit that he is a Christian; when flag burning and nude dancing are protected speech but prayer before a football game is not; when...?

You get the picture.

What we are witnessing is nothing less than a cultural *coup d'etat* fostered upon us by a fashionable elite in the universities, the media, the legal profession, politics, arts and other cultural institutions. The governing classes have decided that we superstitious and backward masses must give up God and become "enlightened" like them. They will do the thinking for us and decide what is best. Pressure is being applied throughout society to reject all vestiges of Christianity and replace it with thought codes of the New Morality—which essentially means that anything goes.

An evangelical group at Washington State's Whitman College came under fire because student bylaws say groups are not allowed to consider one sexual orientation superior to another. New Morally speaking, heterosexuals, gays, bi's, transvestites, pedophiles, sadists, and lovers of animals are all essential equal.

The Pennsylvania House of Representatives passed a bill on November 26, 2002, that may criminalize preachers quoting Bible passages about homosexuality from the pulpit. The bill added crimes against "sexual orientation, gender or gender identity" to a list of possible offenses in the state's Ethnic Intimidation Act. The President of the Urban Family Council, William Devlin, warned Pennsylvania pastors and churches to "obtain some very good liability insurance and contact an attorney if the pastor intends to continue faithfully preaching the Word... The bill is so broad that if you have an attender at your church who feels offended or intimidated by what is said from the pulpit, you and your church leadership will be receiving certified letters inviting you to either a deposition or a court appearance."

It occurs to me that politicians legislating what can be said from the pulpit is *not* proper separation of church and state.

Further evidence of pressure against Christianity and its outdated concepts of behavior and morality can be seen in how tax-exempt status is applied to different nonprofit groups. In a ruling that stretches back to the Warren Court, organizations seeking tax-exempt status "must demonstrably serve and be in harmony with the public interest." The "harmony" of private religious schools and conservative organizations constantly comes under the scrutiny of the IRS or some other branch of government.

However, the status of groups such as Planned Parenthood, PETA, the Sierra Club, Jesse Jackson's Rainbow Coalition, and NOW is rarely questioned, leading one to believe that abortion, socialist health care, animal "rights," forced recycling, and gay rights "demonstrably serve" and are "in harmony" with the public interest while a kid reciting the Pledge of Allegiance "under God" is not.

Would-be assassins of God are spreading out all over the landscape, sniping and ambushing and lying in wait. Express a belief in God and your motives are immediately suspect. Say anything other than "Amen" to New Age beliefs, exhortations, and the inanity of the Enlightened and you are attacked with incredible venom for being a member of the "extreme Right Wing."

Lefties threw a tantrum when newly-appointed Attorney General John Ashcroft invited his staff to pray with him on a voluntary basis before each day's work began. By the outcry, you would have thought him guilty of racism, homophobia, anti-environmentalist, anti-vegetarianism, and anti-Americanism. Besides that, he probably kicks his dog, has oil stock, and cheats on his income tax.

During a prayer breakfast, U.S. Supreme Court Justice Antonin Scalia enjoined his fellow worshippers to "pray for the courage to endure the scorn of the sophisticated world."

He then added, "One *can* be sophisticated and (still) believe in God."

What did he *say?* Did he say *God? God!* The sophisticated media jumped on him like a pack of starving dogs on a biscuit. The Washington *Post* led the attack by asking whether or not, considering the Justice's obvious religious leanings, he could give "First Amendment issues a fair and reasoned hearing?"

The article went on by explaining the issue to us poor stupid folk in the hinterlands: "At issue is whether Scalia's impassioned and remarkably personal defense of Christianity...clashed with his sworn duty to impartially interpret U.S. laws."

Do I get this right? Western law is built on Judeo-Christian ethics evolving from the Bible. So...if Justice Scalia believes in Christianity he can't interpret law? But an atheist, an atheist now, *he* could fairly interpret law. We poor Indians have a tough time understanding such logic.

However, we know enough to keep our moths shut from now on and just go along to get along. Isn't that the objective of such attack gonzo tactics anyhow? To make us shut up? Talk about the First Amendment.

The City of Chicago suspended its support for the Boy Scouts of America—the *Boy Scouts*'; that's like spitting on Mom's apple pie—until the Scouts decide to end their ban on gay Scout leaders and remove "God" from the Boy Scout oath. The Girl Scouts have already made "God" optional in their promise.

Nineteen-year-old Joshua Davey received a Washington Promise Scholarship issued annually to assist students of modest means in funding college. It was cancelled when the State of Washington discovered he intended to use it to study theology at a small religious school.

A Christian nation, howls that cultural watchdog People For The American Way, would be "dangerous... This is a holy war (against Christianity) and we are determined to win it."

Dozens of such organizations devote themselves to "protecting your community" from leaders holding "extreme positions" on school prayer, abortion, funding for the arts, homosexuality, race and other liberal causes, clanging the alarm against Christians' "extreme agenda...(and) family values rhetoric."

With the approval and, sometimes, the collusion of government, the American Civil Liberties Union has assumed the responsibility of ripping from America's heart all vestiges of Christianity, starting with holidays. Prayer, invocations, crèches and Christmas displays on public property have all been declared unconstitutional. Simple common sense was the first thing to fall before the ACLU's ardor. It should be no surprise that eleven percent of all Americans in a survey selected the Easter Bunny as their Easter symbol. Presumably, the bunny died on the cross and is resurrected once a year to distribute colored eggs.

Jersey City booted Santa Claus and Frosty the Snowman off city property after the ACLU successfully argued that they were religious symbols. Talk about the Grinch!

For the same reason of "separation of church and state," New Jersey changed Halloween and St. Valentine's Day to "Fall Festival Celebration" and "Special Person Day." Isn't that just so...so *special?*

The silliness goes on and on. Christmas trees are now routinely referred to as "holiday trees," "unity trees," and even "seasonal conifers." One company lists its holidays thusly: New Year's Day, Presidents' Day, Memorial Day, Independence Day, Labor Day, Thanksgiving Day, and December 25th. Another company had "scheduled down time" in order to avoid naming holidays at all.

The New Orthodoxy intervened when a Harvard dorm proposed to have a "Secret Santa." Secret Santa was changed to "Secret Winter

Snow Friend." Elsewhere, Secret Santas have become "Winter Wizards." In Pittsburgh, even "Sparkle Season" was considered too religious and was renamed simply as "Downtown Pittsburgh: A Holiday Tradition with A New Twist." San Diego's "Christmas on the Prado" became "December Night," while other localities celebrate "Frost Time Festivals." In Albuquerque, Frank Rotelo was fired as high school choir director when it was discovered that his Christmas Concert, renamed Winter Concert out of sensitivity to nonbelievers and atheists, still contained songs with a "Christian theme." I'm really not making all this up.

The mere *threat* of a lawsuit forced the National Park Service to remove from the Mojave National Preserve an eight-foot cross used for Easter gatherings and as a World War I memorial. Kara Russell's fifth grade principal wouldn't permit her to sing *The First Noel* in her Nevada school's Christmas Pageant for fear of being sued. Even the mention of Christmas was so controversial in Voorhees, New Jersey, that, said a school district spokesman, "we were to the point where people were objecting to red and green sprinkles on cookies..."

Already, the Supreme Court (as of this writing) is scheduled to rule on the constitutionality of "under God" in the Pledge of Allegiance. The Sixth U.S. Circuit Court sided with the ACLU in ruling that Ohio's state motto, *With God All Things Are Possible,* is illegal. I predict it won't be long until *In God We Trust* is replaced on legal tender with something more appropriate and sensitive. Perhaps *In Government We Trust.*

Maryland's ACLU Director Susan Goering sent the U.S. Naval Academy a letter following the Fourth Circuit Court of Appeals order for VMI to cancel its supper prayer. The letter said, "We believe that when you have had a chance to review the 4th Circuit's opinion, you will agree that the Naval Academy's mandatory lunchtime prayer cannot pass constitutional muster, and will therefore cease the practice."

First of all, the prayer was not mandatory. Secondly, imagine the arrogance of this bunch of lawyers! Where is Shakespeare when you need him? *The first thing we do, let's kill all the lawyers.*

The Academy told the ACLU to go pound sand. But, of course, lawyers and courts that declare same sex sodomy a right and ban Christmas and the Ten Commandments will not be deterred for long.

Even the mere sight of Christians may soon become offensive, unconstitutional, and therefore a violation of separation of church and state if they appear in public and on public property. May I suggest we start relegating them to the Catacombs, isolating them in ghettos, fining them for going to church, confiscating their Bibles, tossing them in jail for "proselytizing," disenfranchising them, and prohibiting them from holding office?

Christians pollute the environment on top of being culturally dangerous. "Christianity is not an environmentally friendly religion," declared Ted Turner, one of the richest men in the world and Jane Fonda's ex-husband.

Finally, during the 2000 presidential election, the Anti-Defamation League cautioned vice-presidential candidate Joe Lieberman about references to his Jewish belief in God. The League blistered him a letter warning that "appealing along religious lines, or belief in God, is contrary to the American ideal."

What? Belief in God is *contrary* to the American ideal? The American ideal must surely have changed while I wasn't looking. I'm just a poor Indian country boy from the Ozark Mountains, unsophisticated enough to accept there must be some Greater Power than we spindly, squabbling humans. I know that a good revival now and again in an abandoned one-room schoolhouse kept a lot of us rowdies out of other people's watermelon patches while we were growing up. A little threat of the hellfire that awaited thieves and liars went a long way in keeping us on the narrow path. Had that narrow path been as wide and tolerant and nonjudgmental and sensitive when I was a kid as it is now, there wouldn't have been a watermelon safe within three counties.

SECTION IX
SEX

"We just did a show on a father who married his daughter and a mother who slept with her son... It is elitist to say they shouldn't be seen and they shouldn't be heard."
Sally Jessy Raphael

CHAPTER TWENTY-FIVE

Had Karl Marx made his remark today about religion being the opium of the people, he would have been immediately dead wrong. *Sex* is the opium of the people. Sex attracts attention, sex sells. It's sex, sex, sex—from the third grader learning how to stretch a condom over a banana to an intern earning her kneepads in the Oval Office. We are working hard to reduce sex to its most vulgar, physical and commercial level, further cheapening ourselves and our society.

"We just did a show on a father who married his daughter and a mother who slept with her son..." said TV hostess Sally Jessy Raphael. "It is elitist to say they shouldn't be seen and they shouldn't be heard."

That used to be called incest. Perversion. Now it's called show biz and accepting it is part of being tolerant, nonjudgmental and a "better person."

Is it my imagination or wasn't there a time not so long ago when we would have been *ashamed* for such things to be known about us, much less appear on national TV for everyone to paw over? Not anymore. Sexuality has entered the amoral sphere of relativity and shame is undoubtedly a construct of the whole male oligarchy attempting to suppress the healthy natural urges of historically oppressed groups.

So what's the big deal? Everybody does it. Of course. But it isn't the fact that everybody does it that I find contentious. After all, everybody defecates too, but most of us don't go around taking dumps in Times Square or the Smithsonian. The problem is *when* and *where* and *how* and *with whom*. The problem is that *tolerance* has been extended to apply to all behavior, no matter how abhorrent, after which that behavior is celebrated and mainstreamed. Pants and panties are falling as moral restraints and barriers drop. *Get it on!* is the new rallying cry. It doesn't even matter with whom or what or how many, all behavior being equal. After all, pedophiles, sadists and beast-ophiles have needs too.

"Kiss and tell" books and movies make celebrities of Monica Lewinskys and Paris Hiltons, whose primary talents appear to be public receptacles of lust. Can you believe these girls don't even have the good graces to *blush?* Can you believe they are considered role models? Can you believe that the names "Monica" and "Paris" are among the most popular nowadays for new female babies. That's exactly what I want—my daughter Monica or Paris to grow up and become just like her namesake.

Sex has moved from the private bedroom to the public arena. Contracts, regulations, and consent forms have taken the place of candy and roses and Valentine cards.

Antioch College enacted a "Sexual-Offense Policy" which required students to obtain verbal consent before kissing or fondling or dropping their drawers. The policy, as spelled out in a school regulation, permitted and apparently condoned almost any behavior as long as everyone was first asked, including group sex orgies.

"If only one person wants to initiate moving to a higher level of sexual intimacy in an interaction," the policy stated in part, "that person is responsible for getting the verbal consent of the other person(s) involved before moving to that level... If sexual contact and/or conduct is not mutually and simultaneously initiated, then the person(s) who initiates sexual contact/conduct is responsible for getting verbal consent of the other individual(s) involved..."

Is this all utter madness or what?

A lucrative new field is about to open up for ambulance-chasing lawyers following the Kobe Bryant rape scandal. Sex contracts. Celebrities are already asking their lawyers to draw up contracts to be presented to groupies prior to any trysts. The contracts require the potential sexual partners to answer such questions as:

Kissing? Close-mouthed, open-mouthed, tongue, no tongue...?

Touching? On the outside of the clothing? Inside the clothing? Breasts? Inside the underwear...?

Penetration? Missionary, doggie, penis, tongue...?

Just how much weirder, I ask you, can things get? A lot. All in the name of sexual equality and tolerance.

After the subject of legalizing gay marriages came up following the victory for same-sex unions in Vermont, Dr. Laura Schlessinger of radio talk show fame conducted an experiment by asking listeners who supported such "marriages" if they also thought siblings should be allowed to marry each other.

Of the hundreds of responses Dr. Laura received, all but one said *Yes.* Brothers *should* be allowed to marry sisters, brothers brothers and sisters sisters, if that was what they wanted and "they loved each other."

In June 2003, the Supreme Court ruled in Lawrence v. Texas that sodomy was, essentially, a constitutional right. Senator Rich Santorum (R-Pennsylvania) spoke for a bunch of us dissenters when he said, "If the Supreme Court says that you have the right to consensual sex within your home, then you have the right to bigamy, you have the right to polygamy. You have the right to incest, you have the right to adultery... Does this undermine the fabric of society? I would argue that yes, it does."

It not only undermines society, it will eventually destroy society when all types of perversions become "normal."

The American Psychiatric Association, which declared homosexual practices normal, is now flirting with downgrading pedophilia. Formerly, the APA's Diagnostic and Statistical Manual contended that merely "acting upon" one's urges toward children was sufficient to diagnose pedophilia. Not anymore. One can now molest a three-year-old and not be psychiatrically ill if his actions do not cause "clinically significant distress or impairment in social, occupational or other important areas of functioning." In other words, the guy can violate his grade-school niece or nephew and be considered perfectly "normal."

The Center for Reproductive Rights (CRC) wants to legalize sexual relations between "age mates," whatever the hell that's supposed to mean. Only sexual activity between an adolescent (say twelve years old?) and a "much-older person" (say 50?) should be deemed statutory rape and therefore necessary to report.

You have to wonder to what wacky and sick depths Americans are capable of taking our sexual behavior in public. Consider the following:

The *average* age at which a child is now taught the technical skills of using a condom is eleven years old...

More than 100,000 condoms were ordered for competitors at the Sydney Summer Olympics, in colors including gold, silver and bronze...

A current New York City hot spot named *La Nouvelle Justine,* after a character out of a novel by the Marquis de Sade, is a place where "snickering suburbanites bring friends on their birthdays for public spankings..."

The State University of New York at Albany sanctioned a sadomasochistic club on campus, using student funds...

A Manhattan store called *Toys In Babeland* featured an annual "Masturbate-A-Thon" with proceeds, so to speak, going to charity...

San Francisco's Department of Health issued a new motto: *Making every penis a healthy penis...*

CHAPTER TWENTY-SIX

Daniel Patrick Moynihan referred to the process by which our culture is conditioned to accept, indeed embrace, all forms of bizarre, outlandish or dangerous behavior as "defining deviancy down." As sex is the most intimate and personal part of humans, perhaps the nature of a society can best be judged by its sexual behavior. If that is so, then we may be in real trouble. Deviancy seems to have become the norm.

For example, it wasn't that long ago when most respectable newspapers rejected personal "Lonely Hearts" ads. You know the type: *Single white female would like to meet compatible man.* That's tame for these days. Take a look at the following "personals" that appear regularly in today's newspapers, respectable and otherwise:

—Curious heterosexual couple seeks gay male for fun night (or maybe two). Help us fulfill a fantasy.

—Very oral giving SWM (single white male), 46 YO, in shape, very eager to please, seeking females who love receiving oral pleasures. You will not be disappointed. Age/race/weight unimportant. All calls answered.

—Sex clubs are noisy and expensive. Have free orgies at my cozy Lauderdale home. SWM, attractively mature, BD (bondage), ritual, wife consignment experience. Sandwiches/humiliation? Doggie threesomes? "Masked" confidential videos made. Uninhibited lustiness.

Sex, the raunchier the better, has become big business. You can get virtually any perversion your little heart desires by letting your fingers do the walking. Ads offering everything from group orgies to S&M torture appear next to *Houses For Sale, Pets* and *Autos.* How about these:

—Get off in 10. Hot live phone sex. 10 min, for $10. Credit cards...

—Come spank us! Fantasy role play. Full EQ (equipped) dungeon. Exp. Mistress. $30 sessions...

—Swingers Club. Fun & discreet—Meet singles & couples on the Confidential Connection...

—Gorgeous Latin She-Male. Naomi. I will fulfill all your fantasies...

—Adult Videos. Looking for new female starlets. Actresses needed for adult videos. Must be attractive 18+. No experience needed...

—Hedonism at the club. Ladies, bi, bi-curious or just on the wild side? Come party with us...

Prostitutes, who these days like to refer to themselves as "sex workers" in the "sex trade," have a tough time making ends meet, so to speak, because of all the amateur competition. They have had to vary and expand their repertoires in order to compete. One industrious young woman of the night constructed a portable toilet with an opening in the underside into which her client could stick his head. So there he lay squinting up through the toilet seat while the hooker urinated and defecated in his face while she watched re-runs of *Seinfeld* on TV.

Think she has a corner on the market? Nope. There are now groups who specialize in "Golden Showers" and the like and meet regularly, hopefully, in each other's toilets.

It's damned confusing sometimes.

In the movie *GI Jane*, Demi Moore keeps yelling "Suck my dick!" Never mind that she doesn't have one. Women's magazines publish articles with titles like "Testosterone Isn't Just A Guy Thing Anymore" and "How To Feel Him Up In The Elevator." Genders are becoming so merged that it's frequently difficult to define what *is* a man and what *is* a woman.

Confusion developed in San Antonio, for instance, when Jessica Wick applied for a license to marry Robin Manhart. Two lesbians? Huh-uh. Not that simple anymore. You see, Jessica had been born a man, but had had her/his penis surgically chopped off to turn him into a woman. Then he turned right around, as a woman, and became a lesbian. Stay with me here. If he/she has a thing for women, why didn't he stay a man in the first place? Far be it for me to have the wisdom to figure these things out.

In Britain—and if it happened in Britain it'll soon cross the Atlantic—the British House of Lords passed the Gender Recognition Bill which will allow a man/woman to be recognized legally and politically as a woman/man even if he/she possesses a full set of male/female tackle. If you are a man who wants to be known as a woman, or vice versa, public authorities will issue you a new birth certificate with your new sex of choice written in. All that is required is a certificate from a registered medical practitioner or a psychiatrist practicing in the field of "gender dysphoria" and evidence that you have been living as a member of your new sex for the past two years. You don't have to have sex reassignment surgery. In other words, a person with a penis can still be legally a woman.

Among other British exports to America might be included the fad of "dogging," in which men and women go out trolling for anonymous sex in parks, parked cars, behind the bushes or any other convenient spot.

Jean Cocteau's maxim that the problem with the 20th Century (also the 21st) is that stupidity has started to think doesn't quite go far enough. We have now come to regard stupidity *as* thinking, as an equal with philosophies on the meaning of life and death. We actually listen and nod our heads wisely at the bombast of idiots and fools rather than speak up and risk being thought judgmental, close-minded, sexist, homophobic, racist and certainly, all in all, not a very good or tolerant person.

"Just this year I was introduced to the sadomasochistic community..." began a letter published in the Austin *American-Statesman.* "I
was pleasantly surprised to find a group of people with a higher degree
of compassion, sensuousness and communication skills than I have
found elsewhere... I did find their dedication to safe, sane and consensual behavior—counter to guilt-ridden shame-based sexuality—to be
refreshing...

"While the diversity of people involved in sadomasochistic practices is broad enough to involve all types...the vast majority are good,
responsible citizens just like the rest of society... (To suggest otherwise)
encourages bigotry and has been used to spread racism, sexism and
hatred... (of those) targeted for scapegoat or is a minority..."

In other words, if you don't agree with me that it's rational and
normal for us to meet in basements, tie each other in chains, beat bare
butts with hair brushes and whips, call each other dirty names, make
one another crawl and grovel, dress up in leather and lingerie, hang
weights from our testicles, and urinate in each other's faces—then
you're judgmental and *you* probably have a sex hang-up. Deviancy is
made to appear normal by insisting that it first be regarded as normal.

Part of the sadomasochistic scenario, taken only a small step forward, ends in *snuff* films in which the female is purportedly tortured
and killed on the screen to satisfy perverse tastes. Americans are the
world's largest importers of such materials. That says bunches about
the state of American culture and American sanity.

To insist that perversion affects only "consenting adults in the privacy of their own homes" is false at its very core.

In 1993, the International Lesbian and Gay Association (ILGA),
which received consultive status in the United Nations as a human
rights organization, joined NAMBLA (North American Man-Boy Love
Association) to stand for "youth liberation." They seek to abolish age-
of-consent laws so that young people can enjoy the "right to sexual and
social self-determination." In other words, to quote NAMBLA, "sex by
eight or it's too late." Surely it won't be long before NAMBLA, along
with other "sexual minorities" such as the incestuous and necrophilia-
oriented, will be invited to take their proper seats at the UN.

Far fetched?

The American Library Association recommended to teens a website called *Go Ask Alice*, which featured sexually explicit information
for young people about anal sex, oral sex, masturbation and sadomasochistic role playing. *Alice* informed a Christian boy that he might want
to have sex because "sometimes you can't know what's best for you
until you sample your options." Presumably, *Alice* offered such options
as homosexuality, group gropes and a tryst with Dumbo the elephant at
the local zoo.

Alice gave some rather unusual advice about pets.

"Several things might make sex with animals, also known as bestiality, appealing," she counseled, then listed them. "It can be forbidden, secretive and/or exciting. An animal doesn't kiss and tell, nor does the animal complain about performance or desire orgasm. You are in control of the when, where and how... *Alice* has confirmed with several veterinarians that STD's (sexually-transmitted diseases), including HIV, cannot be transmitted from animals to humans, and vice versa..."

It can be most reassuring in this age of STDs that FiFi won't give you the clap in your "relationship."

I'm really not making this up.

Bill Clinton, whose legacy consisted of the spectacle of the President of the United States engaging in oral, cigar and phone sex in the Oval Office, greatly accelerated the removal of shame and stigma attached to bad sexual behavior. The most powerful man in the world exploited a 21-year-old intern and the behavior was not looked upon as offensive. In fact, he became even more popular and was called heroic for standing up against "puritans" and those who were "judgmental." *Hero* these strange days has lost its original definition.

Tommy Hilfiger ads hawking clothing appeared almost immediately. In one of them, a luscious young Monica look-alike in bare feet, black leather pants and a come-get-it look was curled up provocatively on the President's desk with the American flag in the background. In another, the same young lady knelt on the blue Oval Office rug, her knees over the Presidential Seal, eagerly looking up.

The advertising executive responsible for the campaign explained that the ads actually enhanced the president's allure by bringing the scandal "to fantasy as opposed to the tawdry reality."

"We wanted to use a theme that the White House represents to the American people—a symbol of hope," said designer Hilfiger. "Our White House is all inclusive. Anyone could be president."

Anyone *was* president. Isn't it heartening, a tribute to our inclusiveness, that even a pervert may grow up to become president—and be celebrated for it?

Sex columnist Anka Radokovich claimed Clinton revived her career. "When I started writing, I felt like I was morally judged. But with Clinton, with Monica going under the table and having that reported, that changed the whole sexual dialogue in America, which was great for my career and me."

A Los Angeles computer salesman ran an ad in the LA *Times* touting how his prices were "dropping faster than the president's pants." But even Clinton's pants were dropping no faster than America's sense of morality. Standards of behavior have plummeted so low it is virtually impossible to come up with a good moral judgment anymore.

A U.S. Navy wife discovered that a chief petty officer on a nuclear submarine was using the code name "Boysrch" (Boy Search) in advertising over the Internet, proclaiming to the world that he was a pedo-phile. His on-line profile listed his marital status as "gay" and his hobby as "driving around, boy watching and collecting photos of young studs." As a *Personal Quote*, he used, "My God, he's got a nice butt, and I know because I'm a bootyologist!"

His command attempted to boot *his* butt out of the navy under the military's "Don't Ask, don't tell" policy. Commander-in-Chief Clinton intervened and ordered the navy to keep him on active duty long enough for him to file a court order blocking his discharge. After all, gays are a protected minority class, even pedophilic gays—and we must not be judgmental.

Unfortunately, in this Brave New World of the Enlightened and the Compassionate, common sense isn't as easily transmitted as AIDs. Of course it is "judgmental" to point out that license and liberty are two separate and even opposing concepts. License in behavior very fre-quently marks the loss of personal freedom. Sexual license is quite compatible with socialist totalitarian governments. The Soviet Union at the height of its revolutionary communist power, while it was dispatch-ing hundreds of thousands of its citizens to gulags, permitted free love and provided abortion on demand.

Human beings, Thomas Jefferson wrote, are "inherently independ-ent of all but moral law." Men who defy that law are not free. Slaves at first to their own passions, they eventually succumb to political tyr-anny. Men cannot sustain a democratic government who cannot govern their own passions.

SECTION X
GAY ISSUES

"Heather's favorite number is two. She has two arms, two legs, two ears, two hands—two mommies. Momma Jane and Momma Kate...
From children's book *Heather Has Two Mommies*

CHAPTER TWENTY-SEVEN

"In retrospect, lighting the match was my big mistake," Eric explained to bemused doctors. "But I was only trying to retrieve the gerbil."

Eric was suffering from second-degree burns and a broken nose when admitted to the Salt Lake City hospital, a result of a "felching" accident. Felching is an odd practice in which gay men stuff furry little animals up each other's rectums in order to experience some sort of sensuous pleasure.

Eric explained how things started going wrong. "I pushed a cardboard tube up Kiki's rectum and slipped Raggot, our gerbil, *in.* As usual, Kiki shouted 'Armageddon!', my cue that he'd had enough. I tried to retrieve Raggot, but he wouldn't come out again. So I peered into the tube and struck a match, thinking the light might attract him."

A hospital spokesman took up the story: "The match ignited a pocket of intestinal gas and flame shot out of the tubing, igniting Mr. (Eric's) hair and severely burning his face. It also set fire to the gerbil's fur and whiskers, which in turn ignited a larger pocket of gas further up the intestine, propelling the rodent out like a cannonball."

The burning gas scorched Eric's face and the impact of the gerbil broke his nose. Kiki suffered first and second degree burns to his anus and lower intestinal tract.

Today's radical gay movement uses the language of "civil rights" and "constitutional rights" to demand acceptance of virtually any depraved behavior. Stuffing a gerbil up your anus *isn't* depraved? According to the mass media, such practices are merely "alternative lifestyles." Reflective of the any-perversion-is-our-perversion mentality, society has been brainwashed to remain silent about it. Suggesting people behave with some decency is an affront. Suggesting to a gay man that he stop having anal sex, or stuffing gerbils, is homophobic and a hate crime.

During a "Literature and Cultural Diversity" lecture at UNC-Chapel Hill, a student expressed mere disagreement with pro-homosexuality comments. His instructor, Elyse Crystall, said his disagreement "constituted hate speech and is completely unacceptable..." The student, she went on was "a white, heterosexual, Christian male (who) can feel entitled to make violent, heterosexist comments and not feel marked or threatened or vulnerable."

When it comes to violence, gays are much more at risk from other gays, contrary to the urban myth about homophobic rednecks bashing homosexuals whenever they go out for a night of fun. I was a Tulsa, Oklahoma, police homicide detective for nearly ten years, during which time I investigated a number of violent crimes involving homosexuals.

I began searching the gay community for a suspect whenever a homosexual turned up murdered, not the community at large. Take the following case, for example:

Mohawk Park was a known gay hangout. As soon as the sun set, gay men started cruising the park, eyeing and being eyed, rendezvousing with each other for quick, sweaty trysts in their cars, in the woods, or in the public restrooms. Men furtively scouted the *Men's* until they received the right come-on. A quick oral or hand job among the stench of urine and other equally unpleasant odors, and then they were back out cruising again.

For the more demure, "glory holes" were drilled through the partitions that separated the toilet stalls. A man seeking pleasure simply walked into one of the stalls, stuck his member through the glory hole and promptly received service by his next-stall neighbor. Anonymous sex at its best, no face-to-face contact. Simply face to member, as it were.

We found a corpse shot in his own car beneath the pecan trees with his pants around his knees. Turned out, as it often does, that he was drilled by a jealous and resentful lover while giving and receiving blowjobs in the front seat.

Not *all* gays are promiscuous and crass and depraved. I'm sure there are committed same-gender couples who live otherwise normal and unblemished lives. However, they are, by far, the minority. Research suggests promiscuity of strenuous proportions to be the norm among male homosexuals; 43 percent of gays have had 500 or more partners *each*. Even Andrew Sullivan, an eloquent advocate of gay marriage, wrote that he always defended "the beauty and mystery and spirituality of sex, even anonymous sex."

Say whatever you want, the practice of strangers, or even friends and acquaintances, ramming penises into orifices never intended for that purpose and engaging in practices so bizarre as to defy the imagination and the capacity of the human body to take abuse seems neither normal nor natural. Yet, far be it for me to question the curious rituals of homosexuals. I need to start with that disclaimer. After all, I'm nothing if not a "sensitive, tolerant, nonjudgmental" Indian boy.

I learned one thing well in the Ozark Mountains where I grew up: You live and you let live as long as the other fella doesn't try to knock down your fence. If two gay guys want to stuff rats, tarantulas, boa constrictors and other things up their buns in the privacy of their own boudoir, so be it. I don't *care* what *anybody* does in his/her/their/its own bedroom. Sex should be private. I get teed off, however, when bearded, paunchy guys start prancing around in bras and high heels in public, stepping on my fence while demanding that I accept and embrace their behavior. If I don't, I'm a bigoted, closed-minded homophobic, intolerant, judgmental redneck redskin. In claiming special acceptance, privilege and protection for simply being gay, they are ramming their sex down our throats (pun intended). In coming out of the closet, they have made "sexual orientation" the most public part of them. That's how they define themselves.

Since gays themselves have made homosexuality and the forced acceptance of it upon the public their primary driving issue, I think perhaps we should take a hard look at exactly what being gay entails. I fully expect to be savaged in the mass media for doing this. To dare suggest that being homosexual may not be something to celebrate instantly makes me a Nazi, a gas-chamber operator, a hate monger...

But... *Duck!* Here I go!

CHAPTER TWENTY-EIGHT

The American Psychological Association withdrew homosexuality as a mental disorder, then began beating the drums for "affirmation." The idea that being gay is normal, may even be *more* normal than a man and a woman together, has made enormous inroads into the news media, education, arts, religion, and indeed into all our institutions. What started off asking for tolerance soon sought acceptance, and now demands mandatory affirmation and the moral equivalency of heterosexuality.

"We have to be more open about sex, and we need to speak out to tell people that sex is good, sex is wonderful," cajoled former Surgeon General Jocelyn Elders. "It's a normal part and healthy part of our being, whether it is homosexual or heterosexual."

Adolf Hitler maintained that you had to start with children if you wanted to change a culture. The process of changing culture through children has been going on in the United States and the Western World for the past two generations, subverting education to support and enhance a liberal politically correct agenda that includes gay and "alternative" lifestyles. Gays, said Kevin Jennings, executive director of the Gay, Lesbian and Straight Education Network, "need to receive support from their schools. They need to receive affirmation." Kids must be taught to "*value* homosexual relationships."

A New York teacher's guide called *Children Of The Rainbow* reminded educators that some pupils may come from households in which one or both adults are gay. It urged teachers to encourage first graders to "view lesbians/gays as real people to be respected and appreciated." In accomplishing this worthy goal, it recommended certain readers for six-year-olds. No more *Dick And Jane*. Now, it has to be *Susie And June* or *Dick And Stevie*.

In *Gloria Goes To Gay Pride,* Gloria's mother explains that "Some women love women, some men love men, and some women and men love each other. That's why we march in the parade—so everyone can have a choice."

"Heather's favorite number is two," begins a passage in *Heather Has Two Mommies*. "She has two arms, two legs, two ears, two hands—two mommies. Momma Jane and Momma Kate."

Daddy's Roommate is about a boy whose father is divorced and living with a new partner named Frank. According to the book, for *first graders*, "Being gay is just one more kind of love." Daddy and Frank "work together...eat together...sleep together."

"It is very important that children learn early on that there are different family structures other than the traditional one," explained New York public school chancellor Joseph Fernandez.

Family structures? *Homo sapiens* would be on their way toward the fate of saber tooth tigers and passenger pigeons if the world had to depend upon gay "families" for their ultimate survival.

Curriculums in New York public schools, where condom usage is taught in the fourth grade, include glossary material explaining such terms as *Dental Dam*: "A piece of latex that can be placed over the vulva during oral sex to protect against transmission of viruses that may be present in vaginal fluids, or over the anus during analingus (oral sex of the anus)."

Seattle school administrators and teachers in lower grades are trained to provide "gay-positive classrooms."

Harvard University research associate Arthur Lipkin developed a curriculum to aid high school teachers in including gays in history, literature and psychology lessons.

"If schools get beyond looking at gay youth as the problem and look at the homophobic atmosphere instead, we'll get some positive results," said San Francisco educator Robert Birle.

If you should so much as question any of this, you had better be prepared to be stonewalled and sneered at by school officials, savaged by the press and denounced as a homophobic hate monger. You may even be arrested for a "hate crime."

Two suburban Boston fathers, Brian Comenker and Scott Whiteman, found this out when they objected to the gay agenda in the Massachusetts public schools.

The Annual Conference of the Boston Chapter of GLSEN (Gay, Lesbian and Straight Education Network), a conference sanctioned by the state, partly supported by tax money and attended chiefly by students and educators, declared its purpose to be the training of teachers and students in developing programs that "challenge the anti-gay, hetero-centric culture that still prevails in our schools." GLSEN pushed its agenda down to even kindergarten level with themes such as "What is a Boy/Girl?" and "Freedom To Marry." Instructor lesson plans and books with titles like *Queering Elementary Education* accompanied the theme proposals.

Comenker and Whiteman attended the GLSEN conference and secretly audio-taped workshops with topics such as "Early Childhood Educators: How To Decide To Come Out At Work Or Not;" "From Lesbos to Stonewall: Incorporating Sexuality Into A World History Curriculum;" and "The Struggles and Triumphs Of Including Homosexuality In A Middle School Curriculum."

One workshop for "youth only, ages 14-21," was called "What They Didn't Tell You About Queer Sex & Sexuality In Health Class." It was a raucous session led by two Massachusetts Department of Education employees, Margot Abels and Julie Netherlands, and an AIDS educator from the Massachusetts Public Health Agency, Michael

Gaucher. Seventh graders in the session had their consciousnesses raised on everything from "felching" to "fisting," a practice in which one partner rams his entire hand up the other's rectum.

Doesn't all this sound perfectly "normal" to you?

Gaucher asked teens present how they knew whether or not they had had sex. One kid, apparently confused because of examples set by President Bill Clinton, asked if oral sex was really sex.

"If that's not sex," Gaucher squealed, "then the number of times I've had sex has dramatically decreased, from a mountain to a valley, baby."

He guided a shy young participant into talking about which orifices needed to be filled in order for sex to have occurred. "Don't be shy, honey, you can do it." He then explained how lesbians experienced sexual bliss by rubbing clitorises together and how male ejaculate tasted "sweeter if you ate celery beforehand."

During a question-and-answer session, he demonstrated the proper hand position for "fisting." Abels in turn described the practice as "an experience of letting somebody into your body that you want to be close and intimate with." It put you, she said, into an "exploratory mode" and was "an experience of opening yourself completely to another person."

All in the name of good, clean, informative fun.

When word got out that the two fathers had taped the conference, Superior Court Judge Allan van Gestel issued a gag order prohibiting them, the news media and even the state legislature from disseminating or discussing the audios. The Board of Education called them "slanderers." The chairman of the Governor's Commission on Gay and Lesbian Youth denounced them in the press.

Have we indeed all gone mad in that the two fathers who objected became the villains in this sordid little episode?

It's an exercise in superfluity to go beyond public schools and education to look at how children are being conditioned throughout society to embrace homosexuality and all the other crazier aspects of our New Enlightened culture.

During San Francisco's 1992 Gay Pride Parade, President Bill Clinton's appointee for Assistant Secretary for Fair Housing, Roberta Achtenberg, rode in a white convertible with San Francisco Municipal Court Judge Mary Morgan. Morgan's seven-year-old son rode in the car with the two women as they passionately hugged and kissed. A sign on the side of the convertible read *Celebrating Family Values*.

An article in Minnesota's St. Paul *Pioneer Press* reported on the "authenticity" of modern Scouting.

"For those of us who remember the Girl Scouts as the quiet girls in class who wore their green uniforms on Wednesdays," the piece began, "encountering Katze Ludeka can be quite an eye-opener... Rather than stitching doilies and tea cozies, the talented seamstress has created her own costume company specializing in 'fetish-wear.' Instead of going for the Gold Award...by reading to senior citizens, Ludeka pushed to start her own support group for at-risk teens called Queer Youth Exist. For her Gold Award application... Ludeka is submitting her work with gay, lesbian, bisexual and transgender teens, with the support of her troop..."

Pressure to accept, to affirm, to embrace homosexuality as natural and normal extends into every institution of American society. Being branded gay, once a social stigma, is now looked upon as so normal that being exclusively *heterosexual* is almost a disgrace in certain enlightened circles.

New York City councilwoman Christine Quinn (D) became embroiled in a scandal over rumors that she had dumped her longtime girlfriend in order to have a fling with—No, not that!--a *man!* Quinn spokesperson Maura Keany issued a public statement denying the affair and affirming the fact that the good councilwoman was still a lesbian.

The man in question also stepped forward to save Ms. Quinn's bacon. He couldn't be having an affair with her, he said, because "I am not now, nor have I ever been, a heterosexual..."

CHAPTER TWENTY-NINE

A significant part of homosexuality focuses almost exclusively upon sex and the obtaining of it in any way possible. This is not merely an aberration in an otherwise exemplary alternative lifestyle. Douglas Crimp, a professor of visual and cultural studies at the College of Rochester, New York, explains how many men first become involved in the gay life.

"(They) initially find out that they are part of a community, or find out that they are what we call 'gay' when they follow their sexual desires to a place where they can rent a pornographic video or go to a bookstore and have anonymous sex."

Notwithstanding that to most of us a *bookstore* would be the last place we would expect to have sex, anonymous or otherwise, the neophyte is then ushered into a bizarre world that is endlessly touted as being as normal as any other. Gay bars, bath houses and sex clubs form the nucleus of gay life in most larger cities.

"The phenomenology of a sex club encounter is an experience of world making," proclaimed gay activist Michael Warner. "It's an experience of being connected not just to this person but to potentially limitless numbers of people and that's why it's important that it be with a stranger. Sex with a stranger is like a metonym."

Ads seeking sex with strangers appear in most gay publications and many mainstream ones as well.

"The Circuit" is an international series of weekend dance parties attended by tens of thousands of men where drug use and the bathhouse ethic of anonymous sex with multiple partners is the real name of the game. *Circuit Noize,* an inside publication promoting the scene, describes how The Circuit provides gay men the chance "to enter the altered world where man-to-man sex is not only accepted, but is celebrated. When The Circuit comes to town, that town becomes an instant gay ghetto full of hot men who are behaving as queer as they care to be."

Such wholesale promiscuous behavior is what led to the AIDS plague. In the beginning, the disease was almost exclusively among gay men until it spread through IV drug use and bisexuality. It is still most prevalent among gay men. Yet, how often do you hear anyone in the press or the liberal intelligentsia pointing that out? It's almost a "hate crime" to suggest that most HIV sufferers get that way *because of their own behavior.* It's politically correct to view them as victims of some awful scourge like cancer, against which they are powerless, instead of willing participants acquiring contamination on their hands and knees in private little cubicles in the backs of bathhouses.

Celebrities, government officials, college professors, the usual leftwing suspects, wear ribbons to show their sensitivity, hold quilting bees for victims, march for more government aid, give benefit concerts, lament the dreadful circumstances by which fate just *happened* to select gays to infect—and woe be to anyone insensitive enough to suggest limiting the spread of HIV by limiting indiscriminate behavior.

"This (limiting behavior) offends the fundamental requirement of a just society that people have the right to intimate associations that allow them to explore, experience, and give sexual pleasure to others and to derive sexual pleasure themselves from their intimate contacts with other people," said Kendall Thomas from an organization called Sex-Panic.

How long do you suppose it would take cities to close down whore houses, hooker bars, sex clubs and other enterprises if it were discovered that promiscuous *heterosexual* sex was transmitting and spreading some horrible affliction? Doors would be busted down and squirming half-naked bimbos would be carted off to jails and sanitariums by busloads while the populace cheered. I'm merely pointing out how our focus has been conditioned to protect, condone and accept certain social aberrations as long as they're politically correct aberrations.

In 1995, the Gay and Lesbian Alliance Against Defamation named Gabriel Rotello "Outstanding Journalist of the Year," after which he then became *persona non gratis* in the gay community when he published a book arguing that gay men's sexual behavior was in large part responsible for the AIDS epidemic. Suddenly, he was "openly hostile to gay sex." His views "repudiated the legacies of the gay movement." In taking "the moral high ground by denouncing the sex lives of queers," he became a reactionary whose ideas were a threat to gay liberation.

Things went even crazier when New York City attempted to stem AIDS by promoting guidelines for bathhouses, sex clubs, porn theaters and other "public sex" venues. About the only requirements of these guidelines was that clubs distribute condoms, make sure patrons used them, and that all areas of clubs be open for monitoring. There could be no closed "private resting rooms" with doors locked. City health codes already prohibited "penetrative sex" in public places and commercial establishments, but these laws were rarely enforced when it came to gays.

The uproar and outrage over "sex police" began immediately. You would have thought a bunch of bubba gay bashers had been turned loose to run amuck.

"I felt something as significant as my being gay, as my Mexican and Italian heritage, as my struggle with HIV was being robbed from me," complained former gay porn star Tony Valenzuela after being chastened for engaging in penetrative sex in a monitored club.

The owner of a sex club called The Attic asked patrons to remove their trousers when they entered in an effort to thwart monitoring. Inspectors, on the other hand, were required by their jobs to remain fully clothed while on duty. They were therefore easy to spot when the entire dance floor was otherwise filled with men dancing in their BVDs, Fruit O' The Loom or favorite *Victoria's Secret* selection.

City officials soon amended the guidelines because of pressure from the "sensitive" and "inclusive" loud crowd. Inspectors were instructed to enforce law only in instances where they observed penetrative sex *without condoms.* Screw on the dance floor if you wanted, just as long as you wore a condom and the inspectors could *see* that you were wearing one.

"(The establishments) have baskets of condoms," said one observer. "They have posters on the walls. Once a week...somebody will set up a table and give out information about HIV testing and brochures about safer sex, and in the meantime unsafe sex is going on all over the place."

Government continued to try to stem the AIDS epidemic using sensitive politically correct guidelines. The Food and Drug Administration issued a special waiver allowing the use of rapid HIV test kits in "outreach settings." More than 250,000 kits were purchased at a cost of two million dollars and distributed to health clubs, bath houses and sex clubs.

"Agreements with law enforcement, owners of social venues such as bathhouses and sex clubs, neighborhood associations and other key partners should be established before testing activities begin," advised a Center for Disease Control document entitled *Advancing HIV Prevention: Interior Technical Guidance For Selected Intervention.*

CDC guidelines recommend counselors take a "nonjudgmental" approach. Essentially, the government made peace with behavior that spread the virus.

"For clients with several high risk behaviors," say the guidelines, "the counselor should help clients focus on reducing the most critical risk they are willing to commit to changing. The step does not need to be a personal behavior change."

Heavens! Don't even suggest that the gay's stripping off his jockey shorts in the back room of a sex club is what will give him AIDS. There must be no morality judgment involved.

The San Francisco Department of Health tried a different approach to AIDS control with a new public service campaign called "Healthy Penis...making every penis a healthy penis." I'm really not making this up. The ads show cartoon images of smiling, friendly erect penises with personalities, faces and attitudes. It also shows unhappy penises with syphilitic sores and other afflictions. One sore named Phil (syPHILis) wears silver shoes and an earring.

Does it work? Gays continue to infect each other and the rate of

AIDS is climbing. Some *purposefully* infect one another while expecting straight Americans to fund this death party.

There was "something empowering about the idea of sharing someone else's HIV," wrote Stephen Gendin, the HIV-positive vice president of *POZ* Magazine.

In a speech given at Yale University, Douglas Crimp lamented over how AIDS had affected the gay lifestyle.

"Alongside the dismal toll of death," he pontificated in a scholarly manner, "what many of us have lost is a culture of sexual possibility: back rooms, tea rooms (toilets), movie houses, and baths; the trucks, the piers, the rumble, the dens. Sex was everyplace for us, and everything we wanted to venture: Golden showers and watersports (urination in sex), crosskicking and rimming, fucking and fist fucking. Now our untamed impulses are either proscribed once again or shielded from us by latex."

My poor heart reaches out to such victims.

CHAPTER THIRTY

While gays and their supporters champion tolerance and "freedom of sexual choice" on the one hand, on the other they express bitter intolerance of anyone who might disagree with them. Raw coercion, not persuasion, guides the movement to force the unqualified acceptance of homosexuality upon every American institution, including religion. The movement will never be happy until it forces America to legitimize homosexuality in every respect.

The story of Dan Savage, a gay sex columnist for *Slate* electronic magazine, illustrates the passionate lengths to which some in the gay movement will go to suppress opposing points of view. He infiltrated the Gary Bauer presidential campaign of 2000 and, when he caught the flu, attempted to sabotage the campaign by infecting Bauer and his staff with the virus. His plan, he admitted in *Slate*, was "a little malicious—even a little mean-spirited—but those same words describe the tactics used by Bauer and the rest of the religious right against gays and lesbians..."

He coughed in the faces of staffers, handed the candidate a pen he had kept in his mouth while his own virus raged. Then, "much as it pains me to confirm a hateful stereotype of gay men—that we will put anything in our mouths—I started licking door knobs. The front door, office doors, even a bathroom door. When that was done, I started in on the staplers, phones and computer keyboards. Then I stood in the kitchen and licked the rims of all the clean coffee cups drying in the rack..."

After all, *anything* is justified when you're fighting against the evil, homophobic, racist, sexist, specie-ist, capitalist... You get the picture.

Even the Boy Scouts—Is *nothing* sacred!—became free prey after the U.S. Supreme Court ruled 5-4 that Scouts had the right to ban gays from leadership positions. Six Boy Scouts leading the Pledge of Allegiance at the 2000 Democratic National Convention were booed and spat upon by delegates unhappy to see them on the platform.

"It was pretty insensitive," said one delegate, speaking *not* of the booing but instead of the Scout presence at a Democratic Party function. How *dare* the Boy Scouts show their homophobic young faces where their mere appearance might make honest homosexuals feel disrespected.

Incredible pressure is on throughout the society to validate homosexuality and diminish heterosexuality. The agenda of the Gay Movement and of the entire political correctness campaign is directed toward transforming society into an enlightened reflection of itself. The Enlightened are determined, through persuasion if possible, through pressure and coercion if necessary, to bring us all around to accepting virtually any damned thing, celebrating it even. Recalcitrants will end up in padded rooms where Big Nanny and Nurse Ratchett administer generous doses of social Prozac to force us to behave in a proper *enlightened* manner.

"Being queer is more than setting up house, sleeping with a person of the same gender, and seeking state approval for doing so..." writes Paula Ettelbrick in *Lesbians, Gay Men And The Law*. "(B)eing queer means pushing the parameters of sex, sexuality and family, and in the process transforming the very fabric of society..."

How much clearer can it be put? Transforming the very fabric of society...

We are rapidly heading toward a time when it will be a *crime* to express any disapproval of homosexuality. "Racist" speech is already illegal in most of western Europe, down to the point of even *noticing* that there might be a racial difference between folks. Europeans and American leftists are now agitating to ban "homophobic" speech. Those in America who think the First Amendment protects speech had better look again.

When William Cohen was Secretary of Defense, he ordered the establishment of a plan in the military for curbing offensive speech, derogatory remarks and jokes regarding homosexuals. Similar policies are widespread in virtually all government institutions and, under government pressure, in most private ones as well. You can now be punished for merely voicing an opinion against the radical gay movement. There are places in the world, even in America, where an anti-gay opinion is considered a "hate crime."

Pope John Paul II criticized the World Gay Pride March in Rome as "offensive to Christian values" and said homosexuality is "objectively disordered" and "against natural law." The Dutch magazine *Gay Krant* filed a criminal complaint against him on the grounds that he violated anti-discrimination laws. "Incitement to discriminate" is illegal in the Netherlands.

"The Local Law Enforcement Enhancement Act of 2000," if passed in some form within the next few years, provides the federal government with a hierarchy of crimes in which those based on "sexual orientation" receive harsher penalties. Citing civil rights, the U.S. government appears eager to stifle any perceived threat against "gay rights" and to increase "hate crimes" laws. Take the case of homosexual Matthew Shepard as an example.

Shepard's story blitzed TV, radio and print when he was murdered, generating literally thousands of media features. He became a "poster boy" for "hate crimes" legislation. Rhetoric made headlines nationwide about how *all* society, being homophobic, was guilty for the crime.

According to Deborah Mathis of Gannett News Service, Shepard's murder was inspired by "the Christian Right per se and some particular members on Capitol Hill have helped inflame the air so that the air that these bad people breathed that night was filled, filled with the idea that somehow gays are different, and not only are they different in that difference, they're bad and not only are they bad, they are evil and therefore evil can be destroyed... It's the air filled with hate..."

Inspired by Shepard, Attorney General Janet Reno argued that hate crimes were epidemic. She urged hate crimes law be expanded in definition to include not only race, color, religion and national origin but also disabilities, gender, and sexual orientation.

"People who commit these crimes against gays and lesbians have to face the same penalties," bellowed Kim Mills of the Human Rights Campaign.

Under traditional American law, people who commit similar crimes *do* face similar penalties. The politically correct crowd does not want equity; it demands special protection to elevate the status of protected groups.

While Matthew Shepard's murder continued to make headlines, virtually nothing appeared in the media when a pair of gay men murdered 13-year-old Jesse in Arkansas. The men duct-taped the boy, drugged him, blindfolded him, gagged him with his own underwear, tortured and repeatedly raped him with a variety of objects. There were no marches over his death, no protests, no lamentations of how he must have suffered. *All* society was guilty for Matthew Shepard. No one dared suggest that *all* homosexuals were guilty in Jesse's murder. When it comes to gays, American institutions have been conditioned to accentuate the positive and downplay the negative.

Jesse and Shepard were each killed by murderous scumbags. Yet, the crime against Shepard is somehow perceived to be much worse than that committed against little Jesse.

Mindsets like this influence government policy decisions and open the way for ever greater "protection" of gays and for the restriction of behavior and attitudes toward them. It will inevitably lead to further legislation that can be used against law-abiding citizens who don't share the pro-homosexual viewpoint. The Netherlands mentality is not far away—and to hell with the First Amendment.

A court in Denver forbade a mother to tell her child that being homosexual is wrong and threatened her with criminal contempt of court if she exposed her daughter to any ideas "that can be considered homophobic."

The complication began when mother and daughter joined with Mom's lesbian lover to form one of those wonderful new family styles bequeathed by the sexual revolution. Mom eventually became a devout Christian, concluded that homosexuality was a sin, and split the sheets with her lesbian lover. The court awarded joint custody to both little mommies, although the real mother's lover had no blood or legal relationship to the child. The ban on "homophobia" was included in the court order. Anybody want to make a bet on how confused that poor child is going to be when she grows up?

When Bill Clinton was president, he advanced the Gay Agenda more than any other public official in U.S. history. After all, the homosexual lobby had donated more than five million dollars to his various political campaigns. A typical politician will break off pieces of his soul, providing he has one, and sell them for that kind of money.

Clinton boasted of appointing one hundred open gays to senior administrative positions; he created a White House liaison to gays with salaries paid by taxpayers; offered national asylum to immigrants claiming persecution due to sexual orientation; mandated controversial AIDS awareness training sessions for government workers; pushed to allow homosexuals to openly serve in the U.S. military; endorsed major gay rights legislation; appointed an open lesbian as a federal judge; selected a surgeon general who stated homosexual sex was healthy; and was the first president to be interviewed by a homosexual magazine, *The Advocate,* which included explicit and erotic gay photos in the same issue.

Whenever a President of the United States puts the power and weight of his office behind a movement, you can bet it will soon carry the weight of law and that opportunists and other branches of government will quickly take up that same banner. U.S. Census Form 2000, for example, listed "unmarried partner" as an option for a relationship.

Ford, General Motors and Chrysler jointly announced that they would offer benefits to gay partners of employees who have shared "a committed relationship for no less than six months." No such benefits were offered to cohabitating heterosexual couples.

In 2003, New York established Harvey Milk High School for gay students by claiming the students were being harassed and discriminated against in conventional schools. There were problems with crime almost immediately in this school, as in most NYC institutions of education. Male students were arrested for dressing up as female prostitutes, soliciting clients in Greenwich Village, then pretending to be vice cops to shake them down for money.

Wait. It gets even crazier.

The American Psychological Association published the "Rind Study" which purported to show that homosexual acts were not harmful to young boys, even when they occurred between men and boys. In fact, said the study, "quite a few of the boys remembered their childhood sexual experiences positively."

The University of Chicago's "Queer Safe Campus" association asked for gender neuter bathrooms because feminists, gays, transgenders and assorted other related groups did not feel comfortable going through doors marked either *Men* or *Women.* How about a third door marked *Other?*

Homosexual "marriage" is the next major step in the radical gay agenda. "Why should society discriminate against our love?" goes the argument. Marriage is for people who love. Homosexuals love. Ergo, denying one the fundamental right to marry whomever (or whatever?) one wishes is a denial of civil and human rights.

"Once you say that actresses Ellen Degeneres and Anne Heche, or two men auditioning for the leads in *La Cage Aux Folles,* are the equivalent of a family conforming to God's law and maintaining the cradle of civilization," journalist Paula Ettelbrick contended, "the fabric of society is irreparably rent and, in the words of Cole Porter, 'anything goes.'"

Gossip columnist Jeanette Walls, with a totally straight face, reported the important news of the breakup of that celebrated lesbian couple, Anne Heche and Ellen Degeneres. Heche had reportedly had an affair with a *man,* Colley Laffoon. "Anne really wanted to have a kid with Ellen, too..." went the column.

How, pray tell, were these two women supposed to have a kid *together?*

"But," the column went on, "Ellen wanted her to stay home and give up her career. Coley is much more supportive of her career and the idea of her being a working mom..."

Isn't that touching? It's so...so 21st Century.

On December 21, 1999, the Vermont Supreme Court branded the preference for heterosexual unions as mere bigotry and ruled that homosexual couples are entitled to the same benefits and protections as wedded couples. Governor Howard Dean (Yep, the later presidential candidate) then signed into law a bill granting gay couples "civil unions" with nearly all the benefits of marriage, the first such law in the nation. Of course, the pressure didn't stop with that.

On November 18, 2003, an unelected Massachusetts judge declared the state constitution *guaranteed* gay couples the right to marry, not just to "civil unions" as in Vermont. This followed the Supreme Court's ruling in June striking down the Texas ban on sodomy. Declared Massachusetts' Chief Justice Margaret Marshall: "We declare that barring an individual from the protections, benefits and obligations of civil marriage solely because that person would marry a person of the same sex violates the Massachusetts Constitution."

Things really went wild after sodomy was no longer proscribed anymore, anywhere. San Francisco started the hysteria of love after newly-elected Mayor G. Newsome attended President George Bush's State of the Union speech in January 2004.

"What Mayor Newsom heard was discrimination..." pontificated CNN's Bill Schneider. "The 36-year-old mayor is looking to the future.

Younger Americans are much more inclined to favor same-sex marriage. It's like their civil rights issue."

More than 3,000 gays "married" each other in one hectic, ribald San Francisco week in February 2004. On March 3, Portland, Oregon, also decided law allowed gay unions; county officials issued hundreds of license to homosexual couples.

"We're just here to make it official," said Paul Harris, holding the hand of James Griener. "We're here to make honest men of each other."

I ask you, ain't that just too sweet?

Four states allowed homosexual marriages in February and March before a general outcry from "the Vast Right Wing Conspiracy" forced officials to act and shut down the factories. Ironically enough, perhaps in an unintended endorsement of the Enlightened agenda, the same Massachusetts high court that ruled normal marriage to be an unconstitutional form of bigotry actually suggested that if "the legislators were to jettison the term 'marriage' altogether, it might well be rational and permissible..."

Naturally, politics of the heart must not be exclusive in a society sensitive toward everyone and to all behavior. Room must be made at the table for everyone and for every combination of everyone. Homosexual marriage inevitably opens up even more unusual combinations.

One of the newest things, according to *Time* Magazine, is "polyamory," a limp euphemism for polygamy. The *Time* article profiled April Divilbiss and "the two men she calls her husbands...an odd but functional family."

In Milwaukee, a cohabiting brother and sister argued for marriage and the right to continue rearing their three children. They *love* each other, their attorney reasoned. How can society possibly discriminate against their love?

Once gay marriage is established, no logical reasons remain to deny a marriage certificate to any other couple or combination of couples. What will prevent someone from marrying his bowling league or his sister's son, her Siamese cat or Raggot the gerbil?

It's going to be tough for me to accept a mixed marriage between my cousin and her Doberman.

Various aggregates like these are already showing up in Christian churches seeking "affirmation" and "inclusion." In 2003, the Episcopal Church ordained its first openly-gay bishop, right in the middle of the Catholic scandal of gay priests abusing alter boys. And the Boy Scouts are condemned for not wanting gay leaders!

Religion is the last major institution of American society to resist the pervasive philosophy of total permissiveness, but it is rapidly crumbling. I doubt it will resist for long. After all, isn't it a Godly thing to be "tolerant" and "open of human natural inclinations to love more?"

First, the church is told to stay out of political matters in order to avoid the church-state compromise. Then it is told to stay out of the morality business, since it shouldn't impose its morals upon the rest of society. Gay rights advocates insist that God has changed His mind. He didn't *really* mean His admonishments against certain behavior. God is no homophobe. Besides, God couldn't have understood modern culture back then.

"You shall not lie with a male as one lies with a female; it is an abomination," (Leviticus 18-22)

"Neither fornicators, nor idolaters, nor adulterers, nor effeminate, nor homosexuals...shall inherit the Kingdom of God." (St. Paul in 1 Corinthians)

Seems clear enough to me. I'm beginning to think Heaven may be a very lightly populated place.

In a novel by Sinclair Lewis, *God's Little Acre*, a bunch of cracker farmers set aside one acre upon which anything produced belonged to God. However, suspecting treasure was buried on the farm, the crackers kept moving God's little acre from place to place to prevent its restricting their ability to mine wherever they pleased. The morality of religion has become God's little acre, to be moved whenever it threatens any kind of restrictions upon man's baser nature.

What else is left once the church, the last bastion of morality, abdicates its responsibility? God's little acre will disappear as the last roadblock to mandatory affirmation of literally any behavior.

SECTION XI
ENVIRONMENT

Home, home on the range,
Where the greens and the bureaucrats play.
Where often is heard a discouraging word,
And the skies grow more cloudy each day.
Updated rendition of an old cowboy croon

CHAPTER THIRTY-ONE

The sky is falling! The sky is falling!

Remember when declining average earth temperatures led us to fret about an approaching *ice age?* Americans were warned all through the 1970s that catastrophe was upon us. Glacier ice would spread south from the Arctic and north from the Antarctic. Armadillos were retreating south from Nebraska. Heating bills would rise. You could snow ski on Miami Beach.

"Earth may be headed for another ice age," direly warned the New York *Times.*

"Intensive Northern hemisphere glaciations...a full-blown 10,000-year ice age," clamored *Science* magazine.

Newsweek joined the clamor with forebodings of "ominous signs (that) the Earth's climate seems to be cooling down... Meteorologists are almost unanimous (that) the trend will reduce agricultural productivity..."

Then, one day, suddenly, almost overnight, it seemed, *global warming* set in and scientists were again "almost unanimous" that Alaska would turn into a desert. Leonardo Di Caprio, being an actor and young esteemed celebrity, which naturally makes him an authority on about everything, led the mantra.

"There is a global emergency going on..." he cried. "The earth is heating up and everyone's future is at risk."

"Climate extremes would trigger meteorological chaos," shrieked Senator George Mitchell. "Raging hurricanes capable of killing millions of people; uncommonly long, record-breaking heat waves; and profound drought that could drive Africa and the Indian subcontinent into mass starvation..."

Al Gore worried that the unusually hot summer of 1988 was the "*Kristallnacht* before the warming holocaust...the most serious threat that we have ever faced...(W)e must act boldly, decisively, comprehensively, and quickly, even before we know every last detail about the crisis..."

The sky is falling! The sky is falling!

Earth experienced greater warming between the 10th and 15th Centuries than it is likely to see within foreseeable generations. Satellite measurements show *no* warming between 1979 and 1996. Although the press and environmentalists constantly report that scientists have reached a consensus that global warming is real, having apparently dismissed a previous consensus that *global cooling* was real, the exact opposite is true among these scientists. There is no such consensus. While it is reported that "scientists agree that failing to respond to the threat (of global warming) could prove disastrous," a survey discovered

179

that 67 percent either disagreed or were uncertain about the proposition. A Gallup survey of climatologists found 82 percent believed global warming was *not* occurring or that there was insufficient evidence to draw that conclusion.

The national media reported that "thousands of scientists" had signed petitions alerting the public to the danger of global warming. Actually, only *ten percent* of the signatories had backgrounds in climate science. Most were environmental activists who had read Al Gore's *Earth In The Lurch*. Among them were landscape architects, a practitioner of traditional Chinese medicine and a gynecologist.

The opinions of those who might question the theory of global warming, said Al Gore, himself a self-declared authority, "should not be given equal weight with the consensus now emerging in the scientific community about the gravity of the danger we face..."

Paying too much attention to doubting Thomases, he went on, "undermines the effort to build a solid base of public support for the difficult actions we must soon take..."

Could it be that much of the pollution we suffer derives from the foggy thinking of our enlightened superiors and their agendas to transform the world?

In George Orwell's prophetic novel, *1984,* his fictional despotic government constantly required an enemy outside the walls to divert the attention of the miserable enslaved citizens within the walls. The government was always at war, and whichever enemy it faced at the moment had *always* been the enemy. History was constantly being rewritten to make it conform to new realities.

Does this not sound hauntingly similar to "global cooling" and "global warming?" A few short years ago, global cooling was the enemy. Now, it's global warming. Great pains are taken to assure us that global warming has *always* been the enemy.

We must be protected from it, our consciousnesses raised. We must heed the environmental colored ribbons worn by our betters and have our awareness lifted. Big Nanny knows what is good for us.

"We have to offer up scary scenarios, make simplified dramatic statements, and make little mention of any doubts we might have..." admitted environmentalist Stephen Schneider. "Each of us has to decide what the right balance is between being effective and being honest."

As in much of political correctness, effectiveness and agenda trump honesty every time. Much of the environmental movement to "save the planet" is made up of the wacky Left, some of whom even advocate that humankind voluntarily go extinct in order to save insects and rodents and reptiles.

"Environmentalists now say that the only way to assure the *complete* recovery of the earth is if all humans are eliminated from the planet—will you join us?" goes a *Bizarro* comic strip by Piraro.

Dark humor like this is amusing precisely because it contains an element of truth. It wouldn't have been funny at all before the environmental movement. There would have been no context for appreciating it. Today, however, when groups *do* advocate such a thing, the cartoon takes on an entirely new, even scary, connotation. Perhaps some family trees deserve extinction because of their stupidity.

Even more ominous than the obvious wackos, however, are those who use the environmentalist movement to further political aims. Of all the politically correct movements in our society, perhaps the environmental one is not only the wackiest but also the most threatening when it comes to human liberty.

"The whole aim of practical politics is to keep the populace alarmed..." observed H.L. Mencken, "and hence clamorous to be led to safety—by menacing it with an endless series of hobgoblins, all of them imaginary."

Paul Johnson, author of *The Quest For God,* described a former Marxist as being undaunted by the intellectual collapse of communism as a system for promoting prosperity combined with equality.

"What we can now turn to are far more attractive and exciting forms of action—race politics, sexual politics, environmental politics, health politics," said the Marxist. "There are other forms of action which will emerge in due course whereby we will transform and overthrow existing society."

CHAPTER THIRTY-TWO

Global warming alarmists (formerly global cooling alarmists) envision a world plagued by catastrophic flooding, war, terrorism, economic dislocations, drought, crop failures, mosquito-borne diseases, tragedy, melting ice caps and growing deserts. Pervasive pessimism about the future is the hallmark of today's environmental orthodoxy. Seldom a day passes that newspaper headlines fail to herald some new environmental crisis lurking over our heads. To these people the sky is always falling. No wonder they always look so uptight.

"One day the story may be about global warming," writes Steven Hayward. "The next it may be about overpopulation, air pollution, resource depletion, species extinction, sea-level rise, nuclear waste, toxic substances in our food and water. Especially jarring is the implication in most of these stories that you and I are the enemy—that our affluent lifestyles are chiefly responsible for upsetting nature's balance; polluting our cities, skies and oceans; and squandering the natural resources that sustain us. Unless we change our thoughtless and wasteful ways, we are reminded, the earth will become a very inhospitable place for ourselves and our progeny... The clear implication of this viewpoint is that the earth was a better place before humans were around to despoil it..."

I agree. When I was growing up, the U.S. had only half the population it has now. I would prefer a land with no fences and few towns where this old Indian could take out across the plains with a few ponies and a few squaws and go wherever the hell I pleased. But that's not the way it is.

On Earth Day each year, events around the country encourage people to restore America to the time before Chris Columbus came over and ruined everything. Never mind that the idea of the Noble Savage living in reverent harmony with his environment before the evil white man came is a load of BS. Pre-Columbian man absolutely ravaged his environment. That's a brutal fact. The average man's existence prior to the modern age may be characterized as brutish and short. Those idiots who suggest otherwise get most of their impressions from an Audubon calendar and wouldn't know a skunk from an alley cat. Ignorance, however, is no impediment to the modern radical environmentalist determined to save the world.

San Francisco, that bastion of enlightenment and progression, warned its residents that they must modify their behavior or the city would no longer be "sustainable." The city's Department of the Environment (Yep, it really has one) drafted a "Sustainability Plan" in which a "sustainable society" was defined as one which meets its needs without sacrificing the ability of future generations and "non-human forms of life" to meet theirs.

The plan reads like a Stalinist five-year plan for managing virtually everything. Food stamp users would be educated to shop at farmers' markets; campaigns would be initiated to put "a fruit tree in every yard;" city-wide quotas would be established on the production of certain vegetable crops; there would be secure bicycle and roller skate storages built at transit stations to reduce the use of internal combustion engines; guests in hotels would be encouraged to have their towels replaced less frequently in order to reduce the use of water in unnecessary laundry; and, naturally, there would be more sex education and self-esteem programs established for youth...

That wasn't all. In order to prevent "environmental degradation and resource depletion that jeopardizes our fragile ecosystems," citizens would be exhorted, urged or ordered to limit the use of such things as scented personal-care products, curtail "everyday activities" such as barbecues and fireplaces, and make "dramatic changes to almost every economic transaction." What that means, simply put, is that the "caring professions" with their regulations and laws would swarm all over the masses who, without proper education and supervision, would carelessly foul the city and the contiguous planet.

Media mogul Ted Turner is typical of the "caring professions" when he smugly announces that it is up to him, and others like him, to *save the world.*

"Most of my time and effort now is going to try to save the human race and make things better for human beings and the other creatures that live on this planet," he said.

It disturbs me when rich, powerful elites, the Enlightened like ole Ted, are going to save the human race. Generally that means somebody is going to get screwed big time. What does their saving the world mean for most of us peasants out here? Alan Carruba, founder and director of the National Anxiety Center, answered the question by listing items we must learn to live without if we follow the dictates and orders of radical environmentalists. It is by no means a complete list, but it provides an idea of where we may be heading:

No more than one child per couple; no disposable diapers; no air conditioning; no automobiles; no motorcycles; no pesticides; no herbicides; no powered lawn mowers; no personal water vehicles; no plastic intravenous bottles; no plastic packaging; no plastic *anything;* no new homes; no perfumes; no air travel; no chlorine; no meat; no fish; no zoos; no rodeos; no circuses; no pets; no hunting; no fishing; no camping; no hiking; no mining; no logging; no oil extractions; no nuclear power; no synthetic fibers; no leather and furs; no...

Ban this, get rid of that. Curtail, regulate, pass a law...

Genetically modified crops to allow farmers to grow more food on less land? No way!

DDT and other pesticides that have virtually eliminated malaria, yellow fever and other plagues? Ban 'em. Besides, they might destroy some endangered variety of mosquito or tick.

Freon essential to millions of air conditioners and refrigerators? Get rid of it, even though freon is a heavy chemical that cannot even reach the ozone.

Chlorine in drinking water? Make a law against it, even though its elimination will likely result in outbreaks of cholera and other infectious diseases.

The wackos' latest enemy is the flush toilet. Larry Warnberg, featured speaker at the first annual international Dry Toilet 2003 Conference in Tampere, Finland, wants to prevent developing nations from going down the drain the flush toilet route. He advocates Solar Composting Advance Toilets (SCATs) which use earthworms to "provide mixing and aeration" and which "need to be emptied at six to twelve month intervals, depending on loading." Folks, we called these "outhouses" when I grew up.

The World Conference on Global Climate Change proposed phasing out the use of diesel fuels, limiting production of some crops, requiring "plowless" agriculture and restricting livestock production and the use of fertilizers.

Wonder who's going to feed all those starving children in China?

Thanks to environmentalists, we now know what is causing the depletion of the ozone layer. It's cow flatulence. That's right. Farting cows. Environmentalists with the vocal support of vegetarians now demand that cattle production be curtailed in order to save the planet. In New Zealand, which signed onto the Kyota Protocol, farmers pay a "flatulence tax" of about $300 per farmer per year to research "lower greenhouse gases" from livestock.

I personally suspect we have more of a gas problem from Washington D.C. than we do from Montana.

Environmental "scientists" recently announced they had discovered the root cause of violent crime. *Dirty water.* That's right. The theory espoused by Dartmouth College's Roger Masters, among others, asserts that polluted water causes brain damage, which then turns ordinary people into violent criminals. The crime problem has been solved: Give our kids bottled water!

Wonder if Roger has been drinking any of that polluted water?

That noted environmentalist Al Gore weighed in on the wacko side when he blithely stated, "The Pacific Yew can be cut down and processed to produce a potent chemical, taxol, which offers some promise of curing certain forms of lung, breast and ovarian cancer in patients who would otherwise die. It seems an easy choice—sacrifice the tree for a human life—until one learns that three trees must be destroyed for each patient treated."

So, Al, grow more trees.

This guy almost became president.

You get the idea. Yep. Let's all go back to Rousseau's "Noble Savage" and live squalid lives both brutish and short. Most of us common men will be stuck in hovels barely eking out our daily bread while the civilization degenerates around us and we grow bitter and angry at our betters. After all, you don't really think *they*, the Enlightened, are going to live like that, do you?

Famed environmentalist Robert F. Kennedy Jr. joined with Walter Cronkite in fighting the installation of off-shore wind farms off Cape Cod. "I love wind energy," he said—*but not in my back yard.*

Let the middle and lower classes conserve. The Enlightened Elites want another vacation home and a jet. Billionaire entertainment exec David Geffen wants to run the public off "his" Malibu public beaches in order to preserve them for...himself and his rich friends.

What has truly gone nutty is our neglect of a reasonable balance between civilization and environment. The balance has shifted to those who have, in effect, gone bonkers and are attempting to coerce the rest of us into following them over the cliff and into the sea. We seem to have lost a base of reality, skewed and distorted our vision to the point that Julie Butterfly trespassing in the top of a tree for two years, crapping off a limb and dropping her litter for others to pick up, has become the ultimate symbol of sensitivity and caring. The weird, the bizarre and the illogical have taken over the environmental movement while the rest of us stand back in bewilderment. Who is going to listen to reason when everyone is running about shouting that the sky is falling?

"You'd probably avoid Don Lundberg on the street," began an article in *Audubon* Magazine. "With a pant leg stuffed in his sock and a black bowler hat perched on his ponytail, he looks like a person who might grab your lapel and warn you of the Second Coming...

"Lundberg's purpose in life is to halt the construction worldwide of all new roads and parking lots... (He) has declared concrete roads to be the enemy of all mankind. 'We think if new roads are stopped, a lot of good things will follow from that,' he says in explaining why he started the Alliance For A Paving Moratorium...

"When you sit down in his cramped storefront office and listen to him talk," *Audubon* concluded, "it's the SUV-driving, forest-chopping, mall-building mainstream that looks nutty..."

Using scare tactics, the politically correct intellectual class knows it can dominate the media and convince the semi-educated to demand and vote for whatever happens to be the ribbon-wearing hustle of the moment. Scaring the pants off 'em works.

"Without the Kyota Agreement," President Bill Clinton warned, "ice caps will melt and huge lowland areas in the United States, including big portions of central Florida, could be completely flooded..."

The people who worry about global warming today are the same ones who preached against global cooling yesterday. Back then, some of them wanted to spread soot over the polar ice caps so they would melt and counteract the cooling. You see, truth doesn't really matter when it comes to the righteous crusade to save the world. Environmentalists and other Enlightened are determined that we unenlightened rabble will follow their plans for Utopia, no matter the cost in human suffering, no matter if it's earth warming or earth cooling or if spotted owls crap all over the White House lawn and timber grows in Brooklyn. People are going to be whipped into line.

Recently, the New York *Times* ran a front page report which stated in alarming terms how open water was found at the North Pole for the first time in 50 million years. It had to retract the story a few days later; the Arctic is ten percent water *every* year and has probably always been that way. The retraction, however, was in a small piece hidden deep inside the paper which hardly anyone noticed. The original story soon became established fact among environmentalists. *Watch out! Watch out! Water at the North Pole proves global warming.*

After much repetition, such items become truth which no one questions and to which everyone responds without the use of intellect. A freshman at Eagle Rock Junior High School won first place at the Greater Idaho Falls Science Fair by showing how susceptible Americans have become to alarmists practicing junk science and spreading fear of everything in our environment.

His project urged people to sign a petition demanding strict control of or total elimination of the chemical "dihydrogen monoxide." It is a dangerous chemical, he pointed out, because: it can cause excessive sweating and vomiting; it is a major component of acid rain; it can cause severe burns in its gaseous state; it contributes to erosion; it decreases the effectiveness of automobile brakes; it is found in the tumors of terminal cancer patients; and accidental inhalation can kill you.

He asked 50 people if they supported the chemical's banning. Forty three said yes, six were undecided, and only one knew the chemical to be banned was—water.

Children are particularly susceptible to propaganda tactics of radical environmentalists who word arguments in such a way that opposing them means you must be *for* dirty water and killing off the spotted owl. Feed the little darlings such crap early and they'll grow up to become Breatherians (eliminate mankind in order to save the planet) or will end up sitting in the tops of tree by the time they're in college.

Saturday morning cartoon villains are now eco-criminals like Dr. Blight who schemes to "take pollution to new heights," or like Sly Sludge who turns national forests into toxic waste dumps. The Teenage Mutant Ninja Turtles have written a book, *ABCs For A Better Planet*, which warns kids against acid rain, promotes "animal rights" and encourages them to become environmental activists.

"Write to your government leaders at every level. Don't buy or use products that hurt the environment. Get your folks and friends to do the same..."

No wonder the little darlings are all becoming paranoid and hyper enough to require Ritalin.

The Green Lobby created the Environmental Media Association which pressures writers and producers into slipping propaganda into movie and TV scripts. You get educated the "proper way" while you're being entertained the "enlightened way." Ain't the Modern Enlightened grand!

In the environmental movement, as in most of the Enlightened crusade, there is an underlying agenda. Home grown activists demonize virtually every area of American civilization with the stated goal of destroying it and replacing it with... Well, they're not quite sure what to replace it with, but whatever it is will be *better.*

"Primary on the list of things environmentalists want banned are corporations and the concept of national sovereignty," warns Alan Carruba.

"On ecological grounds," insists Amherst professor Leo Marx, "the case for world government is beyond argument."

"The immediate source of the ecological crisis is capitalism," added Leftist Murray Bokchin, "which is a cancer in the biosphere. I believe the color of radicalism today is not red (as in communism), but green (as in environmentalism)."

"There is no other single force that has opened up the private sector to the public more than environmental regulations," darkly proclaimed Dr. Richard Allison, professor of environmental management at the University of Houston. "There is no such thing as private industry anymore. It's all public."

When Al Gore was senator, he introduced the World Environment Policy Act of 1989, a blueprint for Big Government to commandeer the global economy for ecological purposes. The bill is still around, waiting for the right moment. When passed in its present form, or slightly modified, it will specifically charge government with the task of intruding into your house, garage, car, work place, medicine cabinet, pantry, or chicken house to dispose of anything environmentalists believe to be harmful to the earth.

Civilization, Gore wrote in his tome *Earth In The Lurch (Earth In The Balance),* is a dysfunctional family... (which requires) wrenching transformation...by new central organization principles."

Now, *that's* scarier than the sky falling.

CHAPTER THIRTY-THREE

Government and environmentalists have lost all patience with us polluters and destroyers of the earth's eco-systems and have teamed up on a mission of mercy to save the world and all its little creatures, leading to bizarre abuses by both government and environmental lawyers. The message is clear when it comes to people, their property rights and individual freedom: Get out of the way or get crushed.

"We hear Mother Earth, and she is crying," wailed former Congresswoman Claudine Schneider.

Take the Endangered Species Act of 1973 which was intended to protect plants and animals in danger of becoming extinct, no matter the economic cost or the species' impact or role in the environment. In other words, some bug almost no one has ever heard about, which literally serves no known purpose and is on its way to extinction anyhow with or without the presence of mankind, a process that has happened thousands of times in the history of the planet, and government will spend millions of tax dollars and move people to save it. Affected citizens have almost no recourse under the law.

Of the millions of species of life on earth, the U.S. government has selected some 1,500 to place on the endangered list for protection—and the list keeps growing. People who kill or harm them face fines of up to $200,000 and a year in jail.

So far, Northern Spotted Owls have curtailed logging in the Pacific Northwest; grizzly bears delayed road building in Montana; an eyeless crustacean smaller than a grain of rice delayed plans for an airport in economically strapped Virginia; San Antonio had to slash its water supply because of the Texas wild rice plant, the Fountain Darter and the San Marcos salamander; an 18,000-acre preserve was set aside around Palm Springs for the fringe-toed lizard; Oregon and Washington may have to remove dams to protect sockeye salmon; Oregon denied waters from dams to farmers in need of irrigation because of a sucker fish...

Homeowners within designated areas of Riverside County, California, faced $10,000 fines and jail time if they cleared brush or created firebreaks *on their own land.* The brush was necessary, environmentalists argued, as habitat for the endangered kangaroo rat. Twenty-nine residents who followed the rules lost their homes when a catastrophic fire swept through 25,000 acres of rat habitat.

It killed the kangaroo rats too.

Elderberry bushes grew up in and around the original levees of the Yuba County Water District in California, weakening them. When the District petitioned the feds to restore levees along the Yuba and Feather Rivers, officials learned the bushes were "protected habitat" for the Valley Longhorn Elderberry Beetle—although *not one* of the bugs had ever been found there.

The federal government forced the water district to construct an 80-acre mitigation site for the non-present beetles ($2 million) and build a large pond near the project for the unseen insects. Local experts complained that the pond weakened the levees. Their warnings went unheeded.

Floods came. The weakened levee failed. Water flooded 500 homes, 9,000 acres of private farmland, displaced 35,000 people and killed three of them.

The Valley Longhorn Elderberry Beetle has still not been seen in the area.

The construction of a needed hospital in San Bernardino, California, was halted because of the Delhi Sands Fly, the first fly ever to land on the federal endangered species list. *Eight* flies located on the construction site were all it took. No one knew if there were *really* eight flies—or if the same fly was counted eight times.

First, the feds ordered construction to cease, then commanded San Bernardino County to spend $220 million to set aside two acres of dune sand for the little fly, each of which lives about two weeks.

That still wasn't enough. Then, the feds drew up maps of proposed corridors linking fly reserves in different cities, hoping the forced purchase of these corridors would provide a "route" connecting "fly reserves." Theoretically, the route would encourage the flies—either eight of them or one counted eight times—to go from place to place and "re-colonize."

The dispute between the hospital builders and the environmentalists continues over eight years later. As for the Delhi Fly, no one can be sure he will stay on the "proposed paths linking the reserves." Perhaps little maps could be issued to them.

The National Center for Public Policy Research publishes an annual *National Directory of Environmental and Regulatory Victims* who have been "hounded by excessive, irrational application of asinine rules promulgated by ivory-tower ideologues against common sense." Here are some recent victims:

Viola Allen, a 72-year-old ailing widow, needed to sell her eight-acre tract of land near Lynnwood, Washington, in order to have enough money to move out of her deteriorating home. For eight years, environmentalist lawsuits prevented her selling it on the grounds that a tiny stream in a ditch going through the property was vital for salmon. Never mind that the creek went completely dry every summer and not a single salmon, lost or otherwise, has been seen in that neighborhood for at least 44 years.

"If salmon are going to get to Tunnel Creek," said the widow, "they would have to sprout legs and walk up there..."

Immigrant Taung Ming-Lin from Taiwan arrived in the United

States in 1997 where he purchased 720 acres of land near Bakersfield, California, on which to grow herbs and vegetables. He got into trouble with the federal government because of his farming. Two dozen state and federal agents in helicopters descended upon the poor man with search warrants, seeking evidence that he "did knowingly take and aid and abet the taking of an endangered species of wildlife, to wit, Tipton kangaroo rats."

The agents tramped his fields taking pictures and looking for animal parts. They seized his tractor and disc as evidence of the crime and threatened to arrest him and fine him $300,000.

"It's just incredible," exclaimed his lawyer. "You see this sort of thing and you think: This can't be America. It has to be some other country."

It's America all right, in the New Sensitive Age.

Michael Rowe of Winchester, California, had the same rat problem. When he applied for a building permit to construct a home on his twenty acres, he was informed he couldn't build because his land was part of a kangaroo rat study area. He would have to shell out $5,000 to survey his property for the rats. He was out of luck for a new home if even a single rodent were found.

If no rats were found, he would be permitted to develop— providing he paid the government a "mitigation fee" totaling nearly $40,000 to buy land elsewhere for a rat preserve. When I was a cop, we called schemes like that *extortion*. You got your butt thrown in jail for it.

The most famous example of government abuse started in 1994 when the Democratic Party chairman of Piatt County, South Carolina, asked Peg Bargon to make a dream catcher for Hillary Clinton when she visited the area. A "dream catcher" is an Indian craft constructed of a circle of boughs, woven string and feathers. That was when Mrs. Bargon's troubles began.

Federal agents raided her house and arrested her for illegally possessing a single eagle feather used in the making of Hillary's present. Her five-year-old son had picked it off the ground at the local zoo. Peg lost her job and spent $10,000 in legal fees before finally pleading guilty to a federal felony. She was fined $1,250 and placed on probation.

Government abuse, ineptness and stupidity. An editorial in *The Wall Street Journal* said the Federal Environmental Agency was worthy of an "Award for Environmental Lunacy." People encouraged by the FEA installed $10,000 "odorless outhouses" in national forests which were supposed to use solar power to vent out smelly air—and built them *in the shade.* These same people used the wrath of the federal bureaucracy to punish anyone caught howling back at the wolves in Alaska's Denali National Park with the justification that "interaction in the park should be spontaneous."

When Boy Scout Robert Graham, 14, got lost while hiking in New Mexico's Pecos Wilderness, the U.S. Forest Service refused to allow a helicopter to land and pick him up when he was found. That would violate the Wilderness Act. Robert spent another 26 hours alone in the elements after having already survived two days.

However, a short time previously, the same U.S. Forest Service promptly let a helicopter land in Idaho's Frank Church River of No Return Wilderness to recover an injured gray wolf.

In rural New York, a 72-year-old man beat a timber rattler senseless with his cane after it bit him. The snake later died—get this!--on the *operating table.* The old man was accused of killing a member of an endangered species and threatened with a $1,000 fine. I'm not making this up.

Michigan environmental officials reacted to reports of dams on Spring Pond by firing a cease-and-desist letter to the property owner. "It has come to the attention of the Department of Environmental Quality that there has been recent unauthorized activity on the above referenced pieces of property... A permit must be issued prior to the start of this type of activity..."

The property owner possessed a sense of humor. He fired a letter back. "Are you trying to discriminate against my Spring Pond beavers or do you require all dam beavers throughout this state to conform to said dam request?"

"They have taken our land," protested Mrs. Beth Morian of Texas after Federal Fish & Wildlife froze all development on her Davenport Ranch to protect a small bird called the black-capped vireo. "We want to see species preserved, but people should have a place too."

I predict there will come a day in the foreseeable future when government will lock all wildlands away from any form of human contact. People will have their own place all right—stuffed into grimy, crowded cities. Kangaroo rats, three-toed lizards and Delhi sand flies will roam the forests, deserts and plains. No one will ever see them, but won't it be satisfying to just *know* they're out there? That should be enough to make us feel awfully good about ourselves.

Home, home on the range,
Where the greens and the bureaucrats play;
Where often is heard a discouraging word,
And the skies grow more cloudy each day...

SECTION XII
ANIMAL RIGHTS

"A rat is a pig is a dog is a boy."
PETA's National Director

CHAPTER THIRTY-FOUR

PETA (People for The Ethical Treatment of Animals) is only one more example that this nation is truly coming unglued at the core. It holds that meat eating is "holocaust on your plate," that, as PETA founder Ingrid Newkirk bleated, "six million people died in concentration camps, but six *billion* broiler chickens will die in slaughterhouses this year." This woman is *serious.* You have to be mentally ill to equate the life of Anne Frank with that of a chicken on its way to see Colonel Sanders.

Newkirk further maintained that "if I had more guts, I'd light a match" to animal research laboratories.

PETA's Bruce Friedrick added, "It would be great if all the fast food outlets, slaughterhouses, laboratories and the banks that fund them exploded tomorrow... Hallelujah to the people who are willing to do that."

Animal Liberation Front (ALF) and Earth Liberation Front (ELF), to which PETA donates tax exempt funds, are home-grown eco-terrorists willing to shout "Hallelujah" and go out and bomb things to end *speciesism.* In February 2002, FBI counter-terrorism chief James Jarboe told a House Committee that ALF/ELF had committed more than 600 criminal acts in the U.S. since 1996. Examples of some of these acts include: arson that destroyed luxury homes under construction in San Diego, during which terrorists left a banner proclaiming "Stop Razing Nature. The ELFs are angry;" and an August 2002 fire-bombing of a U.S. Forest Service Research Center in Pennsylvania, followed by a chilling ELF communiqué stating that "while innocent life will never be harmed in any action we undertake, where it is necessary we will no longer hesitate to pick up the gun to implement justice."

According to these people—and their numbers are growing—*speciesism* is equivalent to *racism, sexism, look-ism, homophobia-ism; able-ism* and all the other *isms* designating protected classes in a society so chock full of victims that you actually need a score card to tell who's who. Their goal is "total animal liberation." Animals will not be "exploited" in any form by humans. No meat, no milk and cheese, no woolen underwear, no seeing eye dogs, no pampered poodles, no horses... You get the point.

How *dare* a human think he is superior to or better than a shrimp or a tick or garter snake. The mere thought is enough to make PETA-philes cry out over the pain they feel for our "non-human brethren." They dream of that Utopian day when all animals and plant life have social and legal rights equal to mankind. No lab rats in cages, no zoos, no more chickens in every pot, and no "non-human companions" unless the dog agrees to it. All life to the zealots of the Animal Rights movement is equivalent. After all, as PETA contends, "a rat is a pig is a dog is a boy."

"The life of an ant and that of my child should be granted equal consideration," opined Michael W. Fox, Vice President of the Humane Society of the United States.

In writing about a five-year-old boy who had had open-heart surgery, Dr. Jerry Vlasak said the child's life was "no more or less important than any other animal's life, no matter how much (the father's) emotions tell him otherwise."

If you'll pardon the *speciesist* expression, motorists on an interstate through Florida went ape when they spotted a cow standing knee deep in water in a marshy field. Dozens of frantic people called the Florida Highway Patrol to report an animal about to drown. Now, we farm boys who grow up knowing the difference between bullshit and a straw hat understand that cattle wade into water to cool off and escape heel flies. That so many people lost their minds over this bovine seeking relief illustrates how far humankind has distanced itself from our roots and demonstrates why animal righters have gone so goofy.

Columnist Michael Sasser, my son, points out that most of them are city folks who hardly know one end of Bambi from the other. They are three or four generations removed from calloused hands and red sun burnt necks. Sentimentality and ignorance is common currency for those whose major interaction with animals is through a petting zoo or Discovery Channel. They think the talking animals on cartoon shows and anthropomorphic movies such as *Babe* the talking pig are real.

As a rancher, I breed, rear, train and use horses. I have a lot more respect and regard for a good honest roping mount than I have for many people. One of my beautiful yearlings broke his leg. It could not be repaired. I broke down and cried when I had to shoot him.

I like all animals, but I know the difference between humans and animals and accept their ranking on the value scale. If I had to make a choice between my horses, much as I love them, and my wife or children or grandchildren or friends, guess which will have to go? We have an ethical obligation to treat animals humanely; we do not have any sort of obligation to assure them "equal rights."

Still, being sensitive and caring and nonjudgmental, we are expected to go along with all the goofiness of the animals rights movement and accept a fool's paradise as the real world. We are being compelled, shamed and coerced into changing our view of the world to include the delusions, fantasies and madness of asylum inmates turned loose among and on us.

Spot, be a good doggie and go fetch my newspaper. That's unlikely to happen much longer. That's *slavery, speciesism.* An adjunct law professor at Harvard Law School, Steven Wise, said his goal was to

"break down...the legal wall of separation between animals and man..."
Sound absurd? It wasn't that long ago that federal protection for fat people and victims of "look-ism" seemed equally absurd.

CHAPTER THIRTY-FIVE

Do they put something in the water out there in San Francisco?

One night, as on any other, there were a number of shootings, stabbings, beatings, rapes and the like in the city. But one particularly heinous crime got everyone worked up more than all the others. Street sweeper Jack McGann discovered the first little corpse near Union Square.

"At first I thought it was shot," he explained to sensitive San Francisco cops. "But then I found the other three, and that many dead pigeons pointed to poison."

Fifteen more murdered pigeons indicated a mass homicide.

"One of my officers saw one pigeon literally fall from the sky," lamented Captain Vicky Guldbech of the Department of Animal Care and Control.

Police launched a full-scale investigation. More cops showed up at the pigeon crime scene than normally attended a human homicide. Out of respect for the deceased, small shrouds were placed over the remains. Authorities promised to get to the bottom of this heinous felony and prosecute the culprit or culprits to the full extent of the law. I wouldn't have wanted to be found in San Francisco that dark day with a pigeon feather stuck in my Stetson.

God bless America. As the comedian Yakoff is always saying, "Only in America..."

Bill Maher, host of ABC's "Politically Incorrect," which wasn't, declared that actor Christopher Reeve deserved what he got when he was paralyzed in a horse riding accident.

"I took it as animal abuse," he said. "Most people go, 'Are you kidding? Horseback riding is horseback riding.' Well, you know, at one point people said the same thing about slavery... If you try to make a horse jump over something that it doesn't want to jump over, I think it really should throw you off its back."

While you might assume that the Left with all its zany antics and posturing would be loaded with fun and humor, it simply ain't so. Even when the Enlightened Ones are at their most ridiculous, as in investigating the murder of a pigeon, they are totally serious—zealots on a solemn mission to "make a difference" and "change the world." Sometimes it's hard to believe they can't *not* be spoofing us all. Take, for example, the Fuzzines.

The Fuzzines are an animal rights subculture that dresses up like animals. They *really* believe they are cheetahs or dogs or rats or whatever trapped in human form, born that way, like homosexuals, waiting for the day when science makes trans-species operations possible. We have "gender choice," so why not "species choice."

A schism recently developed in the happy veldt of the Fuzzines that set the fur to flying. The Fuzzines went at each other fang and claw, so to speak. It started when the Reform Fuzzines broke away from the Orthodox Fuzzines. The Orthodox wear full-body "fursuits" of their totem animals. The heretic Reforms began wearing only face wear and carrying the stuffed animals of their choice. The Orthodox were outraged.

I know such wackiness is hard to believe, but, I'm really not making this up. This is all grave business to a lot of folks out there in Looneyville.

Take the matter of Socks, the former Clinton First Cat at the White House.

A Seattle group calling itself "Cacophony" attributed magical powers to the Enlightened Tabby. Members handed out a brochure assuring prospective converts that "Socks, the First Feline, is a powerful wonderworker who gave her owners the White house, and is still granting wishes to those who petition him in writing."

I wondered how Bill Clinton ever became president. Perhaps Al Gore should have petitioned ole Socks before he started his presidential campaign.

During his tenure in Washington, Socks received more mail than most senators—more than 200 letters a day. He got so much mail he was assigned his own zip code. He even had a fan club to handle the correspondence and publish his fan club letter. Paid for with tax money, naturally. Letters began with, "Dear Socks...when you read this..."

Apparently, Socks can read, which is a step ahead of forty percent of America's public school fourth graders.

This only illustrates the delusional and fanciful way so many of these poor wackos view animals, insects, reptiles, and birds. In their minds, animals and people truly are the same thing.

"Do you know what shams those smiling chicken pictures in supermarkets are?" a letter published in PETA's *Newsletter* began. "More than four billion chickens in America each year do not have a single happy moment in their lives. They go immediately from shell to hell. I know chickens are capable of happiness because of a little tan and yellow hen named Butterscotch. When I visit her farm, she runs down the path to me and makes little hops up and down at my feet until I pick her up. Then she snuggles into my arms, contented as any cat I've ever held... She has taught me that chickens are sensitive individuals with their own special intelligence..."

Sensitive? Special intelligence? Spare me the sentimentality. It's a chicken.

A friend of mine, Les Cobb, is a big game hunting guide in Alaska. The Bambi attitude that has swept the Lower Forty Eight has reached into the tundra and glaciers and forests of this wild land. Hunting is an evil that must be eliminated as quickly as possible.

Les was present, along with other big game guides, at a meeting in which the Federal Game Department dispatched a woman wildlife biologist to listen to guides' complaints that wolves were decimating caribou and moose herds. The biologist was the typical liberal New Englander morally opposed to all hunting; mostly she was outraged at the concept that anyone should find pleasure in the pursuit. She declared the wolves should not be hunted to control their population. A process known as *immunocontraception* should be utilized instead. Immunocontraception was developed to control the deer population— and didn't work with deer any more than it would work with wolves.

Deer in certain areas had caused so many problems that, rather than allow them to be hunted, animal righters wanted to control them through experimental technology. The idea was that females could be shot with a tranquilizer dart and given a contraception. They could then be darted again a few weeks later and then every year thereafter to keep them sterile. Obviously, these people have never hunted deer.

Les listened in astonishment to the lady's proposal to sterilize wolves. He clambered to his feet, a big rough man with a direct action mentality and little tolerance for absurdities.

"Lady," he rumbled, "them wolves are *eating* them caribou, not *fucking* them."

Such nuances, of course, go unrecognized in the world of animal rights, where the real goal is as much political as it is humanitarian and idealistic. Underlying the movement, beneath the wacky surface of pigeon investigations, "fursuits," and sensitive chickens lurks the true agenda of "reformers" bent on molding a New World in their own image.

"In the academic world," announced a member of Rutgers' Federalist Society, "especially in law school, it's better to be a Marxist than a Republican. The problem with Marxism, of course, is that it never took place in the First World, where it was intended to take place. It failed in the Second World, and it has been and is increasingly being rejected in the Third World. So all that's really left is the animal kingdom."

God help the animal kingdom—the Marxists of the future.

CHAPTER THIRTY-SIX

"Raised awareness" and law compose the two attack fronts of the animal "equal rights" movement, both of which are designed to weaken our values and common sense and replace them with a new Enlightened consciousness. Law steps in for the knockout punch once common sense is on the ropes.

PETA is the largest of the animal rights groups with 700,000 delusional members and a pot full of deep-pocket celebrities who raise nearly $20 million annually for the cause. The target of all this money and power is the gullible, the naïve and the young.

"There is an animal holocaust going on!" activists cry as they show up almost everywhere to protest in their animal suits and naiveté.

They demanded the town of Fishkill, New York, change its name because it incited cruelty to fish. Fish, said a protestor, are our brothers and sisters. Hooking one is the moral equivalent of gaffing your grandmother.

What?

"While fish do not express pain and suffering in ways that humans easily recognize," preached another, "they do gasp and struggle when caught. Moreover, fish have been known to go out of their way, and even risk their lives, to aid others in trouble."

Knock, knock! Fish *eat* fish, even their own grandmothers.

"Fish have individual personalities, too. They talk to each other, form bonds, and sometimes grieve when their companions die... Fish also enjoy companionship and develop special relationships with each other. And since they enjoy tactile stimulation, they often gently rub against each other."

Only rednecks and those with unraised consciousnesses would dare question such truths.

"Tree hugging is fine—as long as you don't interfere with hunting and fishing," declared Debra Dean, the unenlightened host of TV's "The Honey Hole" fishing show. "If you (interfere) in Texas, the fishermen will call the game warden to arrest the protestors, after they beat the hell out of them."

What a Neanderthal attitude. Long live Texas!

For animal righters, the "Oscar Mayer Weinermobile" is a personification of all evil. They follow it around wherever it goes, picketing and chanting, wearing placards and scaring small children. The Weinermobile, explained PETA's Bruce Friedrick, "is very, very fun (for children). Which is why it's so insidious. It's selling the idea that eating hot dogs is fun. When in fact it is a violent, bloody business."

Since children—along with the perpetually childlike—are particularly susceptible to PETA-phile propaganda, eco-radicals concentrate much of their efforts on converting the young. The younger the better, as with sex education, environmentalism and all the other canons of the Leftist faith.

PETA goes on periodic McDonald's "Unhappy Meals" tours to distribute colorfully-illustrated lunch boxes to kids at schools and on playgrounds. The illustrations show anthropomorphic chickens and pigs being prepared for slaughter.

The organization's "Save Our Schools" program features Gil the Fish and Larry the Lobster preaching against "the unnecessary torture of fish... (and) the cruelty of fishing."

It's working. The majority of American children are so removed from nature that most of their impressions about it come from cartoon shows.

"Can't we just pass a law against fishing?" asked one student.

This kid will grow up to be a liberal.

Animal righters demand Wyoming change its license plate featuring the silhouette of a cowboy riding a bucking bronco, because the symbol "promotes and glorifies" abuse of animals. They demand the use of fur be outlawed. They demand pets be granted special considerations in domestic violence situations to "reduce the risk for women *and their pets...*" They demand...

When demands and propaganda fail to work, or to work fast enough, the impassioned resort to other means of "consciousness raising."

Eco-terrorists periodically break onto fur farms to release minks from their cages. They bomb cooperatives producing or selling mink feed. Although most of the little critters when released die of exposure and from fighting each other, the Animal Liberation Front declared the releasing of the minks "an act of love... Even if some of them died, at least they had a shot at freedom."

Courts commonly treat such extremist criminals with consideration and leniency. After all, their "hearts are in the right place." Legal activists build upon this attitude to bring the force of law behind the movement. Eventually, we will all be compelled to go along. These people never give up. They are on a crusade for goodness against evil. And, naturally, lawyers are eager to cash in on the latest anti-something crusade, whether it be against asbestos, tobacco, fat foods, guns, or keeping animals as pets.

Boulder, Colorado, and San Francisco are removing all references to "pet owner" from municipal ordinances and replacing them with "pet guardian." The term "guardian," said Elliot Katz, president of In Defense Of Animals, is more "sensitive" to animals. Besides, pet *ownership* implies that humans are superior to animals, which everyone with an Enlightened consciousness knows is not true.

San Francisco's Commission of Animal Control and Welfare voted to ban calf roping and steer wrestling at future rodeos because the live-stock "are not willing participants..."

Talk show host Bob Barker and other animal activists wanted Congress to enact a law against using elephants in traveling shows such as circuses...

Bruce Friedrick, spokesman for PETA, promised it would soon be "illegal to eat meat..."

Pending legislation in Pennsylvania would make it a crime to leave a pet alone in a car while the "guardian" is out of sight...

"Animal law" is a specialty now taught at the "best" law schools. A fat "Animal Legal Defense Fund" has been established to promote proper animal rights campaigns through the courts. A scholarly journal on the subject is published. Law firms dedicate themselves to this latest cultivation of "rights."

Professor Gary Francione, head of the Rutgers University Animal Rights Law Center, argues that animals are rights holders and morally equivalent to humans. Any use of them for food, clothing, medical research, or even as pets is an unconscionable violation of their rights.

"The reality is that we progressives like to think that we have eschewed all vestiges of slavery from our lives, but the reality is that we are all slave owners," is how he puts it. "The plantation is the earth, sown with the seeds of greed, and the slaves are our nonhuman sisters and brothers."

In stumping for a new and glorious era of animal legal rights, lawyers fuel the litigation explosion and further embolden Left Wingers to infringe upon the liberties of humans. Absurd as it may seem, animal lawyers and others of the ilk are succeeding in instilling within Americans feelings of guilt and reservations about the use of animals. They are even convincing courts to award animals quasi-human status.

At "doggie death row trials" involving certifiably vicious dogs, "character witnesses" and animal behaviorists are allowed to testify on the defendants' behalf... "Canine rage" is now a legal defense; there is no such thing as a bad dog, only a good dog having a bad hair day...

Dogs who bite small children are afflicted with "interspecies dyslexia." In other words, they can't tell a child from another dog...

Bring on the race card. Laws against pit bulls could exacerbate the dog's "antisocial tendencies." It's "canine racism" to discriminate among the breeds...

It's not the dog's fault if it commits a crime, it's society's fault. The New York Supreme Court ordered an Akita dog that mauled a two-year-old child to undergo psychiatric evaluation...

Where have we heard all this psychobabble before? Psychobabble for animals reflects the psychobabble in society at large.

"We're pushing the envelope until we can press a case in which the animal is the plaintiff," said Joyce Tischler of the Animal Legal Defense Fund.

"A great ape will appear in the courtroom," New York *Times* reporter William Globerson predicted. "A lawsuit, perhaps protesting the ape's life behind bars, will have been filed in the animal's name. The ape will then testify in sign language or using a voice synthesizer to support the claim that, contrary to centuries of law, it has legal rights, including a fundamental right to liberty... (A) growing group of lawyers and legal academics say they are plotting strategies to bring such a suit, perhaps within a decade."

I can hardly wait to see a rat testify in the ape's behalf, followed by a bright lobster expounding academically on its life of suffering in human-imposed poverty. Certainly, Congress will have to enact a civil rights law protecting animals from *speciesist* discrimination and providing them legal remedies through the courts. Perhaps an affirmative action program? How about reparations for past sins committed against their ancestors.

Are all these people smoking something?

Speciesism is the Left's newest victim group added to the trinity of racism, classism and sexism. What you have to understand is that "animal rights" is not a movement in itself separated from all the other "progressive" campaigns. The ultimate goal of everything from radical feminism and arts and culture to gay issues, the environment, animal rights and all the other "causes" is to destroy capitalism and democracy in America and replace them with an Enlightened socialism of the state. It is a dream not unlike that of Stalin or Hitler. All you have to do is listen. These people are not shy about expressing their ultimate aims.

"Rejecting speciesism," Gary Francione continued, "requires the rejection of the exploitation of all who are oppressed under capitalism... This country and other industrial countries are deeply dependent on animal exploitation to sustain their present economic structures... To the extent that you associate personal freedom with things like health care and education, one might say that maybe Cuba is a more free place..."

Bring ole Karl back out of his grave and dust off his Marx.

Ironically enough, the more society comes to value animals, the less it seems to value humans.

In Norman, Oklahoma, an animal sanctuary offered a $200 reward for the apprehension of kids responsible for severing a bullfrog's left foot. While the amphibian was being lovingly treated at Wild Care Foundation, an abortion clinic not far away was being paid by government to perform late term abortions. Viable fetuses, *live* children, were being killed inside their wombs.

Tell me where I'm wrong in seeing this as a serious twist of ethical priorities.

"It is wrong to assume that fetuses have rights just because some animals do," declared an internet site that promotes both abortion on demand and animals rights.

Peter Singer, professor of Bioethics at Princeton University and considered the founder of the animal rights movement, has elevated abortion to its next ultimate level. He claims infants have no moral right to live and looks upon infanticide as an ethical act. Seriously ill or afflicted people should also be killed if it will enhance the happiness of family and society.

Here is the way his reasoning progresses: "Personhood" does not necessarily mean human, nor is a human necessarily a "person." "Personhood" includes all mammals—dogs, cats, ferrets, mice... All "persons" have equal rights—a rat is a pig is a dog is a boy—and all "persons" have greater rights than "nonpersons."

Are you following this?

Infants, even if healthy, are among those humans who are not "persons" because they are not yet self aware over time and lack the ability to reason. They are "non-persons," along with other such human "non-persons" as those suffering from cognitive disabilities like Alzheimer's disease. As "non-persons," they retain no more moral status than other forms of life Singer labels as "non-persons"—human embryos, fetuses, fish, snake eggs and, presumably, conservatives.

"It is difficult to see the point of keeping such human beings alive," Singer maintains, if by their continuing to live they will cause "unhappiness" to their parents and others and if "their life, in the whole, is miserable."

I am much less concerned about the rights of animals than I am about maintaining sanity in a world going insane.

SECTION XIII
PROPERTY

"A welfare recipient has a greater property interest in her welfare check than a homeowner has in protection of her real property."
Clint Bolick, Institute for Justice

CHAPTER THIRTY-SEVEN

My stepdad grew up during the Great Depression. His family were "Okies" like those John Steinbeck wrote about in *The Grapes Of Wrath*. They lost their Dust Bowl farms and many of them made the torturous trek to California looking for work. Few of them found it.

The experience severely marred my dad. Forever afterwards, he was terrified of any government contact. He actually trembled in fear if stopped by a traffic cop. He wouldn't even walk into a courthouse if he could help it. He refused to own property because he was afraid of losing it, suspicious of the "guv'ment comin' out an' takin'" it when they want to." Because of dad's fears, my brothers and I were reared as gypsies, like migrant workers following the crop harvests. We never had a real home. We lived in a dirt-floored former chicken house, a converted barn, a log cabin, rental shacks abandoned on other folks' property.

It was difficult to understand him when I was a kid. Today, however, much as I hate to admit it, I'm beginning to experience the same kind of fear. I have come to the startling realization that everything I own is subject to the approval and benevolence of government. Through its various agencies, government has the option to control or to actually seize on one pretext or another anything I own.

No citizen has the right to the use of his own land if a government inspector discovers a wet area on it, no right to the cash in his bank account if an IRS agent decides he might have dodged taxes, no right to his building if it becomes a "historical site," no right to build his home if zoning regulations forbid it, or if a bald eagle has built a nest there, or if the government wants the land in the "public interest..."

"A welfare recipient has a greater property interest in her welfare check," said Clint Bolick of the Institute for Justice, "than a homeowner has in protection of her real property."

My wife and I were going to build a new home on our ranch. There are no other houses nearby. Nonetheless, we had to *pay* to get a building permit from County Planning. That was also when I learned I had to have *permission* from government if I wanted to build a barn, a chicken house or a swimming pool. I had to beg for *permission* to make any kind of improvement to my own property.

Do I own it or not? I asked.

Well, yes.

But government is the final authority on how I can use it?

Yes, again.

Then I don't *really* own it. Property becomes meaningless if government admits you hold title to a property but at the same time forbids you to live on it, improve it, sell it or transform it. Once the right to acquire, hold or dispose of property becomes conditional, so does everything else that constitutes America's core. Property and liberty are inseparable. As Balint Vazsonyi pointed out in *America's 30 Years War*, those societies that indulge in the large-scale "legal" taking of lives start by taking property through government action.

I was a cop for fourteen years. I was in the military, active and reserve, for 29 years. I believe in America, in patriotism, in personal liberty and in personal responsibility; that used to be called liberalism. I am also, now, scared to death of my own government. Of the control it has assumed over my life and property.

I received a letter from the Internal Revenue Service, that most dreaded missile any of us who are self employed can receive. I was being audited. *You are summoned...*it began. I am *summoned?* Am I a citizen or am I a subject to be summoned to the castle at the king's pleasure?

I appeared at the castle with trepidation in my heart, although I knew I had nothing to hide. Intimidation is the name of the game. Keep the masses scared and they'll keep coughing up the dough. Government wanted to know every aspect of my life.

How do you live? Do you have a safe deposit box at the bank? What do you keep in it? Do you keep any cash? What kind of car do you drive...?

I felt guilty of *something*, even though I knew I wasn't. It was up to me to *prove my innocence*, not to the IRS to *prove my guilt*. I realized at that chilling moment that anything I possessed had to meet the approval of government—or government could take it away from me.

That was scary.

In this Brave New World infested by the indulged, the delusional, the sensitive, the Enlightened and the downright demented, property has become the most useful method in the struggle to transform society. Envy, class warfare and resentment have attached stigma to property of every kind, including education and personal accomplishment. The noble pursuit of "social justice" has deemed that if you possess more than your neighbor, then you must have acquired it unfairly or won it illegally in "life's lottery."

CHAPTER THIRTY-EIGHT

The concept of private property has been so narrowed that government no longer considers taking it a violation of a person's rights unless he is physically ejected from his land. Government automatically assumes it has the right—and it certainly has the power—to control anything in which the community can be perceived to have even a vague interest. Bureaucrats assume frightening and discretionary power over ordinary citizens.

"The *public interest* in the use of *private land* must be defended," asserted Arnold Berke, editor of *Historic Preservation.*

Ronald Angelocci in Michigan dumped several truckloads of soil on his back yard because a family member had acute asthma and plants growing there exacerbated it. The Army Corps of Engineers had him *jailed* for violating the Clean Water Act.

John Taylor, 80, of Mt. Vernon, Washington, was at first denied a permit to build a small modular home on his lot because the U.S. Fish & Wildlife Service claimed it would harm a bald eagle's nest located 90 feet away. Fish & Wildlife finally relented, but only if Mr. Taylor agreed to comply with certain terms. He must contribute money to a salmon restoration project because eagles eat salmon; he must build two eagle platforms; he must donate money to a bald eagle exhibit. Finally, he would not be permitted to mow his lawn or allow children to play on it between the months of November and July when the eagles were nesting.

Is it necessary to mention that Mr. Taylor *owned* the property?

Reasoning such as this and the resulting attacks on private ownership of property have become pervasive throughout government, especially among Enlightened politicians. Take, for example, Howard Dean, governor of Vermont and a Democratic presidential candidate in 2004. He left the Episcopalian church, he said, because the Episcopalians had too much respect for private property rights.

"Dean himself made a decision about religion in the early 1980s," reported the Boston *Globe,* "opting to leave the local Episcopal Church when it sided with landowners seeking to preserve private property in lieu of a bike path in Burlington." Dean told the *Globe* he didn't think opposing the bike path "was very Godlike" and thought it was "hypocritical of me to be a member of such an institution."

Undoubtedly, granted the power, he would have seized private property for the better benefit of bike riders.

Congress recently extended federal control of property by banning billboards within the "limit of vision" of certain U.S. highways. Not only that, but farmers were also told they could not have their farm machinery and equipment parked within sight of passing motorists.

211

Fuel storage tanks would have to be moved "so as not to be unsightly to highway users."

Isn't it typical of the Wacky Left that anyone who objects to such high handedness is branded an *extremist*? I'm an *extremist* if I don't want hikers, bikers and campers trodding across my ranch? I'm an *extremist* if I choose to sell a portion of my land for a profit rather than donating it to the Gay Youth Bird Watchers Association? It must be because I'm simply not "socially aware."

Law is stuffed with technicalities that permit cunning lawyers to do whatever government wants done to you. Government can take your property while saying it really isn't.

Lorna LeBlanc of Rochester, New York, sought to supplement her income by investing in a small rental property. The single mother of two closed on the property before discovering that the previous owner had been forced to rent to a low-income Section 8 tenant. She was now expected to accept $31 a month rent for property whose expenses alone totaled more than $400 a month. The Rochester Housing Authority prohibited her from either ejecting the government-subsidized tenant or demanding more rent. She was stuck with supporting her renter. Charity by decree.

The New Jersey Meadowlands Commission forbade the owner of twelve prime acres of real estate from developing it, thereby reducing the land's value to almost nothing. The owner sued to reclaim his property. He lost. Officials successfully argued that since the landowner was receiving $13 a year as rent from a billboard, the land was still "economically productive." Thus, government had not violated the owner's rights.

What kind of goofy reasoning is that? You don't really *own* your land.

In Issaquah, Washington, David Kelly, who had two kids in Little League, decided to build a baseball field on a 28-acre horse pasture owned by his mother. City inspectors shut the field down as soon as it was built, claiming it was illegal. Why?

First, Tibbetts Creek which ran through the property was a government-designated flood plain; the baseball field jeopardized salmon in the creek. Secondly, the baseball diamond constituted a public park which must therefore meet safety and traffic standards. To meet these standards, the City Council wanted Kelly to pay for various reviews and permits which would cost up to $5,000. Kelly refused to pay. The park remains closed.

"This is a matter of one individual who didn't like being told what to do," City Councilman Bill Conley scolded.

Imagine that!

In today's climate, if you own *anything*, certainly if you work harder and own more than your shiftless neighbor, you are automatically suspected of having interests that run counter to the greater social good of the community. You are not being the new "Soviet Man." You are against *equality.* You probably earned your possessions anyhow by working too hard.

A friend of mine owned an 80-acre pastureland near Tulsa, Oklahoma, upon which existed a small lowlands that held water during the wet times of the year. *Shazam!* A wetlands! The federal government refused to allow her to build on the land, to farm it, or even to run cattle on it. In essence, government took it over. The only right she had left was to walk around and look at the "wetlands." And, oh, yes. She still had the right to pay taxes on it.

Land you cannot use is not yours. If she had attempted to use it anyhow, she would have been prosecuted as a dastardly eco-criminal, much more dangerous than some scumbag who mugs you on the street. The scumbag is a scumbag only because of his deprived social environment. The eco-criminal is such because of *greed.*

Have you noticed how criminals on TV and the movies are increasingly of the environmental type instead of killers and robbers. Big corporations and the "evil rich" are being depicted as eco-criminals who deliberately pollute the planet at the expense of all us little helpless people. Laws are being championed throughout the United States that would allow confiscation of the assets of corporations that violate environmental law.

"Environmental crime is no less a crime than theft and blackmail," declared William Reilly, when he was chief administrator of the Environmental Protection Agency. "And more and more assuredly, if you do the crime you'll do the time."

Florida builder Ocie Miller and his son learned that the hard way when they were sent to prison for two years each for placing clean sand on a quarter-acre lot they owned. Burglars seldom get that much time.

Within cities, suburbs and development tracts, a citizen's use of his own property is presumed illegal until approved by multiple zoning and planning commissions. Zoning laws restrict and, in certain instances, even prohibit the use of private property, all in the "public interest." The righteous despotism of the New Enlightened rises its head everywhere to administer and regulate citizens and their property.

Floosmore, Illinois, banned pickup trucks from its streets, even from private driveways. Coral Gables, Florida, requires Spanish tile roofs on children's playhouses in back yards. Malibu, California, enacted a zoning code that requires nonconforming houses to be torn down in twenty years. In Los Angeles, which prohibits home-based businesses in residential neighborhoods, even freelance writers and artists are legally prohibited from working in their own homes. A woman in Laguna Beach, California, was prosecuted for building her picket fence six inches too high, while not far away a family could not move into a new home because the house had been painted the wrong shade of white. Pasadena, California, proposed banning residents from having weeds in their yards.

Nothing is more amazing than the capacity of people to attempt to regulate and govern their neighbors. That capacity is multiplied tenfold when the attempt is made in the name of "social justice" and "community interest."

In addition to the thousands of *Catch-22* laws and regulations by which the use of your property can be restricted and regulated, federal agents can now seize private property under more than 200 different statutes. Fish and wildlife violations, environmental concerns, suspected criminal activity, zoning regulations, historic confiscations, wetlands, eminent domain, taxes... These are only a few of the excuses by which government can confiscate private property.

Within the last ten years, for various purposes involving taxes, the Internal Revenue Service has seized over twelve *million* bank accounts and pay checks, placed liens on the homes and property of over three million people, directly confiscated more than 100,000 houses, cars and other items of property, imposed over 100 million penalties on people for late payments or allegedly paying insufficient taxes, and audited roughly fifteen million American families and businesses with the designed intent to pressure people into paying more taxes than they actually owed.

Summoned is the right word for when the IRS calls you to its office to be further fleeced, bled and extorted—and the money then sent to Washington to be redistributed by the Enlightened.

Government is greedy. Don't steal... The Government hates competition.

Former White House Chief of Staff Leon Panetta (under Bill Clinton) endorsed a scheme in 1995 to separate Charles Hurwitz in Texas from a valuable piece of property coveted by the federal government. "Budgetary constraints," Panetta wrote, "have made it impractical to acquire such an expensive tract of land through outright purchase."

Therefore, pressure was put on the Texan to convince him to surrender his land at a cheaper rate. The government filed suit against Hurwitz over a Texas Savings & Loan that had failed in the 1980s, in which Hurwitz's company was a minor investor. The message was clear: Give us the land; we'll settle the suit. That was exactly what happened.

Give Big Nanny what she wants—or Big Nanny will simply take it.

"Asset forfeiture" exists and is proliferating because of a legal technicality that allows government to claim that it is suing only the item of property, which has somehow violated the law on its own, and not the property's owner. The dodge goes all the way back to medieval doctrines in which the King could take whatever he wanted by claiming the donkey or cornfield or whatever violated some law.

The ploy works just as well today in America as it did in Seventeenth Century England. It is up to the owner to prove that his house, car or the cash in his wallet is innocent. A tough thing to do. He may have committed no crime whatsoever—but his cash may have passed hands somewhere in a drug case. Therefore, the cash is guilty. Seize it! Uncle Sam will then decide which bureaucracy is more deserving to distribute it among which constituency.

In 1998 alone, the Federal Justice Department confiscated 42,454 cars, boats, airplanes, houses, stocks of cash and other items of property valued at more than $600 million. Those numbers continue to rise year by year.

Federal and state agents accused Richard Smith and his 75-year-old father of poisoning eagles. They charged onto the Smiths' Texas ranch and seized Richard's pickup truck. Then they tracked down his father and took his pickup truck too. No charges were ever filed against the Smiths due to lack of evidence—but government kept the pickup trucks. The trucks are still doing hard time.

Darryl Ward was murdered in Pittsburgh. Prosecutors claimed that since he was *probably* a drug dealer, all his previous income was guilty and subject to forfeiture. Even though his wife, Anna, and her three small children were never implicated in any crimes, even though Anna had her own legitimate business, the government took everything the widow owned, including furniture and the children's toys. It even attempted to take the dead man's life insurance. Anna and her children had to go on welfare in order to survive.

Confiscation, or the threat of it, is turning into a useful tool by which government can control people while it transforms America into a "happier, more equal" society. Suffolk County, New York, considered an extension of law to allow local officials to confiscate property in connection with any *misdemeanors*—such as permitting your dog to poop on the sidewalk or sitting in your car on a government parking lot smoking a cigarette. There goes your dog and your car.

It won't be long until automobiles photographed by automatic cameras violating traffic laws will be deemed guilty and seized; until your tractor that accidentally runs over a rattlesnake and causes it to suffer mental anguish and whiplash will be tried in court, found guilty and turned over to the Audubon Society; until your back yard grill is deemed eco-criminal in emitting too much smoke, convicted and taken out and turned into the blade for a non-polluting, eco-sound windmill.

No wonder lawyers and politicians are held in such low regard.

Through law, lawsuits and coercion, people are being discouraged against making their own choices in regard to property. We are even being conditioned away from regarding property as exclusively ours;

there is arguably a "public interest" in even the jockey shorts we wear, since they must some day be discarded and disposed of in a way that affects or involves other people. In demonstrating its ability to bankrupt and destroy people who are stubborn enough to resist and foolish enough to think they actually own what they think they own, government loosens that vital bond between owner and property and introduces fear. My step dad's phobia against ownership, if nothing else, demonstrates that fear and freedom cannot exist together in a world going crazy around us.

SECTION XIV
GUN CONTROL

"Outlaw all guns, and put all gun owners in jail."
Rosie O'Donnell

CHAPTER THIRTY-NINE

Two *kindergarten* boys were suspended from school in New Jersey after being nabbed red-handed playing cops and robbers at recess—using their fingers and thumbs as guns. At a California elementary school, a nine-year-old was threatened with suspension when a teacher found snapshots in the boy's book bag of him and his brother shooting at a range—where they were supervised by their aunt, a certified police firearms instructor. A 21-year-old water fountain depicting two children in a water fight in Santa Fe was altered because one of the children was shooting at the other with a squirt gun. The water gun was changed to a hose. Whenever the classic musical *Annie Get Your Gun* is performed in some "progressive" cities, any song with a reference to "gun" in it cannot be sung.

Nothing drives Lefties wackier than guns. The *mention* of guns, the *thought* of guns, anything that *looks* like a gun is enough to drive them rabid. They have demonstrated they will do virtually anything to eradicate the Second Amendment from the Constitution. Big Nanny's many little busybody children *shudder* at that Right Wing extremist Thomas Jefferson's observation that "No man shall ever be debarred the use of arms. The strongest reason for the people to retain the right to keep and bear arms is, as a last resort, to protect themselves against tyranny in government."

During Senate confirmation hearings for John Ashcroft, President George W. Bush's attorney general nominee, Ted Kennedy from Massachusetts laid into Ashcroft about his strong support for the Second Amendment. He demanded Ashcroft *apologize* to the American people for having once used the above Jefferson quote in a speech.

Federal government attorneys arguing a gun case before the Fifth Circuit Court of Appeals in New Orleans contended that individual Americans have no rights under the Second Amendment. Government, continued the attorneys, has full authority to ban and confiscate any firearm it wishes—without the Constitution getting in the way.

"Are you saying the Second Amendment is consistent with a position that you can take guns away from the public?" Judge Will Garwood asked U.S. Attorney William Mateja. "You can prevent ownership of rifles, pistols and shotguns from all these people? Is that the position of the United States?"

"Yes," Mateja replied.

"Is it the position of the United States that persons who are not in the National Guard are afforded no protection under the Second Amendment?"

"Exactly."

Need anything else be said about the intent of government and the

anti-gun lobby toward the Second Amendment? Big Nanny and the
Enlightened know best. Most of the rest of us are intimidated into keeping our mouths shut and our heads ducked. After all, no one should
have the right to go against our superiors, our betters, our Enlightened
keepers.

"Just by signing on to a point of view or certain social agenda,"
said actor Charlton Heston, then-president of the National Rifle Association, "you become part of the preferred class. By quietly agreeing
that corporate America is inherently evil, or that southern Christians are
somewhat dumb and misguided, or that guns are dangerously prevalent,
or that Asian lesbians have more informed views, or that any us-versus-
them class concept is superior, you sign on and you're one of the elite."

And the elite say we bigoted, sexist, racist, insensitive, gun-toting
rednecks are going to have to give up guns as another step toward a
"safer, gentler" society, another step toward complete government control.

Fitting, isn't it, that the same folks who want gun confiscation and
gun eradication are the same folks who: ban the Ten Commandments
and Christmas nativity scenes; file charges against you for spanking
your child; put you in jail for running over a kangaroo rat; sit in the
tops of trees and preach to the rest of us for being greedy; push legali-
zation of drugs, pedophiles, gay marriages, human-animal sex and
porn; want to outlaw SUVs, sugar, junk food and underarm deodorants;
want two mommies or two daddies for children; insist that a seven-
month-old fetus is not life while protecting with threat of fine and jail
the egg of a buzzard; fire you for using a word like *niggardly* which
could *sound* offensive...?

Incrementalism is the method government uses to desensitize the
public to expansive government authoritarianism. If one set of rights
can be diminished and eventually lost via regulation, so too can every
other Constitutional right. Citizens can claim all the rights they want,
but if they show themselves unable or unwilling to defend these rights
from aggressors and encroachers, those rights are little more than a
howling wind.

A chilling and prophetic story about the future of America made its
rounds over the Internet. According to the story, you're sound asleep
when you hear a thump and muffled whispers outside your bedroom
door. Two men have broken into your home. You have been burgled
several times before. You search for your shotgun and surprise the
thieves. One of them brandishes what appears to be a crowbar. You fire
in self-defense.

You know *you're* in trouble even as you call the police. Your shotgun is unregistered; most guns have been outlawed for years.

One of the intruders dies. Police arrest *you* for First Degree Murder
and Illegal Possession of a Firearm. Although both thieves have been

arrested numerous times, the press presents them as choirboys. *Loveable Rogue Son Didn't Deserve To Die* boldly states one headline. The surviving thief sues you. He'll probably end up owning your entire house instead of only your TV and silver. When you go to court, prosecutors portray you as a vicious, vengeful gunman who intended to kill the misguided youth. The judge sentences you to life in prison.

Sound insane? It *is* insane, but it happened just that way in Norfolk, England. On August 22, 1999, Tony Martin killed one burglar and wounded the second. In April 2000, he was convicted and is now serving life in prison. The wounded burglar, incidentally, is still free.

When cultures go bonkers, they seem to turn everything upside down.

Something similar to this is going to happen in the United States. If not this year, then the next year or the year after that. You can bet on it. The American media and the noisy elite are busy painting all gun owners as mentally unstable, as kooks, or as criminals-in-waiting. Liberal politicians have launched a *blitzkrieg* to register and eventually ban and confiscate all firearms.

"Outlaw all guns," suggested air-brained TV personality Rosie O'Donnell, "and put all gun owners in jail."

CHAPTER FORTY

A column in the University of Oklahoma student newspaper clearly illustrates liberal reasoning when it comes to guns or anything else of which the Enlightened disapprove. The column complained that "easy access" gun laws permitted "criminals, youth and the mentally disabled to quickly and easily kill as many random people as they want." People have guns. Ergo, it follows that these people will use them in unacceptable ways—such as shooting poor, defenseless, misguided, disadvantaged thugs who break into your house in the middle of the night.

Geology professor David Deming possessed the unmitigated gall to point out the female columnist's illogical reasoning. She had "easy access" to a vagina, he said, which enabled her to "quickly and easily have sex with as many random people" as she wanted. It didn't necessarily follow, however, that she would.

Campus feminists filed sexual harassment charges against him for his sexist remarks.

You have to understand liberal thought processes, difficult as it is. The more liberal you are, the less you're grounded in reality. At the same time, you feel somehow morally obligated to assume guardianship over the rest of us. When it comes to guns, the gun control crowd is out there howling all over the landscape.

During her successful campaign for a New York senate seat, Hillary Clinton led elementary school students in a "pledge against gun violence."

"Would you tell your parents something for me?" she asked, wide-eyed in that phony manner of hers that passes for sincerity. "Ask them if they have a gun in the house, please lock it, or take it out of the house. Will you do that as good citizens?"

The government is here to protect and take care of you good little citizens. Turn over your guns and brains and lives to us. We care! We feel your pain!

An article on Hillary's website began with the banner, *Hillary Calls On Students To Stay Away From Guns.*

Two days later, ironically enough, she paid a visit to Robert E. Bell Middle School in Chappaqua, New York. Armed Secret Service agents and dogs rushed about while kids stood outside their classrooms being frisked.

Diana Schneider's seventh-grade daughter called home. "Mommy, I'm scared. There are men in the halls with guns."

"Despite her anti-gun advocacy trips to suburban schools," said Mrs. Schneider, "the only person bringing guns into my kid's school was Hillary Clinton."

People like Hillary Clinton, Rosie O'Donnell and Chicago Mayor Richard Daley are obviously more valuable and responsible than the rest of us. They head a long list of Enlightened Elites who demand that the rest of us disarm while they retain their own armed bodyguards.

"All gun owners should be registered and licensed by the government exactly as we register automobiles," proposed a Tulsa *World* Letter to The Editor, "because all gun owners are a potential threat to society."

So are automobile owners, bicycle riders and short-order cooks with sharp knives. Perhaps we should also register reporters, TV commentators, filmmakers, politicians and authors to reduce *their* potential threat to society. Also churches. Definitely churches whose non-sanctioned philosophies run contrary to those collectivist ones of the new socialist state. What counts in the gun battle, as throughout the cultural wars, is emotional appeal. Reality is subjective to that.

At the 1996 Democratic National Convention, Bill Clinton claimed the Brady Bill had "stopped 60,000 felons, fugitives and stalkers from getting handguns." Seven days later, in another emotion-grabbing speech, he upped the number to 100,000. By April 1999, he was using 250,000 as the number—ballooning it up to 400,000 in July. Of course, Bill Clinton was truth-challenged, but so are a number of other politicians, activists and media people when it comes to promoting their pet causes, of which gun control generally heads the list.

The so-called Million Moms March on Mothers Day 2000 was a public relations coup primarily because of the way it was promoted by a mainstream press that continues to demonstrate its bias against guns. *U.S. News & World Report* described Donna Dees-Thomases, the organizer of the march, as "a New Jersey mother of two small girls (who) came up with the idea while watching frightening television coverage of an August 1999 shooting at a day care center in Granada Hills, California..."

Nowhere in the mainstream was it so much as mentioned that Dees-Thomases was a longtime liberal activist and former Democratic Senate staffer with family ties to Hillary Clinton. Guns aren't about kids shooting kids. That's simply the emotional catch phrase. Guns are about the use of political power.

While the anti-gun marchers were referred to by the press in glowing adjectives, mothers who marched at the same time in support of Second Amendment rights were called "pistol packing mommas." The Tulsa *World* headlined the Millions Moms March with *Tulsa Mothers Rally For More Gun Safety.* The secondary story on the Second Amendment moms began with *Anti-Ban March Here Draws 300.* Notice the difference, other than in the larger, more prominent display of the Million Moms story?

"Mothers pushing strollers, balancing toddlers on their hips and marching arm-in-arm with their teenagers served notice Sunday that they are a 'vocal, determined minority' demanding attention to the need for gun safety..." was how the Million Moms story began its lead.

Here was the lead for the counter march, with an entirely different flavor. "More than 300 flag-waving, sign-toting people marched on Mothers Day to protest the Second Amendment from 'vultures' who are trying to rip it to shreds..."

"We have just witnessed one of the great spontaneous events of our democracy..." gushed Mortimer B. Zuckerman of *U.S. News & World Report* about the Millions Moms.

Spontaneous? It couldn't have been more organized.

"...A million moms across the country marching on Mothers Day to plead for federal gun control laws," *U.S. News* continued. "The shadow across the march was the National Rifle Association. It has opposed virtually every gun control initiative in a period of gun outrages... Have the moms got any chance at all?"

How *dare* the evil NRA defend a Constitutional right! When film maker Spike Lee was asked what should be done with NRA president Charlton Heston, he snapped, "Shoot him with a .44-caliber Bulldog."

But shoot him in a *sensitive* way. Right, Spike?

If the Million Moms really were concerned with saving children's lives, maybe they should be marching against automobiles, bicycles, swimming pools and medical doctors. More children under age five die every year drowning in buckets than from gunshot. *Toys* cause 144,000 accidental injuries annually compared to 2,000 for guns. The 700,000 physicians in the United States account for 120,000 accidental deaths each year, while eight million gun owners account for about 1,500 accidental deaths annually. Your family doctor is *nine thousand times* more dangerous statistically than your .44-caliber Bulldog.

Ban-the-gun ads deplore 4,000 "children" killed every year by firearms. They never mention that "children" is defined as "20 and under" and that the vast majority of these deaths result from criminal acts by late-adolescent dopers, common thugs and gangsters.

According to the latest available data from the Center for Disease Control, which annually ranks accidental deaths by categories, accidental deaths for "children" under age twenty were as follows: automobiles-8,113; drowning-1,269; smoke and fire-723; mechanical suffocation-529; guns-306.

The statistics for accidental deaths for children from birth to age fourteen were automobiles-2,608; bicycles-2,010; drowning-1,010; pedestrian-675; guns-142.

So what? *Guns* are evil.

Linda Chavez of the Center for Equal Opportunity explained on Public Broadcasting why she bought a gun.

"If you're someone like me, who lives out in a rural area—if someone breaks into my house and wants to murder or rape or steal all my property, it'll take half an hour for a policeman to get to me."

Scoffed Bonnie Erbe, former legal correspondent for NBC Radio/Mutual Network, "... I would bet that you have a greater chance of being struck by lightning, Linda, than living where you live, and at your age, being raped..."

Erbe later e-mailed Chavez her condolences: "I know and accept your insecurities. And I expect insecure people, and especially conservatives, to lie and play games... I suggest you get into therapy. Otherwise, you're going to continue to be miserable and in denial the rest of your life..."

In other words, if you disagree with the Enlightened, there must be something wrong with you that can only be corrected through therapy, sensitivity training, or reeducation. Send Chavez to the gulags to get her mind straightened out.

The Second Amendment argument is framed in such a way that you must be in favor of kids killing kids if you oppose restrictive gun controls. A banshee cry rises across the nation every time a gun incident occurs. That some two-bit off-kilter punk chooses to go on a rampage is the direct fault of every gun owner in the United States.

Singer Lorna Luft fired a note to Charlton Heston after the Columbine High School shootings. "I hope you're happy now."

Denver Mayor Wellington Webb told the NRA, "Don't come here. We don't want you here."

Incrementally, raw emotionalism and a concerted drive by the Enlightened are winning the public relations campaign when it comes to gun control. Sooner or later, the rednecks in America will be reprogrammed to accept the loss of yet another constitutional right. You can't fight the moms, the media, all those sensitive people out there who know best. You can't fight the government. You can see it coming.

High school senior Jennifer Shotoing won national championships in shooting for four consecutive years. She was summoned to the principal's office when she submitted an informal photo of herself with an AR-15 match grade rifle for the school yearbook. She was lectured about "assault weapons" and ordered to withdraw the photo because it "promoted violence."

Make-A-Wish Foundation came under withering fire from the wacko anti-hunting, anti-gun and animals rights groups when it granted Eric Ness, 17, his wish. Ness had brain cancer and a dream of going brown bear hunting in Alaska. Since then, the Foundation has rethought its policy, deciding that "it is not in the best interest of the children we serve for us to continue considering wishes that involve firearms, hunting bows, and other hunting or sport-shooting equipment."

What a bunch of spineless wienies.

"Any time a citizen of the United States of America...is shamed into silence because he or she embraces a view at odds with the cultural elitists," exclaimed Charlton Heston in frustration, "that citizen has been 'taken captive.' His freedom has been curtailed."

CHAPTER FORTY-ONE

Although gun control advocates insist their goal is not to disarm American but instead merely to make America *safe*, they are ingenious at outright lying. The leaders of countries which end up banning and confiscating guns didn't suddenly get up one morning and say, "Well, this is the day. Let's go out and take all their firearms." The process began much earlier with permits and gun registrations and controls in order to condition people to accept that fateful day.

Lawsuits against "Big Tobacco" has predictably led to the same kind of lawsuits against "Big Sugar," "Big Autos," "Big Junk Food," and, inevitably, "Big Guns."

"We have the capacity," smugly announced Elliott Spitzer, Democratic Attorney General of New York, "to squeeze (gun) manufacturers like a pincers and hurt them in the marketplace. We are bigger than the NRA."

Government is bigger than any other entity in the United States—and it keeps growing. That's part of the madness.

The U.S. government got in the lawsuit act after the National Taxpayers Union Foundation, among others, filed suit against firearms manufacturers on tobacco grounds—that gun violence and resulting medical costs were leaving cities and states strapped for manpower and money. It was a "health issue." The Department of Housing and Urban Development (HUD) said its 3,200 public housing authorities filed class action lawsuits to recover billions of dollars in alleged damages for costs of criminal violence. Urban mayors had already filed similar suits, looking for deep, easy pockets to raid for their expensive social projects.

Look out, Big Autos. You're next.

"Gun makers can agree to modest, reasonable steps that will cut the flow of guns to juveniles and criminals," lectured a Los Angeles lawyer, "or they can continue to write very large checks to their attorneys."

Do what we say—bring money—or we'll hound you out of business. Thousands of pressure points by both government and gun control advocates are being applied throughout the United States to get rid of all guns, step by predictable step.

The Oakland area of California intentionally attempted to drive legitimate firearms retailers out of business by imposing a sales tax that was *twenty times* higher than that required from other businesses.

Denver-based Citibank Corporation informed the Nevada Pistol Academy that its checking account was being cancelled because the bank, as a matter of policy, banned service to anyone who made or sold firearms.

The American Academy of Pediatrics, which supports banning all handguns, semi-automatic rifles and shotguns, urged its member doctors to ask child patients during examinations if guns were kept in their homes. The doctors were then supposed to counsel parents about the danger of guns and recommend their disposal. The AAP handed out instructional packets on how to deal with "challenging individuals" who might object to the crusade.

The Buyback Program, using tax money to "buy back" guns, was one of the most hare-brained boondoggle ever to come down the pike. The Clinton administration appropriated $15 million to its "Buyback America" program, which Clinton termed "an important part of my administration's comprehensive strategy to reduce gun violence in America." Never mind that it was not authorized by law. Never mind that it didn't work. Few of the buyback guns came from high-crime neighborhoods. Those that did were old guns being turned in to get money to buy new guns.

Las Cruces, New Mexico, paid $50 cash and two $25 tickets to see a boxing match for each firearm turned in. Washington D.C. went so far as to trade kids basketball tickets, books and crayons for their *toy* guns. One little boy resisted so strenuously that his mother had to pry his toy pistol from his hand. Another didn't have any toy guns. He went to a nearby Dollar Store and bought a red plastic sword for one dollar and traded it in for basketball tickets. Shrewd little kid. Capitalism at work.

I'm sure Washington D.C. must be a safer place for tourists now that toy guns and red plastic swords are in police custody.

Does anyone seriously think the Enlightened will ever stop until we're all slaves to their mad vision? Fun houses at carnivals used to have those big footsteps on the ground that you followed to the House of Horrors. America is in the process of following such footsteps. Liberties are lost incrementally, not in one fell swoop. It won't be many more years until the United States goes the way of other countries in banning and confiscating firearms. Britain, Australia, Turkey, the Soviet Union, China, Germany, Guatemala, Uganda...

"I have seen lines of submissive citizens," Charlton Heston wrote of English and Australian gun confiscations, "whose only alternative is imprisonment, bitterly surrendering family heirlooms—guns that won their freedom—to the saw blade and blast furnace."

Radio commentator Paul Harvey likes to broadcast what he calls, "A History of Gun Control Laws."

Turkey, he pointed out, enacted gun control in 1911. From 1915 to 1917, 1.5 million Armenians were rounded up and exterminated.

The Soviet Union initiated gun control in 1929—and twenty million dissidents were rounded up and killed between 1929 and 1953.

China established gun control in 1935, then proceeded to kill twenty million of its own citizens between 1948 and 1952.

Hitler imposed gun control on Germany in 1938. Thirteen million Jews, gypsies, homosexuals, mentally ill people and other "undesirables" went to the gas chambers between 1939 and 1945.

Cambodia bit the bullet in 1956. The country exterminated one million "educated" people from 1975 to 1977.

Guatemala made the list in 1964. More than 100,000 Mayan Indians were marched to their deaths between 1964 and 1981.

Uganda bought into gun control in 1970, then suffered the executions of 300,000 Christians within the next nine years.

All told, more than 56 million victims lost their lives in the last century following gun control. Does that make any impression on our sensitive national do-gooders? None at all. The only time Lefties make sense is when they're talking to each other. America must be disarmed in the name of a safer society.

"I propose," said Hillary Clinton, "boosting the federal investment in technology research so that we could create gun detectors that could scan city streets and pinpoint guns, reducing the need for stop and frisk."

Why not at the same time boost federal investing in technology so we can scan city streets and read the minds of those who might be contemplating robbing a bank, littering with a candy wrapper or writing a nasty letter to a politician? Is this kind of thinking scary or what?

Even though gun control is coached in terms of curbing crime and reducing violence, its real purpose is to limit the ability of citizens to resist intrusion from whatever source it originates. Government is not, has never been, a benevolent entity. Power should be viewed with suspicion, always. We should be especially suspicious of the weird, the wacky, and the ideological do-gooders. Whenever and wherever they take over, a bunch of us end up in gulags.

"To those who desire a cultural hierarchy with an elite in power," said Charlton Heston, "a gun is a threatening symbol of equality of power."

American anti-gunners are fond of toasting England as an example of a "safer society" because of its anti-gun laws. That is one of the many delusions of our homegrown authoritarians who can lift a skunk's tail, get squirted, and still call it a house tabby.

Britain experienced a century of incremental gun laws, so-called "sensible measures that all reasonable people can agree on," before it outlawed all handguns in 1996. Since then, the overall crime rate in England and Wales has risen until it is higher per capita than in any of America's fifty states.

Robbery, sex crimes, crimes of violence, property crimes and auto theft are twice as high in Britain as in the United States. The average Brit is twice as likely to have his home burgled while he's in it. Two thirds of all Brits will have their property broken into at some time in their lives.

If, by chance, a Brit does happen to have a gun and uses it to defend himself and his property, heaven help him. He has a better chance of getting tossed behind the Big Walls than does the offender.

How much more insane can a society become?

Australia experienced similar phenomena when it banned and confiscated firearms following a media- sensationalized mass murder.

Australian Prime Minister John Howard and his anti-gun government had already instituted every move in the gun ban playbook before the murder occurred. There had been buybacks, licensing and registering before the murder provided an opportunity for the government to impose a ban on all handguns, semi-automatic and pump action rifles and shotguns. More than 660,000 private firearms were confiscated, sawed up and sold for scrap metal.

The violent crime rate immediately accelerated. Overall homicide rates rose by 3.2 percent, 300 percent in the state of Victoria. Assaults went up 8.6 percent and armed robbery increased by 44 percent. There were similar dramatic increases in break-ins and assaults on the elderly. Unable to defend themselves, citizens locked themselves in their homes behind iron bars.

Louis L'Amour was right. People in the Old West *were* a lot nicer to each other when everybody had a gun.

Those same big footsteps on the ground that led England, Australia and all the other "progressive" countries to gun confiscation are clearly visible in America.

Senator Jack Reed, D-Rhode Island, introduced a bill entitled the Handgun Safety and Registration Act of 2000. When it and its subsequent riders eventually pass, they will place gun control under the authority of the *Internal Revenue Service,* those same sensitive, friendly folks who come out and seize your house, your lawn mower and your firstborn if you fail to give Big Nanny every dime she thinks you owe. Under this bill, all handguns would be registered with the Bureau of Alcohol, Tobacco and Firearms, then listed on the taxpayer's annual tax return. Handgun owners would be required to pay a $50 annual tax on each gun.

"(Tax) returns and return information with respect to taxes imposed..." the proposed bill states, "shall be available on an online format for inspection by or disclosure to officers and employees of any federal law enforcement agency, and any state or local law enforcement agency, whose duties require such inspection or disclosure..."

You don't have to be a brain surgeon to see where this is headed. Fifty dollars tax this year, a hundred next, two hundred the year after that...

In 1996, Congress passed the Lautenberg Domestic Violence Prevention Act. It created one million new felons overnight. Under this law, any person with a domestic violence misdemeanor on his record found in possession of a gun—or even a single bullet—could be fined $250,000 and slammed into the slammer for ten years. In some states, the mere shaking of your fist in your wife's or "significant other's" face can get you permanently stripped of the right to go squirrel hunting. A number of cops had to give up their guns and their jobs.

Starting in 1999, Connecticut police no longer need a search warrant to enter a private residence and confiscate firearms. Under the new law to "curb gun violence," police were empowered to confiscate firearms based on nothing more than a personal belief that the gun owner might be a danger to himself or others. All your ex-wife has to do is call the police and tell them you're a dangerous person. There goes your deer rifle.

The zeal to snatch guns away from the public continues to become more frantic each year.

The sheriff's department in Onondaga County, New York, assigned a deputy to read the local obituaries each day looking for deceased gun owners. Under state law, relatives are required to turn in licensed pistols within fifteen days of an owner's death or be charged with a crime for failing to do so. Local funeral directors cooperate by notifying the bereaved about the law.

"We are sorry about your husband, Mrs. Jones. Leave the arrangements to us. Oh, by the way, did he happen to own a gun...?"

It's not government's business to know what a law-abiding citizen does or does not own—unless government is already contemplating making guns illegal. Don't say it can't happen in America. It is happening.

This is all scary, but know what is *really* scary? The thought of only government having guns. To people like Hillary Clinton, Rosie O'Donnell, Ted Kennedy and Jack Reed, privately owned guns are a dire threat to public safety while government machine guns pose no threat, even when pointed at a cowering child.

Before dawn on April 22, 2000, heavily armed federal agents in Miami, Florida, raided a private home to seize a six-year-old illegal immigrant, Elian Gonzalez, whose mother died getting him out of communist Cuba to freedom. The agents ignored a court order denying them the authority to make the seizure. They grabbed the child anyhow at the point of automatic weapons and left in their wake shattered doors, a broken bed, roughed up Cuban Americans and two NBC cameramen writhing from stomach kicks and rifle butts to the head. A famous photograph showed the boy cowering in the arms of a Cuban fisherman while a helmeted policeman pointed an automatic rifle at them.

This was the first time in the history of the United States something like this had occurred. Raw government power on display—and to hell with due procedure. It must have been a chilling flashback for those Jews who remembered the Holocaust.

Attorney General Janet Reno justified the action because "we knew guns were in there." Besides that, she said, "One of the things that is so very important is that force was not used... It was a show of force that prevented people from getting hurt... As I understand it, if you look at it (the photo) carefully, it shows that the gun was pointed to the side, and the finger was not on the trigger."

The boy "was not taken at the point of a gun..." asserted Deputy Attorney General Eric Holder. "They were armed agents who went in there who acted very sensitively."

You should be *sensitive* when you point a gun at a child.

Instead of indicating rightful outrage, polls showed over sixty percent of Americans agreed with the action. The only thing MSNBC's Brian Williams was concerned with was that the incident might "stir up the right wing wackos." Elian Gonzalez was sent back to Cuba.

New York *Times'* Thomas Friedman said the raid "warmed my heart." He said the photo of it should be "put up in every visa line in every U.S. consulate around the world, with a caption that reads: 'America is a country where the rule of law rules.' This picture illustrates what happens to those who defy the rule of law and how far our government and people will go to preserve it."

It certainly does that.

"Who would have imagined in the wake of Kent State thirty years ago," wrote Miami columnist Michael Sasser, "that when 135 armed troops raid the home of a private citizen in Miami charged with no crime that half of America would be sitting on its collective ass watching it on CNN and rooting for the guys leveling deadly weapons at a child?"

SECTION XV
PRESIDENT BILL CLINTON

"Playing with the president was weird. He shot a 90. At the end of the game his scorecard said 84."
Bryce Molder, NCAA golfer

CHAPTER FORTY-TWO

Why should I single out former President Bill Clinton for an entire section in a book bearing a title like *Going Bonkers: The Wacky World of Cultural Madness?* Simple enough. Bill Clinton, a living parody of cultural insanity, could well be the poster-child for the title. He personifies and symbolizes all the political correctness wackiness that now holds America captive. He is an amusing lunatic who has done more harm to the nation than any public figure in our history.

The Clinton White House will be remembered as a soap opera in its comic relief and high daytime TV drama. Like *The Jerry Springer Show*. Populated with tacky characters and strewn with even tackier episodes. *How I Slept With Two Women And Their Cocker Spaniels.* That sort of fascination.

Heading the zany cast is The Man himself, the Arkansas Traveler, the Man From Hope. A buffoonish, self-absorbed Faustian character who solicits cash from Chinese gangsters, kowtows to a scheming wife, holds trysts with comely servants in the Oval Office john like a randy Billy goat, bombs other countries to divert attention from his personal peccadilloes, and blames everyone else when he's caught.

Abe Lincoln was wrong in a sense. While you can't fool *all* the people *all* the time, you don't have to. All you have to do is fool enough of them to keep getting elected.

Bill Clinton first invaded the national consciousness when he gave a keynote speech for Michael Dukakis at the 1988 Democratic National Convention. His speech was so long that when he finally got to "in conclusion," the audience actually stood up and cheered. Four years later, he became president and wore down the nation the same way.

His scheming wife is now a senator from New York. We will never get rid of them. They're like bad hillbilly relatives who come for a visit and decide to stay while they pawn your TV, seduce your daughter and invite over all their rowdy friends on parole from the state pen.

Clinton took office promising "the most ethical administration in history." What a sick joke. His White House holds the dubious honor of breaking all records for the most number of convictions and guilty pleas; of cabinet officials who resigned under fire; of independent investigations; of White House lawyers; of Presidential legal bills; of witnesses who fled the country or pled the Fifth; of foreign illegal political donations accepted; of key witnesses who died unexpectedly...

No other sitting American president has, in no particular order of importance, been impeached; recommended for disbarment from the legal profession; found guilty of violating the privacy act; held in contempt of court; fined for giving false and misleading answers under oath; accused of using military force in bombing raids to divert attention from his other misdeeds; forced to settle a sexual harassment suit; accused of rape...

No other sitting American president has done business with so many shady characters; been pals with so many convicted felons; rented out the Lincoln Bedroom like Motel 6 to big contributors; solicited donations from drug dealers, spies and international arms smugglers; been accused of obstruction of justice, witness tampering and perjury; misused the FBI; politicized the Justice Department and the IRS; received a more-or-less public blowjob in the Oval Office...

No other sitting American president ever married Hillary Clinton.

He was described as the "first black president," the "first gay president," the "first Indian president." Whatever the hell all that means when what you see looking at him is a depraved white cracker from Arkansas. He was the first president to compare himself to Martin Luther King, Nelson Mandela and Jesus Christ. He was the first to appear on TV with a warning across the screen: *Sexually Graphic Material.*

"If the deponent is the person who has oral sex performed on him, then the contact is...not with anything on that list, but with the lips of another person. It seems to me self-evident that that's what it is..."

Whatever he did, he always claimed it was in the interest of the American people. "I need to get back to work for the American people." One blowjob coming up for the American people.

He compared his travails during the impeachment crisis with those of blacks and gays, "people who've been targeted, who've been publicly humiliated and abused." He knows how to play the victim game. He was actually quoted as saying how his "journey," meaning all the scandals, while exhausting, would surely be good for us. According to him, he had saved the Constitution.

Oddly enough, sickening enough, a large portion of America cheered and, along with the national press corps, largely ignored the damning reality of the emperor going mad. That such a man was elected, then re-elected, to the most powerful office in the world says more about the state of balance of American sanity than it does about him.

"This is a good man," Charles Grodin asserted on his TV show. "This man will be considered one of the best human beings to hold the office of the president..."

Geraldo Rivera chimed in with, "I think his judgment has been impeccable. He's been a brilliant president..."

"A distinguished record that will go down in history as a virtuoso performance," said Vice President Al Gore.

News anchor Dan Rather, representing the important news media, fawned on the Clintons: "If we could be one-hundredth as great as you and Hillary Rodham Clinton have been in the White House, we'd take it right now and walk away winners..."

It is so difficult to parody parody.

"I would be happy to give him a blowjob just to thank him for keeping abortion legal," declared *Time* contributor Nina Burleigh. "I think American women should be lining up with their presidential kneepads on..."

"Obviously," said White House spokesman Joe Lockhart in defending his boss against scandals, "the President probably has more experience than any living human being about how deep in the gutter some people can go."

Obviously.

Straight-faced, with no intent of irony, Clinton proclaimed a National Character Counts Week 2000.

"One of our greatest responsibilities as adults and citizens," he pontificated, "is to ensure that we teach our children, by word and deed, the values that will help them develop into men and women of strong character."

Just *try* to parody that.

"The next time we elect a president," cracked David Letterman, "I am begging you, for the love of God, will somebody please do a background check?"

CHAPTER FORTY-THREE

It says something disturbing about American society and its collective moral sanity when Bill Clinton and Hillary consistently top the list of "Most Admired People." Either folks aren't paying attention, they don't care, or they admire depravity. For an eight-year period, a sociopath governed the nation and at least half the country didn't give a damn. In fact, they thought it was just fine. This, *this,* was the presidency of the United States under Bill Clinton:

Elizabeth Birch, executive director for the Human Rights Campaign, described meeting Clinton at a gala political dinner she attended at the White House. Referring to herself as a "lesbian Monica" while addressing the Lesbian, Gay, Bisexual, Transgendered Association in California, she said, "I could be Monica Lewinsky. I gave (Clinton) a tie. I've got a lot of raw-playing video, and I do believe that when he hugged me at the national dinner, there was a little cupping—I shouldn't say this—of my breasts."

Comedian-actor Robin Williams was the guest speaker at a fundraising event attended by Clinton and Vice President Al Gore. Although Williams' routine was peppered with its usual filth and profanity, it was covered live on TV's C-Span. The camera showed Clinton and Gore howling with laughter when Williams spotted a small child in the audience and wisecracked, "Hello. There's a child in the front row. We've learned some new words."

When Democratic anti-tobacco lawyer Stanley Chesley volunteered his Cincinnati estate for a party fundraising event, a big white tent was set up and furnished with gold chairs and place settings, candelabras and flowers flown in from Chicago. It was cold outside, a few degrees below freezing. Four big heaters were set up in the tent to keep the 120 guests from freezing.

Along comes Bill, smooth-talking Bill... He asked that all the heaters be turned off so everyone could hang onto his every word—except for the space heater behind the podium that kept him warm.

He went on for about a half-hour while the guests sat and shivered. At least five guests were so angered they demanded the return of their $10,000 checks. About half retreated to the warmth of the house while Clinton was still speaking. So absorbed was Clinton in himself and what he had to say that he hardly noticed.

He *does* feel our pain.

Because of the adroitness with which the president got himself out of the various scandals in which he became implicated—at least 43 separate ones by last count, including his pardon-signing-for-pay marathon during his final hours in office and his stealing White House furnishings on his way out the door, he became widely and, in some circles, affectionately known as "Slick Willie."

When Illinois entrepreneur Jack Wagner, who sells novelties tweaking Clinton for fun and profit, attempted to trademark "Slick Willie" as his logo, the U.S. Commerce Department turned him down.

"The evidence clearly shows that the name 'Slick Willie' is a nickname which refers to President Bill Clinton," trademark examiner Karen Bush informed Wagner by letter. "Furthermore, the evidence shows that the nickname is not a complimentary name and is used in a disparaging manner, indicating that the president has a lack of character."

Lack of character? Bill Clinton?

"Playing with the President was weird," said NCAA golfer Bryce Molder after playing a round of golf with him. "He shot a 90. At the end of the game, his score card said 84."

The FBI withheld national security information from Clinton because he couldn't be trusted with it. The President of the United States *could not be trusted.* FBI Director Louis Freeh wrote a memo to Attorney General Janet Reno saying that information developed during the campaign finance investigation, which centered around illegal contributions from the Communist Chinese, should not be shared with the White House.

Some politicians, it seems, will sell off parts of their souls to the highest bidders.

Hillary, it seems, is much admired in Red China where the Communist Party and media institute at Bejing's Academy of Social Services picked her as a shining example of a successful manipulative orator, a model for apparatchiks to emulate. The Reds were particularly impressed with Bill's and her ability to successfully brand opponents as mere Republican extremists without credibility.

Satan says to Bill: "I have a deal for you. I'm going to give you the most powerful job in the world. I'm going to give you the most beautiful women doing whatever you want. I'll even make it so people send you money, even thousands of dollars. There's just one thing I want in return—your soul."

Bill: "So what's the catch?"

Chuck Colson told a story on TV about how he had been in England for a dinner. Someone raised a glass and said, "To the Queen!" Americans and Brits stood to toast Her Majesty.

Then someone raised a glass and said, "To the President of the United States."

The entire room erupted in laughter.

Joe Eszterhas wrote a book, *American Rhapsody,* that featured "Willard," the Talking Presidential Penis. Long before the Monica Lewinsky intern-on-her-knees-in-the-Oval Office scandal, it was widely known, even among the public, that our loveable Bill had a hard time keeping Willard behind a zipper. It was said, not entirely tongue in cheek, that Clinton spent so much time getting so much sex that it was hard to believe he had any spare time for illegal fund raising.

Al Gore to Clinton: "I never slept with my wife before we were married. Did you?"

"Hmmm. What was Tipper's maiden name?"

Clinton came to town with the perfumed shadow of Jennifer Flowers hanging over his political head. Soon, it would be credibly known that he forcibly raped a woman when he was attorney general of Arkansas; that he invited a stranger to his hotel room during a fundraiser, dropped his drawers—

Why does Bill Clinton wear boxer shorts?

To keep his ankles warm.

—and invited her to put "it" (Wilbur) in her mouth; groped a supporter in the Oval Office...

There were so many of them that a dedicated section of his campaign team went around quelling "bimbo eruptions" through bribes and threats.

Pre-Clinton, even a smutty remark to a woman, if you were a public figure, got you tossed out on your butt. Now, however, Lefties were in a dither to protect shoddy behavior which, to them, was explainable and not particularly shoddy at all. After all, these were new times of sexual freedom, an age in which sensitive, enlightened people were nonjudgmental.

"The president's enemies are enemies of sex," proclaimed *Playboy's* Hugh Hefner. "Hillary is right. There is a conservative cartel out to get the president—and anybody else who is openly sexual... The attempted character assassination of Clinton may be the final battle in this century-long culture war... We have a Playboy in the White House. And depending on the poll, as many as 65 percent of Americans think that's just fine."

Clinton and the White House will probably end up being a sexy TV sitcom.

"If you take someone like the president who a lot of women would find attractive," said Clinton apologist Gene Lyons on *Meet The Press*, "(and) make him President of the United States...and you sexualize his image with a lot of smears and false accusations so that people think he's Tom Jones or Rod Stewart, then certain irreducible numbers of women are going to act batty around him."

Sounds like ole Gene is acting a bit batty himself.

Steve Schragis of Carol Publishing made an offer for a book entitled *Dreams Of Bill,* in which women had sexual fantasies about Clinton.

"This caught my eye," Steve admitted. "I have to admit I'm a big fan of Bill's and I can see dreaming about him. I haven't yet, but who knows?"

How does Bill Clinton define safe sex?

Whenever Hillary is out of town.

Then Monica Lewinsky met Bill—and Bill displayed his typical libido. The resulting scandal was repeatedly dismissed by apologists as being "just about sex." It *was* about sex. But it was also much more than that. It was about character. Not only that of Bill Clinton, but also, as it turned out, about the character of those who defended him, apologized for him and, in the process, condoned and assisted America's further slide into cultural insanity. In one sense, it was also about the character of the American people.

Monica came to Washington as a girlish, naïve 21-year-old to work in the White House as an intern. Quite understandably, she was taken by the glamour and power. Easy pickings.

"My heart skipped a beat," Monica wrote later of how she felt when she met the president. "My breathing came a little faster and there were butterflies fluttering in my tummy."

Flirtations began quicker than you could mutter Victoria's Secret. Our poor, gullible President was ensnared by this predatory female. All she had to do was lift her skirt and show him her thong underwear.

"A small, subtle, flirtatious gesture," as Monica described it.

John P. Siegal theorized in the *Wall Street Journal* that he believed the Clintons "have learned guilt-free separation of sex and intimacy. A sexual act is not about domination or submission, nor is it about making love or an expression of intimacy, nor even a fleeting moment of passion or overwhelming animal attraction. It is simply fun, another individual performacne sport in which one casually engages one's friends and acquaintances, like golf, tennis, jogging or shooting baskets..."

Let the games begin.

The world soon heard of the president's and Monica's romping in the Oval Office and in the Oval Office toilet, of when, where, and how many times Monica performed oral sex on him, of their hours of midnight "phone sex," of his creative use of a cigar, which he stuck into his mouth afterwards and proclaimed to "taste good."

Of how she fellated him while he was on the phone with a member of Congress discussing the war in Bosnia. Of how she goosed "the Big Creep" on a rope line and sneaked "to squeeze the President's penis..."

Then... Then...she realized she "had fallen in love" with the President of the United States. And, presumably, with Wilbur.

It wasn't that way with the President. No, sir. No way. The only thing Bill was trying to do was *help* that girl. Presidential aide Sidney Blumenthal said the President who feels our pain was merely "ministering" to a "troubled girl... He ministers to troubled people all the time... He's done it dozens if not hundreds of times. He does it out of religious conviction."

Right. But who was on whose knees?

"You're president," Blumenthal recalled saying to Clinton. "These troubled people can just get you in incredible messes, and you just...you have to cut yourself off from them."

"It's very difficult for me to do that...given how I am," Clinton responded. "I want to help people."

The fun began. For awhile there, the entire world seemed to go as wacky as the White House. It was the golden era of political humor.

In Moscow, as the President addressed the Duma, a female heckler shouted from the crowd, "Bill, take off your trousers and show us what a sexual boss you are."

German Chancellor Gerhard Schroeder offered Clinton a box of cigars. Was he sincere, or was it a poke at the Monica incident? Clinton, it was reported, stopped laughing and looked irritated.

"Officials" at the Asian Pacific Economic Cooperation summit held in Vancouver asked a tobacco shop to cover up a cigar display in order not to "offend the U.S. president, who is known to enjoy an occasional cigar."

Nearby, a sign was spotted outside the Penthouse strip club: *Welcome, Prez Clinton. Our lips are sealed.*

The TV series *Law & Order* referred to a blowjob as a "Lewinsky" on one of its programs.

When actress Sophia Loren arrived at the White House New Years Eve dinner, Elizabeth Taylor whispered to Bill, "I hope you are not going to spend the whole evening staring at her boobs."

"I don't do that anymore," Clinton reportedly responded.

Monica appeared in an interview with Barbara Walters. Afterwards, incredibly enough, shelves and warehouses containing her favorite lipstick that had left love marks on Wilbur came under siege. Women begged for the opportunity to buy the Club Monaco brand "blaze" lipstick and "bare" lip liner so they could look like Monica.

"Any woman alone with him for five minutes would have done exactly the same thing," Monica insisted in excusing her behavior.

I would hope Mother Teresa or Margaret Thatcher would have had more self-control.

As at any other time when a Clinton scandal broke, the President could always be seen with Hillary on Sundays walking out of church with the biggest Bible he could carry. The Reverend Jesse Jackson, who was having his own extramarital fling as it turned out, rushed to the White House to commiserate with his friend and presumably offer spiritual advice. A Pentecostal preacher and his wife rode the bus from Louisiana to Washington to bring solace to the haggard president. The preacher reminded the President that the devil lives and that in the world there are dark forces and dark men. Undoubtedly, he meant the pesky Republicans who were trying to bring our beloved president to his senses.

New Age psychobabble ran as thick as Arkansas sorghum molasses.

"Clinton does not want sex, he wants love," proclaimed Roger Rosenblatt in *Time*. "He never got enough as a kid (dead father, abusive stepfather, absent mother) and he cannot get enough of it now. Anyone who is not given sufficient love as a child will spend the rest of his life looking for it, and so he has..."

"...If we look at this as a family problem, his only real option is to seek marital and sexual counseling and then, maybe, make it a kind of crusade," recommended the San Francisco *Chronicle*. "'I face my problem, world. I get help. That's not shame. Hillary and I are, after all, just another Baby Boomer couple struggling to make sense of our lives.'"

Newsweek's Jonathan Alter asked Clinton whether he might seek psychiatric therapy.

"This is a crazy question..." Clinton snapped. "Why are you asking me this question?"

After all, he had the support of the Enlightened Elite.

"Mr. President, we love you!" gushed Geraldo Rivera. "I want to hug you. I want to hug you..."

"After all Bill Clinton has done for us," trumpeted former Arkansas Senator Dale Bumpers, "it's time for us to celebrate his presidency and to do something for him."

At a breakfast, Clinton requested that people pray for politicians and journalists so that Americans could "rid themselves of this toxic atmosphere of cynicism." After all, the President hadn't done *anything* wrong. Those *other* politicians were doing *him* wrong.

"We're cooperating fully. We're not claiming privileges. It's enough," said suffering First Lady Hillary. "*We're* the President." (Emphasis added)

President Clinton looked resolutely into the camera's eye, right into our eyes. "I repeat, I have not had sexual relations with that woman, Ms. Lewinsky."

"Can you name one president that has told more lies than Clinton?" a reporter asked White House spokesman Joe Lockhart.

"I don't think I'm going to take that question."

When White House press aid Mike McCurry was asked if he really wanted to know the truth about Monica, he quickly responded, "God, no. No. No. I really don't want to know. Knowing the truth means that you have to tell the truth."

No, it doesn't.

"The bolder the lie and the more brazenly imposed on the public," wrote Thomas Disch, "the more admiration the liar is accorded."

And Clinton, quipped Senator John Kerry, was "an exceptionally good liar." John Kerry should know, as America was soon to discover in his own adroitness at the art during the 2004 presidential campaign.

"The President looked me in the eye and told me (he had not had sex with Monica Lewinsky)," said Senator Robert Torricelli of New Jersey. "And I'm not upset. You want to know why? Because I never believed him in the first place."

Two John Hopkins University researchers said the President might have experienced sexual amnesia—a loss of memory brought on by passionate sex—during the various court hearings over whether or not he had lied under oath.

"...There is no testimony or no proof that President Clinton knew he was wrong when he looked at (the special counsel's definition of sex)," said Clinton Attorney Greg Craig.

Clinton took the position that while Monica was having "sexual relations" with him, *he* was not having "sexual relations" with her. According to him, "any person, reasonable person" would recognize that Ms. Lewinsky in performing oral sex on him was engaged in "sexual relations," but he was not.

Clinton trouble shooters were prepared to defend their hero against all charges, no matter how outlandish. The White House had more lawyers, on the public dole, naturally, than the First Dog had fleas. The defense was based on the liberal credo: Clinton didn't lie, but it didn't matter even if he had; character didn't count, only public liberal policy; sex was a private matter, even if it was in the Oval Office; taking sexual advantage of a young female employee was only wrong and illegal in the private sector; it wasn't fair, damnit, it just wasn't right to expect the President of the United States to be anybody's role model...

The percentage of those who believed Clinton innocent was less than eighteen percent. The disturbing thing was, nobody cared. It was time for the country to "move on."

Why is Monica Lewinsky switching parties?

Because Democrats left a bad taste in her mouth.

CHAPTER FORTY-FOUR

Sleaze and abuse in the White House began the day the Clintons assumed office. It wasn't enough to simply fire the White House Travel Office staff and put in Clinton cronies from Hollywood. Travelgate's chief victim, Billy Dale, was prosecuted with virtually no evidence of wrongdoing, other than having been in the way. A jury finally took less than thirty minutes to acquit him. Having the IRS audit him was merely a form of punishment after the fact.

Clinton and his administration quickly established a pattern of truth obfuscation, government abuse, destruction of opponents, and corruption. Corruption didn't rub off on that bunch of Arkansawyers when they got to Washington; they brought corruption and sleaze with them. Bill Clinton was the man in the center who led the way into the muck, abusing government power, running roughshod over ordinary citizens and personally soiling himself at every opportunity.

Anyone who criticized him was immediately branded a fanatic, an Extreme Right Wing "Clinton hater," while his apologists portrayed him as a dedicated public servant cruelly savaged by scandalmongers and conservative attack dogs. He might have been a sleazebag, but to the Left and all its politically correct minions he was *"our* sleazebag."

Besides, it seemed, the whole country was too sleazy to care anyhow. What difference did it make if Clinton and his public-paid cartel destroyed those who got in his way? Weren't his so-called victims all sexists, racists, bigots, polluters, and animal abusers anyhow, and didn't they all wear deodorants, carry guns and drive energy-guzzling SUVs?

Juanita Broaddrick accused Clinton, credibly, of having raped her in 1978. Feminist Susan Estrich, who normally pounced on a sexual harassment incident faster than a duck on a June bug, jumped up in defense of her "friend, the President." She branded Clinton female critics as "the catty version of male chauvinism...peroxide blonds...a new brand of babes...bunnies who are, almost to a babe, against sex..."

If you were a female raped, groped or lewdly propositioned by Bill Clinton, you were "a babe against sex." You were supposed to keep your mouth shut. If you didn't, Clinton and his bunch would destroy you. After Juanita Broaddrick went public, her cat mysteriously disappeared and a stranger on the street approached and warned her she should keep her mouth shut. The IRS audited her. Coincidences? I was a cop too long to believe in such coincidences.

Sonya Stewart, former Commerce Department employee, didn't believe in coincidences either. She expressed fear for her "personal safety and livelihood" after she accused the White House of thwarting efforts to expose corruption involving Commerce Secretary Ron

Brown.

In the aftermath of the Elian Gonzalez affair, after the six-year-old refugee was forcibly returned to Cuba by federal authorities, the boy's relatives remaining in Miami suffered government retribution as a result of their struggle against the federal government. They had their lives threatened and official intrusions made into their financial and personal affairs. Judge Rose Rodriguez, who issued a controversial ruling saying the boy should not be seized by force, thereby getting in the way of what the White House wanted to do, was suddenly indicted on a trumped-up charge of illegally accepting a campaign donation.

Can you image Bill Clinton having the chutzpah to accuse anyone else of accepting illegal campaign donations?

"The road to tyranny, we must never forget, begins with the destruction of the truth."

You're not going to believe this, but that's a direct quote from— *Bill Clinton.* The man should know.

The Monica Lewinsky affair was only the latest in a long line of erupting scandals—and it most certainly would not be the last. If you had poked a stick in a nest of polecats, you couldn't have created a bigger stink than the Clintons did in spraying stench on everything around in order to make themselves smell better.

Poor lovelorn Monica was suddenly depicted as a predator entrapping the President in order to garner publicity, not much better than that trailer house trash Paula Jones, part of a vast right wing conspiracy to get the Clintons. Anyone who so much as dared question Clinton became a target. James Carville and George Stephanopoulos promised a "scorched earth policy" during which everyone who had skeletons in his closet would be exposed if he didn't back off.

Hustler publisher and renowned pornographer Larry Flynt offered a million dollars to any woman who could prove she had had sex with members of Congress or high government officials who were Clinton enemies, the accounts of which he would then publish in his nudie magazine.

Flynt is most certainly a reputable citizen I would want to have in my corner were I involved in a sex scandal. He was even invited to the White House. Most folks I know out in flyover country wouldn't invite him to a hog butchering.

"I find it very difficult to see why anyone would be a Republican," Flynt rasped. "They're so callous and bigoted and insensitive to both race and gender."

Don't these people *know* any other mantras?

Linda Tripp, who exposed the scandal, was vilified and ridiculed in the press. The IRS investigated her and she was eventually charged with a felony for illegally recording her telephone conversations with Monica.

Special Prosecutor Ken Starr, a good and decent man, was singled out for trashing by the rancorous and indignant Left.

"I mean, let's face it, America," ranted James Carville, "that's the kind of clown that you've got in there—a spineless, gutless weasel... Most people want Ken Starr to stop his slimy, skuzzy, little sleazy sex investigation... This is a war. And I'll tell Mr. Starr...that I'm going to be on the phone all day with reporters talking about Mr. Starr and talking about people in his office...I'm going to be spreading court records around."

Go, team, go!

Major General Larry Smith was forced to retire after being accused of sexually harassing the army's highest-ranking woman by attempting to kiss her. No free gropes in this man's army unless you're the commander-in-chief.

"I hope (the general's 'victim') will empower and encourage more women to be brave enough to come forward if they have been sexually harassed or assaulted," exclaimed Democratic Representative Carolyn Maloney of New York.

This woman was "brave" to "come forward." Clinton accusers were "trailer park trash, bimbos and sluts." Don't these people understand irony and hypocrisy?

Military authorities were instructed to warn officers and enlisted alike that "contemptuous words...insulting, rude and disdainful comments" about Clinton would be punished. Even repeating jokes about the commander-in-chief and Monica could lead to prosecution under military law.

Air Force Major General Harold Campbell, who had won a Silver Star in Vietnam, gave a speech at an Air Force banquet during which he referred to Clinton in no uncertain terms as "draft dodging...gay loving...pot smoking... womanizing..." He was reprimanded and confronted with the real possibility of serving one year in prison and loss of $66,000 a year in retirement pay.

What would it take to get Clinton to do the noble thing and resign, as Richard Nixon had?

"(Not even) a delegation made up of the Father, the Son and the Holy Ghost," responded a White House source.

Seventy-two hours after Clinton's grand jury testimony about the scandal, he had Afghanistan bombed because of terrorists. At the same time, he bombed an aspirin factory in the Sudan that was almost certainly blameless of any acts of terrorism. The day before he faced an impeachment vote in the House of Representatives, he ordered another bombing of Iraq. Coincidences?

There were a few "wag the dog" comments about how the attacks were timed to take public attention away from Clinton's troubles. Nonetheless, the vast majority of Americans, led by a Clinton-supportive media and an army of cackling Lefties, went placidly along with it.

"In the unlikely event he is pushed from office," editorialized *Newsweek*, "it would take only weeks, maybe just days, before a vast national remorse set in. We destroyed our loveable rogue prince of prosperity over this...?"

In other words—for Christ's sake, just leave the poor corrupt sonofabitch alone!

Senate Majority Leader Trent Lott was one of only a few with the guts to speak up. Clinton's whining, he said, was absolutely bizarre.

"It shows you something about his thinking and judgment that he has. Look, he disgraced the office. He did things in the Oval Office that are absolutely still incredible and then he lied about it. Only a scofflaw could flippantly diminish the abuses of power, the contempt of court, the felonious perjuries, subornation of perjury, obstruction of justice, lying to the American people—and let's not even get into Chinagate—as merely private wrongs."

"I don't care if you have proof that he raped a woman, stood up and shot her dead," said a member of the Republican leadership, "you're still not going to get 67 votes" to convict him of impeachment charges in the Senate.

He wasn't convicted. It was not America's finest hour. Like Sir Galahad, Bill Clinton stood up and fought for a very noble cause—and he prevailed.

"...I was right to stand and fight for my country and my Constitution and its principles..." he boldly asserted. "The right thing to do is the right thing... What was good about (the impeachment) was that we protected and saved the Constitution."

What a hero!

"It would have been a tragedy if we lost him..." said Andy Rooney on CNN's *Larry King Live*. "Yet...there was no question, if we went by the rule of law, he'd be out of there."

America, it seemed, deserved Bill Clinton and all he represented. "I voted for Bill Clinton twice, and I'd vote for him again," his legions still howl. Given his track record and slimy antics, that's like supporting West Nile Virus. He was a soft man for a soft age, the ideal president in an era of *Oprah*, psychobabble, endless therapy and endless obsession.

Vote for him once, shame on me. Vote for him twice, I'm a total idiot. The corruption, wackiness and phoniness continued in the White House until the day Bill Clinton left. Nothing symbolizes more this man's lack of character, lack of a core, than his little show on the Normandy Beach in France during D-Day celebrations. While a score of cameras followed him, he knelt pensively where stones, the only stones on the beach, had been planted beforehand. With battle ships in the background, he arranged a little cross in the sand with the stones and his lips moved in a little prayer—all as though he wasn't being watched and recorded by an invasion of dopey photographers and TV cameras willing to believe this was *real*. I doubt if the man has ever known a real moment in his life, other than when Hillary tosses furniture at him.

He finally made it to Vietnam, after having illegally schemed not to be drafted when there was actually war going on there. He promised beforehand not to apologize for the Vietnam War, as he had apologized for slavery and so many other things.

"He has been wanting to go to Vietnam for a long time," said Bettina Gregory on the evening news.

"I'm glad to be here..." he said when he arrived.

From now on, you can bet on it, he will be telling people, "I went to Vietnam."

You simply cannot invent parody better than this.

Every three days on the average found him out stumping at another Democratic fundraiser or hustling cash for his legal bills or his presidential library.

"We raised a great deal of money that was totally and one hundred percent legitimate," said Dan Fowler, former Democratic National Committee co-chair.

And the part of it that wasn't?

"The man of the people," noted Richard Reeves of Universal Press Syndicate, "has been selling off pieces of himself for these past eight years. How much is left then? Not much, just the anger of uninvited guests who have the temerity to suggest this is corruption."

He would have been a good Caesar of the decaying Borgia or Caligula type. Power, he had the power, and everything else was nothing. He averaged signing a new executive order or policy-making decision every week, nearly every one of them politically correct to whip America into shape.

"Stroke of the pen. Law of the land. Kinda cool," marveled aide Paul Begala.

Clinton searched for his legacy like it was the Holy Grail. Two Norwegian public relations agencies and a Norwegian politician said White House lobbyists tried to enlist their aid in making *Doctor* William Jefferson Blythe Clinton a Noble Laureate. He was always so damned disappointed to have been born in a period of history which lacked great causes with which he could grapple.

"I feel like I was born out of my time," he once lamented. "I should have been president during the Second World War."

In the meantime, Monica Lewinsky was asked if she wanted to reacquire and sell the infamous semen-stained blue dress that bore the Presidential Seal of Approval.

"What sort of girl do you think I am?" she retorted.

And White House Security found large numbers of the Clinton administrative staff downloading hard core pornography from the White House Internet, including gay, teen and bestial sex acts.

This was the real Clinton legacy.

During his last weeks in office, the President brought in a film-maker to immortalize the occasion—Wes Craven, director of *Scream* and *Nightmare On Elm Street* and other horror movies. Seems a fitting choice to me.

He ended his tenure as he began it. He allegedly sold presidential pardons during his last hours, in complicity with his brother and Hillary's brother. A family affair scandal. Enter with a scandal, leave with a scandal.

Staff trashed and vandalized the White House offices and stripped Air Force One of everything except its navigational system. Bill and Hillary even took the White House silver when they left and had to return it when they got caught.

At a Sony Studio event in Hollywood, organizers inadvertently positioned President Clinton before a large movie billboard that seemed to sum up the man's entire life. The movie being advertised was *The Hollow Man*.

Hollow or not, it seems he and Hillary will be with us from now on—writing their books, speaking, trying to stay in the headlines, building a legacy (or overcoming one). Now a U.S. senator from New York, Hillary wants to be president so bad we can all taste the bitterness with her. I wouldn't be surprised if she and Bill don't move back into the White House one day. Disappointed, outraged, most certainly, but not surprised. The arrogance of these people. They actually think they are Royalty.

Senator Hillary kept an American Airlines passenger jet waiting for an hour and a half because she couldn't make it to the airport on time. Does that remind you of how Bill held up air traffic at LAX for two hours while he got a $200 haircut? Finally, here comes an unapologetic Hillary with her entourage of bodyguards and flunkies on her way to make a book signing for her new tome *Living History*.

Would AA have held up a flight even five minutes for you or me? You got to be kidding. My God, will the American culture never rid itself of the Clintons and their breed?

SECTION XVI
CRIME

"The (New York) Times has printed two op-ed submissions in which readers apologized for being mugged. Both said they understood their attackers' feelings perfectly, felt sorry for them, and only wished they could have done more to help."
William Tucker, The American Spectator

CHAPTER FORTY-FIVE

Mark David Chapman, the convicted killer of Beatle John Lennon, made his plea for parole by saying he thought the late musician would *want* him released from prison. "I think he would be liberal; I think he would care."

Weird thing is, the guy is probably right.

A few years ago, a famous cartoon showed two pinheads looking down upon the battered body of a mugging victim.

"My, my," said the one to the other, "the person who did this really needs our help."

I was a cop for fourteen years—four in Miami, Florida, and another ten in Tulsa, Oklahoma, where I was a homicide detective. In addition, I was Director of Criminal Justice at American Christian College in Tulsa. I learned something about crime and even more about criminals during that time.

I have seen children scalded to death and beaten with clothes hangers by addict parents; robbery victims shot down in cold blood for twenty bucks or less; girls snatched off the streets for the pleasure of a gang of predatory males; punks who felt they had a legitimate right to steal from you because they thought you had more than they... Brutes and bullies whose personal self-interest took precedence over their victims' possessions and lives.

And then I saw them all cleaned up for court and looking pathetic and contrite while our goofy society, conditioned to be compassionate and sensitive and tolerant and nonjudgmental, felt guilt for sending the worthless perps to jail where they belonged.

Criminal: I'm sorry I raped that old woman and beat her to death with a hammer.

Liberal: He said he's sorry. Besides, she was old. Our concern should be with him. He's got a full life ahead of him. I feel the pain in his heart that could drive him to do such a desperate act...

During the 1992 Los Angeles riots four black thugs, members of a street gang, dragged Reginald Denny from his truck, robbed him, kicked him senseless and dropped a concrete block on his head. Denny's only offense was driving white through a black neighborhood. The assailants were caught on videotape in one of the most violent and senseless assaults of the decade.

But guess what? Denny was still in the hospital, unconscious, when slogan t-shirts began to hit the market: *Justice For The LA 4. Let My People Go.* Jesse Jackson even appeared to protest the punks' incarceration. After all, it wasn't *their* fault that they had damned near killed a man. It was *society's* fault. It was the fault of *institutional racism.* It was the fault of *capitalism.* It was the fault of everything except

252

the thugs themselves. They were, after all, members of a politically protected class. Besides, Denny shouldn't have been driving down that street.

"The support (for the offenders)," said CORE's (Congress on Racial Equality) state chairman, "has come because so many people feel that there but by fate could be one of their relatives."

That is scary.

"The greatest fears (black people) have are not of gangs," said Comptom City Councilor Patricia Moore, "but of the criminal justice system."

That is simply not true. I worked the ghettos as a cop. Most victims of black gangs are black people. Besides that, why be afraid of the criminal justice system? It has become as politically correct, as sensitive and caring and, believe it or not, as *nonjudgmental* as the military, or education, or religion or any of our other institutions.

A student at Temple University wanted to know if it was racist for him to fear being robbed again after he had been mugged by a young black man when his car broke down in a "bad" neighborhood. Another student, James Trudeau, admonished him to be more careful in blighted, high-crime neighborhoods. The professor then scolded *both* students, saying it was inherently racist to characterize *any* neighborhood as unsafe.

Wait a minute. As a cop working "salt-and-pepper teams" with the Miami, Florida, police department, I saw neighborhoods where it wasn't safe to drive through in an *Abrams tank.* That ain't racist, that's common sense.

A small-time hustler took a shot at me when I was a cop. He was a 23-year-old dope pusher with about five thousand bucks and a sheaf of government food stamps in his pocket. No job. Just welfare, food stamps and dealing dope. An "understanding" judge sentenced him to six months in the county jail, reduced to time served, for shooting with intent to kill a police officer.

"What if he had hit me?" I asked.

"There is no evidence that he actually *intended* to shoot you."

No evidence? The guy was pinging rounds at me and there was no proof of *intent?* That guy wasn't shooting baskets, Judge.

Since no one is considered responsible for his own behavior, no one is held accountable. Vicious criminals are now victims of their environment while the real victims are shunted aside and made to feel almost guilty for wanting to see justice done. *Criminals* are the ones who deserve our sympathy and our help. All they have to do is say *I'm sorry* and Lefties will swarm all over themselves attempting to bring them back into the fold. A mugging never reflects the character of the mugger; it reflects the character of the entire society.

"The people who write for, and read, the New York *Times* make your skin crawl," William Tucker wrote in *The American Spectator*. "The *Times* has printed two op-ed submissions in which readers *apologized* for being mugged. Both said they understood their attackers' feelings perfectly, felt sorry for them, and only wished they could have done more to help."

CHAPTER FORTY-SIX

Psychoanalyst Dr. Maurice Marcus blamed the Denver Super Bowl rioting on—*man's ancestors.* His theory held that fans watch football, see the physical aggression and then can't resist the urge to knock a few heads of their own. They can't help it, you see, because the violent ancestors in their brains took over.

Can anyone recommend a psychoanalyst for *this* guy?

The attorney for Erik and Lyle Menendez, who brutally plotted the slaughter of their indulgent parents in order to receive an early inheritance, devised one of the most original defense strategies of the century. Snails, the attorney said, *snails* explained the crime. The brains of the brothers had been "rewired, the same way a snail's could be."

Snails don't have brains; apparently, neither do some lawyers. The brothers were convicted of murder, snail brains or not, and then the jury was asked to please go lenient on them. They were now, after all, orphans.

Hubert Napier stabbed a woman to death on Roosevelt Island in New York—then explained to the jury that he wasn't responsible because he had a multiple-personality disorder.

An Oklahoma woman killed one woman, went to prison, was paroled, then promptly killed her live-in female lover. She couldn't be punished, she said, because she had a mental problem.

Rashid Baz opened fire on a van crossing the Brooklyn Bridge and killed an 18-year-old rabbinical student. His excuse? He grew up in Lebanon and suffered from post-traumatic stress syndrome.

Wouldn't it be refreshing to go to court one time and hear some defendant stand up and say, "Judge, I did it because I got pissed at the guy?" Instead, it is *never* the perpetrator's fault. It's disturbing how willing courts and juries have become at accepting outrageous rationalization for outrageous behavior.

For example, there was: the "Twinkie Defense" (Impairment through the toxic effects of junk food); the "Black Rage" defense, in which the judge "understood" the rage a black man felt every time he saw a white person; the "Steroid Defense;" the "XYY Chromosone Defense;" the "Mob Mentality Defense;" and various other defenses in syndromes such as "urban survivor" and "post-traumatic stress..."

If the perp isn't responsible for his own behavior, then someone or something else must be. The law seems to increasingly indicate that not even a criminal engaged in his trade is responsible if he can find a handy deep pocket to sue.

Police interrupted two muggers forcibly robbing an 80-year-old man in a New York subway. Police shot one of them as they fled. It left him partially paralyzed. He accused the police of excessive force and sued, winning a $4.3 *million* judgment. The U.S. Supreme Court upheld it.

Whereas he might have only gotten ten bucks off the old man, he became a multimillionaire—he and his lawyers—by mugging the system.

In Hialeah, Florida, two dope dealers arranged to meet "customers" on the parking lot of a Ramada Inn. They ended up getting shot in a drug dispute, whereupon they sued Ramada Inn on the grounds that if the motel had provided adequate security the shootings could have been prevented. They were awarded nearly $2 million in a jury verdict. Even criminals should enjoy proper security while conducting their transactions.

We stand back, *some* of us, cluck our tongues, shake our heads and wonder where the hell common sense went. In the meantime, society drifts further and further away from plumb. In the ranching trade, we say that "the pond has turned over" on hot summer days when some phenomena causes the scum and debris that has settled at the bottom to suddenly convulse and come to the top.

The pond of modern culture, it seems, has turned over.

Each year, the Phillips Exeter Academy gives its Edmund E. Perry Award for "diversity and cultural awareness." The award was named for a graduate of the Academy killed while trying to mug a plainclothes cop. Isn't that an award to inspire?

I nominate thirteen-year-old Nate Brazill for the award. He brought a gun to school one day in Palm Beach, Florida, where he shot and killed his teacher.

"When you meet him," said his attorney, with absolutely no intent at irony, "you're going to see that he is what makes America great. He's intelligent, sensitive, caring...just a wonderful kid."

So this "sensitive, caring" kid came to school one day and shot down his teacher. Certainly sounds to me like he's "what makes America great."

Through some bizarre twist of logic, violent and vicious criminals have been turned into aggrieved and offended victims of our society. Such an approach is especially effective if these "victims" have learned to parrot the correct rhetoric to assist the Left in working on the nation's collective guilt for being "judgmental" and expecting criminals to be judged.

Convicted rapist/murderer Willie Horton was let out of prison on a "weekend leave." He had raped and killed a woman, then was let out of jail to go see a movie and munch a Big Mac! While out, he raped another woman. The Left, inexplicably, took up his cause. He took up the Left's rhetoric.

"The public does not know the real Willie Horton," he sermonized. "I think I'm intelligence, sensitive, caring and honest..."

Does he know the right words or what? "I'm certainly more mature than when I was initially incarcerated..." At least he didn't kill his second victim. "I understand myself better. I know who I am. I'm certainly wiser today. I read more, care more, feel more..."

Toss in a little psychobabble and you have the Lefties goo-goo-ing all over you.

The "sensitive" and "caring" are always willing to provide a platform for every unrepentant and defiant wretch that comes along if he will help "expose the system."

In Texas, Gary Graham pled guilty to *ten* armed robberies and was convicted of the execution-style slaying of Bobby Lambert in the holdup of a Houston supermarket. He was sentenced to die. The Reverend Al Sharpton and Amnesty International representative Bianca Jagger flew down to protest his execution. So did Reverend Jesse Jackson. Where *hasn't* Jackson shown up?

In his last statement, Graham cried out that he was being lynched. "I die fighting for what I believed in."

Isn't that stirring? Sort of like, "I know not what course others may take...but as for me give me liberty or give me death!" What *did* Graham believe in? The right to rob people, to kill them if they got in the way?

"He was amazingly upbeat," gushed Jackson over the executed killer. "There were no tears shed. He had a sense of inner peace. He feels he was being used as a kind of change agent to expose the system..."

See what I mean?

The guy was a vicious dirt bag, Jesse. Dress him up, clean him up, call him a victim and a martyr—and he's *still* a dirt bag.

There is a natural progression from excusing and justifying criminal behavior and rewarding it to the final step of championing it. Making heroes of violent outcasts is one of the most bizarre trends of modern culture. It simply illustrates the depravity to which current liberalism has sunk.

Mumia Abu-Jamal, whose real name was probably something like Robert Smith, is on Death Row for the murder of New York police officer Danny Faulkner. There has been no dispute but that he committed the murder. The Left came on the scene because of his being a Marxist with a high-sounding African name who claims to be the "political prisoner" of a trial unjustly conducted. Understand one thing: If you are a member of a protected group convicted of a crime, then it must not have been a fair trial.

He has since become a *cause celibre* for the wacko fringe. The mention of his name is enough to bring out the intelligentsia in defensive droves. Five thousand of his supporters, including realty-challenged celebrities like Ed Asner and Susan Sarandon, rallied in

Madison Square Garden.

Former New York City Mayor David Dinkins told the crowd that the jailed martyr needed "a new trial, an unbiased judge and a competent lawyer... It's not just Mumia Abu-Jamal's nightmare, it's *our* nightmare. If they come for me in the morning, they can come for you in the afternoon..."

"We must fight the establishment," shrieked Ed Asner. "This fight is for the nation's soul. Mumia must not die!"

Abu-Jamal is in *such* demand. For a while, he presented his socialist tirades on National Public Radio, paid for by tax money. The Quixotic Center of Hyattsville, Maryland, filed an anti-censorship lawsuit against Public Radio when it halted the killer's raving commentaries.

Antioch College hosted the unrepentant Marxist murderer as its commencement speaker in 2000. What an inspiration that must have been. College President Bob Devine complained that opponents tried "very hard to keep one man's voice from being heard." At the same time it invoked its "free speech" mantra, however, the college was imposing a politically correct campus-wide speech code and maintaining a de facto ban on conservative speakers.

If another cop had shot Abu-Jamal while Abu-Jamal was shooting the first cop, do you really think that cop would have ever been a commencement speaker *anywhere?*

There are few faster ways to identify yourself as a redneck hick in intellectual circles than to use words like "evil" to describe certain persons. Endless books, movies and other discourses try to explain away evil as an "illness." They avoid ascribing evil to Hitler or Stalin or Lenin. They justify communism, humanize pedophiles and in general debunk assorted pathologies while, in effect, championing the conditions under which they are allowed to breed.

Homemarkers are ostracized by radical feminists and ridiculed for bringing children up in the home rather than in day care centers;

Parents who spank their children to discipline them are accused of being abusive and subjected to criminal charges;

Politicians, celebrities, sports figures and others in the public eye commit egregious personal acts and crimes and are excused rather than held accountable for their behavior;

Academic excellence and civic responsibility now come second in schools to the teaching of sexuality and "self-esteem." Anyone who advocates the teaching of the Three R's and the Ten Commandments is an old-fashioned Far Right relic;

We are constantly bombarded with the idea of a corrupt America that is racist, homophobic, sexist, and all the other ready labels. We are told that the rich are the only evil, that they own everything and oppress the rest of us. The poor are glorified as victims who have no chance except that provided by the Enlightened.

The environment is being destroyed, the sky is falling, and deodorants and aftershaves will eat a hole in the ozone...

At the same time that conditions breed deterioration and we become more understanding of delinquents and scofflaws, government is busy criminalizing entire new ranges of behavior, politicizing crime as every other aspect of our society is being politicized.

CHAPTER FORTY-SEVEN

"Frank" came home late one night from driving cab and decided to sip a suds and watch a little TV. He got angry at one of those offensive lawyer commercials, dialed the number on the screen and drunkenly lambasted the barrister's answering machine. He was foolish enough to leave his name and number in case the lawyer wanted to respond.

The lawyer did. Police charged Frank with committing a hate crime—*against a lawyer*. It was the first hate crime in Illinois directed at a TV lawyer commercial.

On the one hand, a drunk raving into an answering machine is a hate criminal, despised and abhorred and deserving of getting tossed into the can. On the other hand, we trivialize the behavior of those criminals we've turned into "victims."

Orlando, Florida, convicted a man of having sex with a girl and knowingly infecting her with AIDS. Judge Deb Blechman sentenced him to nine months *probation,* and then she really threw the book at him. From now on, she ordered, he would have to obtain a witnessed signed permission statement from all sex partners, male or female.

"The judge was looking for some way to make his future partners *absolutely* aware that he was HIV positive," explained the perp's attorney, "and I was looking to protect him from partners who would say they weren't warned."

Isn't that an *enlightened* approach? What about the 16-year-old girl already infected and facing a miserable death? I suppose she doesn't matter. AIDS is, after all, a politically correct disease and mustn't be discriminated against.

Dennis Cayse of Ohio was convicted of drunk driving. "Everybody" knows alcoholism is a disease. The U.S. Supreme Court ruled that it was "caused and maintained by something other than the moral fault of the alcoholic." There was a time not so long ago when sots endangering others went to jail. Not anymore. Judge James Hapner sentenced Cayse to live within walking distance of a liquor store or bar.

"It's my hope that he'll walk to get his beer and wine rather than drive..." Hapner said.

Don't count on it, judge.

It took centuries of struggle to get rid of the idea that a crime against a king or a duke, or a crime committed by a king or a duke, should be treated differently than the same crime committed by or against a dirt farmer or a simple merchant. That principle is in the process of being reversed through political correctness. We are reverting back to a darker and more dangerous age when punishment need not fit the crime but instead varies according to who commits the crime and against whom it is committed. It is politically correct to enforce "hate crimes" against a drunk ranting over a telephone but incorrect to toss him in jail for driving under the influence. Federal legislation now bases the harshness of punishment on the group identities of the victims and offenders rather than on the actions of individuals involved.

There is now a distinction between ordinary crime and "hate crime." You may be punished for what you did, true, but that punishment will be magnified by what you were *thinking* when you did it. For being motivated by thoughts your government deems unacceptable. Your government is much more eager to investigate one sort of crime over another.

A witness testifying before Senate hate crime hearings in California said he received a memo from the U.S. Attorney's office saying the federal government lacked resources and would therefore no longer investigate or prosecute certain kinds of robberies and embezzlements. He was surprised, however, when shortly after he received the memo a small army of federal agents and U.S. attorneys showed up in Bakersfield to inquire into an altercation involving racial epithets and symbolic watermelons.

It was a perfect example of federal priorities. Rob a bank—no time for that crime. Call somebody a "watermelon head"—Boy, are you in deep trouble.

Equality under the law is lost whenever crimes are invented that can only be committed against protected groups and which protected groups cannot commit in return.

If a husband explodes and beats an unfaithful wife, that's a hate crime against women, protected under hate crime statutes. If *she* stabs a philandering or drunken husband, she probably did it because he drove her to it. Besides, she was likely suffering form PMS.

When gay Matthew Shepard was beaten and killed, it was a hate crime for which we were all guilty because of our alleged homophobia. When two homosexuals sexually molested and murdered a young boy in Arkansas, it barely made the national news. It was certainly not considered a hate crime.

If you're a white man walking down Pennsylvania Avenue and get mugged by a gang of black guys, that's a simple mugging. Cops may or may not investigate. But if you're a black guy strong-armed by white punks, that's a *real* crime, a *hate crime,* and it'll likely make the *Six O'Clock News.*

Guess which of these two incidents is most likely to occur. Let the Reverend Jesse Jackson answer that one.

"There is nothing more painful to me at this stage in my life," he said, "than to walk down the street and hear footsteps and start thinking about robbery—then look around and see somebody white and feel relieved."

We are repeatedly reassured that we'll all still be equal before the law under hate crime statutes, but George Orwell had a better grasp of reality in his *Animal Farm*. Some animals are more equal than other animals. If government can make laws to enhance penalties for crimes motivated "by reasons of racial bigotry," how long can it be before hate crimes also include writing a letter to the editor questioning racial or other social policies? How long before certain speech becomes a hate crime? If you think it won't happen here, ask John Rocker, the Atlanta *Braves* pitcher who expressed disdain for single motherhood, immigrants and homosexuality in a *Sports Illustrated* interview.

He was suspended from baseball, fined, sent to sensitivity training to get his mind right, then demoted to the minors—all for his temerity in voicing a strong opinion. Lefties went into apoplectic fits; they would have given him the Death Penalty if hate crime laws permitted it. I'll bet you a dollar to a donut that Reverend Jackson and crew wouldn't have been outside the prison on a candlelight vigil either while Rocker was absorbing the needle.

The furor over Rocker hadn't even died down before another athlete, Richard Casey, Penn State's star quarterback, spotted a white off-duty cop out with a black woman. Ironically, the white cop, Patrick Fitzsimmons, was the "Tolerance Training Instructor" for the Hoboken, New Jersey, police department.

The black football player berated the black woman for associating with a white man. Then he and his friends literally beat the cop to the ground. Security cameras captured the entire incident on tape. Casey was arrested six blocks away, his boots still spattered with blood.

Want to bet on whether or not *he* was suspended, fined, demoted and sent to sensitivity training?

Penn State's coach refused to condemn him. The university opened an "investigation" that went nowhere. Casey's high school guidance counselor said he was "one hundred percent behind him." While Rocker was lambasted in the press for merely uttering a few words, Casey's incident involving a lot more than words barely spilled enough ink to make it to these pages.

At about the same time that Hillary Clinton was doing volunteer legal work for the Black Panthers, who were promising in song and slogan to "off pigs" and were in fact killing cops and each other, I was a cop working the black ghettos of Miami, Florida, with a black partner, Charles Daniels. Our job was to protect black people against black criminals, and it was one hell of a job. Crime in the ghetto was ten times as high as elsewhere.

Blacks still commit a disproportionate amount of crime. Statistically, black offenders commit up to sixty percent of all violent crimes, the victims of which are overwhelmingly black. That's why blacks are represented in disproportionate numbers among the prison population, not because of racism or discrimination. I'll be called a racist for even pointing that out.

As a cop, was I suspicious of young black men? If Daniels and I spotted four black scumbags prowling somewhere they didn't belong, acting hinky, you bet they got checked out. Eight times out of ten our instinct were right and we ended up saving some poor sucker from getting knocked over the head or his TV ripped off.

It had nothing to do with race. I was just as solicitous of the safety of potential black victims as I was of white victims, and the same was true of Daniels. Daniels and I were cops and we were close friends. The only black and white we saw on the job was that involving right and wrong, good and evil, criminal and victim.

These days, you police aggressively, you try to protect citizens by *being* a cop, the next thing you know you're accused of "racial profiling." Another name for racial profiling on the streets is called "common sense." The idea that a cop isn't supposed to be observant and use common sense is one of the most insane things ever imposed upon society through political correctness. I get a report of two black mugging suspects in a green car, who am I going to stop? Two *white* guys in a green car just to keep from racial profiling?

If I know that seventy percent of the burglary suspects in my patrol beat are black guys, or that eighty percent of the dope dealers are Hispanics, do I racially split up my rolling stops fifty-fifty or thirty-thirty-thirty or whatever simply to satisfy the need to eliminate racial profiling?

So-called "black leaders" are now demanding parity in the jails and prisons. In other words, it's not the crime that counts, it's race. Overlook crimes by certain races in order not to put into jail disproportionate numbers. Isn't that also racial profiling?

Whatever happened to common sense?

You're not even supposed to *talk* about race—unless it portrays protected groups in a positive light. The NAACP violently objected to the National Institute of Health holding a conference at the University of Maryland to explore possible links between genetics and crime.

"When you deal with sensitive issues, you have to be conscious of how these issues are going to be perceived," scolded Jim Williams, director of public relations for the NAACP.

The conference was stopped. If it isn't politically correct, don't even touch it. Don't do it, don't say it, don't even *think* it.

"Some might want to keep silent about the facts for fear that publicizing the true nature and magnitude of interracial crime might give...aid and comfort to America's white racists..." wrote economics professor Walter E. Williams. He's black. That irrelevant fact has to be pointed out to keep him from being called a racist. "Silence is perhaps one of the most effective recruitment tools for racists. They can use our silence for proselytizing disaffected whites with demagoguery about how hate crimes are not important unless a black is the victim... If there's to be racial good will and harmony, at a minimum we must be willing to confront ugly truths. One of those truths has to do with interracial crime. We all readily condemn highly publicized racial violence, such as.... (the) brutal murder of James Byrd by white supremacists in Jasper, Texas. However, there's little notice and condemnation of interracial crime when whites are victims."

Jared Taylor, president of NewCentury Foundation, invited roughly 400 print and electronic media to a press conference at Washington's National Press Club to report on the foundation's newly-released study, *The Color of Crime*. Among its findings was that in ninety percent of all interracial crimes a white was the victim of black while a black was the victim of white in only ten percent of the cases.

Fourteen reporters showed up for the briefing. Only the Washington *Times* and C-Span reported on the study. One reporter said he would like to write a story but doubted he could get it past his editor.

All 400 reporters would have undoubtedly showed up were these statistics reversed. Can you imagine the outcry were black the victim of white ninety percent of the time? My God, there would be a crisis. There would be marches and congressional hearings. People would be demanding action. Jesse Jackson would come out of his corner raging.

You have to confront truth in order to confront and solve a problem. A society gone politically correct concocts its own "truths," then defends them no matter the facts.

After three young men in Washington D.C. were killed delivering Domino's Pizza and a third stabbed in the face with a knife, Domino's instructed its drivers to deliver in certain high-crime neighborhoods only if the customer came out and retrieved the pizza from the driver at the car. According to federal court lawsuits, that was blatant racism since most of the muggings occurred in black ghetto areas.

So what if the delivery drivers were routinely mugged and killed? Get out there and deliver that pizza and duck the bullets and knives. It's the sensitive thing to do. Door-to-door pizza delivery is an inalienable constitutional right.

What kind of insanity forces people to become victims of crime in order to avoid the hard facts and do something about them?

The New York *Times* complained in a headline that *Crime Keeps Falling, But Prisons Keep On Filling*. The *Times* is the second most politically-correct newspaper in American, behind the Los Angeles *Times*, which explains why the connection beween crime and prison was so difficult for its writers to make. Knock, knock! If you put a thief in prison, he's not out on the streets stealing from you.

The Associated Press recently reported a dramatic change in thinking among corrections officials across the country. States, the AP said, are moving away from the lock 'em up and throw away the key attitude of the 1980s and 1990s and are starting to focus on drug and alcohol treatment, job training and education. What he overlooked, of course, is that the 1980s and 1990s "lock 'em up" attitude was the result of runaway crime in the 1960s and 1970s.

"In the 1980s," said Mary Ann Saar, Maryland's secretary of public safety and correctional services, "we began putting people away for a longer period of time, giving them less opportunities for drug treatment and education, and we abolished parole. But, hey, has it worked? I think an honest person would have to say it hasn't worked."

Really? This was the exact same argument made in the 1960s and 1970s that resulted in soaring crime rates. It was only when hard liners took over in the 1980s and 1990s that crime rates began to fall.

Studies show that every time the prison population increases by 1,000 inmates, society gets four fewer murders each year, 53 fewer rapes, 1,200 fewer assaults, 1,100 fewer robberies, 1,600 fewer burglaries, 9,200 fewer larcenies and 700 fewer auto thefts. Those 1,000 criminals are busy little reprobates when they're left alone in the cities.

Yeah, but... But a state pays a public school only $6,000 a year to educate a student while it costs $34,000 a year to keep a prison inmate. Does that make sense?

Not unless you calculate that the average criminal is responsible for $53,900 annual damages to society when he's not behind bars. An inmate is a bargain when you look at it like that.

Yeah, but... But criminals are only criminals because they're poor and disadvantaged and members of a minority. It isn't *fair* to incarcerate them.

Doesn't anyone ever stop to think that their *victims* are also largely poor and disadvantaged and members of a minority?

It is so bizarre to note how Lefties fight to release muggers, rapists and common scum from justice because they're *disadvantaged*, you understand, while at the same time they clamor for more law and more punishment and greater government control over behavior they perceive as being supremely more dangerous.

A panhandler outside a café might be doing everything but mugging passersby and that's considered protected behavior. A New York federal judge ruled that panhandling was "speech" and therefore protected under the First Amendment. Inside the café, however, in Manistee, Michigan, Janie Barton made a private comment to her mother that she wished "these damned spics would learn to speak English." *That* was a jailable offense and not "speech."

Although the target of her "hate speech" did not hear or understand her, an off-duty sheriff's deputy did. Jamie was convicted of a misdemeanor charge of "insulting conduct in public" and sentenced to 45 days in jail.

Insults are now crimes.

In Gloucester, England, cops don disguises and infiltrate local restaurants to try to catch customers using insulting criminal speech. Does anyone doubt but what "Speech Squads" will soon be undercover in restaurants and bars in Milwaukee and San Francisco? There'll probably be a TV hit series, *Speech Squad.*

Government snooping into our everyday lives continues to seek quicker and more technologically efficient ways to keep track on all of us. Can it be much longer before Big Nanny installs monitors in our homes, a la *1984*, and sows spies thickly among us, a la Josef Stalin, to make sure we don't say anything politically unpopular or commit some thought crime?

Boyish behavior such as playing cops and robbers or shooting water pistols is considered threatening and therefore subject to censure, counseling and "reeducation." In North Carolina, students were invited to participate in a program called WAVE (Working Against Violence Everywhere). They were rewarded for spying on other students and reporting those who mentioned *anything* that might be considered a prelude to threatening behavior—including ownership of a water pistol.

As attorney general, Janet Reno urged kids to turn informant on parents, siblings, relatives or anyone else they overheard making ethnic remarks in their homes. If junior overheard you tell a Polish joke or utter an off-color remark about the fairer sex he was to report you by "talking to your parents, teacher, religious leader, counselor or some other adult with whom you feel comfortable."

If the culprits happened to be unenlightened parents, the child was taught to seek out someone "in authority" to which to report them. Mom and Dad may even have committed a hate crime for which they could be prosecuted.

Human spies are, while effective, a bit old-fashioned and unreliable. Electronic monitoring is the wave of the future. Traffic cameras are currently being installed across the nation to monitor our driving habits and punish us accordingly. Overtures have even been made to place cameras at strategic locations on city streets to keep an eye on the public 24 hours a day. In Germany, a traffic camera caught a man expressing his distaste for it by flashing it "the finger." He was convicted of "offending the police." It's a sign of things to come in America.

Government is watching you, making a list of who's naughty or nice.

The FBI deployed a system known as CARNIVORE to allow law enforcement agencies the capability to intercept and analyze e-mail.

The U.S. Secret Service contracted with a New Hampshire company to field a national identity database using the photographs of all drivers' license applicants in the nation.

The Federal Justice Department attempted to pass legislation—"Cyberspace Electronics Security Act"—that would allow police to obtain search warrants and secretly enter homes or offices to disable security on personal computers as a prelude to a wiretap or a further search.

The spy satellite Echelon operated by the National Security Agency was discovered scanning millions of phone calls, e-mails and faxes each hour, searching for key words. "Niggardly," perhaps?

Professors at the University of Pennsylvania say that microelectronics and medical imaging are bringing us closer to a world where mind reading is possible. "Researchers may one day find brain activity that correlates with behavior patterns such as tendencies toward alcoholism, aggression, pedophilia, or racism," explains Arthur L. Caplan, chairman of trhe Department of Medical Ethics.

Consider the ramifications of this development.

"Let's say I show you a series of photographs of people from around the world," Caplan says. "And every time a black face appears, you get a different brain pattern. I start to suspect that you are different in your reactions to blacks than you are to others—or whatever the group is..."

Tendencies could well become a thought crime.

All this is viewed as necessary and acceptable by so much of the Left in order to keep the rabble in line. The Enlightened Elite know best how to define crime and control it. Ordinary punks are not criminals if they can be viewed as *disadvantaged.* The Enlightened, being superior people, should also be above the law and free to dictate it to us little people in the middle between *disadvantaged* and *enlightened.*

Sara Jane Olson, nee Kathleen Soliah back in the 1970s, was a "soldier" in the Symbionese Liberation Army and a fugitive for over 25 years on charges of planting bombs under police cars. Supporters showed up everywhere to offer aid and comfort after she was finally nabbed. Among her liberal celebrity supporters was Bernadine Dohrn, former leader of the Weather Underground, who herself spent eleven years underground before emerging to become a lawyer working on "family policy issues."

"I'm looking at that era to try to figure out what took place and what society can understand from it," Dohrn pompously stated.

That is so typical of Enlightened arrogance. *We* learn something from what the liberals undergo. Whatever happens to them is good for us—and they'll still respect us in the morning.

William Ayres, Dohrn's husband, who had also been a fugitive, offered his assessment of it all.

"Guilty as hell, free as a bird."

SECTION XVII
GOVERNMENT

"When you deal with the government, you're really afraid. You're afraid to think the wrong thoughts. It seems like I have to ask my attorney if I want to go pee-pee."

Mike Welbel, accused by
Federal Government of hiring discriminations

CHAPTER FORTY-EIGHT

Some of the best analysis about government is being done by comic strips. After all, but for the very real and serious impact it exerts over our lives, government is a comic strip. In the strip *B.C.*, the Midnight Skulker leaves a philosophical question scrawled on the side of a cliff in the moonlight: *God uses the leaders we choose to show us what we are—How do you like us so far?*

Many of us choose not to look in the mirror and answer that question. We may not like the answer of what we are. We willingly give up to others our abilities of reason and discrimination and let them do our thinking for us. That way we don't have to be judgmental about anything. We can all be moderates and trot down the middle of the road bleating mindless euphemisms while our sensitive and enlightened shepherds take care of our lives for us.

Every vote should count. That became the mantra in Florida during the 2000 elections drama when pregnant dimples, hanging chads, and lottery tickets were counted and recounted. *Every vote should count.* Incredibly enough, a quarter or more of Americans did not even recognize the names George W. Bush or Al Gore. For those of you in Palm Beach, Florida, those were the names of the two major presidential candidates. Scary thing is, some of the people who didn't recognize the names actually *voted.* Political workers went out, picked them up, gave them donuts, hauled them to the polls and told them who to vote for.

It was even worse during the mid-term elections of 2002. Having lost the 2000 Presidential election, the party of Political Correctness and Hanging Chads seemed willing to do anything to win the midterms. Dozens of stories of voter fraud and attempted fraud popped up in the weeks before November 5th.

Arkansas native Ms. Deborah Willhite abruptly resigned her position as Senior Vice President of Government Relations and Public Policy for the U.S. Postal Service amid allegations that she engineered the cutting of 500 postal jobs in Arkansas so it could be blamed on Republican Senator Tim Hutchinson in a tight reelection race.

In Florida, convicted felons, including one man serving life for attempted murder, illegally registered to vote, as Democrats, in Duval County.

Lyle Nichols was arrested for voter fraud in South Dakota for, as *The Argus Leader* put it, "...suspicious cases in which documents were submitted in the names of people who were deceased or too young to vote... Nichols turned in 226 registration cards, most of which were fraudulent."

Such attempts at fraud occurred in South Dakota, Nevada, Iowa, Connecticut, Oklahoma, Texas, Rhode Island and other states. Election officials allegedly sent out unsolicited absentee ballots, petitions loaded with forged signatures, and covered up vote-buying schemes. In the Minnesota town of Coates, population 163, a total of 94 newly registered voters listed their addresses as Jakes Strip Club.

It got so bad that Russia and Albania sent poll observers to Florida to "assess whether mid-term elections in Florida meet international standards of democracy."

Sometimes I think we don't know enough, or care enough, about our own liberty to maintain it. The Chicago *Tribune* published a poll showing how nearly a third of Americans believe the First Amendment (that's the one about free speech) is *too lenient*. Another eleven percent said they didn't know if it was or not.

Increasingly, our job as citizens is not to actually know anything about government but instead simply to sit in the spectator cheap seats and cheer or boo the Enlightened. Mostly, you're expected to cheer, because if you happen to boo the wrong ones you will likely find yourself accused of racism, homophobiaism, sexist, judgmentalism, etc, and kicked out of the stadium. Citizen stupidity in this strange theater of the absurd is exceeded only by the arrogance and matching stupidity of the Elite on stage.

When Tennessee legislators met resistance in passing a state income tax, Representative Mary Ann Eckles declared, "The people of my district don't know what they need. They haven't studied it like I have."

Representative Bob Patton went even further in his contempt for voters: "All those e-mails we get—I just wipe them off. I don't read them. I'd like them to know they're wasting their time."

The state budget negotiator, Representative Tony Head, told an audience that decisions on important state matters ought to be made by legislators and not left to the people. "We don't need a referendum to make our decisions. We're the ones who are supposed to be educated and know about the issues."

Why do we let the politically and socially anointed push us around? The main reason is that most of us choose to ignore the insanity around us. If social workers have the power to snatch children from their homes, that's none of my business as long as they don't snatch mine. If some farmer accidentally runs over a sacred rat and has his tractor confiscated... Well, I don't even own a tractor.

Politicians gain control over aspects of our lives by keeping up a constant barrage of hysterics while claiming they, and only they, can save us from dangers ranging from fatty foods and tobacco to global warming and the return of the Nazis. Politicians do not want constituencies who *think*. People who think for themselves see things for the way they really are. Politicians prefer Americans who are easily led, easily distracted, and satisfied with spin over truth. In the process, we permit ourselves to be indoctrinated according to the Bible of the Enlightened.

Bruce Tinsley, author of the *Mallard Fillmore* comic strip, had his Mallard duck character describe how politically correct schools will treat America's Independence Day in this new millennium: "Independence Day was started a long time ago by some right-wing gun nuts who didn't want to pay taxes. They wrote about God and militias a lot, so you can see right away who we're dealing with here...They had some control issues with the British that ended up cheating us out of the fabulous British health care system."

Out of the mouths of ducks.

Kabandu, a gorilla at the Boston zoo, interrupted a press conference by a bunch of politicians when he lobbed poop at them. A keeper said the event frightened Kabandu. Perhaps we should all be frightened. Kabandu might have come up with a good idea. Heap it on them rather than letting them constantly heap it on us.

"Political language," wrote George Orwell, "is designed to make lies sound truthful and murder respectable, and to give an appearance to pure wind."

CHAPTER FORTY-NINE

The rallying cry of politicians nationwide has become a single mantra: "Tax 'em, hammer 'em, regulate 'em, and seize 'em." Washington views taxes the way Roman tax collectors did under Emperor Trajan—as the means to feed a hungry and constantly growing government. At the beginning of the Twentieth Century, less than ten percent of a person's wealth and income went to taxes. Today, the various levels of government extract nearly *sixty percent* of our earnings one way or another. In addition, less than a century ago, government regulated and controlled few of the personal and commercial affairs of American citizens. Today, government's greedy fingers poke into every corner of our private, business, social and personal affairs. It's virtually impossible to find a single area of our daily lives that isn't somehow overseen, managed, restricted, or commanded by government.

Worse than that, so many Americans now *demand* government protection and subsidy at the expense of our neighbors and underneath the cloak of benevolence. The American way was supposed to encourage hard-earned success; instead, like everything else in the New Enlightened Society, that premise has been turned upside down. Success is now penalized and heavily taxed, while sloth, failure and dependence is rewarded. Take from the productive and redistribute to the nonproductive. No nation can thrive forever with that kind of philosophy.

"From the time they get up in the morning and flush the toilet, they're taxed," said California Governor Arnold Schwarzenegger. "When they go and get a cup of coffee, they're taxed. This goes on all day long. Tax, tax, tax."

After all, the government knows better how to spend our money that we do. Former-President Bill Clinton led the liberal opposition to any kind of tax cuts for Americans.

"We could give it all back to you and hope you spend it right," he said, then alliterated how it was best the money stay in Washington so politicians and bureaucrats could spend it.

What audacity, what pomposity this politician possesses to assume that I shouldn't have more right to my own earnings than the government does. You would think from all the hot air generated from the Potomac that government owns all money and parcels it out to us like an allowance. We can't be trusted with it all at once.

We rubes and hicks out here? Give us a little show, a pat on the back, a doggie treat, and a brandishing threat of the whip if we misbehave, and we remain tractable and compliant, willing to be milked dry without further complaint.

Some pol is always bleating about how government "can't afford" to let the peasants keep a little more of our own money. It ought to be the other way around. We can't afford *them*. We got rid of a British king a little over 200 years ago, but now we've anointed a whole bunch of new kings who spend our money as if it were theirs. Well, not exactly. Nobody would spend their *own* money so foolishly. They spend a good chunk of tax money, first off, on *themselves.*

Many of us expect to work most of our lives paying in Social Security in order to draw a monthly $1,000 stipend for our last few years. Politicians not only control their own wages, they also vote themselves lavish special retirement packages. Although senators and congressmen pay not a dime into Social Security or any other retirement fund, they can serve for as few as six years in Washington, retire, and continue to draw regular pay for the rest of their lives. Our tax money allows them to live in retirement luxury in Florida or somewhere in the Caribbean. A retired senator may draw as much as seven or eight *million* dollars from the government dole during his "sunset years." No theme trailer parks in Tampa for this bunch.

Representative Zoe Lofgre, D-California, expressed indignation over a House vote that would have required candidates for federal office to reimburse the government for their political travel costs, calling the proposal "petty and unchivalrous." Hillary Clinton's use of U.S. Air Force aircraft in her campaign for the New York senate seat came to one million dollars. She agreed to reimburse less than $33,000 of that. Fleece the taxpayers for the rest of it.

"I have found that it is not easy to stop spending the taxpayers' money," admitted Bill Bradley, democratic senator from New Jersey.

And spend it they do—like drunken sailors on a clip strip. Drunken sailors, however, run out of money sooner or later, sober up, and go back to the ship. Pols never sober up and run out of money as long as they have taxpayers to roll in a waterfront alley. That's why they can so recklessly blow our cash.

New York spends $39,500 per year on *each* homeless person. One $700,000-a-year-program convinced only *two* homeless people to accept housing.

The U.S. Department of Agriculture spent $97 million on a single "vehicle;" $20 million on painting garages in California; and $11 million for a microscope. It lost, *lost,* $5 *billion* in taxpayer funds.

"The bottom line," said the USDA Inspector General, "is that we don't know (where the money went)."

USDA's financial officer, Sally Thompson, then asked Congress for an additional $100 million—so she could look for the missing money with "new accounting procedures."

Six small defense contractors charged the Pentagon for perks such as: baseball tickets, including parking, $14,000; running shoes to improve employees' health, $5,800; maintenance of a 46-foot sport-fishing boat, $62,000; liquor, $24,000; management conferences in Bermuda, Grand Cayman Islands, Jamaica, Hawaii and Mexico, $383,000...

"Emergency" spending by Congress included $750,000 for grasshopper research in Alaska; a subsidy for researching decaffeinated coffee in Illinois; $1.1 million for the care and handling of livestock manure in Starkville, Mississippi, out of which came an official warning from the Occupational Safety and Health Administration (OSHA) that manure could make barn floors slippery and therefore dangerous.

We cowboys out here with it all over our boots needed to be told *that* by the government?

How about these other noxious abuses of the public treasury: $750,000 for a Baseball Hall of Fame; $350,000 for a Rock and Roll Hall of Fame; $200,000 for the Maxine Waters (D-California) Employment Preparation Center; $150,000 for office renovation for Senator Robert Byrd (D-West Virginia)?

Other spending items approved by the White House and the house and Senate Budget Committee included: $615,000 to renovate a skating rink in Plattsburg, New York; $84,425 for posters commemorating the first settlers of Muskegan, Michigan; $312,000 for a sculpture memorial of Princess Diana, to be erected in Lake Ozark, Missouri; $2.1 million to establish a Skateboard Hall of Fame; $3 million to fund a Miss District of Columbus pageant; $12,600 to replace waffle irons in the Congressional dining room; $230,000 to study the sex habits of house flies; $27,000 to study why prisoners want to escape; $400,000 to distribute information on the correct way to cut toenails; $100,000 to find out why Americans don't like beets...

A Montana group requested tax money to cook a three-ton hamburger in order to make the Guinness Book of World Records. A grant from the National Science Foundation helped Dr. Alex Lobkowski answer the important question of, "Do candy wrappers make less noise when you unwrap them slowly...?"

Government maintains a delicate balance between, on the one hand, picking the peasants' pockets for more money by threatening to curtail "needed" social services, then soothing them on the other hand by doling out enough gratuities to keep them from storming the gates.

"What is free money and how can you get it?" begins an ad by the National Grants Conference which helps Americans get to the government trough. "For anyone who's in business or even wants to start their own business, you can get a $6,000 or more subsidy, courtesy of the U.S. Congress, that you never have to pay back..."

"I went down and applied for grants. They gave me $50,000," said Louis Wilson, a construction company owner. "With that $50,000 I was able to buy better equipment and with the better equipment I was able to get bigger jobs. I made a lot of money after that and I didn't have to pay that grant back."

"When I received that grant," reported Mary Orlando, "I felt like I just won the lottery. I used the money to fix up the house. I later sold it for $58,000. I made a $36,000 profit, and I never had to pay back the grant money."

Where do these people think this money comes from? For government to favor some with windfalls requires the seizure of it from others.

The bell began to toll the end of freedom and liberty the moment the public discovered it could vote itself largesse from the public trough. Every hog in the pen is now squealing and fighting in a mad struggle to get to the slops, to get his share. Pols have discovered the best way to keep power is to buy it.

"This week is tax week," columnist Michael Sasser wrote, "when our tithing go off to Washington to provide for the common defense, promote the general welfare and, well, build highways. Then the other 90 percent of our donations can be used to support the bureaucracy and pay off the sycophantic voters who support the establishment in exchange for a check."

The city of New York employs 353,000 people, one in every 21 residents. Put your voters on the payroll and guess what they will vote for—more government.

Half of all federal employees, about 900,000, work at jobs that are not inherently governmental in nature, which could be done cheaper and more effectively in the private sector. But do you really think their numbers will do anything but increase? Government knows it has their votes and intends to keep them.

Democratic Representatives Elijah Cummings wanted to make sure they stayed happy. He introduced a "Federal Workforce Digital Access Act" that would buy each federal employee a brand-new personal computer, along with unlimited internet access. Subsidized by tax money, naturally.

No one in government is ever compassionate with his own money, but he'll constantly come up with new scams to spend ours. Increasingly in Western democracies, the political Left is using public cash to sponsor and support liberal goals and ideals. It decides a person's morality based on his positions on social issues, then contrives to reward or punish him accordingly. Public institutions, populated by those with the "right" views, are thus corrupted to support an agenda. Those with the "wrong" views are condemned and reeducated.

AmeriCorps created in 1993 is one of the biggest Leftist scams of the century. By 1999, 50,000 people were on its payroll. "Volunteers" are paid a salary in addition to receiving health insurance, emergency dental care, free child care, and an education award. None of these bennies affect how much they receive in food stamps and housing subsidies. *The American Spectator* called AmeriCorps a federal relief project for nightclub comics.

Take all the politically-correct issues heralded by the wacky Left and you'll find AmeriCorps involved in nearly every one of them, with government sanction and government money.

AmeriCorps recruits carried out "undergarment drives" to collect used bras and panties for a women's center; volunteers in Buffalo helped run a government program to pay children five dollars for every toy gun they turned in; others in Lone Pine, California, put on a puppet show to warn four-year-olds about earthquakes; Charleston workers went door to door seeking businesses to apply for government-subsidized loans; throughout the nation, recruits exerted great effort in identifying and locating potential new recipients of food stamps and other welfare programs; a federal education grant proposed to place assistant AmeriCorps teachers all over Mississippi to teach students how to read—but the assistant teachers were only required to read at an eighth grade level...

After a goal was announced to enroll "75 percent of surveyed rural Mississippi residents who are eligible for food stamps" into the program, an AmeriCorps spokesman was asked how recruiting more people for welfare meshed with claims that the organization promoted self-reliance.

"A self-reliant citizen knows what their (sic) opportunities are and figures out how to make use of those opportunities," the spokesman said. How, I ask again, can you parody *parody?*

AmeriCorps provided some $60,000 to support Equality Colorado, an organization that described itself as "dedicated to social change through education, advocacy, and organizing to combat violence and negative attitudes toward GLBT (gay/lesbian/bisexual/transgender) people in our society." The Los Angeles Gay and Lesbian Center received $200,000.

In one project, AmeriCorps members distributed information to students implying they should report to school authorities any time they heard a student make a derogatory comment to another student. An example of a derogatory comment was explained as "one person not being invited to a lunch table."

Guess how all this bunch votes as a block. Give me more government! Give me more government!

Not that long ago, American colonists held a "tea party" in Boston Harbor in protest of what they considered an odorous tax. That tax is *nothing* compared to how Americans are taxed today to support a growing bureaucracy and an increasing proportion of our population dependent upon bureaucracy and taxation for its livelihood.

Film comedian W.C. Fields once cracked that, "The major responsibility of a president is to squeeze the last possible cent out of a taxpayer."

Money is power. The power to tax is the greatest power there is, and the greatest potential source of tyranny and abuse in a democracy. The average American pays more in taxes of one form or another than he spends for food, clothing and shelter *combined.* "Tax Freedom Day," that day of the year when the taxpayer has earned enough to pay for government and starts spending money on himself, comes later and later each year. It is now about May 3, meaning that we work from January 1 to May 3 before we earn enough to spend a dollar on a new pair of shoes for the kids.

Americans should be storming the castle, dumping tea in the harbor, throwing the rascals out. Instead, we bleat placidly and seem conditioned to being fleeced in order not to appear "selfish" and "greedy" by the loony Left's different schemes to relieve us of our earnings and apply them to goofy causes. Walter E. Williams points out that nowhere in the Constitution do we find authority for up to three-quarters of what Congress taxes and spends. There is no constitutional authority for farm subsidies, bank bailouts, food stamps, midnight basketball...

Government is absolutely ingenious at finding new ways to squeeze the turnips. When Oklahoma needed a new fleet of cars for its highway patrolmen, it hiked speeding fines and turned troopers into revenue collection agents. To hell with public safety and all that. Catch them speeders. We need new cars.

It used to be said that the only sure thing in life were taxes and death, and that you could escape one only by doing the other. Not anymore.

Colma, California, a suburb of San Francisco, devised a method to tax the dead. Squeeze every possible cent out of them while they live, then tax their headstones when they die. Gravesites will be levied $5 per grave, per year, into perpetuity.

All taxes are always unto perpetuity. Once enacted, even a "temporary" tax for some so-called needed social service is rarely repealed. On May 25, 2000, the House of Representatives finally voted to repeal a federal telephone tax originally passed to finance the Spanish American War.

Another telephone tax had already replaced it anyhow. The Telecommunications Act of 1996, sometimes called the "Gore Tax" in tribute to its leading proponent, then-Vice President Al Gore, was established by the Federal Communications Commission (FCC). The Telecommunications Act tacked a hidden fee on all long-distance telephone service in order to pay for Internet connections for "underprivileged" schools, libraries and health care facilities. In addition, the regulating act created the Schools and Libraries Corporation to oversee the project, adding another bureaucracy to government with thirteen employees in Washington, 84 independent contractors, and a chief executive with an annual salary of $200,000 and a $50,000 "performing bonus." Total, so far, $2.5 *billion*.

Watch government grow! A billion here, a billion there, and pretty soon you're talking some real change.

In addition to Americans paying taxes, they also shell out another $230 *billion* annually simply trying to figure out the federal tax code and comply with it. Americans spend 5.4 billion hours each year sweating over tax papers. That's the equivalent of three million people working full time—in addition to 93,000 IRS employees with their $63 billion annual budget.

You might expect all our money that *does* go for legitimate government needs to at least be spent efficiently.

"After almost 30 years of delays caused by planning and environmental challenges," the New York *Times* reported, "the last stretch of Interstate 287 between Mortachle and Mahwah, N.J., is to be opened next month—six months ahead of schedule."

The Federal Reserve Bank and the Internal Revenue Service are the most powerful institutions in the United States. According to House Hearings, the IRS has customarily used threat, coercion and intimidation in its enforcement of tax laws, assuming virtual dictatorial powers over citizens. The potential for political tyranny is almost limitless. The Clinton administration fanned that potential into full flames during that president's reign. If Clinton could twist institutions of government to serve his own political ends, so can future presidents. Not only can they, but they will, which Clinton proved.

IRS auditing and threats of auditing became the main weapon in the Clintonistas' arsenal to force enemies and critics to back down. During Clinton's eight years in office, the IRS pounced upon an unprecedented number of conservative organizations and private citizens who may somehow have displeased Bill and Hillary. Among those selected for IRS attention were The Heritage Foundation; Western Journalism Center; National Center for Public Policy (audited twice); Americans for Tax Reform; The National Rifle Association; Citizens Against Government Waste; the *National Review;* Citizens For A Sound Economy; Oliver North's Freedom Alliance...

Not one organization favorable to a liberal cause was audited. The Reverend Jesse Jackson has *never* been audited, in spite of questionable records and nonprofit donations spent on a mistress to keep her in luxury after she gave birth to Jackson's illegitimate baby. Powerful liberal politicians are virtually immune from IRS attention; government knows its friends.

When Joe Farrah, founder of the conservative nonprofit Western Journalism Center, was singled out for IRS attention, a federal agent admitted to Farah's accountant that it was politically motivated.

"This is a political case and the decision is going to be made at the national level," he said.

Then-Secretary of Energy Hazel O'Leary warned one of Farah's donors that he would lose his federal contract if he continued his support of the Journalism Center.

Not only conservative organizations and nonprofits were singled out for IRS attention by a corrupt administration. Individuals received the same kind of attention.

"The IRS has audited a mathematically improbable series of the president's (Clinton's) critics," wrote syndicated columnist Ann Coulter.

Among those who drew the administration's ire and the IRS's scrutiny were:

Billy Dale, former head of the White House Travel Office, after he was fired to make way for Clinton cronies;

Bill O'Reilly, Fox News, a frequent critic of the Clinton administration;

Kent Masterson Brown, whose lawsuit forced Clinton to release the membership list of Hillary's health care task force;

Jean Lewis, the investigator whose transgressions against the Clintons consisted of taking seriously her duty to investigate Whitewater;

Linda Tripp, whose audiotapes of Monica Lewinsky spurred the Clinton sex scandal. Tony Snow reported on Fox News that Tripp's lawyer received credible evidence that "the White House legal team had asked (an investigator) to root through Tripp's trash and perform a back audit on her tax returns;"

Paula Corbin Jones, who filed sexual harassment charges against Clinton—and won—over an incident that occurred in an Arkansas hotel room;

Gennifer Flowers, one of Clinton's "bimbos" in Arkansas, who unwisely talked about it;

Former Miss America Elizabeth Ward Gracen, who also talked;

Juanita Broaddrick, who credibly accused Clinton of having raped her when he was attorney general of Arkansas...

Government and its elected and appointed representatives utilized personal power to crush or intimidate citizens whom bureaucrats considered a threat. They did it because in this insane New World that political correctness tyranny has built in America, they knew they could get away with it. Corruption in the power to tax and in law enforcement is merely one indication of tyranny on even larger scales.

CHAPTER FIFTY

When Tipper Gore, wife of then-Vice President Al Gore, went to Honduras to view the devastation of Hurricane Mitch, a press spokesman briefed American TV networks on how to capture the action for home consumption.

"She's gonna be shoveling mud. Then she'll wipe the sweat from her brow, like this. Make sure you get that shot, all right?"

The perfect photo op. Staged, faked and phony, lies and light, as are many political events. Tipper came out dressed in jeans and did eight shovels full of mud. She straightened and, sure enough, wiped her brow while pretending the cameras weren't present and that she really *was* working. She appeared on all the TV shows the next morning.

"In Honduras..." she said, her voice soft with empathy and compassion, "we joined the effort to clean up the school that will become a medical facility... That night I slept in a tent outside a shelter with homeless families..."

Maybe I'm overreacting, but I'm offended by such condescension. Should my house get blown away by a tornado and my neighbor comes over, scoops *eight* shovels of mud out of what used to be my vestibule, then goes on TV wiping sweat and saying how much he helped me and shouldn't I be grateful, I'm certainly not going to elect him to office and give him control over my life.

But we do it all the time, fall for symbolic gestures and "I feel your pain" ads. In a society in which symbolism trumps substance, we seem ever more willing to accept more and more minute government regulation of our lives. For every eight shovels full of mud, we also get eight of bullshit and ten times eight of regulations. After all, the Enlightened *care* about us. They want to take care of us. The result is that we have created a New Priesthood of Enlightened Elites who do what they damn well please to us because we yahoos have proved that, for eight shovels full of mud, we'll pretty much go along with anything. In turning America into *the* Regulating Society, the sensitive and the Enlightened consistently act as though nothing is as dangerous as insufficient government power. The recipe for progress appears to be more law, more regulation and more penalties.

We are being regulated down to the type of toilet we can flush, the content in the material of our drawers, the thoughts we can express in public. The Federal Registrar in 1999 contained 71,161 pages of regulations, a four percent increase over the previous year. More than 4,000 new rules and regulations are issued by federal government agencies every year, more than 30,000 new ones within the last seven years. The annual U.S. cost of imposing all these regulations exceeds Canada's entire gross national product.

To put this in perspective, the Lord's Prayer is 66 words, the Ten Commandments 199 words and the Declaration of Independence 1,300 words. The U.S. Government's regulations on the sale of cabbage alone totals 26,911 words. A Florida ordinance required 346 words to explain "buttocks" in an anti-nude dancing ordinance so as not to violate "freedom of artistic expression." See if you can figure this one out:

"The area at the rear of the human body (sometimes referred to as the gluteus maximus) which lies between two imaginary lines running parallel to the ground when a person is standing, the first on top of such lines being one-half inch below the top of the vertical cleavages of the nates (ie., the prominence formed by the muscles running from the back of the hip to the back of the leg) and the second or bottom line one-half inch above the lowest point of the curvature of the fleshy protuberance (sometimes referred to as the gluteal fold), and between two imaginary lines, one on each side of the body..."

Back in 1945, Lloyd Olsen of Fruita, Colorado, fancied a chicken dinner. He caught his rooster Mike and chopped off his head. Instead of ending up on *that* Sunday's menu, however, Mike ran around "like a chicken with his head cut off," so the story goes, for a full eighteen months before he finally succumbed.

Brigades of Mikes running around with their heads cut off and armed with visions of a "new egalitarianism" now run mindlessly throughout America imposing their Utopian visions upon us poor slobs. Nothing escapes the regulators.

The U.S. Department of Agriculture issued a regulation to reduce the size of the average hole in Swiss cheese from eleven-sixteenths of an inch to three-quarters of an inch. DOE, the Department of Energy, decreed that the typical top-loading washing machine that controls ninety percent of the market uses too much water and energy. Therefore, more-expensive, less-efficient front loading machines will be forced upon the public. DOE had already made a similar ruling about flush toilets.

In the tyranny of the therapeutic state, enlightened little despots arrive with misty eyes and quivering lips to give us "help" whether we want it or not. Take the "Twinkie Tax," for example, another step in government's taking over and managing for individuals what was formerly considered personal. Dictating for us what constitutes acceptable and unacceptable values and attitudes.

It began, of course, with the Enlightened discovering a new "victim" class—the fatties. Naturally, overeating wasn't the fatties' fault, no more than sucking smoke into their lungs was the fault of cigarette smokers. People don't really have choices; we're victims. The Enlightened looked around to see who or what was victimizing the lard butts and, lo and behold! What did they see—junk food! Big Macs and Whoppers and Domino's pizza and the Colonel's fried chicken.

Bumper stickers appeared: *Tax Fast Foods.* Neo-Puritans held press conferences and published reports alleging the dangers not only of bicycles, skateboards, golf courses, and trimming your own toenails but also of hot dogs, steaks, Mexican and Chinese food, popcorn, ice cream, hamburgers... We heard tearful testimony of lives lost through overeating, of related health problems, of the trials and tribulations of "victims" pursued by sinister chocolate and cunning butterfats.

America, cried Kelly Brownell, director of Yale's Center for Eating and Weight Disorders, lives in a "toxic food environment... There is no difference between Joe Camel and Ronald McDonald."

Look out, Ron. You're about to eat the silver slug and be buried next to Joe Camel.

Isn't it my own business if I turn into an Indian lard butt by stopping every morning at Daylight Donuts? Not in this wacky New World where Big Nanny is watching and feeling our pain.

"Hide the ham, guard the gravy, and hold on to your hamburger!" warned Steve Dasbach, Libertarian Party's national director. "The calorie cops are coming after us. If you don't stop them, the grease Gestapo will do to fatty food what they've already done to cigarettes."

Yale's Center for Eating and Weight Disorders wants to *make* us eat less junk food by government's subsidizing the sale of healthy food, increasing the cost of "non-nutritional" foods through taxes, and regulating food advertising to discourage unhealthy practices.

The Center for Science in the Public Interest (where do they get these titles?) declared that tax on Whoppers and Keebler's Oreos "makes eminent sense." It demanded a ban on "junk food" advertising.

U.S. News & World Report hailed the "Twinkie Tax" as one of "16 Silver Bullets: Smart Ideas To Fix The World."

The New Republic said tax on fatty foods "can actually be a less intrusive policy than regulating tobacco."

Barry M. Polkin, professor of nutrition at the University of North Carolina, wrote that, "...Our research shows that strategically altering prices can potentially lead to better health... Changes in government subsidies, taxes, and public health services can literally change the menu..."

All the wackos joined the crusade. Vegans demanded an end to the sale of meat and its replacement by carrots and sprouts. Animal righters insisted that no product from an animal held in slavery be used. Environmentalists wanted a fat-free environment. Politicians demanded strict controls over candy ads...

And then...and *then*, along came Big Nanny.

The Colorado legislature declared dieting as the state's "official health policy" and passed the Obesity Prevention Act that described "fat people as suffering from a disease." Victims.

"Politicians..." went a news release, "want the state to look at ways of ensuring citizens do not overeat at meals."

How are they going to do that? Send undercover cops to restaurants to catch you at it?

"Your honor, I observed the defendant order *two* bags of French fries, when the Surgeon General explicitly states that excess consumption constitutes a risk to health and therefore a violation of Section..."

Sound far-fetched? I'm really not making this up. Have you read the rest of this book?

Colorado, the news release continued, would also produce an annual "fat report" to "see if tougher measures are needed."

Such as? Suing Big Fat Foods? Fining grocers and padlocking their doors? Casting recidivists into jail and sending first offenders to "re-education classes" next door to "sensitivity training?"

We ordinary citizens are simply too weak-minded to know what is best for us. We are little children who need government to protect and look over us. That was what the Big Tobacco issue was all about, protecting us sheep from our own behavior, although government and a bunch of lawyers reaped one hell of a windfall on their own in the process.

You have to be an idiot to smoke cigarettes in the first place—but we all have to be completely bonkers to accept government measures to protect us from cigarettes.

In addition to laying prohibitive taxes on tobacco, government has now warned tobacco companies that if the number of smokers under the age of eighteen has not been cut in half by a prescribed time limit, cigarette producers will be fined $3,000 annually for *each* underage smoker in the U.S. It will be interesting to see how *that* is calculated.

The do-gooders, naturally, are in the front ranks to help government stamp out cigarette butts. When California passed Proposition 99 and raised tobacco taxes to new, even higher levels, the Americans For Nonsmokers' Rights Foundation, yet another support group, began compiling an enemies list of people it suspected of secretly working for Big Tobacco. It passed the list on to interested government contacts.

Texas teens caught smoking must pay a $250 fine and attend (what else?) a "tobacco awareness class" or lose their driver's license. In Pleasant Plains, Illinois, guilty underage smokers are sent to a "tobacco education class." I hope it's a more honest class than New History or New Math in public education.

Massachusetts attempted to enact a law requiring urine tests for nicotine. In Sylvania, Ohio, convicted teen smokers may satisfy community service by participating in "sting" operations to catch store clerks selling Camels or Marlboros to underage customers. The federal government nationwide urges states and municipalities to use fifteen-

or sixteen-year-old kids in their tobacco stings against businesses.

In San Diego, voluntary compliance of the ban against smoking in public places, especially in bars, did not work. Therefore, police vice squads went undercover to bust the notorious barroom smokers.

"What we want to do is create paranoia," said Police Sergeant Sam Campbell. "We want smokers to be paranoid about being cited for breaking the law. If paranoia gets compliance, I can live with it."

But can *we* live with it?

Doesn't anyone find it crazy that at the same time we are in deep national discussion about legalizing all kinds of drugs, even providing needles and drugs themselves at taxpayer expense, we are cracking down on tobacco and Twinkies?

"In the name of ideals such as income equality, sex and race balance, affordable housing and medical care, orderly markets, consumer protection, energy conservation, to name a few," writes economist Walter E. Williams, "we have imposed widespread government controls that have subordinated us to a point at which considerations of personal freedom are but secondary or tertiary matters... Taking tiny steps toward the goal, we will ultimately get there—totalitarianism, a reduced form of servitude."

But Big Nanny will be compassionate toward us in our servitude— or at least toward some of us, those in protected categories. Can "means-tested justice" be far from American courts where it will join "hate crimes" and other forms of justice designed for various groups? It has already reached England.

Traffic offenders in England will now be fined according to their means. New guidelines issued by British courts state, "The fine should be a hardship depriving the offender of the capacity to spend money on luxuries, but care should be taken not to force him or her below a reasonable subsistence level."

If I have a good job and am responsible with a few bucks in the bank, I might have to pay five hundred dollars for running a stop sign in order for the punishment to "be a hardship..." But if I'm an irresponsible ne'er do well and part-time petty thief, I might only pay five dollars for the same offense.

How exactly do you determine an individual's fine? By the size of his house, the year of his car, his salary before or after taxes? What kind of message does that send? Let us go out there and, in every way we can, chastise those who are ambitious, frugal and successful.

Government's true role in society is to prevent evil. It invariably creates evil when it endeavors to do good. Government uses bad means—coercion, confiscation, fines, punishment—to achieve what the Enlightened see as good ends—helping people. We would be tossed into jail as extortionists and common thieves if we did half the things government does. The liberal philosophy seems to be that the more people government can bring to their knees in supplication, the fairer society becomes.

Mike Welbel owned Daniel Lamp Company in Chicago. All 26 of his employees were minorities--21 Hispanic and five black. Nonetheless, two Equal Employment Opportunity Commission feds in pointy shoes and power ties paid a visit to inform him that, according to the local population, he should be employing 8.45 black workers instead of the current five.

To make up for past discrimination, the EEOC ordered Welbel to spend $10,000 in newspaper ads to seek out those blacks who had applied but had not been hired by his company—and pay them $123,991 in compensation.

He couldn't do that, he responded. It would drive him out of business and then everyone would be out of a job.

So what?

"When you deal with government," Welbel said, "you're really afraid. You're afraid to think the wrong thoughts. It seems like I have to ask my attorney if I want to go pee-pee..."

A deal was finally struck. Welbel gave the government $30,000 to settle the issue, plus another $20,000 to pay to people who hadn't been hired. But the nightmare continued.

"We report everything to the government," he said. "We keep all kinds of records of who applies, who is hired, who is not hired, why they are not hired. We're really busy record keeping for the government... It left a stigma in my mind. Sometimes I'm afraid I'm thinking the wrong thoughts...asking people the wrong questions when they apply... You can get paranoid from this kind of thing. You're always afraid you're not doing the politically correct thing..."

Hey. *I'm* paranoid about writing this politically incorrect book. Reckon the IRS will audit me again next year or that my name will go down somewhere in the federal government as a potential "hate crimes' suspect?

We have all heard of Stalin's and Khrushchev's "five year plans" and "ten year plans" for minutely regulating every aspect of the economy and every facet of an individual's life in order to create a "new communist man." Over and over again, the Enlightened tell us they have the same kinds of plans for the United States. Why don't we listen to them?

"I am a socialist at heart," declared media mogul Ted Turner on a trip to China.

Notice he didn't stay in China.

"If we are to avoid the eventual catastrophic world conflict," said Walter Cronkite upon accepting an award from the United Nations' World Federalist Association, "we must strengthen the United Nations as a first step toward world government... We Americans will have to give up some of our sovereignty."

In an interview with the German magazine *Der Spiegel*, Senator Hillary Clinton (D-New York) praised her husband's close ties with Europe. "For eight years we were on the right course to a globalized and integrated world, which is coming one way or the other... A single unified world is a perspective we Democrats had not successfully made clear."

"Nationhood as we know it," lectured former Deputy Secretary of State Strobe Talbot, "is obsolete: all states will recognize a single, global authority. National sovereignty wasn't such a good idea after all."

Part of the Enlightened plan includes world government. What would World Government entail? A single world military that could enter the U.S. and arrest you without due cause; a world court with power over the U.S. Constitution; world taxes; a world religion such as that described in the Christian book series *Left Behind*; brain washing of children (more so than now); gun confiscation; seizure of all private property; encouragement of deviancy in any form...

More government is exactly what we need—concentrated at the highest possible level. It is amazing how so few of us notice Mike the chicken as he scurries heedlessly about imposing greater and greater restrictions upon individual liberty.

"Decisions about motherhood and abortion, schooling, cosmetic surgery, treatment of venereal diseases or employment," Hillary Clinton wrote, "where the decisions or lack of one will significantly effect the child's future, should not be made unilaterally by the parents."

No, ma'am. The *state* should make such decisions.

"There is no act of treachery or meanness of which a political party is not capable," warned Benjamin Disraeli.

Especially is that true when the Enlightened have their eyes set on a goal that "will make a difference." They continue to devise new and devious means of keeping track of us and forcing us to "do good," inventing new lexicons as did the Nazis and communists to disguise their true intent. Coercive power is increasingly prettied up, subterfuged and coached in the misleading language of Newspeak of which George Orwell was so contemptuous.

Does any of the following Newspeak from Nazi Germany ring a bell?

The invasion of Poland in 1939 was called a "police action." Withholding of money from paychecks—taxes—was referred to as "voluntary contributions." "Urban renewal" described the razing of a

Jewish synagogue. People were taken into "protective custody" and "relocated" or "resettled"—in ovens.

Most of these terms and many others of the same obfuscation have found their way into our own government lingo. "Contributions" means taxes. "Investments" is a general word for government spending, much of it pork and most of it certainly not invested. Being allowed to keep more of your own money through reduction of taxes is deemed "wasteful spending" or "irresponsible spending" by government. "Affirmative action" is a high-priced word for cheap quotas.

It's easier to swallow quinine if you mix sugar with it to disguise it. But it's still quinine. We're made to feel guilty and anxious if we don't swallow it without complaint.

The backs of checks used to warn us not to "fold, spindle or mutilate." Technology is providing government new means with which to fold, spindle, mutilate, number, identify, catalogue and pigeon-hole citizens for easier tracking and control. Americans have shown ourselves surprisingly compliant to about anything government heaps upon us as long as government pork keeps coming to salve our consciences and special interests.

We already have Social Security numbers, without which we become virtual non-citizens unable to get a job, apply for credit, buy a home, get a driver's license, go to school... Children when they are *born* are now issued a number. The 1996 Health Insurance Accountability Act would have required everyone receive an "identifier" at birth that would follow him throughout life.

Minnesota transportation officials planned to equip automobiles so they could be tracked by satellite wherever they went in order to assess fees and taxes based on where, when and how much one drove.

Internal Justice Department memos concocted justification to permit "intrusive investigative activity" by the FBI, ATF, U.S. Postal Inspectors, U.S. Marshal services and other federal agencies. It would allow them to compile dossiers on non-politically correct groups such as the National Conference of Catholic Bishops (opposes abortion), National Rifle Association (pro-Second Amendment), National Taxpayers Rights Foundation (opposes excessive taxation and waste), and the Christian Coalition (Far Right Wing).

Marvin Goodfriend of the Federal Reserve Board proposed government use new technology to penalize citizens who do not spend their cash as fast as government wants. A sort of frugality tax.

"The magnetic strip (on U.S. currency) could visibly record when a bill was last withdrawn from the banking system," he explained. Feds could then impose a "carry tax" to discourage "hoarding" of currency.

What comes next? Numbers tattooed on our foreheads? Monthly reports to government on our activities, travels, expenditures? It *could* happen.

Does government have the right to do such things? It has the power. That's what counts.

Liberty is lost in inverse proportion to the growth of government. All around us, if we open our eyes, we can see the symptoms of freedom's defeat—the Constitution overthrown; public schools turned into propaganda centers for political correctness and the Enlightened socialist agenda; colleges that no longer teach history or logical thought processes but which concentrate upon "esteem" studies and "ethnic" and "gender" studies; an aggressive cultural war waged against religion, tradition and all standards of right and wrong; degradation of moral frameworks; destruction of patriotism and the ideals of hard work, individualism and success...

"One of the ugliest aspects of totalitarian societies," Thomas Sowell wrote, "is having children inform on their parents. We have already gone much further in that direction than most Americans realize..."

Schools across the United States commonly require children to keep diaries and fill in questionnaires about their parents—in order, of course, to protect the children from potential abuse and counteract non-politically correct ideas.

Spying for government extends well beyond children and parents, however. We are rapidly becoming a society in which everyone must be suspicious of everyone else as a potential informant whose revelations or lies can and do ruin lives.

Billboards provide 800-numbers for informants to call to report excessive exhaust fumes from their neighbors' cars, litterers, suspected child abuse, or noncompliance with scores of petty rules and regulations.

My year-old grandson needed his diaper changed while we were driving in the car on an expressway. My wife took him out of his car seat for a few minutes to administer that task. A few days later we received a letter from something called The Safe Kids Coalition. It warned us that a "citizen" had observed us driving with an "unsecured child" and threatened punishment.

A father whose son received a black eye while playing baseball expressed relief that it happened during summer vacation. Otherwise, it would have been reported by school authorities and a child investigation begun.

You must remember. Big Nanny is always watching.

"Unique to this century has been the marriage of sinful men, of powerful governments and technological progress..." wrote R.J. Rummel, author of *Death By Government.* "The more power the government has, the more it can act arbitrarily according to the whims and desires of the elite..."

The New York *Times* reported in 1999 that the Clinton administration "summoned six drug company executives to the White House...and reprimanded them for running advertisements critical of President Clinton's plan to offer free prescription drug benefits to everyone on Medicare..."

They were summoned? Reprimanded?

Does no one have the guts anymore to tell government to stuff it where the sun doesn't shine? Telling government "it's none of your business" does not mean anarchy. Cynicism about government is not a "hate crime," as some people would have us think. In a society rapidly going bonkers, it might be well for us to remember the warning of retired author, economist and journalist George Koether before we all end up in cages.

"We'll never get a world without government," he wrote, "but I believe we must organize and maintain a strong antigovernment movement simply to keep the beast in its cage."

One year when I was a kid, we were so poor Dad had to do something dramatic and against our principles—accept charity. He signed up for what he called "gimpy groceries"—free government surplus commodities for the poor. He was too proud to go after them himself. I was about twelve, so he sent me with a gunny sack to tote home the free bacon.

At the giveaway barn, one of the government workers started shoving us into line. I flared back that he didn't have the right to push me around. He replied with a phrase I have never forgotten.

"Boy, if the government feeds you, it'll do what it damned well pleases."

SECTION XVIII
WAR ON TERROR

"Anyone who would blow up the Pentagon would get my vote."
Professor Richard Berthold
University of New Mexico

CHAPTER FIFTY-ONE

"Americans are bedeviled by fantasies about terrorism," a former State Department counterterrorist specialist said a mere two months *before* the 9-11 terrorist attacks against the U.S. "They seem to believe that terrorism is the greatest threat to the United States and that it is becoming more widespread and lethal... And they almost certainly have the impression that extremist Islamic groups cause most terrorism. None of these beliefs are based on fact."

Say what?

It's not like there weren't enough signs that this guy, Larry C. Johnson, shouldn't have known what he was talking about—the bombing of Pan Am Flight 103; the 1993 World Trade Center bombing; the bombing of the Marine barracks in Lebanon; the 1996 attack against U.S. troops living in the Khobar Towers in Saudi Arabia; the bombing of American embassies in Africa in 1996; the sabotaging of the USS *Cole* in 2000... So what were U.S. leaders doing all this time while Osama bin Laden and his cohorts plotted to transport catastrophe to American shores?

For one thing, they were all busy showing compassion and understanding. President Bill Clinton changed the term "rogue nations" to "nations of concern" out of sensitivity for their national self-esteem. A former ambassador from the Carter administration said we should look at "root causes" for why Americans were hated, that we should understand the "alienation" and "sense of grievance" against us by people in the Middle East. Old-time nasty spies had to be made kinder and gentler, so CIA officials forced agents to attend sensitivity training classes and sew diversity quilts. Clinton ordered the CIA to purge any spy who had contacts with unsavory foreign nationals. From whom did he expect to get information on anthrax letters or hijacked airplanes—the Pope, Mother Teresa, a White House intern?

Even when U.S. retaliation occurred, it was seldom more than a weak girl fight. Clinton did nothing in 1996 when nineteen U.S. military men were killed in a bombing of the Khobar towers in Saudi Arabia, nor in 2000 after terrorists blew up the USS *Cole* in Yemen, killing seventeen. Sudan detained two operatives of Osama bin Laden's two days after the bombing of American embassies in Africa; FBI Director Louis Freeh wanted them extradited to the U.S., but the White House refused.

Finally, *finally,* Bill Clinton declared bin Laden the world's most dangerous criminal. "Sticks and stones may break my bones, but words will never harm me." A few Tomahawk cruise missiles were lobbed into empty al Qaeda training camps in Afghanistan. Some more were shot at a "chemical weapons" plant in Sudan—which turned out to be a legitimate aspirin factory. That cost the American taxpayers a million or so to replace. Then the American government sat back and waited with its thumbs figuratively up a particularly unsavory part of the anatomy.

Forbearance merely invited more contempt and audacity. What else were terrorists to think but that the United States was weak and ripe for the plucking? They took a look at the U.S. and what did they see after more than a decade of sensitivity classes and feminization of the nation's institutions? They saw a President of the United States who dodged the draft and had to be taught how to salute; mighty warrior women in the military threatening to sue because of "sexual harassment" and, in the case of an army female helicopter pilot, refusing to fly because babies had a "constitutional right" to be breast fed on time; the odd concept of "Bobby Has Two Daddies" and "Lisa Has Two Mommies," of a nation whining about "rights" while getting in touch with its feminine side.

Perhaps Osama's biggest mistake was in failing to strike while Bill Clinton was still president.

"Bill Clinton never had his shot at greatness," lamented Chris Matthews of the San Francisco *Chronicle*. "He could lower the jobless rate, balance the budget, and console us after the Oklahoma City bombing. But he never got the opportunity George W. Bush was given (on September 11): the historic chance to lead."

Personally, I would feel much more comfortable with Clinton in the Oval Office john. It's easy to imagine his official response—maybe a Tomahawk fired at an isolated cave in the Hindu Kush, followed by hand-wringing summits and jeremiads on how to repair our image in the Islam world to make Muslims like us better.

Instead, George W. Bush became president. He declared a War On Terror with the support of a surprising majority of America. In Baghdad, Uday Hussein became deeply depressed. The former director of Iraqi television remembers Uday exclaiming, "This time I think the Americans are serious. Bush is not like Clinton. I think this is the end."

For awhile after 9-11, it appeared America's Cultural Wars would stand down. Conservative pundit George Will noted some welcome changes. America's mind, he noted, was no longer so open that everything of value fell out. Gone, he said, was the intelligentsia's consensus that the only absolute is relativism—the doctrine that all values are mere "social constructs," thereby arbitrary and temporary.

Sorry about that, George. It didn't last long. The Twin Towers were still smoldering when the Enlightened rushed in to *understand* our enemies, to try to determine if *we* did something to provoke the attack, if *we* somehow might have done something wrong to *deserve* the attack.

"They have good reason to hate us..." declared Bill Clinton. "After all, we sent the crusaders to try and conquer them."

Huh? I say again, *Huh?*

Three days after 9-11, Madonna climbed onstage in Los Angeles and exhorted the audience to pray that America did not retaliate. The ACLU printed and distributed a pamphlet in seven languages telling potential terrorists how to legally avoid answering police questions. Professor Eric Foner of Columbia University began the waterfall of anti-American rhetoric with, "I'm not sure which is more frightening: the horror that engulfed New York City or the apocalyptic rhetoric emanating daily from the White House." And Reuters ran a photo of Ground Zero with the caption *Human rights around the world have been a casualty of the U.S. "War On Terror" since 9-11.*

In other words, stand back, don't do anything that might piss off the Islamics. This time they might *really* hurt us. For one of the few times in my life I have to go along with Georgie Ann Geyer.

"We were sure that the terrorist attack would awaken us from some of the moral lethargy and cultural vulgarity that have so long threatened us," she wrote on March 14, 2002. "Well, we ought to wake up again, because during these last six months we've slipped back into our old habits. In fact, we hardly missed a beat..."

CHAPTER FIFTY-TWO

Lest we think the wackiness is over, that the events of 9-11 jarred us back to some semblance of sanity, listen and watch the inmates squirming and crying out in their anguish and think again. The Left's critique of America's many failures in the social arena became subdued for, oh, entire *days* before the offensive led by academics, the media, liberal politicians, lawyers and all the other usual suspects resumed in full howl. One major sign of what historian Crane Britton called a "markedly unstable society," a society going bonkers, is the appearances of bunches of loud intellectuals herding around the gullible, the malleable, and the stupid. Even before a single U.S. soldier went into combat or one missile was fired in the war on terror, the America-is-always-wrong crowds took to the streets and air waves in strident protest and complaint.

Professor Robert Jensen, University of Houston, avowed that the attacks on the World Trade Center and the Pentagon were "no more despicable than the massive acts of terrorism—the deliberate killing of civilians for political purposes—that the U.S. government has committed in my lifetime."

"It took these terrorists years to plan the kind of destruction we have wreaked on other countries in a matter of days to weeks," asserted Lisa Mann of Wake Forest University. "America is not a nice country."

University of Wisconsin protestors broke into an Iraqi song and Professor Richard Berthold of the University of New Mexico harmonized with, "Anyone who would blow up the Pentagon gets my vote."

Many of these wacky people didn't even know how they should *feel*, much less think, about the terrorists. The University of Pennsylvania summoned a gaggle of neuroscientists to consider the problem of whether terrorists should be viewed as venal or demented, evil or deranged, wicked or merely suffering from an exculpating mental disease. By the time it's all over, I predict, the terrorists will themselves be considered *victims*.

Media mogul Ted Turner has already started the terrorists-as-victims movement. The nineteen al Qaeda hijackers, he said admiringly, were "brave at the very least..."

He further pontificated with, "The reason the World Trade Center got hit is because there are a lot of people living in abject poverty out there who don't have any hope for a better life."

Let me get this straight. I become a jihad junkie because I'm poor and therefore crash airplanes full of terrified civilians into buildings full of other unsuspecting civilians? One of the notions of the Enlightened is that there is no such thing as "evil" or "personal choice." The *real* victims are terrorists because we Americans are not nice and we force them to become terrorists because we oppress the world.

"We say to our Muslim brothers: we share your pain," grieved the Right Reverend Jesse Jackson.

"Islam," echoed Bill Clinton in his we-feel-your-pain mode, "is a subtle part of each of us."

What the hell does *that* mean?

Had one of the nineteen skyjackers survived, I'm sure he would by now have attained the status of, say, cop-killer Mumia Abu-Jamal and be inundated with requests to speak at all the best and most progressive universities. In one inspired twist of deep-seated empathy and sensitivity, United Way's September 11 Fund paid the legal bills of suspected terrorists before giving money to the actual victims of their attacks.

You have to understand. It's about "fairness," about "social justice." So we lost 3,000 people. They're dead. Get over it. What's important now is portraying terrorists as "real people" and not misjudging them harshly. After all, we made them do what they did because, well, we're *Americans*.

Reuters News Agency banned the word "terrorist" from its copy in order to show sensitivity to, well, terrorists.

ABC News President David Westin declared that, "For me to take a position this (the attack) was right or wrong, I mean that's perhaps for me in my private life...but as a journalist I feel strong that's something I should not take a position on."

Mr. Westin, let's start at the beginning. There were babies, little kids, grannies, gramps, pregnant women and others on those airplanes. It's not wrong to hijack them and crash them into buildings? Can you say moral compass?

Channel 12 News in Long Island banned American flags and red, white and blue lapel pins from its newsroom. Management wanted to avoid appearing biased "one way or another."

Huh?

School officials in Broken Arrow, Oklahoma, removed "God Bless America" signs from their schools for fear someone would be offended. Berkeley banned U.S. flags from city fire trucks for the same reason. Florida Gulf Coast University ordered "Proud To Be An American" signs removed from campus in order not to offend international students.

Let's not be proud to be an American even in our own country.

The Declaration of Independence, the Ten Commandments, Jesus in a manger, the American flag, indeed the essence of America still seems to offend hell out of about everyone if you judge by the selective outcry. Tennessee Democratic legislator Henri Brooks, former membership chairman of the NAACP's Political Action Committee, refused to stand for the Pledge of Allegiance, declaring, "This flag represents the former colonies that enslaved our ancestors."

And *freed* them, Henri, when no other nations in the world were doing so. Remember that, Henri?

Raved black Senator Wayne Bryant of New Jersey regarding the Declaration of Independence: "You have nerve to ask my grandchildren to recite the Declaration. How dare you! You are now on notice that this is offensive to my community."

Is it just me, or is it strange that all these people can be offended by so much of America while yelling diversity and demanding acceptance of about everything that is anti-American? Hardly a peep has been heard from anyone, for example, about artwork outside the new Central Library in Memphis, Tennessee, where a hammer and sickle are imbedded in large letters in the sidewalk at the front door, along with the *Communist Manifesto* quote, "Workers Of The World, Unite."

Can it be that our intellectuals pine for the good old days when the hammer and sickle had a chance of bringing social justice to the world, albeit by killing or enslaving reactionaries and the unenlightened? Might not the survivors of Soviet political gulags appreciate the irony of it? Or the millions who were executed to effect a workers' Utopia?

Can it be these people long for the destruction of the very country that protects and maintains their lunacy? You might think so by the hue and cry that went up from sea to shining sea when the war on terror began. Listen to them.

"I have a confession," declared *Salon* executive editor Gary Kimaya after the start of the Iraqi war to unseat dictator Saddam Hussein. "I have at times, as the war has unfolded, secretly wished for things to go wrong. Wished for the Iraqis to be more nationalistic, to resist longer. Wished for the Arab world to rise up in rage. Wished for all the things we feared would happen. I'm not alone. A number of serious, intelligent, morally sensitive people who oppose the war have told me they have had identical feelings...Wishing for things to go wrong is the logical corollary of the postulate that the better things go for Bush, the worse they will go for America and the rest of the world."

We aren't fighting fair. If the United States went out there on the ground and fought "mano-a-mano" with al Qaeda and the Taliban, wailed Senator Joe Biden, Chairman of the Foreign Relations Committee, the Islamic world would more likely remain supportive of the U.S.

Why not make it swords? At dawn?

"If the word 'cowardly' is to be used," Susan Sontag wrote in protest over applying *cowardly* to *terrorists*, "it might be more aptly applied to those who kill from beyond the range of retaliation, high in the sky, than to those willing to die themselves in order to kill others."

What on God's earth are these people smoking? I've been in combat. When people are shooting at me, trying to kill me, I'd hurl the moon down on them if I could. Wonder how long it'd take Biden and Sontag to start yelling "Nuke the bastards!" were they tossed into a terrorist enclave?

It's almost like these people *hope* we lose in order that they may be proved right.

Nine days into the Iraq campaign, Jess Bacharach grandly announced, "The war is over and we have lost...surrounded and forced to surrender."

Yale professor Immanuel Wallerstein warned of a "long and exhausting war... Swift and easy victory, obviously the hope of the U.S. administration, is the least likely outcome. I give it one chance in twenty... Losing, incredible as it seems, is a plausible outcome."

During recent past decades, said Pat Buchanan, Americans have seen their God dethroned, their heroes defiled, the culture polluted, values assaulted, the country invaded, and themselves demonized as extremists and bigots for beliefs they and their ancestors have held for generations. Although Americans might have come together in the grief that followed September 11, the unity had already faded by the end of the month.

"Nowhere at present is there such a measureless loathing of their country by educated people as in America," said Eric Hoffer.

Out of the loathing continues the nation's terminal insanity. Subsequent events should be enough to convince you that there can be no truce in the cultural wars, even if America is at war.

Disney released a new TV movie, *Cadet Kelly*, about young ladies attending a military academy. A *military* academy, mind you, and the movie blazed this disclaimer across the screen: *No real guns were used in the making of this movie.*

Airport security guards are encouraged to randomly strip-search passengers, even 80-year-old women in wheel chairs, in order to avoid "racial profiling" the very category of people from which 99.9 percent of all terrorists have hatched during the past decade.

Lawyers rush in wherever other fools dare to tread. Attorneys for Global Exchange, a San Francisco-based (where else?) advocacy group, demanded compensation from the U.S. for unintended victims of the bombing in Afghanistan.

In a bold stand for diversity and tolerance out on the Left Coast, Mario Obledo, president of the League of United Latin American Citizens and recipient of the Medal of Freedom from President Bill Clinton, asserted that, "California is going to be a Mexican state. We are going to control the institutions. If people don't like it, they should leave."

Finally, New York City decided to erect a statue to commemorate firefighters who died in the WTC on 9-11. The statue would be copied exactly from a photograph except for one aspect. In order to be more sensitive and politically correct, the three *white* firemen in the photo would be transformed to one white, one Hispanic, and one black.

In my opinion, that doesn't go far enough. What about us Indians, Irish, Jews, females, people of gender, the fat, the physically and mentally challenged...? Don't we all *deserve* equal recognition?

One consolation is that not everyone out there on the Looney Left is unpatriotic. Planned Parenthood Inc. began distributing red, white and blue condoms so people could go out and, to coin an old military phrase, f___ for Old Glory.

"Sometimes our differences run so deep," President George W. Bush noted in his inaugural address, "it seems we share a continent but not a country."

CHAPTER FIFTY-THREE

When I was a kid growing up in the Ozarks attending a one-room school, a kid named Albert was the local bully. He was bigger and meaner than everyone else and terrorized even the man-and-wife teachers. After he beat me up for about the third time, blacking both eyes and busting my nose, my dad and Uncle Johnny drove me to his house. They handed me a butcher knife and told me to "cut him."

We were a bunch of hillbilly half-breeds who handled our own problems. The law wasn't part of the equation. I jumped out, yelled at Albert and charged him waving the butcher knife. I was about eight or nine years old, small for my age, and Albert was thirteen and big for his. But when he saw the knife and realized I intended to use it, that kid spooked. He took off down the road with me hot in pursuit. I chased him for over a mile before he finally got away.

Know what? That kid never beat me up again. From then on, remembering that big knife, he treated me with deference and respect. Point being, do you think I would have obtained the same results by trying to reason with him, for "understanding" and having "compassion" for circumstances in his life that led him to become a bully? Don't kid yourself. He would have crunched me even as I "felt his pain." I didn't then—and still don't—give a damned what caused him to bust my nose. That he crunched my nose and would continue doing so unless stopped was what concerned me.

Bullies, whether they are individuals, states or terrorist groups, will step on others and take things from them until somebody stands up and stops them. That's a fact the Enlightened never seem to understand. Bodies from the Pentagon and the World Trade Center hadn't even been recovered before the "compassionate community" took its predictable stand in the terrorist fray. We should have seen it coming. The Enlightened find it easy to rationalize, apologize for and defend those who become enemies of our country. They have blamed American for all the world's ills for so long that a little thing like a bunch of ratty terrorists stealing airplanes full of innocents and crashing them into buildings full of other innocents isn't about to change them now.

Maybe if we weren't such a big, powerful, successful country, the other countries in the world wouldn't hate us. Columnist Richard Reeves was among the first to take up the banner of appeasement. "Most Americans," he scolded in that self-righteous tone of the Enlightened, "don't give a rat's ass for the poor and sick, the desperate and the crazy of the world..." What he proposed was more foreign aid. Give "Albert" more money, a sort of bribe, obviously, to keep him from crunching our noses again. We'll give you money if you'll be good to us.

Former President Bill Clinton gave him a quick amen. "We cannot have a global trading system without a global economic policy, a global health care policy, a global education policy, a global environmental policy, and a global security policy," he railed. "In effect, we have to create more opportunities for those left behind by progress, thus reducing the pool of potential terrorists by increasing the number of potential partners. To start with, there should be another round of global debt relief."

In other words, redistribute American wealth. A liberal's guilt can never be assuaged until everyone is equally poor.

The most frivolous people in the universe---celebrities—led the mantra.

"I'm an American tired of lies," declared actor Woody Harrelson in an article in the London *Guardian*, "and with our government it's mostly lies." He then informed readers that the U.S. goal was to wipe out "non-white" nations.

"(Osama bin Laden) has been out in these countries for decades building schools, building roads, building infrastructure, building day care facilities, building health care facilities, and people are extremely grateful," said author Alice Walker. "He's made their lives better. We have not done that."

How many times have Bill Clinton, Ted Kennedy, Ted Turner, Alec Baldwin and others of this tribe of supplicators commented upon the lives or deaths of those brave American service people killed in battle in Afghanistan and Iraq. It's easy to count them, even if you are a public school graduate: None. Yet, the outraged Enlightened took up arms in support of Jihad Johnny, the American Taliban Johnny Walker who was apprehended fighting for the Afghan Taliban against his own country. Here was a figure, scroungy and traitorous though he was, who could be transformed into an idealistic warrior on a spiritual crusade against the evils of corporate America.

"There is no evidence so far that he actually did the United States any harm," declared Michael Kinsley. "He played some unknown but small and ineffectual role in defending Afghanistan from an attack by the United States."

"He was just a good kid who ended up in the wrong hands," said a family friend.

This "good kid" was in the same age bracket as those American soldiers he allegedly conspired to kill and some of whom have in fact been killed.

"We want to give him a big hug," said his father. "I also want to give him maybe a little kick in the butt for not telling us what he was up to."

Isn't that just too precious? That little kick in the butt should have been administered a long time ago. But then, of course, the Enlightened don't do such things to their children, do they? It might damage their self-esteem. Even as the bombing of Afghanistan began and, later, the attack on Iraq, the U.S. delivered food, clothing, blankets and other relief supplies to the suffering populations. How many other countries have declared war and then in the process provided humanitarian aid to alleviate the suffering of the enemy's civilians? Again, even if you attended public school, it's easy to count them. But, naturally, no matter what the U.S. does it is never enough.

ABC News reporter Dan Harris complained that the war itself was interfering with the delivery of humanitarian aid.

"Some humanitarian aid workers were saying this effort is little more than propaganda," he announced. "The attacks have significantly hampered a large humanitarian effort, and the U.S. food drops simply can't compensate for that."

Stop the war. Leave the poor terrorists alone. Bring money.

Besides, said ABC's Barbara Walters, we have more important terrorists at home.

"Since September 11," she lectured, "the word 'terrorist' has come to mean someone who is radical, Islamic and foreign, but many believe we have as much to fear from a home-grown group of anti-abortion crusaders."

Right on, Barbara. These anti-abortionists are bound to start hijacking airplanes and wiring themselves with bombs to blow up kids in pizzerias.

Western elites seem indifferent to the fate of civilization, even hostile toward it. They rage on in a revolution of their own definition, the goal being to deepen America's sense of guilt, to disarm and paralyze the West while they extract endless apologies and reparations until the West is either destroyed or its wealth and success transferred and redistributed to the rest of the world.

In 2003, the Athens Bar Association filed a criminal complaint with the UN's International Criminal Court against British Prime Minister Tony Blair, alleging Britain's military actions against Iraq constituted "crimes against humanity and war crimes." The ICC also brought charges against President George W. Bush, Israeli Prime Minister Ariel Sharon, Deputy U.S. Defense Secretary Paul Wolfowitz, U.S. Attorney General John Ashcroft, and National Security Advisor Condoleezza Rice. These people and British allies, the court asserted, were a greater world menace than Saddam Hussein, Muammar Ghadafi (appointed by UN to czar its Human Rights Commission) Yasser Arafat (Nobel Prize for Peace in 1994), or North Korea's Kim Jung Il.

See what I mean about parody?

"This is a brief moment in history when the United States has pre-eminent military, economic and military power," said Bill Clinton in a

speech at the 2002 World Congress in Sydney. "It won't last forever."
He sounded like he looked forward to the fall.

Lack of familiarity with the tenets and foundations of Western culture may partly explain disturbing reactions we have seen against all
things American by the Enlightened Elites of our society. Americans no
longer seem to have a sense of freedom or of history. Today, not one of
the 55 elite colleges and universities rated by *U.S. News & World Report* requires a course in American history in order to graduate. Many
of them, however, do require courses in black history, women's history
or some other politically-correct history.

Did you know, for example, that Muslim explorers arrived in
North America before Columbus and became Indian chiefs among the
Algonquin and Iroquois tribes? That when Europeans finally reached
the New World they met chiefs with names like Abdul-Rahim and Abdullah Ibn Malik? Of course, this is all a bunch of bunk distributed
through a PC 540-page *Arab World Studies Notebook*, a "history"
primer for secondary-school teachers. In keeping with the line of BS,
none of it was sourced in any way (in other words, for those of you in
Palm Beach County, it was all *fiction* passing as fact). The *Notebook*
also claimed Yasser Arafat was president of a newly created state
called Palestine and that present-day Palestinians are descendants of the
Biblical Canaanites.

See what I mean? Truth is what the Enlightened want it to be and
to hell with the facts if they get in the way.

The dumbing down of America, what Americans believe they
know, is truly scary. In a recent survey, 29 percent of the respondents
declared the Constitution guaranteed them a job; 42 percent said it
promised health care; 75 percent thought it provided for a high school
education; and, most alarming of all, 45 percent thought the Marxist
creed "From each according to his abilities, to each according to his
needs" is part of the Constitution of the United States.

Eighteenth Century scholar Alex Fraser Tyler of Scotland devised
what he called the mysteries of the "Nine Cycles" in every civilization.
Every society, he said, went from bondage to spiritual faith; from spiritual faith to great courage; from courage to liberty; from liberty to
abundance; from abundance to selfishness; from selfishness to complacency; from complacency to apathy; from apathy to dependence; and
from dependency back again to bondage.

The Nine Cycles, I propose, should have a Tenth inserted, that being from apathy to ignorance, then from ignorance to dependency.
Apathy and ignorance on the part of the people, arrogance and cultural
insanity on the part of the Enlightened can result in but one ending:
disgrace and loss of freedom.

While the War On Terror may be won, the cultural wars may already be lost. Insanity may have already fallen upon the West.

CONCLUSION

"America will eventually succumb to a 'depraved taste for equality' in which the majority of citizens will gradually surrender to an 'all-powerful form of government (that) provides for their security, foresees and supplies their necessities, facilitates their pleasures, directs their industry and...spare(s) them all the care of thinking and all the trouble of living.'"

Alexis de Tocqueville

CHAPTER FIFTY-FOUR

By now it should be clear that the lunacy of political correctness has no bounds, that it has indeed transformed itself into a pathology of cultural insanity. In her book *The Burden of Bad Ideas: How Modern Intellectuals Misshape Our Society,* Heather MacDonald concludes that the "Enlightened Elites" are creating "an upside down ideology... The acolytes of liberalism, many of whom hold lustrous positions in government and academia, spiritually maintain the irrational, not to mention the antirational. Ideology clouds their vision. They bid their fellow Americans believe all sorts of nutty propositions about human behavior in order that they be considered 'compassionate and caring.'"

Social pathologies of political correctness in the United States have disturbing ideological roots in history. Both the Soviet Union and Nazi Germany displayed many of the same aspects of political correctness that are so prevalent in modern-day America. Political correctness and its attendant dark wackiness did not begin with the spoiled campus radicals of the 1960s.

"The primary task (of society)," said Adolf Hitler, "is to service what is socially correct."

Being a Nazi under Der Fuhrer was considered "politically correct." Followers called themselves "The Children of the New Age of World Order" and looked down with contempt on everyone else. Anyone who questioned Nazi high-handedness was branded a "conservative reactionary." As Hitler and his Brown Shirts began the nationalization of education, health care, transportation, national resources, manufacturing, and law enforcement (all guns were confiscated), they seized homes, businesses, bank accounts and personal belongings of conservative citizens. Public schools rewrote history and Hitler youth groups taught children to report their parents for anti-Nazi remarks. Pagan animism, secularism, became the state religion. Christians were widely condemned as "right wing fanatics." Millions of "un-PC" books were burned. Unmarried women were encouraged to give birth out of wedlock. Evil was declared as being good, and good was condemned as being evil...

Does that all sound familiar?

Hungarian Marxist Georg Lukacs, a Hitler-Stalin contemporary, initiated a philosophical movement which became known as "cultural terrorism." The only way a communist revolution could succeed, he wrote, was for it to first annihilate old values world-wide. The old values would then be replaced by new ones created by the revolutionaries. With that in mind, he established a radical sex education program in Hungarian schools. Children were taught that middle-class family standards were out of date and restrictive, that monogamy was abnormal.

Old values were replaced with ideas of free love and unrestricted sexual access. Religion, he lectured, denied mankind its worldly pleasures. Women were urged to throw off the "yoke of oppression."

He said the restructuring of society along socialist lines required "a long march through the institutions." The march began with schools and colleges and quickly overtook the theater, cinema, seminaries, newsrooms, magazines, the arts and even sports and sciences. Each area would be politicized into an agency of the revolution.

Naturally, he depended upon the Enlightened to guide, direct, teach, and ultimate coerce his radical ideology upon the stupid masses.

Sound familiar?

Persons who go insane don't usually do so all at once. Same thing with a culture. The process of going bonkers depends upon delusion, without which conflicting and extremist ideas cannot be widely accepted. Those who are deluded rarely recognize their own self-deception. They assume that if *they* see purple people eaters and polka-dotted skies, pretty soon mass hysteria will have lots of people seeing them. Those who *don't* see become the loonies and outsiders and end up in "sensitivity training."

A society sliding into madness will experience periods of lucidity and rationality. Although these periods appear to offer hope for the return of sanity, they are merely interludes during which the graph line of sanity continues its relentless descent toward total lunacy. It is frightening how little time it has taken to dismantle and destroy cultural standards which took ages to construct.

The antics of the Enlightened can be amusing in a twisted sort of way. After awhile, however, the amusement turns to stunned disbelief. Funny Uncle Fred may be comical. Funny Uncle Fred given an ax is something else. We have given axes to legions of impassioned Uncle Freds who have assumed the sacred mission of either committing the entire culture to the asylum or destroying it. It is ironical that in attempting to mold the "New Man," our sensitive, compassionate Enlightened have subscribed to the philosophies of men like Hitler and Stalin, the worst mass murderers in history. We are all going to be assisted into mass-cultural suicide, whether we want to go or not.

In 1999, the American Hemlock Society held a "Self-Deliverance New Technology Conference" in Seattle during which it introduced a new suicide machine called the "Exit Bag." Described in the handouts as a "hand-made customized plastic bag for use in self-deliverance," the Exit Bag is marketed with compassion and sensitivity out of consideration for those who would be *self-delivered.*

It is "made of a clear, strong industrial plastic. It has an adjustable collar...for a snug but comfortable fit. It is extra large...to reduce heat build-up. It comes with flannelette lining inside the collar so that the plastic won't irritate sensitive skin. And it comes with an optional terrycloth neckband to create a 'turtleneck' for added comfort and snugness of fit. This is particularly useful for terminally-ill people who had lost a lot of weight and neck bulk..." It will be "discreetly" shipped to customers in a plain brown box.

Former Colorado Governor Richard Lann was one who apparently saw potential in the Exit Bag. He declared that he elderly should "consider making room in the world for the young by simply doing with less medical care and letting themselves die." There will come a day, I predict, when laws will be enacted whereby old folks, the "mentally- or physically-challenged," the culturally unenlightened and other undesirables who pollute our environment with their politically-incorrect existences will be ordered to "self-deliver" in the name of "social justice."

Another step into cultural insanity. America being coached, assisted and forced into killing itself as a culture. Call it the "Exit Bag."

NOTES ON SOURCES

The material contained in this book—quotes, anecdotes, facts and information—has been collected over a period of nearly a decade. Much of the material has been previously published in various periodicals, official documents, books, electronic media, and other sources. Rather than footnote, a tedious and overwhelming task, disruptive to the reader, I have condensed references and arranged them by Sections for those readers who might like to review primary sources and conduct more extensive research into this modern phenomena of cultural madness. I would like to give credit where credit is due. Unfortunately, some of my sources, clippings collected over the years, were left undated or missing essential features that would permit easy recall. I must be forgiven for my oversight, as I did not intend writing a book when I first started collecting them. Nonetheless, I have listed in this source list as much of each reference as possible under the circumstances. Thank you for your understanding, forbearance, and tolerance, if you will forgive me the use of that oh-so-PC word.

INTRODUCTION:

Accuracy in Academia, letter dated Jan 28, 2002
Buchanan, Patrick J. *The Death of The West* (St. Martin's Press, NY, 2002)
Cato Institute Letter, dated Apr 22, 2002
Cato Policy Report, Nov/Dec 2001
Hannan, Daniel. "New World Order," *The American Spectator,* Jan/Feb 2002
Kaczinsky, Ted. Unabomber Manifesto
The Limbaugh Letter, Jan 2002
National Review, Jul 1, 2002
Schlessinger, Dr. Laura. Radio program of Feb 28, 2002

SECTION I—VICTIMS:

Accuracy in Academia. "Politically Correct Top Ten List," 2000
The American Enterprise, Jul/Aug 2003
The American Spectator, Jul 1996
   Ibid, Aug 1996
   Ibid, Sept 1996
   Ibid, Mar 1997
   Ibid, Feb 1998
   Ibid, May 1998
   Ibid, Jun 2000
Bennett, William J. *The De-Valuing of America* (Touchtone Books, NY, 1992)

Black, Jim Nelson. *When Nations Die* (Tyndale, Wheaton, Illinois, 1994)

Boortz, Neal. Commencement address, Texas A&M, 2003

Bork, Robert H. *Slouching Toward Gomorrah* (Regan Books, NY, 1996)

Bruce, Tammy. *The Death of Right and Wrong* (Forren Books, 2003)

Carlson, Margaret. *Time,* Dec 6 1993

Cheney, Lynn V. *Telling The Truth* (Simon & Schuster, NY, 1995)

College English, Mar 2000

Davenport, Jim. *Associated Press,* May 24, 2000

Detroit *News,* Jun 11, 1998

Donohue, William A. *The Politics of The American Civil Liberties Union* (Transaction Books, New Brunswick, 1985)

Fumento, Michael. *The American Spectator,* May 24, 2000

    Ibid, Human Events, Jun 9, 2000

Gross, Martin L. *A Call For Revolution* (Ballantine, NY, 1993)

Hanson, Gayle M.B. *Insight,* Jan 3, 2000

Hare, Bruce R. Syracuse University Magazine, reported in The American Spectator, Sep 1997

Heterodoxy, Apr 30, 1996

    Ibid, Jan/Feb 1997

    Ibid, Jun 1997

    Ibid, Sep 1997

    Ibid, Feb 1998

    Ibid, May/Jun 1998

    Ibid, Sep 1998

    Ibid, Oct 1998

    Ibid, Jan 2000

Human Events, Jan 15, 1999

    Ibid, Jun 9, 2000

    Ibid, Aug 25, 2000

Iannone, Carol. *Heterodoxy,* Feb/Mar 2000

Insight, May 3, 1997

    Ibid, Oct 6, 1997

    Ibid, Dec 25, 2000

    Ibid, Jan 3, 2000

Jacoby, Jeff. Column, Boston *Globe,* 1997

Johnson, Haynes. *Divided We Fall* (W.W. Norton, NY, 1994)

Leo, John. U.S. News & World Report, Jan 17, 2000

    Ibid, The Seattle Times, Aug 15, 2000

The Limbaugh Letter, Apr 1998

    Ibid, Jun 1999

    Ibid, Oct 1999

    Ibid, Nov 1999

    Ibid, Jan 2000

Ibid, Aug 2003

Limbaugh, Rush. *The Way Things Ought To Be* (Pocket Books, NY, 1992)

London *Sunday Times*, Jul 13, 2003

MacNelly Cartoon, Chicago *Tribune*, Sep 6, 1997

"Mallard Fillmore" cartoon, Jun 26, 2000

McCain, Robert Stacy. *Insight,* Jun 19, 2000

Miller, John J. *Americans, no more? The Unmaking of America* (Free Press, NY, 1998)

National Review, Oct 9, 2000

Orthodoxy, Sep 1, 1997

Overall, Michael. Tulsa *World,* May 21, 2000

Raspberry, William. Washington *Post* Writers Group column, May 24, 2000

Reader's Digest, Jan 1999

Reed, Fred. "Spare Me The Sensitivity," *Penthouse* Magazine

Robinson, Randall. *The Debt: What America Owes To Blacks* (Dutton, NY, 2000)

Schupack, Deborah. New York *Times* "Letter to Editor," Jan 5, 1997

Shalala, Donna. Speech at University of Chicago, Nov 15, 1991

Smith, Kenneth. Tulsa *World* "Letter to Editor," Jun 12, 2000

Stein, Benjamin J. *The American Spectator,* Jun 2000

Steyn, Mark. The American Spectator, Mar 1998

Stossel, John. On ABC's *20/20*, reported in *Insight,* Mar 6, 2000

Sykes, Charles J. *A Nation of Victims* (St. Martin's, NY, 1992)

Thomas, Cal. *Human Events,* 1998

Tulsa *World,* Jan 14, 2000

Ibid, May 22, 2000

Ibid, "The Americans With Disability Act," Jan 26, 1992

U.S. Census Form for 2000

U.S. News & World Report, Jan 31, 1994

Ibid, Dec 20, 1999

Ibid, May 22, 2000

Vazsonyi, Balint. *The New Absolutes* (Bethany House, Minneapolis, 1996)

The Washington *Times*, July 25, 2003

Woods, Marion J. San Francisco *Chronicles,* Dec 20, 1997

Wright, Jason Ashley. Tulsa *World,* Sep 2, 2003

SECTION II—POLITICAL CORRECTNESS:

The American Spectator, Dec 1997

Ibid, Feb 1998

Ibid, May 2000

Ibid, Mar/Apr 2002

Associated Press. 23 Jan 2000

Beck, Glen. Syndicated radio talk show, Aug 28, 2003
Bennett, William J. *The De-Valuing of America* (Touchstone Books, NY, 1992)
  Ibid, The Death of Outrage (Free Press, NY, 1998)
Bernstein, Richard. *Dictatorship of Virtue* (Knopf, NY, 1994)
Bork, Robert H. *Slouching Toward Gomorrah* (Regan Books, NY, 1996)
Gross, Martin L. *A Call For Revolution* (Ballantine, NY, 1993)
  Ibid, The End of Security (Avon, NY, 1997)
Heterodoxy, May/Jun 1998
  Ibid, Sep 1998
Howard, Philip K. *The Death of Common Sense* (Random House, NY, 1994)
Human Events, Aug 18, 2003
Insight, Oct 18, 1999
  Ibid, May 8, 2000
  Ibid, May 15, 2000
  Ibid, Jul 24, 2000
Jacoby, Jeff. Column, Boston *Globe*
Johnson, Haynes. *Divided We Fall* (W.W. Norton, NY, 1994)
Lefever, Ernest W. Los Angeles *Times,* 1996
Leo, John. U.S. News & World Report, Feb 14, 2000
  Ibid, Mar 20, 2000
  Ibid, Seattle *Times,* Aug 15, 2000
Limbaugh, David. *Human Times,* May 19, 2003
The Limbaugh Letter, 1999
  Ibid, Jan 2000
Limbaugh, Rush. *See I Told You So* (Pocket Books, NY, 1993)
Miami *World,* Jun 30, 2000
National Review, Jul 17, 2000
  Ibid, Jun 30, 2002
Orwell, George. *1984* (New American Library, NY, 1964)
Royko, Mike. Chicago *Tribune,* Jun 1, 1990
Savage, Michael. *The Savage Nation* (WND Books, 2003)
Sykes, Charles J. *A Nation Of Victims* (St. Martin's Press, NY, 1992)
Tulsa *World,* Jun 4, 2000
Watkins, William D. *The New Absolutes* (Bethany House, Minneapolis, 1996)
The Weekly Standard, Jun 26, 2000
West, Woody. *Insight,* Mar 13, 2000
Yoder, Edwin W. Jr. Column, Washington Post Writers Guild, Nov 23, 1993

SECTION III—EDUCATION:

Accuracy in Academia, Politically Correct Top Ten List, 1999

The American Spectator, Dec 1993
Associated Press, Dec 21, 1995
Bloom, Allan. *The Closing Of The American Mind* (Touchstone, NY, 1987)
Bork, Robert H. *Slouching Towards Gomorrah* (Regan Books, NY, 1996)
Bradbury, Ray. *Fahrenheit 451* (Ballantine, NY, 1950)
Broder, David. Column, Washington Post Writers Group, Jul 4, 2000
Collier, Peter and Horowitz, David. *Destructive Generation* (Second Thought Books, Los Angeles, 1989)
De Pasquale, Lisa. *Human Events,* Sep 2003
D'Souza, Dinesh. *Illiberal Education* (Vantage, NY, 1992)
Gabler, Mel and Norma. *What Are They Teaching Our Children* (Vintage, Wheaton, Illinois, 1985)
Geyer, Georgie Ann. Column, University Press Syndicate, Aug 20, 1993
    Ibid, May 25, 2000
Heterodoxy, Jun 1997
    Ibid, Sep 1998
    Ibid, Oct 1998
    Ibid, Nov 1998
    Ibid, Dec 1998
    Ibid, Sep 1999
    Ibid, Oct 1999
    Ibid, Nov 1999
    Ibid, Jan 2000
    Ibid, Feb 2000
    Ibid, Jun 2000
Human Events, Jun 23, 2000
    Ibid, Jun 2, 2003
    Ibid, Aug 11, 2003
Insight, May 17, 1999
    Ibid, Jan 24, 2000
    Ibid, Jan 31, 2000
    Ibid, Feb 7, 2000
    Ibid, Feb 14, 2000
    Ibid, Apr 24, 2000
    Ibid, May 22, 2000
    Ibid, Jun 5, 2000
    Ibid, Jul 24, 2000
    Ibid, Sep 25, 2000
    Ibid, Oct 2, 2000
Jaroff, Leon. *Time,* Apr 4, 1994
Kennelly, Jim. *USA Weekend,* Feb 18-24, 1994
Kimball, Roger. *Tenured Radicals* (Harper/Collins, NY, 1990)

Kincaid, James. *Child Loving*
   Ibid, Erotic Innocence: The Culture of Child Molesting
Kors, Alan Charles, and Silverglate, Harvey A. *The Shadow University*
Lee, Kenneth. *Heterodoxy,* Jun 1997
The Limbaugh Letter, Feb 1998
   Ibid, Apr 1998
   Ibid, Jun 1998
   Ibid, Nov 1999
   Ibid, Dec 1999
   Ibid, Jun 2000
Mallard Fillmore, cartoon, Jul 3, 2000
McQueen, Anjetta. *Associated Press,* Jun 8, 2000
Military, Oct 2003
National Review, Jun 19, 2000
   Ibid, Jul 3, 2000
   Ibid, Oct 13, 2003
Noe, Chuck. *NewsMax.com,* Jul 2003
Ravitch, Dianne. *The Language Police* (NY, 2003)
Reader's Digest, 1993
Rees, James C. *Insight,* May 22, 2000
Reiland, Ralph R. *Insight,* Sep 13, 1999
Roberts, Paul Craig. *Human Events,* Aug 11, 2000
Ibid, *Insight,* Jun 5, 2000
Sachar, Emily. *Shut Up And Let The Lady Teach* (1991)
Sowell, Thomas. Column, Creators Syndicate, Mar 6, 1997
   Ibid, May 17, 2000
   Ibid, Aug 11, 2000
   Ibid, NewsMax.com, Jul 2003
Steyn, Mark. *The Federalist,* Nov 17, 2003
Stotsky, Sandra. *Losing Our Language* (Free Press, NY, 1999)
Stout, Maureen. *The Feel-Good Curriculum*
Sykes, Charles J. *A Nation of Victims* (Regnery, Washington D.C.,
   1998)
   Ibid, Dumbing Down Our Kids (St. Martin's, NY, 1995)
Thomas, Cal. *Human Events,* Jun 2, 2000
U.S. News & World Report, Jan 10, 2000
   Ibid, May 22, 2000
Will, George. Column, Washington Post Writers Group

SECTION IV—FAMILY:

Baskerville, Stephen. *Insight,* Jun 26, 2000
Beck, Glenn. Radio show, Aug 22, 2003
Bennett, William J. *The De-Valuing of America* (Touchstone, NY,
   1992)
   Ibid, The Death of Outrage (Free Press, NY, 1998)

Black, Jim Nelson. *When Nations Die* (Tyndale, Wheaton, Illinois, 1994)

Bork, Robert H. *Slouching Toward Gomorrah* (Regan, NY, 1996)

Bruce, Tammy. *The Death of Right and Wrong* (Forum, NY, 2003)

Collier, Peter, and Horowitz, David. *Destructive Generation* (Second Thought Books, Los Angeles, 1989)

Coulter, Ann. *Treason* (Crown Forum, NY, 2003)

Donohue, William A. *The Politics of The American Civil Liberties Union* (Transaction Books, New Brunswick, 1985)

Houston, Kerri, and Fava, Patricia. *Al Gore: America In The Balance* (ACU, Alexandria, Virginia, 2000)

Human Events, Jan 15, 1999
    Ibid, Aug 18, 2000
    Ibid, Aug 18, 2003
Insight, Aug 28, 2000
    Ibid, Sep 25, 2000

Knight, Robert H. *The Age Of Consent* (Spence, Dallas, 1998)

Levine, Judith. Harmful To Minors: The Perils of Protecting Children From Sex (U. of Minnesota, 2002)

The Limbaugh Letter, Jun 1999
    Ibid, Sep 2003

Rieff, Philip. *The Feeling Intellect*

Savage, Michael. *The Savage Nation* (WND Books, NY, 2003)

Sowell, Thomas. *The Vision Of The Anointed* (Basic Books, NY, 1995)
    Ibid, Column, Aug 23, 2000
    Ibid, Human Events, Sep 15, 2003
    Ibid, Tulsa *World*, Aug 13, 2003

Toussaint, David. "Outward Bound," *Bride's Magazine*, Sep/Oct 2003

Tulsa *World*, Jun 17, 2000

Vazsonyi, Balint. *America's 30 Years War* (Regnery, Washington D.C., 1998)

Will, George. *The Morning After* (Free Press, NY, 1986)

Williams, Walter E. *A Minority Viewpoint* (Hoover Institution Press, Stanford, 1982)

SECTION V—ARTS & CULTURE:

Accuracy In Academia. Politically Correct Top Ten List 1999

America's 1st Freedom, Aug 2000
    Ibid, Sep 2000

The American Spectator, Mar 1997
    Ibid, July 1999
    Ibid, Mar 2000

Bennett, William J. *The De-Valuing Of America* (Touchstone, NY, 1992)
    Ibid, *The Death of Outrage* (Free Press, NY, 1998)

Bernstein, Richard. *Dictatorship Of Virtue* (Knopf, NY, 1994)

Black, Jim Nelson. *When Nations Die* (Tyndale, Wheaton, Illinois, 1994)

Bozell, L. Brent III. *Insight,* May 15, 2000

Bruce, Tammy. *The Death Of Right And Wrong* (Forum, NY, 2003)

Cheney, Lynn V. *Telling The Truth* (Simon & Schuster, NY, 1995)

Collier, Peter, and Horowitz, David. *Destructive Generation* (Second Thought, Los Angeles, 1989)

Coulter, Ann. *Treason* (Crown Forum, NY, 2003)

Goode, Stephen. *Insight*, Nov 1, 1999

Goodman, Ellen. Boston *Globe,* Mar 27, 1998

Gross, Martin L. *The End Of Sanity* (Avon, NY, 1997)

Heterodoxy, Jan/Feb 1997

> *Ibid,* Nov/Dec 1997

Howard, Philip K. *The Death of Common Sense* (Random House, NY, 1994)

Human Events, Jul 21, 2000

> *Ibid,* Aug 25, 2000

> *Ibid,* Sep 15, 2000

Insight, Dec 20, 1999

> *Ibid,* Jun 26, 2000

Jacobs, Alexandra. New York *Observer*

Kennedy, D. James. Coral Ridge Ministries, Jun 2000

Limbaugh, Rush. *The Way Things Ought To Be* (Pocket, NY, 1992)

National Review, Jun 19, 2000

> *Ibid,* Jul 17, 2000

> *Ibid,* Sep 1, 2003

> *Ibid,* Oct 27, 2003

> *Ibid,* Nov 10, 2003

Publishers Weekly, May 3, 1999

Reason, Jan 2004

Rich, Frank. New York *Times*

Schwarzbaum, Lisa. *Entertainment,* Aug 11, 2000

Smith, Dave. Tulsa *World,* Jun 15, 2000

Time, Dec 1, 1997

USA Today, Dec 22, 1998

U.S. News & World Report, May 22, 2000

> *Ibid,* May 29, 2000

Vazsonyi, Balint. *America's 30 Years War* (Regnery, Washington D.C., 1998)

Will, George. Washington Post Writers Group

> *Ibid,* 1997

SECTION VI—THE MEDIA:

Boston *Globe*, Mar 30, 2000

Bozell, L. Brent III. *Insight,* Jun 19, 2000
Buchanan, Patrick. *The Death Of The West* (St. Martin's, NY, 2002)
Buckley, William F. Jr. *Up From Liberalism* (Hillman Books, NY, 1961)
Cheney, Lynn V. *Telling The Truth* (Simon & Schuster, NY, 1995)
Duin, Julia. *Insight,* May 8, 2000
Elder, Larry. *The Ten Things You Can't Say In America* (2000)
Ely, Carl S. *Insight,* May 8, 2000
Feder, Don. *The Weekly Standard,* Jun 19, 2000
Fields, Suzanne. *Insight,* May 8, 2000
Geyer, Georgie Ann. Column, Universal Press Syndicate, Aug 20, 1993
Gingrich, Newt. *To Renew America* (HarperCollins, NY, 1995)
Goode, Stephen. *Insight,* Dec 20, 1999
Goodman, Ellen. Column, Tulsa *World,* Sep 18, 2003
Graber, Doris A. *Mass Media and American Politics* (CQ Press, Washington DC, 1980)
Greider, William. *Who Will Tell The People* (Touchstone, NY, 1992)
Guiness, Oz. *Time For Truth*
Gumbel, Bryant. *Early Show,* CBS, Jun 29, 2000
Heterodoxy, Sep 1998
   Ibid, Jun/Jul 2000
Houston, Kerri, and Fava, Patricia. *Al Gore: America In The Balance* (ACU, Alexandria, Virginia, 2000)
Human Events, May 26, 2000
   Ibid, Jun 9, 2000
   Ibid, Jul 21, 2000
Insight, Feb 21, 2000
   Ibid, May 8, 2000
   Ibid, May 15, 2000
   Ibid, Aug 28, 2000
Janeway, Michael. *Republic Of Denial*
Kilbourne, Jean. *Deadly Persuasion*
Leo, John. U.S. News & World Report, Mar 20, 2000
Limbaugh, Rush. *The Way Things Ought To Be* (Pocket, NY, 1992)
   Ibid, See I Told You So (Pocket Books, NY, 1993)
National Review, Oct 23, 2000
Nordliner, Jay. *National Review,* Jun 19, 2000
The O'Reilly Factor, FOX News, Oct 23, 2000
O'Reilly, Bill. *The No Spin Zone* (Broadway Books, NY, 2001)
Powers, William. *National Journal,* 2000
Ryan, Suzanne. Boston *Herald,* Jul 26, 2003
Schlessinger, Dr. Laura. "Dr. Laura" Radio Program, Jun 8, 2000
Thomas, Cal. *The Death Of Ethics In America* (Word Books, Waco, 1988)
U.S. News & World Report, May 1, 2000

Will, George. Column, Washington Post Writers Group, Apr 3, 2000
   Ibid, The Morning After (Free Press, NY, 1998)
Williams, Walter E. *America, A Minority Viewpoint* Hoover Institute,
   Stanford, 1982)

SECTION VII—MILITARY:

The American Enterprise, Jul/Aug 2003
The American Spectator, May 2000
   Ibid, Jun 2000
Charen, Mona. *Insight,* May 8, 2000
Clinton, Bill. Inaugural Address, Feb 1993
Corry, John. "Dames At Sea," *The American Spectator*
Coulter, Ann. *Treason* (Crown Forum, NY, 2003)
D'Agostino, Joseph A. *Human Events,* Dec 2, 2000
Donohue, William A. *The Politics Of The American Civil Liberties
   Union* (Transaction Books, New Brunswick, 1985)
Gutmann, Stephanie. *The Kinder, Gentler Military* (Scribner's, NY,
   1997)
Hackworth, David. *Military,* Apr 1998
   Ibid, Jan 2000
   Ibid, Jun 2000
   Ibid, SFTTDEFENSEWATCH Magazine, Aug 2003
Heterodoxy, Jan 2000
Human Events, Dec 22, 2003
Hunt, Terence. *Associated Press,* Jun 1, 2000
Insight, May 22, 2000
   Ibid, Aug 21, 2000
   Ibid, Oct 16, 2000
   Ibid, Nov 6, 2000
Johnson, C.R. *Military,* Jun 2000
Limbaugh, David. *How Liberals Are Waging War Against Christianity*
   (Regnery, Wn DC, 2003)
The Limbaugh Letter, Jun 1999
   Ibid, May 2000
Lowry, Rich. *Legacy* (Regnery, Wn DC, 2003)
McDougall, Walter A. "The Feminization of The American Military,"
   Commentary
Military, Aug 2000
   Ibid, Sep 2000
   Ibid, Nov 2000
Minter, Jim. Atlanta Journal and Constitution, Jul 27, 2000
Mitchell, Brian. *Women In The Military* (Regnery, Wn DC, 1998)
National Review, Oct 23, 2000
NewsMax.com, Jul 2003
North, Oliver. *Military,* Apr 2000

O'Meara, Kelly Patricia. *Insight,* May 22, 2000
Paige, Sean. *Insight,* Jun 5, 2000
Powell, Colin. *My American Journey* (1995)
Prince, Phil. E-mail, Aug 22, 1998
Sasser, Charles W. "Women In Combat?", *Soldier of Fortune,* Mar
    1992
Scarborough, Rowan. Washington *Times*
Tulsa *World,* Sep 16, 2003
Vazsonyi, Balint. *America's 30 Years War* (Regnery, Wn DC, 1998)
West, Woody. *Insight,* May 15, 2000

SECTION VIII—RELIGION:

The American Spectator, Feb 1998
    Ibid, March 1998
    Ibid, May 1998
    Ibid, Nov 2000
Associated Press, Mar 26, 1998
    Ibid, Apr 26, 2000
    Ibid, Nov 1, 2000
    Ibid, Dec 2003
Bethel, Tom. The American Spectator, Jul 1996
Bork, Robert H. *Slouching Toward Gomorrah* (Regan Books, NY,
    1996)
Buchanan, Patrick J. *The Death Of The West* (St. Martin's, NY, 2002)
The Constitutional Standard, Jan-Apr 1998
Coral Ridge Ministries Special Report, Oct 5, 2000
Donohue, William A. *The Politics of The American Civil Liberties Un-
ion* (Transaction Books, New Brunswick, 1985)
Greenberg, Paul. Column, Los Angeles Times Syndicate, Jan 25, 2000
    Ibid, Sep 4, 2000
Gross, Martin L. *The End Of Sanity* (Avon, NY, 1997)
Hamlin, Paula G. "Letter to The Editor," Tulsa *World,* Jul 13, 2000
Harper, David. Tulsa *World,* Jul 15, 2000
Heterodoxy, Sep 1997
    Ibid, May/Jun 1998
    Ibid, Nov 1998
    Ibid, Sep 1999
    Ibid, Nov/Dec 1999
    Ibid, Jan 2000
Howard, Philip K. *The Death of Common Sense* (Random House, NY,
    1994)
Human Events, Mar 10, 2000
    Ibid, May 19, 2000
    Ibid, Sep 29, 2000
    Ibid, Oct 27, 2003

Ibid, Dec 22, 2003
Ibid, Jan 5, 2004
Insight, Jan 12, 2000
    Ibid, Apr 14, 2000
    Ibid, May 8, 2000
    Ibid, May 29, 2000
    Ibid, Jun 5, 2000
    Ibid, Aug 21, 2000
Johnson, Haynes. *Divided We Fall* (W.W. Norton, NY, 1994)
Jones, Susan. "Pennsylvania Goes After Thought Crime,"
    CNSNews.com, Nov 28, 2002
Kilpatrick, James J. Column, Universal Press Syndicate, Dec 13, 1999
    Ibid, Sep 18, 2000
Lefever, Ernest W. Los Angeles *Times,* 1996
Limbaugh, David. *How Liberals Are Waging War Against Christianity*
    (Regnery, DC, 2003)
The Limbaugh Letter, Jun 1999
    Ibid, Jul 1999
    Ibid, Feb 2000
    Ibid, Apr 2000
    Ibid, Sep 2000
    Ibid, Nov 2003
Los Angeles *Times,* May 14, 1971
Military, Apr 1998
National Review, 2000
    Ibid, Jun 19, 2000
    Ibid, Oct 23, 2000
    Ibid, Sep 29, 2003
New Oxford Review, Advertisement for "New Age Church"
News Max, Jun 28, 2000
New York *Times,* Dec 24, 1971

Penn, Marti. Battle Creek *Enquirer,* May 28, 2000
Reason, Jan 2004
Rose, Michael S. *Goodbye, Good Men* (Regnery, DC, 2002)
San Francisco *Chronicle,* Aug 14, 1998
    Ibid, Nov 1998
Sowell, Thomas. *The Vision Of The Anointed* (Basic Books, NY, 1995)
Thomas, Cal. *The Death Of Ethics In America* (Word Books, Waco,
    1988)
Tulsa *World,* Aug 7, 2003
USA Today, Oct 5, 1998
U.S. News & World Report, Jan 31, 1994
    Ibid, Dec 20, 1999
Vitz, Paul C. *The Faith Of The Fatherless; The Psychology of Atheism*

Washington, George. First Inaugural Address, Apr 30, 1780
Washington *Post,* Sep 15, 1998
   Ibid, Sep 18, 1998
The Weekly Standard, Jun 19, 2000

SECTION IX—SEX:

The American Spectator, Sep 1998
Associated Press, Jun 7, 2000
Barrett, Michelle. Women's Oppression Today: The Marxist Feminist
   Encounter
Bennett, William J. *The De-Valuing of America* (Touchstone, NY,
   1992)
   Ibid, The Death Of Outrage (Free Press, NY, 1998)
Bernstein, Richard. *Dictatorship Of Virtue* (Knopf, NY, 1994)
Black, Jim Nelson. *When Nations Die* (Tyndale, Wheaton, Illinois,
   1994)
Borewich, Barrie Jean. *My Lesbian Husband*
Bork, Robert H. *Slouching Toward Gomorrah* (Regan Books, NY,
   1996)
Breasts: A Documentary. Video
Carpozi, George. *Clinton Confidential* (Emery Dalton, DelMar, Ca.,
   1995)
Collier, Peter, and Horowitz, David. *Destructive Generation* (Second
   Thought Books, Los Angeles, 1989)
Dodson, Betty. *Sex For One: The Joy Of Self Loving*
Dowd, Maureen. Column, New York Times Syndicate, Aug 19, 1998
Ensler, Eve. *The Vagina Monologues*, a play
The Federalist, Dec 1, 2003
Female Misbehavior, Video
Gabler, Lynn V. *Telling The Truth* (Simon & Schuster, NY, 1985)
Gorin, Julia. *Insight,* Aug 28, 2000
Gutmann, Stephanie. *The Kinder, Gentler Military* (Scribner's, NY,
   2000)
Heterodoxy, Feb/Mar 2000
Hitchens, Peter. *The Abolition of Britain*
Human Events, Apr 1, 1999
   Ibid, Jul 14, 2003
   Ibid, Oct 27, 2003
Insight, Dec 20, 1999
   Ibid, Jun 12, 2000
The Limbaugh Letter, Nov 2000
Military, Apr 1998
National Review, Jul 3, 2000
   Ibid, Jul 31, 2000
   Ibid, Sep 11, 2000

Ibid, Oct 9, 2000
Ibid, Mar 22, 2004
New Times Broward-Palm Beach, Jun 29-Jul 5, 2000
Shurtleff, Phillip. Letter to Austin *American-Statesman,* Jun 5, 1998
Sobran, Joe. Hustler: *The Clinton Legacy*
Sowell, Thomas. *The Vision Of The Anointed* (Basic Books, NY, 1995)
Stewart, Mark. *Insight,* May 22, 2000
Vazsonyi, Balint. *America's 30 Years War* (Regnery, DC, 1998)
Watkins, William D. *The New Absolutes* (Bethany, Minneapolis, 1996)
The Weekly Standard, July 3-10, 2000
Will, George. *The Morning After* (Free Press, NY, 1986)
Williams, Walter E. *A Minority Viewpoint* (Hoover Institute, Stanford,
   1982)
Winks, Cathy, and Semans, Anne. *The New Good Vibration Guide To
   Sex*

SECTION X—GAY ISSUES:

The American Spectator, Nov 1993
Ibid, Jul/Aug 2000
Ibid, Nov 2000
Associated Press, Feb 19, 1994
Ibid, June 29, 1998
Ibid, Dec 20, 1999
Ibid, Apr 27, 2000
Ibid, Jul 15, 2000
Ibid, Sep 13, 2000
Bennett, William J. *The Death Of Outrage* (Free Press, NY, 1998)
Bernstein, Richard. *Dictatorship Of Virtue* (Knopf, NY, 1994)
Bork, Robert H. *Slouching Toward Gomorrah* (Regan Books, NY,
   1996)
Buchanan, Patrick J. *The Death Of The West* (St. Martin's, NY, 2002)
Charen, Mona. *Insight,* Feb 21, 2000
Clinton, Bill. Executive Order 13160, Jun 23, 2000
Coral Ridge Ministries Fact Sheet, Aug 17, 2000
Dreker, Rod. *The Weekly Standard,* Jul 3-10, 2000
Ettelbrick, Paula. *Lesbians, Gay Men and The Law*
Feder, Don. *Insight,* Jun 19, 2000
The Federalist, "Village Idiot," Mar 1, 2004
   Ibid, "DEZINFORMATSIA," Mar 1, 2004
Gabler, Mel and Norma. *What Are They Teaching Our Children* (Vin-
   tage, Wheaton, Illinois, 1985)
Gallagher, Maggie. Letter, Institute For Marriage and Public Policy,
   May 2004
Greenberg, Paul. Column, Los Angeles Times Syndicate
Gutmann, Stephanie. *The Kinder, Gentler Military* (Scribner's, NY,

2000)

Haney, Daniel Q. *Associated Press,* Jul 9, 2000

Hannity & Colmes. FOX TV, May 25, 2000

Heterodoxy, Sep 1997
  Ibid, Nov/Dec 1997
  Ibid, May/Jun 1998
  Ibid, Sep 1998

Horowitz, David. *Hating Whitey and Other Progressive Causes*
  (Spence, Dallas, 1999)

Human Events, Aug 28, 1998
  Ibid, May 19, 2000
  Ibid, May 26, 2000
  Ibid, Jun 9, 2000
  Ibid, July 28, 2000
  Ibid, Sep 29, 2003

Insight, Feb 21, 2000
  Ibid, May 22, 2000
  Ibid, Oct 16, 2000

International Journal of Epiidemiology, 1999

Jacoby, Jeff. Boston *Globe,* Oct 31, 1997

Knight, Peter. *The Age Of Consent: The Rise of Relativism and Corruption of Popular Culture*

Limbaugh, Rush. Radio Program, Nov 25, 2003

Los Angeles *Times,* 1997

Mathis, Deborah. Column, Gannett News Service, Oct 17, 1998

Milwaukee *Journal Sentinel,* Feb 11, 1997

Mitchell, Brian. *Women In The Military* (Regnery, DC, 1998)

Monterrey County AIDS Project Newsletteer, Jan/Feb 1998

Myers, Jim Column, World Washington Bureau, Jul 13, 1996

National Review, Jul 3, 2000
  Ibid, Sep 11, 2000
  Ibid, Oct 23, 2000
  Ibid, Nov 24, 2003
  Ibid, Dec 1, 2003

New Times Broward-Palm Beach, June 29,-Jul 5, 2000

New York *Post,* Jun 8, 1999

St. Paul *Pioneer-Press,* Summer 2000

San Francisco *Chronicle*, Aug 14, 1998

Savage, Michael. *The Enemy Within* (WND Books, Nashville, 2003)

Signorile, Michelangelo. Life Outside: The Signorile Report On Gay
  Men: Sex, Drugs, Muscles, and The Passages of Life
  Ibid, Out, Dec/Jan 1994

Socarides, Charles. *Homosexuality: A Freedom Too Far*

Sowell, Thomas. Column, Tulsa *World,* Mar 24, 2000

Summers, Laura. Tulsa *World,* Jun 20, 2000

Sykes, Charles J. *A Nation Of Victims* (St. Martin's, NY, 1992)
Thomas, Cal. Column, Tulsa *World,* Dec 1, 2003
Time, Jun 3, 1996
    Ibid, Dec 14, 1998
Tulsa *World,* Apr 15, 1993
    Ibid, Jul 13, 1996
    Ibid, Sep 11, 1996
    Ibid, Jun 10, 2000
    Ibid, Oct 19, 2000
    Ibid, Nov 19, 2003
U.S. News & World Report, Jan 31, 1994
    Ibid, May 15, 2000
Web Today, Aug 31, 2000
Weyrich, Paul M. *Insight,* Jul 24, 2000
Wilson, Michael A. *Insight,* Oct 30, 2000

SECTION XI—ENVIRONMENT:

The American Spectator, Feb 1998
    Ibid, Mar 1998
    Ibid, June 2000
Associated Press, Oct 12, 1993
    Ibid, April 23, 1996
Bartlett, Donald L, and Steele, James B. *America: Who Really Pays The Taxes* (Touchstone, NY, 1994)
Buchanan, Patrick J. *The Death Of The West* (St. Martin's, NY, 2002)
Carlisle, John K. Tulsa *World*
Chapman, Steve. Tulsa *World,* Oct 26, 2001
Donohue, William A. *The Politics of The American Civil Liberties Union* (Transaction Books, New Brunswick, 1985)
Farm Bureau Journal, Nov 1996
Fitzgerald, Randy. *Reader's Digest,* Sep 1993
Geyer, Georgie Ann. Column, Universal Press Syndicate, Sep 2, 1997
Gingrich, Newt. *To Renew America* (HarperCollins, NY, 1995)
Gore, Al. *Earth In The Balance*
Gross, Martin L. *A Call For Revolution* (Ballantine, NY, 1993)
    Ibid, The Government Racket: Washington Waste From A To Z (Bantam, NY, 1992)
Hayward, Steven. *The American Enterprise,* Jul/Aug 2003
Heterodoxy, Sep 1999
Houston, Kerri, and Fava, Patricia. *Al Gore: America In The Balance* (ACU, Alexandria, Virginia, 2000)
Horowitz, David. *Hating Whitey And Other Progressive Causes* (Spence, Dallas, 1999)
Howard, Philip K. *The Death Of Common Sense* (Random House, NY, 1994)

Human Events, Oct 2, 1998
   Ibid, May 12, 2000
   Ibid, Jun 9, 2000
   Ibid, Aug 4, 2000
   Ibid, Sep 1, 2000
   Ibid, Sep 22, 2000
Inhofe, Jim. Speech, Jul 28, 2003
Insight, Dec 2, 1999
   Ibid, Jan 24, 2000
   Ibid, May 8, 2000
   Ibid, May 22, 2000
   Ibid, May 29, 2000
   Ibid, June 12, 2000
   Ibid, Jun 19, 2000
   Ibid, Oct 23, 2000
   Ibid, Nov 27, 2000
The Limbaugh Letter, Sep 1997
   Ibid, Apr 1999
   Ibid, June 1999
   Ibid, Oct 1999
   Ibid, Dec 1999
   Ibid, Jan 2000
   Ibid, May 2000
   Ibid, Jul 2000
   Ibid, Sep 2000
   Ibid, Jul 2003
   Ibid, Aug 2003
Ms, May/Jun 1998
National Directory of Environmental & Regulatory Victims (2000)
NewsMax.com, Jul 2003
Pantagraph, Aug 25, 2000
Pombo, Richard, and Farah, Joseph. *This Land Is Our Land* (St. Martin's, NY, 1996)
Reader's Digest, Jan 1999
Snow, Tony. Column, Creators Syndicate, Jul 31, 2000
Tulsa *World,* May 19, 2000
   Ibid, May 31, 2000
Washington *Post,* Aug 9, 1993
Whelen, Robert. *Wild In The Woods: The Myth Of The Noble Eco-Savage* (Institute of Economic Affairs, London, 1999)
Will, George. Column, Washington Post Writers Group

SECTION XII—ANIMAL RIGHTS—

The American Spectator, Oct 1993
   Ibid, Nov 1996

Ibid, Apr 1997
Ibid, Sep 1997
Ibid, Oct 1997
Ibid, Dec 1997
Ibid, May 1998
Ibid, Mar 2000
Ibid, Dec 2000/Jan 2001
Associated Press, May 24, 1997
Ibid, Aug 19, 1997
Ibid, Jun 14, 2000
Ibid, Jun 17, 2000
Bork, Robert H. *Slouching Toward Gomorrah* (Regan Books, NY, 1996)
Donohue, William A. *The Politics Of The American Civil Liberties Union* (Transaction Books, New Brunswick, 1985)
Fink, Jerry. Tulsa *World*
Gross, Martin L. *The End Of Sanity* (Avon, NY, 1997)
Ibid, The Government Racket: Washington Waste From A to Z (Bantam, NY, 1992)
Heterodoxy, Jun 1997
Ibid, Sep 1998
Ibid, Feb/Mar 2000
Horowitz, David. *Hating Whitey And Other Progressive Causes* (Spence, Dallas, 1999)
Howard, Philip K. *The Death Of Common Sense* (Random House, NY, 1994)
Human Events, Jun 16, 2000
Insight, Jul 3-10, 2000
Ibid, Jul 31, 2000
Jacoby, Jeff. Boston *Globe,* Dec 17, 1997
The Limbaugh Letter, Mar 1997
Ibid, Feb 1998
Ibid, Jun 1998
Ibid, Jun 1999
Ibid, Oct 1999
Ibid, Nov 1999
Ibid, Jan 2000
Ibid, Jul 2000
Ibid, Nov 2000
Ibid, Oct 2003
Limbaugh, Rush. *The Way Things Ought To Be* (Pocket, NY, 1992)
National Review, Jun 19, 2000
Ibid, Dec 22, 2003
PETA Newsletter, Mar/Apr 1990
Pombo, Richard, and Farah, Joseph. *This Land Is Our Land* (St. Mar-

tin's, NY, 1996)
Sasser, Michael. *SunPost,* Nov 6, 1997
Schlessinger, Dr. Laura. Radio Program, Jun 9, 2000
Schonholtz, Cindy. *Western Horseman,* June 2000
Time, June 16, 1997
Tulsa *World,* Jun 24, 1996
        Ibid, May 25, 2000'
Weems, George. Lexington *Herald Leader,* Jul 3, 1997
Welch, Aimee. *Insight,* Jul 17, 2000
Western Horseman, Jun 2000
West, Woody. *Insight,* Sep 27, 1999

SECTION XIII—PROPERTY:

Adams Charles. *Those Dirty Rotten Taxes* (Free Press, NY, 1998)
Barlett, Donald L., and Steele, James B. *America: Who Really Pays The Taxes* (Touchstone, NY, 1994)
Bennett, William J. *The De-Valuing Of America* (Touchstone, NY, 1992)
Black, Jim Nelson. *When Nations Die* (Tyndale, Wheaton, Illinois, 1994)
Bovard, James. *Lost Rights*
Buchanan, Patrick J. *The Death Of The West* (St. Martin's, NY, 2002)
Gingrich, Newt. *To Renew America* (HarperCollins, NY, 1995)
Gross, Martin L. *A Call For Revolution* (Ballantine, NY, 1993)
        Ibid, The End Of Sanity (Avon, NY, 1997)
Howard, Philip K. *The Death Of Common Sense* (Random House, NY, 1994)
Human Events, May 5, 2000
        Ibid, Jan 5, 2000
The Limbaugh Letter, Jul 2003
National Director Of Environmental and Regulatory Victims, 2000
Pombo, Richard, and Farah, Joseph. *This Land Is Our Land* (St. Martin's, NY, 1996)
Sykes, Charles J. *A Nation Of Victims* (St. Martin's, NY, 1992)
Vazsonyi, Balint. *America's 30 Years War* (Regnery, Washington DC, 1998)
Williams, Walter E. *Human Events,* Sep 22, 2000

SECTION XIV—GUN CONTROL:

Accuracy In Academia's Politically Correct Top Ten List, 1999
America's 1st Freedom, Jun 2000
        Ibid, Aug 2000
        Ibid, Sep 2000
        Ibid, Nov/Dec 2000

American Guardian, Feb 2000
The American Spectator, Jun 2000
  Ibid, Dec 2000/Jan 2001
Associated Press, May 13, 2000
  Ibid, Jul 31, 2000
Boston *Herald,* Mar 5, 2000
Bovard, James. *Feeling Your Pain* (St. Martin's, NY, 2000)
Donohue, William A. *The Politics Of The American Civil Liberties Union* (Transaction Books, New Brunswick, 1985)
Dougherty, Jon E. *WorldNetDaily.com,* May 27, 2000
Gross, Martin L. *A Call For Revolution* (Ballantine, NY, 1993)
Hanes, Charles. "Letter to Editor," Tulsa *World,* May 25, 2000
Harvey, Paul. *"History Of Gun Control Laws,"* radio broadcast, 2001
Heston, Charlton. *American Guardian,* Mar 2000
Heterodoxy, Sep/Oct 2000
Hornberger, Jacob G., and Ebeling, Richard M. *The Tyranny Of Gun Control* (FFF, Fairfax, Virginia, 1997)
Human Events, May 19, 2000
  Ibid, Jun 16, 2000
Insight, Mar 13, 2000
  Ibid, May 8, 2000
  Ibid, May 29, 2000
  Ibid, Jun 5, 2000
  Ibid, Jun 12, 2000
  Ibid, Aug 28, 2000
  Ibid, Sep 11, 2000
  Ibid, Oct 2000
  Ibid, Nov 27, 2000
LaPierre, Wayne. *American Guardian,* Mar 2000
The Limbaugh Letter, Jul 1999
  Ibid, Nov 1999
  Ibid, Jun 2000
Lott, John R. Jr. *Insight,* July 3-10, 2000
Mack, Richard I., and Walters, Timothy Robert. *From My Cold Dead Fingers* (Rawhide Western, Safford, Arizona, 1994)
Military, Nov 2000
Mincher, Thomas. "Letter To Editor," Tulsa *World,* Jun 5, 2000
National Review, Jun 19, 2000
  Ibid, Jul 3, 2000
NEWSMAX.COM, Mar 16, 2000
Robertson, Joe. "Letter To Editor," Tulsa *World,* May 17, 2000
Sasser, Michael. "Why I Joined The NRA," *SunPost,* Jun 2000
Sowell, Thomas. Column, Tulsa *World,* Jun 2, 2000
Tulsa *World,* May 15, 2000
U.S. News & World Report, May 29, 2000

Wall Street Journal, Dec 9, 1999
Weaver, David. *Comment,* May 16, 2000
Weeks, Byron T. Internet letter to U.S. Senate, May 12, 2000
Zuckerman, Mortimer B. *U.S. News & World Report,* May 22, 2000

SECTION XV—BILL CLINTON:

ABC This Week, Oct 29, 2000
Aldrich, Gary. *Unlimited Access* (Regnery, Washington DC, 1996)
America's 1st Freedom, Jun 2000
The American Spectator, May 1998
    Ibid, Mar 2000
    Ibid, Jun 2000
    Ibid, Jul/Aug 2000
    Ibid, Sep 2000
    Ibid, Dec 2000/Jan 2001
Associated Press, Jul 8, 2000
    Ibid, Nov 16, 2000
Ayers, H. Brand. Chicago *Tribune,* Mar 12, 1998
Bennett, William J. *The De-Valuing of America* (Touchstone Press,
    NY, 1992)
Bovard, James. *Feeling Your Pain* (St. Martin's, NY, 2000)
Brown, Floyd G. *"Slick Willie"* (Annapolis-Washington, Maryland,
    1993)
Carpozi, George. *Clinton Confidential* (Emery Dalton, DelMar, CA,
    1995)
Carville, James. *Larry King Live* TV, Feb 16, 1998
Clinton, Bill. Speech in Connecticut, Oct 15, 1998
    Ibid, Grand Jury Testimony, Aug 17, 1999
Collier, Peter. Weekly Standard
Coulter, Ann. *Human Events,* Aug 21, 1998
    Ibid, Jun 9, 2000
    Ibid, Jul 28, 2000
    Ibid, Aug 4, 2000
Dowd, Maureen. New York Times Syndicate
Esquire, Dec 2000
Eszterhas, Joe. *American Rhapsody* (Knopf, NY, 2000)
Farah, Joseph. *WorldNetDaily,* Jul 12, 2000
Geyer, Georgie Ann. Column, Universal Press Syndicate, Sep 24, 1998
Gibbs, Nancy. *Time,* Feb 9, 1998
Gore, Al. Boston Herald
Greenberg, Paul. Column, Los Angeles Times Syndicate, Jul 25, 2000
Greer, Germaine. Washington *Post*
Grodin, Charles TV program, Sep 4, 1998
Hall, Wiley, *Associated Press,* Nov 6, 2003
Hefner, Hugh. *Playboy,* May 1998

Heterodoxy, Feb 1998
  Ibid, Oct 1999
Houston, Kerri, and Fava, Patricia. *Al Gore: America In The Balance*
  (ACU, Alexandria, Virginia, 2000)
Human Events, Jan 15, 1999
  Ibid, Apr 2, 1999
  Ibid, May 27, 2000
  Ibid, Jun 16, 2000
  Ibid, Jul 21, 2000
  Ibid, Aug 4, 2000
  Ibid, Aug 18, 2003
Hunt, Al. Wall Street Journal
Insight, May 8, 2000
  Ibid, Jun 19, 2000
  Ibid, July 3-10, 2000
  Ibid, July 19, 2000
  Ibid, Nov 13, 2000
  Ibid, Nov 20, 2000
  Ibid, Dec 4, 2000
The Limbaugh Letter, Apr 1998
  Ibid, Apr 1999
  Ibid, Jun 1999
  Ibid, Jul 1999
  Ibid, Oct 1999
  Ibid, Nov 1999
  Ibid, Feb 2000
  Ibid, Jun 2000
  Ibid, Jul 2000
  Ibid, Oct 2000
Lyons, Gene. Meet The Press TV
McRee, Lisa. *Good Morning America,* TV, Sep 10, 1998
Military, Sep 2000
  Ibid, Oct 2000
National Review, Jul 3, 2000
  Ibid, Jul 17, 2000
  Ibid, Sep 11, 2000
  Ibid, Nov 20, 2000
  Ibid, Dec 31, 2000
Newsweek, Aug 24, 1998
O'Reilly, Bill. *The No Spin Zone* (Broadway Books, NY, 2001)
Publishers Weekly, July 5, 1993
Reeves, Richard. Column, Universal Press Syndicate, May 31, 2000
Roberts, Craig. Letter, Aug 15, 2003
Rodriguez, Paul M. *Insight,* Jun 5, 2000
Rosenblatt, Roger. *Time,* Feb 16, 1998

Russert, Tim. NBC, October 23, 1998
Ruth, Henry. Wall Street Journal
Shales, Tom. Washington *Post,* Sep 22, 1998
Siegal, John P. *Wall Street Journal,* Sep 11, 1998
Siegel, Julie. San Francisco *Chronicle,* Sep 4, 1998
Starr, Kenneth W. Speech At Hillsdale College, May 23, 2000
Stewart, James B. Blood Sport: The President And His Adversaries
    Time, Jun 21, 1993
U.S. News & World Report, Aug 1, 2000
Vazsonyi, Balint. *America's 30 Years War* (Regnery, Washington DC,
    1998)
Weinraub, Bernard. New York *Times,* Dec 19, 1998

SECTION XVI—CRIME:

Accuracy In Academia's Politically Correct Top Ten List, 1999
The American Spectator, Mar 2000
Anderson, Curt. *Associated Press,* Jun 17, 2000
Associated Press, Nov 27, 1997
    Ibid, May 17, 2000
    Ibid, Jun 14, 2000
    Ibid, Jun 23, 2000
    Ibid, Aug 5, 2000
    Ibid, Sep 22, 2000
Barr, Bob. Speech at Hillsdale College, Sep 1999
Black, Jim Nelson. *When Nations Die* (Tyndale, Wheaton, Illinois,
    1994)
Bork, Robert H. *Slouching Toward Gomorrah* (Regan Books, NY,
    1996)
Bovard, James. *Feeling Your Pain* (St. Martin's, NY, 2000)
Cheney, Lynn V. *Telling The Truth* (Simon & Schuster, NY, 1995)
Collier, Peter, and Horowitz, David. *Destructive Generation* (Second
    Thought Books, Los Angeles, 1989)
Coulter, Ann. *Human Events,* Jun 23, 2000
Greenberg, Paul. Column, Los Angeles Times Syndicate, Jul 11, 2000
Heterodoxy, Jan/Feb 1997
    Ibid, Sep 1997
    Ibid, Feb/Mar 2000
Horn, Wade F. Tulsa *World,* Jul 23, 2000
Hornberger, Jacob G., and Ebeling, Richard M. *The Tyranny Of Gun
    Control* (FFF, Fairfax, Virginia, 1997)
Howard, Philip K. *The Death Of Common Sense* (Random House, NY,
    1994)
Human Events, Jan 15, 1999
    Ibid, May 19, 2000
    Ibid, Jun 16, 2000

Ibid, Jun 23, 2000
Ibid, Jul 21, 2000
Ibid, Aug 25, 2000
Ibid, Oct 27, 2000
Insight, Sep 20, 1999
Ibid, Mar 6, 2000
Ibid, May 8, 2000
Ibid, Aug 14, 2000
Ibid, Aug 21, 2000
Ibid, Nov 6, 2000
Ibid, Dec 4, 2000
Jacoby, Jeff. Boston *Globe*
Kilpatrick, James J. Syndicated column, Aug 21, 2000
Kolberg, Rebecca. *United Press International,* Jun 3, 1998
The Limbaugh Letter, Feb 1998
Ibid, Apr 1998
Ibid, Jun 1999
Ibid, May 2000
Ibid, Aug 2000
Military, Oct 2000
The Nation, Aug 23-30, 1993
National Review, Sep 25, 2000
Ibid, Nov 6, 2000
Ibid, Jan 22, 2001
New Century Foundation. *The Color Of Crime,* 1999
New Times Broward-Palm Beach, Jun 29-Jul 5, 2000
Olstynski, Jim. "48 Reasons why I Hate Lawyers," WGN Radio, May
21, 2000
Private Eye, Feb 1994
Raspberry, William. Column, Tulsa *World,* Sep 15, 2000
Royko, Mike. Column, Chicago Tribune Syndicate, Feb 22, 1997
Samuelson, Robert. Column, Washington Post Writers Group, Jun 9,
2000
Sowell, Thomas. Column, Creators Syndicate, Oct 22, 1998
Sykes, Charles J. *A Nation Of Victims* (St. Martin's, NY, 1992)
Time, Aug 3, 1992
Tucker, William, The American Spectator
Tulsa *World,* May 18, 2000
Ibid, Jun 14, 2000
Ibid, Sep 16, 2000
Ibid, Sep 28, 2000
U.S. News & World Report, Jan 31, 1994
Ibid, May 15, 2000
Vazsonyi, Balint. *America's 30 Years War* (Regnery, Washington DC,
1998)

The Weekly Standard, Jun 19, 2000
West, Woody. *Insight,* Jul 17, 2000
Will, George F. Column, Washington Post Writers Group
Williams, Walter E. *Insight,* Sep 20, 1999
 Ibid, A Minority Viewpoint (Hoover Institute Press, Stanford, 1982)
Wilson, James Q. *Moral Judgment*

SECTION XVII—GOVERNMENT:

Adams, Charles. *Those Dirty Rotten Taxes* (Free Press, NY, 1998)
Aldrich, Gary. *Unlimited Access* (Regnery, Washington DC, 1996)
America's 1st Freedom, Jul 2000
The American Spectator, Dec 1993
 Ibid, Dec 1998
 Ibid, Jun 2000
 Ibid, Jul/Aug 2000
 Ibid, Dec 2000/Jan 2001
 Ibid, Jan/Feb 2003
Associated Press, May 21, 1995
 Ibid, Sep 17, 1996
 Ibid, Jul 10, 1998
 Ibid, Oct 22, 1998
 Ibid, May 17, 2000
 Ibid, Jun 1, 2000
 Ibid, Jun 8, 2000
 Ibid, Jun 21, 2000
 Ibid, Sep 2000
Bartless, Donald L., and Steele, James B. *America: Who Really Pays the Taxes* (Touchstone Books, NY, 1994)
BC. Cartoon, Aug 10, 2000
Bennett, William J. *The De-Valuing of America* (Touchstone, NY, 1992)
Bernstein, Richard. *Dictatorship of Virtue* (Knopf, NY, 1994)
Black, Jim Nelson. *When Nations Die* (Tyndale, Wheaton, Ill, 1994)
Bork, Robert H. *Slouching Toward Gomorrah* (Regan Books, NY, 1996)
Borst, W.A. *Liberalism: Fatal Consequences*
Bovard, James. *Feeling Your Pain* (St. Martin's, NY, 2000)
Briggs, Joe Bob. *Reason,* Jul 30, 2003
Buchanan, Patrick J. *The Death of The West* (St. Martin's, NY, 2002)
Buckley, William F. Jr. *Up From Liberalism* (Hillman, NY, 1961)
Case, David Wayne. Letter to Rep. Henry Waxman, Oct 24, 2000
Clinton, Bill. News conference, Nov 30, 1999
Clinton, Hillary. Essay, 1978
Collier, Peter, and Horowitz, David. *Destructive Generation* (Second

Thought Books, Los Angeles, 1989)
Competetive Enterprise Institute, 2000 Edition of Ten Thousand Commandments
Connerly, Ward. *Imprimis,* Feb 2000
Ebeling, Richard M. *Notes From FEE,* Nov 2003
Ehrenreich, Barbara. *Time*, Apr 30, 1998
Feder, Don. *Insight,* May 15, 2000
Germond, Jack, and Witcover, Jules. Column, Chicago Tribune Syndicate, May 30, 2000
Geyer, Georgie Ann. Column, Universal Press Syndicate
Gillmore, Dan. Tulsa *World,* Jun 5, 2000
Gingrich, Newt. *To Renew America* (HarperCollins, NY, 1995)
Graber, Doris A. *Mass Media and American Politics* (CQ Press, Washington DC, 198)
Greider, William. *Who Will Tell The People* (Touchstone, NY, 1992)
Gross, Martin L. *A Call For Revolution* (Ballantine, NY, 1993)
   Ibid, The End Of Sanity (Avon, NY, 1997)
   Ibid, The Government Racket: Washington Waste From A to Z (Bantam, NY, 1992)
Gumbel, Bryant. "Public Eye, CBS TV, Jan 28, 1999
The Heritage Foundation Letter, Jul 26, 2000
Heterodoxy, Sep 1997
   Ibid, Nov 1998
   Ibid, Oct 1999
   Ibid, Nov/Dec 1999
   Ibid, Jul 2000
Horowitz, David. *Hating Whitey and Other Progressive Causes* (Spence, Dallas, 1999)
Howard, Philip K. *The Death of Common Sense* (Random House, NY, 1994)
Human Events, May 1, 1998
   Ibid, Oct 2. 1998
   Ibid, Mar 3, 2000
   Ibid, May 19, 2000
   Ibid, Jun 9, 2000
   Ibid, Jun 23, 2000
   Ibid, Jun 30, 2000
   Ibid, Aug 4, 2000
   Ibid, Oct 6, 2000
   Ibid, Mar 3, 2003
   Ibid, Jul 14, 2003
Insight, Dec 6, 1999
   Ibid, Jan 3, 2000
   Ibid, Jan 31, 2000
   Ibid, Feb 28, 2000

Ibid, Mar 13, 2000
Ibid, May 1, 2000
Ibid, May 8, 2000
Ibid, May 15, 2000
Ibid, May 22, 2000
Ibid, May 28, 2000
Ibid, Jun 5, 2000
Ibid, Jun 12, 2000
Ibid, Jun 26, 2000
Ibid, Jul 17, 2000
Ibid, Aug 7, 2000
Ibid, Aug 21, 2000
Ibid, Sep 11, 2000
Ibid, Oct 2, 2000
Ibid, Oct 16, 2000
Ibid, Oct 23, 2000
Ibid, Dec 18, 2000
Jacobs, Joanne. *San Jose Mercury News,* Jan 12, 2000
Jacoby, Jeff. Column, Boston *Globe*
Jennings, Peter. ABC World News Tonight
Johnson, Corky. *Military,* Jan 2000
Johnson, Haynes. *Divided We Fall* (W.W. Norton, NY, 1994)
Johnson, Paul. *A History Of The American People*
Ledeen, Michael. *The American Spectator,* Jun 2000
The Limbaugh Letter, Dec 1997
Ibid, Feb 1998
Ibid, Apr 1998
Ibid, Apr 1999
Ibid, Jun 1999
Ibid, Oct 1999
Ibid, Nov 1999
Ibid, Dec 1999
Ibid, Feb 2000
Ibid, Mar 2000
Ibid, Apr 2000
Ibid, May 2000
Ibid, Jun 2000
Ibid, Aug 2000
Ibid, Nov 2000
Ibid, Nov 2002
Limbaugh, Rush. *The Way Things Ought To Be* (Pocket, NY, 1992)
Ibid, See I Told You So (Pocket, NY, 1992)
Los Angeles *Times,* May 30, 2000
Lucier, James P. *Insight,* May 22, 2000
MacDonald, Heather. *Human Events,* Oct 13, 2000

McCarthy, Eugene. *A Colony Of The World: The United States Today* Military, Jul 2000
    Ibid, Sep 2000
    Ibid, Jan 2001
Mill, John Stuart. *On Liberty*
Morrison, Pat. Tulsa *World,* Jul 2, 2000
National Center For Public Policy Research. Letter dated Aug 28, 2000
National Grants Conference, paid advertisement in Tulsa *World*, May 15, 2000
National Review, Jul 3, 2000
    Ibid, Jul 17, 2000
    Ibid, Aug 14, 2000
    Ibid, Dec 4, 2000
    Ibid, Sep 15, 2003
New York *Times,* Nov 30, 1997
Nugent, *Ted. God, Guns & Rock & Roll*
O'Reilly, Bill. *The No Spin Zone* (Broadway Books, NY, 2001)
Orwell, George. *1984*
Pierce, Michael. *The Federalist,* Dec 1, 2003
Pombo, Richard, and Farah, Joseph. *This Land Is Our Land* (St. Martin's, NY, 1996)
Poole, Patrick. *2000 WorldNetDaily.com,* Jun 27, 2000
Reeves, Richard. Column, Universal Press Syndicate, May 31, 2000
Roberts, Paul Craig. The Washington *Times*, Dec 31, 1998
Rodriguez, Paul M. *Insight,* May 29, 2000
Rose, Michael S. *Goodbye, Good Men* (Regnery, Wn DC, 2002)
Royko, Mike. Column, Chicago Tribune Syndicate, Dec 10, 1993
Rummel, R.J. Death By Government
Sasser, Michael. *SunPost,* Apr 13, 2000
Samuelson, Robert. Column, The Washington Post Writers Group, Jul 28, 2000
Shughart, William F. *Taxing Choice: The Predatory Politics of Fiscal Discrimination*
Sowell, Thomas. Column, Creators Syndicate
    Ibid, Column, Creators Syndicate, Jul 6, 2000
    Ibid, Column, Creators syndicate, Aug 31, 2000
    Ibid, Human Events, Sep 29, 2000
    Ibid, The Vision Of The Anointed (Basic Books, NY, 1995)
Starr, Kenneth. Speech at Hillsdale College, May 22, 2000
Swift, Jonathan. *Gulliver's Travels*
Sykes, Charles J. *A Nation Of Victims* (St. Martin's, NY, 1992)
Thomas, Cal. *The Death Of Ethics In America* (Word Books, Waco, 1988)
Time, Jun 21, 1993
Toffler, Alvin, and Heidi. *The Politics Of The Third Wave* (Turner,

Atlanta, 1994)
Tulsa *World,* May 26, 2000
    Ibid, Jun 2, 2000
    Ibid, Jun 17, 2000
    Ibid, Jul 5, 2000
    Ibid, Jul 9, 2000
Turner, Ted. "Cold War," CNN documentary, Sep 24, 1998
U.S. News & World Report, May 22, 2000
Vazsonyi, Balint. *America's 30 Years War* (Regnery, Wn DC, 1998)
The Wall Street Journal, Oct 1996
Watkins, William D. *The New Absolutes* (Bethany, Minneapolis, 1996)
The Weekly Standard, Jun 12, 2000
    Ibid, Jun 19, 2000
    Ibid, Jul 3-10, 2000
West, Woody. *Insight,* Feb 21, 2000
Will, George. Column, Apr 26, 2000
    Ibid, The Morning After (Free Press, NY, 1986)
Williams, Walter E. *Imprimis,* Aug 2000
    Ibid, A Minority Viewpoint (Hoover Institute, Stanford, 1982)

SECTION XVIII—WAR ON TERROR:

Accuracy In Academia. Letter dated Jan 28, 2002
America's 1st Freedom, Feb 2002
    Ibid, Dec 2002
Bersnak, Rick Jr. Tulsa *World*, Feb 3, 2002
Buchanan, Patrick J. *The Death Of The West* (St. Martin's, NY, 2002)
Coulter, Ann. *Human Events,* Aug 4, 2003
Family Research Council. Letter dated Jun 2, 2002
Geyer, Georgie Ann. USP column, Mar 14, 2002
Hanson, Victor Davis. *Imprimis,* Feb 2002
INS Form
Insight, Nov 12, 2001
    Ibid, Dec 3, 2001
Johnson, C.R. *Military,* Nov 2001
The Limbaugh Letter, Nov 2001
    Ibid, Jan 2002
    Ibid, Feb 2002
    Ibid, Mar 2002
    Ibid, May 2003
    Ibid, Aug 2003
Military, Jan 2002
National Review, Oct 13, 2003
    Ibid, May 17, 2004
New York *Times*, July 10, 2001
North, Oliver. Column, *Military,* Dec 2001

Ibid, Human Events, Aug 18, 2003
Reeves, Richard, UPS column, Mar 8, 2002
   Ibid, Mar 19, 2002
Savage, Michael. *The Enemy Within* (WND Books, Nashville, 2003)
Sherman, Bill. Tulsa *World*, Oct 12, 2001
Sowell, Thomas. Column, Tulsa *World,* Sept 28, 2001
Tulsa *World,* Sep 28, 2001
   Ibid, Mar 8, 2002
Turley, Jonathan. Tulsa *World,* Feb 3, 2002
The Washington *Times.* Promotion letter dated Feb 5, 2002
Will, George. Column, Washington Post Writers Group, Nov 27, 2001
   Ibid, Mar 14, 2002

CONCLUSION:

America's 1st Freedom, Mar 2001
Delbanco, Andrew, *The Death Of Satan*
Fisher-Bacon, Lee Ann. Speech at Hillsdale College, Sep 10, 2000
Heterodoxy, Nov/Dec 1999
Hitchens, Peter. *The Abolition of Britain: From Winston Churchill to Princess Diana* (Encounter Books, NY, 2000)
Insight, Feb 16, 2001
Kaye, Mitchell. *The Bill Of No Rights* (self-published pamphlet, 2000)
The Limbaugh Letter, Dec 20, 2000
MacDonald, Heather. *The Burden of Bad Ideas: How Modern Intellectuals Misshape Our Society* (Ivan R. Dee Books, 2001)
National Review, Jun 22, 2001
Roberts, Paul Craig. "A Nation Divided," *The American Spectator,* Jul 12, 2000
Savage, Michael. *The Enemy Within* (WND Books, Nashville, 2003)
   Ibid, "I Remember The Nazis," *riflewarriors.com,* Jul 22, 2003
Spencer, Thomas R. *Insight,* Jan 15-22, 2001
Vaszonyi, Balint. *America's 30 Years War* (Regnery, Washington DC, 1998)

www.ingramcontent.com/pod-product-compliance
Lightning Source LLC
Chambersburg PA
CBHW031459270326
41930CB00006B/156